Cultural Survival Report 25

THE SPOILS OF FAMINE

Ethiopian Famine Policy and Peasant Agriculture

Jason W. Clay
Sandra Steingraber
Peter Niggli

Cultural Survival, Inc.
Cambridge, Massachusetts

Cultural Survival, Inc.
11 Divinity Avenue
Cambridge, MA 02138
(617) 495-2562

Printed in the United States of America
by Transcript Printing Company, Peterborough, NH

Cultural Survival Report 25
The Cultural Survival Report is a continuation of
the Occasional Paper series.

Library of Congress Cataloging-in-Publication Data

Clay, Jason W.
    The spoils of famine.

    (Cultural survival report ; 25)
    Bibliography: p.
    1. Famines — Ethiopia. 2. Food relief — Government policy — Ethiopia. 3. Peasantry — Government policy — Ethiopia. I. Steingraber, Sandra. II. Niggli, Peter, 1950-   . III. Title. IV. Series.
HC845.Z9F3314 1988   363.8′56′0963   88-28524
ISBN 0-939521-35-0
ISBN 0-939521-30-X (pbk.)

Contents

PART TWO
VILLAGIZATION

Acronyms

BBC	British Broadcasting Corporation
CADU	Chilalo Agricultural Development Unit, Arsi, Ethiopia
CATIE	Centro Agronomico Tropical de Investigacion y Ensenanza based in Turrialba, Costa Rica, a research and educational center focusing on tropical agriculture
CRS	Catholic Relief Service
EEC	European Economic Community
EPDA	Ethiopian People's Democratic Alliance
EPLF	Eritrean People's Liberation Front
ERCS	Ethiopian Red Cross Society
FAR	Fellowship for African Relief; Canadian-based humanitarian relief organization
GLF	Gambella Liberation Front
GOE	Government of Ethiopia
GPLM	Gambella People's Liberation Movement
ICRC	International Committee of the Red Cross
ICVA	International Council of Voluntary Agencies
IUCN	International Union for the Conservation of Nature and Natural Resources based in Gland, Switzerland
LWF	Lutheran World Federation
MCC	Mennonite Central Committee
MSF	Medecins Sans Frontieres; French-based humanitarian relief organization
NGO	Non-Governmental Organization
NRC	National Refugee Commission, Somalia
NSS	National Security Service, Somalia
OLF	Oromo Liberation Front
ORA	Oromo Relief Association; humanitarian organization of the OLF
PMAC	Provisional Military Administration Council
REST	Relief Society of Tigray; humanitarian relief organization of the TPLF
REWA	Revolutionary Ethiopia Women's Association
REYA	Revolutionary Ethiopia Youth Association
RHU	Refugee Health Unit, Somalia
RRC	Relief and Rehabilitation Commission; Ethiopian government agency responsible for all humanitarian operations
SIDA	Swedish International Development Agency
SLM	Sidamo Liberation Movement
SPLA	Sudanese People's Liberation Army; Ethiopian-backed group that controls areas of southern Sudan adjacent to the resettlement areas
TPLF	Tigrayan People's Liberation Front
UNHCR	United Nations High Commission for Refugees
USAID	United States Agency for International Development
WPE	Workers' Party of Ethiopia
WSLF	Western Somali Liberation Front

Introduction

Jason W. Clay

It is now 1988, nearly four years since the onset of the 1984–1985 famine
which elicited the largest humanitarian outpouring in history. Assessing
the scale of the disaster has always proven difficult. During the height
of the famine many estimates indicated that as many as 7 million people were
at risk. By 1986, after famine conditions began to recede, some estimates
indicated that as many as 1 million people might have died. With little supporting evidence, assistance agencies were quick to claim responsibility for
saving the lives of some 6 million people.

The 1984–1985 Famine

During the 1984–1985 famine, journalists, the Ethiopian government and
many humanitarian agencies working in the area told the world that the
famine was the result of drought and other natural misfortunes. Except as
it complicated relief efforts, war was rarely mentioned as a significant contributing cause of famine conditions even though some estimates suggested
that by 1984 more than 40 percent of Ethiopia's total land mass and 30 percent of the population were within war zones.

Journalists and relief workers untrained in ecological assessment made
many public statements about rain patterns, topsoil and crop pests. Yet they
barely mentioned the military campaigns of the Ethiopian army and opposing forces — even though, with more than 300,000 troops deployed within
its own borders, the government boasts the largest standing army in sub-
Saharan Africa. It is telling that few researchers attempted to interview famine
victims systematically about what they perceived to be the cause of their
own starvation. Most agencies continued to claim, for fundraising purposes
anyway, that their relief programs were attacking the famine's root causes.
At best, however, their programs were designed to sustain the hungry until
the rains returned.

1

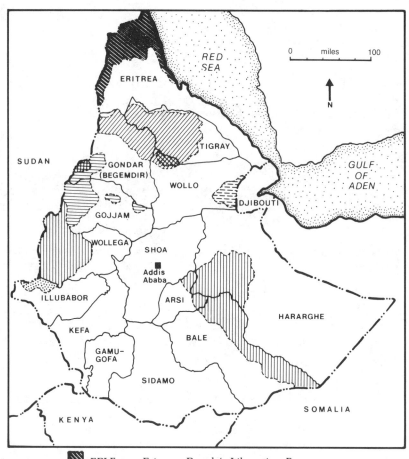

RED
SEA

ERITREA

TIGRAY

SUDAN

GONDAR
(BEGEMDIR)

WOLLO

GULF
OF
ADEN

GOJJAM

DJIBOUTI

WOLLEGA

SHOA

Addis
Ababa

ILLUBABOR

ARSI

HARARGHE

KEFA

BALE

GAMU-
GOFA

SIDAMO

SOMALIA

KENYA

0   miles   100

N

	EPLF	— Eritrean People's Liberation Front
	TPLF	— Tigrayan People's Liberation Front
	OLF	— Oromo Liberation Front
	EPRP	— Ethiopian People's Revolutionary Party
	EPDM	— Ethiopian People's Democratic Movement
	EDU	— Ethiopian Democratic Union
	ALF	— Afar Liberation Front
	GPLM	— Gambella People's Liberation Movement

Evidence from famine victims at the time clearly indicated that the famine of 1984–1985 did not spring from "natural" causes, but originated in a decade of military and agricultural policies implemented by the current Ethiopian government. Once the famine became a reality, the government was quick to exploit its potential to further the very policies that first produced it. Evidence presented in this book demonstrates that famine assistance, provided primarily by Western governments and non-governmental organizations, reinforced the policies and programs that produced the 1984–1985 famine and is enabling the Ethiopian government to consolidate its power. In addition, this evidence shows that assistance from the West helped the government to intensify its resettlement and villagization programs, programs with specific political and military agendas which had, until that date, been implemented on only a small scale in relatively isolated areas.

With "compassion fatigue" as the dominant buzzword, 1986 was a comparatively quiet year for Ethiopia in the international media. Appeals for emergency relief aid yielded to a new sober discourse on the need for long-term development. Following widely publicized accusations of human rights abuses, the Ethiopian government temporarily suspended the resettlement program but continued with its plans to relocate virtually the entire rural population. The less visible villagization program, launched in 1984 and officially inaugurated in 1985 as a national campaign, accelerated in 1986. Implemented first, and most thoroughly, in cereal and grain surplus producing areas, villagization soon reduced food production in these areas so that many former surplus-producing areas could now only meet their own basic needs and no longer produced surpluses for other regions.

Famine Revisited

By 1987, the Ethiopian government and the Western humanitarian agencies once again began to cite statistics about the number of victims of the new impending famine: 6 to 7 million estimated at risk. Only about half these people were said to be concentrated in the northern administrative regions of Eritrea and Tigray; the rest were distributed throughout other parts of the country. The most striking aspect of the 1987–1988 famine, when compared to its predecessor three years earlier, is that the famine-producing policies of the government have caused severe food shortages in a number of southern administrative regions that had been less affected by the earlier famine.

The famine of 1987–1988 came as no surprise to those who had taken the time to examine the causes of the earlier famine and monitor the ways Western assistance was used. In fact, it was predicted in various articles and reports published by the authors of this book. A close examination of the maps of 1987–1988 famine areas in Ethiopia reveals the correlation of these areas with those where specific policies and programs have been implemented.

• In Eritrea and Tigray, famine prevails in areas that are outside the control of the government and as a result are under military attack.

ETHIOPIA – 1984-1985
RESETTLEMENT, VILLAGIZATION & REFUGEES

• In Tigray and Wollo, famine reigns in areas where large numbers of able-bodied farmers were taken, primarily against their will, for the resettlement program.

• In northern Bale, Hararghe and Shoa, famine occurs in areas where production was reduced as a result of the government's villagization program.

• In Wollega, Illubabor and other administrative regions where people have been resettled, famine now prevails because these people are still unable to produce the food they need to feed themselves. The local people displaced from their homes and fields by resettlement also suffer as a result of reduced production.

Famine in Ethiopia is clearly linked to specific famine-producing policies. Furthermore, a close examination of the causes of Ethiopia's most recent famines, coupled with demographic data on population increases, indicates that rain gauges are not needed to predict famine. Since 1985, Cultural Survival's research on the causes of famine in Ethiopia have led us to predict that the conditions currently being created in the country, with the help of Western assistance, will produce famine for decades to come. A recent US AID study corroborates this projection. Its findings indicate that, even with normal rains, Ethiopian food shortages could double to 2 million metric tons by 1992. Such considerations command a detailed analysis of the "band aid" approaches to famine relief that have been operating since late 1984.

In 1988 the Ethiopian government expelled Western assistance agencies from Eritrea and Tigray in the northern part of the country, claiming that agency personnel were in danger in a war zone. At the same time, the government announced a drive for 100,000 additional recruits in the army. A recent treaty with Somalia has allowed the government to move an estimated 10,000 to 20,000 troops from the Ogaden region of eastern Ethiopia into the provinces of Eritrea and Tigray. Most observers agree that these government moves signal an increase in military activity and an intensification of the war with the Eritrean People's Liberation Front and the Tigrayan People's Liberation Front operating in the north. Four UN personnel have been permitted to stay in the area, but their numbers are not sufficient to ensure the appropriate or even humane distribution of relief materials. Furthermore, as of mid-May, three of these "monitors" were not allowed to leave the towns where they were required to stay. Agencies such as the International Committee of the Red Cross, which have insisted on overseeing the distribution of their food and materials, have been asked to leave.

The Ethiopian government has told Western assistance agencies that attempts to reach northern famine victims living in areas outside state control, through cross-border operations from Sudan or Somalia, will be considered acts of war. Some 80 to 90 percent of famine victims in the north live outside the control of the government. As a result, the agencies claim that they now face a dilemma: the government refuses to give them even the minimal monitoring presence necessary to ensure that their help reaches famine victims, while it asserts that all cross-border operations will be viewed as acts of war. This "dilemma" exists only if the agencies insist on delivering most assistance through the government. If getting food to the victims were their primary goal, they would not experience a dilemma. They could deliver food from neighboring countries.

Both during the 1984–1985 and 1987–1988 famines, most assistance agencies have been willing to pay any price, to make any deal, and to compromise their ideals in order to obtain the necessary permission to undertake their programs in government-held areas of Ethiopia. They have not delved into the causes of the famines they claim to be alleviating or the long-term implications of their programs. These agencies became political and military tools of the government in its state-building programs in 1984–1985; they continue to be pawns of the state in the current famine.

The Role of the West

This book serves as a companion volume to an earlier work by Jason Clay and Bonnie Holcomb, published by Cultural Survival, entitled *Politics and the Ethiopian Famine, 1984–1985*. That book examined the causes of the 1984–1985 famine, exploring the manner in which the government launched its resettlement program and its subsequent impact on those resettled as well as those who had been living in the resettlement areas. This volume examines the Ethiopian government's restructuring of family and village life, local politics and food production. Western assistance, intended to relieve the suffering of Ethiopians, has become a key ingredient in the government's efforts to restructure society. It has become the "spoils" of famine, a booty to be plundered by the present state in its ongoing battle to centralize power and wealth.

Prior to 1984 the Ethiopian government had achieved only limited success in its efforts to control the rural economies and societies of various groups living within its borders. The nationalization of land did indeed prove to be a massive affront to the autonomy of individual or communal production systems. It was not, however, initially perceived as such, since local communities and their leaders could decide how land would be allocated. Only when the state began undermining the power of traditional, local leaders through local level organizations—peasant associations—by arranging for chairmen to be appointed by outsiders did many peasants realize the true nature of the evolving system. The peasant associations represented important building blocks in the government's efforts to regulate rural life. They provided the infrastructure for the collection of taxes and "voluntary" contributions, conscription into the army and militia and relocation of families either through resettlement or villagization. Still, their evolution was slow and their presence, while not desirable, was perhaps acceptable to many members.

All this changed during the 1984–1985 famine, when the government utilized the well-organized peasant associations and the chaos of the famine to intensify resettlement and villagization. It soon became evident that the nationalization of lands and even the cooptation of all local organizations represented merely the tip of the wedge in the programs that the government intended to implement, programs which would once and for all alienate peasants from their land, production, communities and national identities.

The government "recruited" for resettlement by denying international food assistance to starving populations until it had identified a quota of resettlement "volunteers." Most of the food for this "carrot-and-stick" operation was provided by the US government through US-based organizations; some came from the World Food Program. Once populations had been resettled, the EEC donated most of the food used to feed them in their new homes.

The government used a similar carrot-and-stick approach to convince peasants to move into new villages. Peasant association officials were given quotas; if they did not meet these quotas, they would be removed from their positions. Only villagized communities could receive any of the government or internationally provided agricultural inputs, famine assistance or social services.

A key aspect of Ethiopia's famine policy is patronage. The political system, dominated by military administrators and urban technocrats, is evolving into an even more elaborate system of patronage than had existed under Haile Selassie. The party and government bureaucracy constitute the life force of the patronage system and, from 1984 onward, Western assistance has represented its most important currency of exchange. International funds help the government to establish tighter control over resistant peasant producers and agricultural resources. In addition to providing the lubricant for the government to orient society from the village level to the Politburo, Western assistance also cushioned the regime from the demands and needs of peasant producers by freeing it from direct reliance on peasant production to feed the cities, army and bureaucracy. The government depended on peasant producers to provide the food necessary to stymie unrest in the army and in urban areas. Western famine assistance, and subsequent development assistance, have reduced that dependency.

The centralization of state power has resulted from the state's ability to separate producers from their lands. To date, the West has been willing to step in and feed those who are no longer allowed to produce their own food. These former farmers thus become wage/food-for-work laborers. The state-controlled systems of production will never be self-sustaining; they will always rely on massive inputs, inputs that the Ethiopian government certainly cannot afford. At this point, Western agencies are being blackmailed. They are told that if they leave, the onus for the resulting starvation will be theirs. Yet if they stay, state power will be further centralized and the situation for peasant farmers will certainly worsen. The Western agencies operating in Ethiopia have been duped; they must now solve the dilemma of how to extricate themselves from their current involvement.

Famine assistance has given the government license to carry out resettlement and villagization programs that dispossessed and then reorganized farmers into state-controlled systems of agriculture. The assistance has enabled the government to continue collecting taxes and contributions, in cash and in grain, from even famine victims. Western famine assistance has thus strengthened the government's hand and made peasants more vulnerable than ever to the vagaries of weather and pest infestations. Thus, the assistance provided by Western agencies has contributed to an overall decline in production and the reliance of the state on peasant producers while it has fueled numerous civil wars.

The Value of Refugee Testimony

Since the West's "discovery" of the Ethiopian famine in late 1984, many conflicting, even contradictory, reports have surfaced concerning the famine itself, the government's resettlement and villagization program and the role of humanitarian assistance in the unfolding disaster. The one clear fact that has emerged from these reports over the past years is that the gap is great between what outside observers claim to hear and what inside observers claim to see. Most of the public observations made by Western humanitarian agency personnel, journalists and high-profile visitors who tour famine areas, resettlement sites and new villages are diametrically opposed to the stories told to researchers and journalists in the liberated areas of Ethiopia and the refugee camps of Sudan and Somalia.

Those who are skeptical about the accuracy of inside reports claim that foreign observers only see showcase camps and villages; that they are assigned government translators; and that they can speak to settlers and villagers only under the eyes of government officials. Those who criticize the reports coming out of refugee camps say that the stories of unhappy, homesick refugees — who are undoubtedly biased against the current government and are perhaps sympathetic to revolutionary groups — are anecdotal at best and unreliable at worst.

Cultural Survival investigators have interviewed more than 500 refugees who have fled Ethiopia since late 1984. We have become convinced that the refugee testimony is both an invaluable and, relative to other sources, accurate source of information. Refugee testimonies corroborate each other over time and space. The reports on conditions leading to resettlement or about life in camps such as Megele are strikingly similar whether the respondents fled in late 1985 and were subsequently transported north to return to their homes or whether they had arrived in Sudan the day they were interviewed in 1987.

The testimonies collected by Holcomb and Niggli in southern Sudan from those who had been resettled themselves or displaced by the resettlement program paralleled those collected by Steingraber in 1986 and again in 1987, regardless of the fact that each year all escapees from resettlement are transported north to the border of Tigray, where they can return to their homes throughout northern Ethiopia.

The descriptions of work schedules and general conditions in Mengele resettlement camp given by Amhara-speaking Wollo Oromo refugees in Damazine resemble those collected with a different translator from people who had fled the same camp but ended up in Yabuus, Sudan. Descriptions of the general procedures as well as specific forms of brutalities that accompanied villagization as told by Anuak from Gambella, Oromo from Wollega and Oromo and Somalis from Hararghe are strikingly similar, even though the interviews were conducted in different languages and years and as far as 1,000 miles apart.

Certain undeniable facts often corroborate the oral testimonies: the wounds, scars and broken ribs on the bodies of those who claim to have been tortured; evidence of malnutrition among children who recently fled the resettlement camp and those whose parents claim that they were more hungry there than they had ever been during the famine in Wollo.

We have found through our research that understatement rather than exaggeration characterizes the narration of the refugees, especially those who have been personally victimized through, for example, torture or sexual assault. Some respondents said that they were too ashamed to describe some of the things that they had witnessed in the resettlement camps or during the process of villagization. Some approached after the tape recorder had been turned off with things they had hesitated to say during the interview. In Khartoum, Anuak refugees sent notes giving information on events about which they were unable to speak. Such post-interview stories and revelations do not appear in this or previous reports, but they certainly influence our interpretation of the validity of the interviews.

In other instances, refugees offered graphic details about daily life in their areas that are shocking to outsiders: regular beatings and imprisonment in peasant associations, villages and resettlement sites; the theft of livestock, grain and household items by the army, militia and peasant association officials; the practices of forcing peasants to work without pay on roads and other public works as well as on the agricultural plots of the local militia, peasant association officials and people in the army; the cultivation, for free, of "communal" plots whose produce is destined for the state. Peasants do not realize that outsiders are unaware that each farmer must contribute a set amount of grain through the local peasant association to various state-identified programs. These practices were common in all the administrative regions in which the refugees had lived – Tigray, Wollo, Hararghe, Illubabor and Wollega.

Virtually all interviewees were farmers who had been producing food all of their lives. They had firsthand experience of the important variables that influence their ability to produce food. At the very least their perspectives, observations and analyses should be compared to those of the bureaucrats, journalists, celebrities and politicians. At the very least they should be sought out to tell us how the crops were growing and who was eating the harvest. In other words, they should be considered expert witnesses.

Just because Western assistance agencies, journalists or diplomats inside Ethiopia find it impossible to speak with peasant farmers in some areas or inconvenient in others, or just because those observers do not have the necessary expertise to elicit reliable information from such sources, does not mean that the testimony of refugee farmers should be dismissed out of hand. On the contrary; refugees offer a window on conditions inside government-held areas where research is restricted. Refugees identify key issues that can be checked, even in government-held areas, where thorough research is forbidden.

Part One | Resettlement

1 | Introduction

Sandra Steingraber

In November 1984 the Ethiopian government announced its intention to resettle 1.5 million peasants. By March 1986, after the program was temporarily suspended, about 800,000 people had been moved, the majority from the northern highlands to the southwest. The program was resumed one year later with plans to resettle between 200,000 and 300,000 by the end of 1987 at the rate of 30,000 each month *New York Times* 11 March 1987; *Christian Science Monitor* 18–24 May 1987).

Recent statements by President Mengistu indicate that the resettlement program will continue indefinitely "until such time as we are able to bring about a balanced settlement pattern" (*Courier* 1986:28). In March 1987, he reported to the Central Committee that 7 million people would ultimately need to be removed from the highlands (Radio Addis Ababa 28 March 1987).

By early 1985, escapees from resettlements in Wollega and Illubabor began crossing the border as refugees. They have continued to arrive in Sudan in small and large groups ever since. By mid-1987, roughly 4,000 escapees from the resettlement camps had been registered as refugees in Sudan. Most of these have escaped from resettlements bordering the Blue Nile province and, once they cross the frontier, are gathered by Sudanese authorities into a holding camp outside the town of Damazine. Before the rains begin each year, the Damazine camp is emptied and the refugees transferred to more permanent camps near Gedaref. Beginning in 1986, Oromo-speaking refugees from Wollo who had been resettled into Wollega began arriving in the Yabuus refugee camp administered by the Oromo Relief Association. As of June 1987, 500 resettlement escapees had been registered there.

These few thousand refugees probably represent only a small fraction of the settlers who have escaped or attempted escape. In 1986, for example, only 23 percent of a group of 3,000 resettlers known to have fled from one settlement site in Gambella, Illubabor, arrived safely in Sudan. The rest presumably succumbed to sickness, thirst or hunger on the journey or had been shot, captured, drowned or kidnapped. An unknown number of settlers also attempt to return to their homelands directly through Ethiopia.

In January 1985, Niggli and Holcomb went to Damazine and systematically interviewed refugees who had been among the first groups of peasants resettled from Tigray and Wollo. Focusing on the conditions for production in the settlers' homelands and on the circumstances of the resettlement, they reported that very few of the settlers had actually been famine victims in their northern homelands. According to refugee testimony, conditions in the resettlement camps were miserable: surrounded by armed militia, settlers were forced to clear land, build huts and labor in producers' cooperatives while subsisting on insufficient rations of donated grain (Niggli 1986; Clay and Holcomb 1986).

Niggli and Steingraber returned to Damazine in March and April of 1986 and independently interviewed members of a second group of resettlement escapees who had arrived after the others had been relocated to the Gedaref camps. Steingraber returned again in May and June of 1987 to interview a third, later-arriving group of escapees. She also traveled further south to talk with Oromo-speaking refugees from Wollo who had recently arrived in the Yabuus refugee camp after fleeing resettlements in Wollega.

The results of the 1986 and 1987 interviews conducted by Steingraber are presented in this part of the volume, which is devoted to resettlement. The first section examines the ecological mandates used to justify the resettlement program as well as the possible ecological consequences for the areas into which the resettlers are being moved and for the Nile River system as a whole. The second section, based on testimonies gathered in the recent interviews in 1987, takes a closer look at the experiences of the resettlers inside the settlements.

Although they constitute one of our only sources of information about the conditions inside the resettlement camps, the testimonies of refugee escapees have heretofore played a small role in the ongoing debate about the wisdom or folly of Ethiopia's resettlement program as it is played out in the Western media. Together with Holcomb and Niggli's 1985 interviews, the testimonies presented here trace the history of the current resettlement program from 1984 to 1987 as experienced by its participants — from those who escaped on the day of their arrival to those who lived in the settlements for nearly three years before fleeing.

Two patterns become strikingly evident when reading through the more than 150 accounts of resettled refugees collected over this three-year period. The first is the increasing militarization of the resettlement camps and their emerging role in the government's campaign against armed opposition movements in the area. The second is the remarkable degree of similarity between the most recent testimonies and the earlier ones, suggesting that — in spite of official reassurances to the contrary — very little about the miserable conditions inside the settlements has changed since 1984.

The close corroboration of these interviews over both time and space also attests to the accuracy of refugee testimony. The stories of settlers who fled the camps of Megele in 1987 — and who are interviewed in Damazine only a few days after arriving in Sudan — support those told by Megele settlers, interviewed in Damazine 18 months earlier, who had long ago been transferred to another refugee camp. They also support those told to Niggli and Holcomb in 1985. Amharic-speaking Wollo refugees interviewed in 1987 in Damazine were asked to describe their work schedules in the resettlement camp of Bambesi; Oromo-speaking Wollo refugees from the same resettlement camp interviewed in Yabuus with a different translator provided similar descriptions. And so on.

Resettlement, like villagization, is in theory and in practice changing the way food is produced and distributed in Ethiopia. The refugees who flee these programs are farmers who have been growing and distributing food all their lives. The following reports are presented with the belief that their perspectives and observations and analyses should be compared to those of the bureaucrats, journalists and relief agencies. At the very least these farmers should be able to tell us how the crops are growing and who is eating the harvest.

2 | Resettlement in 1985–1986: Ecological Excuses and Environmental Consequences

Sandra Steingraber

"We ate the forest like a fire. There was no forest left. We pulled the stumps and cut the limbs. We thought after a year of this, it would get better, but it sent us downwards. We cleared the wilderness; our bodies became misshapen. We had no clothes and no food. When it didn't get any better, we ran away." —Wollo farmer, age 27

In May 1986, a remarkable pair of articles appeared on consecutive days in the *New York Times*. The first, on May 21, quoted Dawit Wolde Giorgis, former head of the RRC, Ethiopia's Relief and Rehabilitation Commission, from his first public interview since he left Ethiopia last October and subsequently requested asylum in the US. In this interview, Dawit claimed that policy rather than drought had been the main cause of famine in the northern provinces of Ethiopia and that certain political priorities, including the resettlement of peasants from the north to the south, were in clear contradiction with human needs. The second article, the following day on May 22, quoted the military leader of the Ethiopian government, Mengistu Haile Mariam, from a rare press conference in which he announced the resumption of the resettlement effort and hailed the program as a bold attempt to relieve, once and for all, the suffering caused by the disastrous droughts in the north.

From October 1984 until March 1986 between 700,000 and 800,000 people — one-half of the targeted population — were taken for resettlement to lands to the south and the west. Of these, less than 600,000 appear to be alive (Jason Clay, personal communication). In October 1985, the RRC said that 8.4 percent of the population in Wollo province and 3.5 percent of Tigray's population had been moved already (RRC 1985:14-16). In February 1986, following Western criticism, the Ethiopian government called for a period of "consolidation" and suspended the program. Its subsequent revival focuses attention on the critical question raised by the two contradictory statements above: Is resettlement a cure for or a cause of hunger in Ethiopia?

Some observers see the resettlement operations in Ethiopia as part of a larger political agenda — namely to consolidate power by increasing the dependency of the peasantry on the central government. The Swiss journalist Peter Niggli compares the relocations to those the Khmer Rouge conducted in Cambodia and to the collectivization of the rural sector in the Soviet Union under Stalin. African scholar Hamdesa Tuso argues (as have many others) that the current resettlement scheme is a continuation of a 100-year-old policy of colonialism which seeks to dispossess the Oromo people of their fertile lands south of the Abyssinian empire (Tuso 1986). The Oromo Liberation Front (OLF) likewise holds that the current resettlement scheme is a new codification for an ongoing historical process of colonization and expansionism. In addition, the Tigray People's Liberation Front (TPLF) objects to the resettlements on the grounds that one of their primary intentions is to depopulate rural areas in the north where liberation movements are active and supported by the local peasants (see TPLF and OLF 1984; OLF 1985a; Clay and Holcomb 1985; Niggli 1985).

With the exception of the TPLF's position, these political and historical considerations have fallen largely outside the bounds of the current debate, which has been limited in the media to discussions of human rights abuses and cost effectiveness in the implementation of the program. Are the resettlers moved by force? Are families split up? Does relocation divert famine relief supplies or hinder relief operations? When the French medical organization Medecins Sans Frontieres (MSF) voiced these concerns and called for a three-month moratorium on resettlement in December 1985, it was expelled from Ethiopia.

Significantly, however, the principle of resettlement itself — as a potential solution to the problem of recurrent famine in the north — has not come under as much public scrutiny as have the human abuses that occur during resettlement's implementation. As the *African Concord* observed, "There has been little quarrel with the principle of the operation. . . . What the majority of critics have condemned is the manner in which the programme is being implemented" (1986:9). Some relief organizations have concluded from this narrowly defined debate that perhaps they should become *more* directly involved with the resettlements — given that the Ethiopian government is firmly committed to the program — to prevent previous abuses that occurred when the government was overseeing its implementation (BBC broadcast March 1986).

Resettlement as a solution to famine in rural Ethiopia is based on three assumptions. First, the land from which the inhabitants are to be moved has become permanently unproductive or its climate so unpredictable that it cannot now or in the near future support the present population. Second, the areas targeted for resettlement in the south and southwest can sustain the sudden insertion of thousands of people, supply their required resources over the long term and not succumb to the same processes of degradation which made their original lands unproductive. Thus, highlands targeted for resettlement in the north are diagnosed as "unproductive," "drought-prone," "overused," "eroded," "precarious" and suffering from "the drought-famine syndrome." In contrast, the resettlement sites in the south are described as "fertile," "virgin," "reliable" and promising "a conducive objective condition for peasant productivity without ecological and climatic risk" (RRC 1984; 1985).

The third assumption underlying the argument for resettlement is, of course, that the agricultural techniques and skills the peasants of the dry, cool highlands use will be appropriate or adaptable to the resettlement sites' different ecological conditions. The RRC does not address this assumption directly but rather stresses the lack of alternative solutions:

> Adverse climatic effects, bad cultivation practices and overgrazing coupled with over-population and over-utilization have rendered the Northern Administrative Regions of Ethiopia drought-prone and unproductive. The inhabitants of these regions have been repeatedly subjected to serious drought which often culminates in famine.
>
> On account of this fact, the inhabitants of the region are left with no alternative other than moving to potentially promising and unutilized areas of the country (RRC 1984:23-24).

This present study addresses both the implementation of resettlement and its ecological viability. The investigation of the circumstances of the resettlements and the conditions in the new settlements is intended to follow up Niggli and Holcomb's study, which was conducted in February and March 1985 and which formed part of Cultural Survival's research (see Clay and Holcomb 1985).

The remarkable similarity in the testimonies of these resettlement camp escapees and those interviewed by Niggli and Holcomb one year earlier reveals that very little about the implementation of the resettlement operations has changed. Meanwhile, the Ethiopian government has continued its reassurances that previous brutalities have been corrected and overcome. Furthermore, the refugee farmers' observations of the ecological and agricultural conditions in both their homelands and the resettlement sites reveal that the resettlement program, as it currently is designed, can in no way be justified with ecological arguments. As is detailed below, the program does not choose as its participants inhabitants of ecologically degraded areas; it does not attempt to halt — or even identify — the processes of ecological destruction in the north; it does not provide the resettlers with the tools, skills, or services needed to adapt to the unfamiliar environmental conditions they have been moved into. Finally, these interviews, together with evidence of the increasing siltation of the Nile River system, suggest that the resettlement program in fact is perpetuating rather than containing an ecological crisis. (The possible ecological effects of resettlement on the Yabuus river system are described in the next chapter.)

Research Design and Methods

In February and March 1986, I interviewed refugees who had recently fled from the resettlement camps in Wollega and Illubabor provinces and who now were living in a temporary camp a few miles outside of Damazine, Sudan. Medical services for the residents as well as food and water distribution were being provided by the Canadian agency Fellowship for African Relief (FAR). In early March 1986, this particular camp held 1,011 people. The camp had begun with the arrival of the first few hundred refugees in January 1985 and was located in a different site from the camp that Niggli and Holcomb visited a year earlier. All of those residents, early escapees from the resettlment camps, were transferred to Wad Kauli in May 1985, and all but 250 (probably from Wollo) walked back to their homes. Thus I interviewed a completely different set of refugees who had had no contact with either the Cultural Survival team or the refugee population the team had interviewed.

Refugees lived in canvas tents, each of which was numbered from 1 to 90; anywhere from five to 15 refugees occupied a single tent. Refugees from Tigray — all of whom had escaped at different times from camps in Gambella, Illubabor — were living in the first 65 tents. Refugees from Wollo — all of whom had escaped from the Asosa camps in Wollega province — occupied the last 25 tents. Wollo refugees had arrived more recently than the Tigrayans, and some continued to arrive in small groups while I was there (see Appendix A for detailed demography of camp population).

I conducted interviews with 54 farmers in 20 randomly selected tents. Because of the close comraderie of tentmates, I made no attempt to single out interview subjects for private questioning and often interviewed several persons at a time, asking the same question to each person in turn. Often those being interviewed consulted each other and nearby family members before answering a certain question. Just as often, spectators who had gathered around to listen would offer their perspectives. Thus, the interviews conducted within given tents cannot be considered completely independent of each other; however, the annotations, comparisons and corroborations that came out of this group dynamic were often important and revealing and can be viewed as advantageous. Moreover I had the chance to interview refugees who had arrived recently and who had not interacted much with their neighbors — one group of Wollo farmers was still erecting its tent. The fact that these newcomers' stories closely matched those of the earlier arrivals is evidence for the accuracy of refugee testimony and strong-

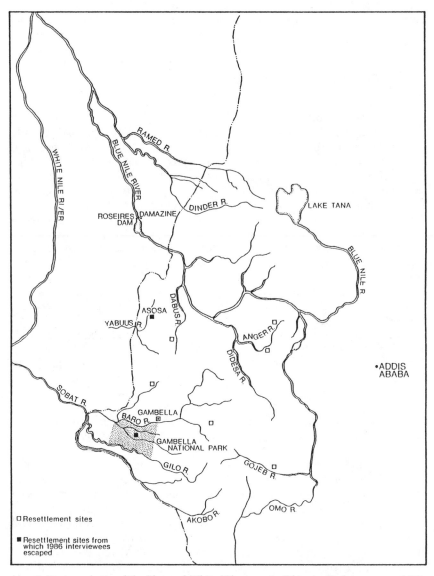

Map 1. Drainage basin of the Blue and White Nile rivers in Ethiopia. By late summer 1985, 600,000 people had been resettled into this area, which has traditionally supported low human populations.

ly suggests that camp residents had not recreated a kind of group history during the time they had been living together in the camp.

The interview was lengthy — often requiring two or more hours to complete. Sometimes during simultaneous interviewing of residents in a particular tent, one or two respondents would leave temporarily during some part of the questioning and then return a bit later, especially if water and food were being distributed. Thus the percentages of responses were tallied according to the actual number of people answering each question, which varies. For questions concerning conditions in the homeland villages, I tallied responses according to the number of respondents from different villages. For questions whose answers were arrived at by group consensus, I tallied the responses of each tent rather than each individual.

My translator was an Anuak refugee from Gambella (one of only two in the camp). He was not a member of any political party and had fled conscription rather than resettlement; he was also much beloved by the camp residents because he had led 200 of the earliest arriving refugees on foot through the forest from Yabuus to Kirmuk. Although his English was excellent, he did not speak Tigrinya. Thus all interviews were conducted in Amharic. One-third of those interviewed from Tigray could converse in Amharic, and at least one farmer in each of the Tigrayan tents was fluent enough in Amharic to translate for his comrades.

In all, I interviewed 5 percent of the camp population from Tigray (38 refugees) and 8 percent of the Wollo population (16 refugees). All of the interviewees were males between the ages of 15 and 68 who had been farmers in their homelands. (Women were present in the camp, but in small numbers; because I was interested primarily in agricultural and ecological issues, I limited my random interviews to the male residents present in the tents when I first entered.)

To investigate the actual process of relocation and the conditions in the settlement, I asked questions adapted from the general survey used by Peter Niggli and Cultural Survival one year earlier. To determine whether the ecological assumptions behind the argument for resettlement were justifiable, I asked refugees about the ecological and agricultural conditions of their homelands and of the resettlement sites (see Appendix B for questionnaire). In addition, I intensively interviewed five farmers who either had been involved directly in planting and harvesting in the resettlement farms or who had lived in the camps for at least one growing season. Farmers chosen for these interviews were those that seemed especially articulate about both agricultural practices and conditions.

Farming in the Homelands

According to the Ethiopian government, the resettlement program rescues and relocates those "who were affected by the drought again and again and could not be rehabilitated in their own area due to its uselessness" (Radio Addis Ababa 9 February 1985, quoted in Niggli 1986:80). According

"The government is trying to kill us. In this new place we don't know the weather and we were given very little food." Tigray farmer, Damazine, Sudan, March 1986.   ©S. Steingraber

to the resettled farmers interviewed in Damazine in 1986, nothing could be further from the truth.

Farming in Tigray and Wollo is carried out in much the same way and has changed little since the times of the interviewed farmers' fathers and grand-fathers. All farmers said they relied on rivers for their water supply and used firewood gathered from nearby forested areas for fuel. All used oxen for plowing and threshing. Tools and plows were inherited or bought from neighborhood craftsmen. None had ever received draft animals or any kind of equipment from the government.

Until they resettled, all of the farmers interviewed had lived their entire lives in the villages where they were born. Their fathers and grandfathers had also lived there. Of 37 Tigrayan farmers, 92 percent said they farmed the same land as their fathers had; significantly, the three who had farmed different land or had land taken away from them said their farms were in Dergue-controlled areas of Tigray. In Wollo, all of the farmers interviewed worked the same land as their fathers, but 25 percent said their plots of land had been reduced since their fathers' time. Irrigation was used by 60 percent of farmers in both Tigray and Wollo—mainly for vegetable fields.

Some of the farmers interviewed, who had lived in liberated areas, mentioned that the TPLF had introduced new crop varieties, but in general all farmers said they inherited the skills of their trade from their fathers and grandfathers. Besides the physical skills of planting, plowing, beekeeping, and so on, each farmer carries with him a vast legacy of knowledge about the rain patterns, soil and ecology of his land and the specific growing conditions required by each crop. For example, these farmers planted an average of 15 crops and some as many as 30. These include various kinds of cereal crops (teff, barley, wheat, sorghum, corn, millet); root crops (sweet potatoes, potatoes, onions); legumes (horsebeans, lentils, chickpeas); and vegetable crops (peppers, beriberi, okra and many others). In addition, most farmers maintained and planted several varieties of each crop. For instance, there are at least three common varieties of teff—white, red and brown. Each has its own planting depth and soil and water requirements, and each commands a different price on the market. In short, a farmer must know the planting schedule, harvesting method and ecological niche of each variety of many crops. Here is the summary of one farmer's planting schedule in Wollo:

> There are six kinds of sorghum I plant: two red kinds, two white kinds and two kinds that are intermediate which ripen very fast. There are also types we eat while the fruit is still green. There are five kinds of teff and three kinds of corn: red, orange and white. Each is planted according to its season, and each has its own time to plant.
>
> In September, I plant chickpeas, then in March, the first kind of sorghum, then in May, two more kinds of sorghum, and then in July, I plant another teff and another sorghum, also oilseeds and peanuts. In August, I plant the last kind of teff. This is according to our laws [see Appendix D for complete text].

All farmers are also plant breeders since they obtain their seeds from the

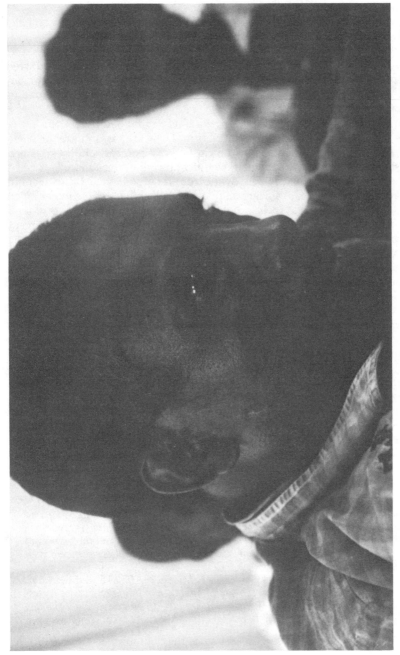

"I don't think there is anything that suits me better than the land my father gave me." Tigray farmer, Damazine, Sudan, February 1986.
©S. Steingraber

previous year's harvest; therefore, they arrange their plots to maintain true breeding varieties of each type of crop. Selection of seed for next year's crop is done before the harvest, mostly in inspecting overall plant vigor but also by selecting for certain characteristics: fast ripening time, for example, is especially important. Some farmers maintain both early- and late-ripening varieties. (See the interviews in Appendix D for more detailed descriptions of planting and harvesting schedules in Wollo and Tigray.)

Sixty percent of the Tigrayan farmers interviewed said the revolution of 1974 brought few changes — good or bad — to this intricate labor-intensive form of agriculture; their farms fell under TPLF control before government land reform spread into their areas. Of the four Tigrayan farmers who lived in Dergue-controlled areas, two reported that they lost land after the revolution. Nine out of 26 Tigrayan farmers (35 percent) said the TPLF made improvements.

Farming practices in Wollo, on the other hand, were greatly affected by the changes that followed the revolution. Nearly all Wollo farmers I interviewed described these changes as detrimental. Unequal redistribution of land and the levying of higher taxes were the most frequently cited complaints.

Some farmers claimed that their best fields were taken "for the government" or were given to people "who could pay more taxes." Some complained that they were left to plow ecologically fragile land ("I remained with the field that erosion attacked"); one said that some farmers in his village ended up with land they had never seen before.

In spite of decreased yields, the farmers interviewed reported that taxes levied after the revolution increased dramatically.

Before my taxes were E$8 [approximately US$4]. Now, for the same amount of land it is E$32. Everyone must also pay for associations.

Each person in the family has to pay taxes, including children. If there is no one to pay, the land is not planted and cattle graze there.

These taxes often required that farmers in Wollo send their surplus grain or animals to raise cash or make payments in kind. These reports, which substantiate those given by Wollo farmers to Niggli and Holcomb in 1985, indicate the systematic impoverishment of Wollo people — independent of ecological or climatic problems.

Although the farmers rarely mentioned long-term ecological degradation as a factor contributing to their problems, all agreed that soil and forest conservation were important for maintaining the well-being of their homelands. Of 36 Tigrayan farmers interviewed, 97 percent said there was forested land near their villages. Their descriptions of these forests greatly contrast with the RRC's portrayal of the areas targeted for resettlement as denuded, barren landscape. According to the farmers, forested land was available for hunting and beekeeping, and supplied firewood, fruit, grazing for domestic animals, charcoal and building materials. The single farmer who reported no forests near his home blamed the lack of tree cover for causing drought.

There was no clear consensus among Tigrayan farmers as to whether the size of the forests had increased or decreased over their lifetimes. Of 24 respondents, 79 percent reported no difference, 8.3 percent said the forests were more extensive now, and 12.5 percent thought the forests were more extensive when they were children. Several farmers mentioned that the TPLF [probably actually REST (Relief Society of Tigray)] had introduced methods of reforestation and woodland management.

We used to cut the forest by dividing it into parts. We cut one part for building and firewood, then we let it build up and cut elsewhere. So there is no difference in the size of the forest. The TPLF taught us how to do this. Previously our fathers used the forest this way, but it was not so prevalent.

We divided the forest into four sections and rotated cutting. Our fathers taught us not to cut down the big trees, but the TPLF taught us this quartering method.

Many of the Wollo refugees who had arrived recently at the Damazine camp were hesitant to answer specific questions about their homelands for fear I would report them to the Ethiopian authorities. Often I chose to eliminate certain questions or terminate the interview when the respondents became visibly ill at ease. Thus the following information was based on discussion with only five Wollo farmers and should be interpreted in this light.

All five respondents said their villages in Wollo were near forested lands, but they were split as to whether these forests had expanded or dwindled over the years. Of the three who reported less forests, one attributed the loss to increased cutting, another to farmers who had turned to selling firewood in an attempt to raise money during the drought, and the third to indiscriminate cutting caused by the nationalization of the forests. Of the two who reported more forests now, one attributed the increase to the government's prohibition on cutting and the other to a government reforestation program. These differences may reflect inconsistencies in the policies of peasant associations in different areas of Wollo.

Only a minority of the farmers from Tigray interviewed experienced severe and constant drought, the pretext for resettlement. Of 34 farmers, about 24 percent said they had never had problems with drought, 41 percent said drought was a moderate problem (other factors were more important) and 35 percent said that drought was bad enough to create shortages and hunger. Significantly, of 20 farmers who reported inadequate rainfall, 65 percent said it only had become a problem since last year, 25 percent said it had been a problem for the last two to three years, five percent claimed it had become a problem since the revolution and 5 percent described the drought as infrequent or sporadic.

More important than drought for these farmers was the loss of crops due to insect pests, especially the armyworm. As in 1985, farmers identified this worm as a major cause of production declines in Tigray. Of 37 farmers interviewed, 89 percent attributed some crop loss to this pest, of which 60 percent reported a total or near total loss. Only four said worms were not a problem for them; two of these said the TPLF had provided them with pesticide. Of those farmers with infestations, all said the worms were a new problem, making their first appearance within the last one or two years. The worm and the drought are not independent evils, since the variety of armyworm now in Ethiopia thrives under dry conditions. But most farmers indicated they could have coped with the drought conditions had worms not arrived. As one explained,

I can plant 10 kinds of wheat depending on the weather.... If there is a drought, I plant certain kinds; if it is cool, I plant other kinds. I plant one kind of wheat that can grow without water. It grew well in the drought, but then the worms finished it too. The drought came on one side and the worms on the other side. There was no harvest last year.

In addition, in 1986 many farmers reported that once the crops were finished, the worms began attacking and devastating the pasture grasses and were thus causing massive cattle die-off. It was this series of events that finally precipitated the decision of farmers to risk traveling to government-controlled areas in the hope of receiving relief aid. (Their abduction and subsequent resettlement is described in detail in the next section of the report.) As one farmer reflected, "Last year we had worms. This is why we got into trouble and how the Dergue was able to fool us."

If the thought that a responsible, grassroots pest management program would do more to improve the quality of life in rural Tigray than a mass transfer of its population seems too obvious, it is nonetheless the only reasonable conclusion one can reach. But it is clear that reasonable and responsible solutions are not what the Ethiopian government is seeking to find for the problems of Tigrayan farmers.

Without identifying the source, I presented farmers with a paraphrased version of the Ethiopian government's argument for resettlement: "Some people say that people from Tigray should be resettled to these new camps because your land is dry and your soil is poor for farming." Farmers were then asked if they agreed with this statement. All 34 vehemently disagreed. One even remarked that "nobody but the Dergue would say this." What then, I asked, do you believe is the real motive behind resettlement? Over 90 percent believed they were resettled because they were supporters of the TPLF; 6.5 percent thought the government was trying to kill them, and one farmer said he didn't have a clue.

We were resettled because we support the TPLF. We used to show them good ways to attack the government.

The drought was only for one year. This is not a good enough reason to resettle us. The real reason is that we are supporters of the TPLF. If they move us, the TPLF can't get food and water.

We could have gone into the town and found work until the drought went away. The Dergue resettled us because we support the TPLF.

The Dergue thinks Tigray is a rebel country, and he is trying to destroy us.

For the resettled Wollo farmer, drought was undeniably a severe problem. Of 17 farmers, 87 percent said they had lost crops to drought, and 76 percent described this loss as severe enough to cause hunger. All said that the drought conditions have persisted since the revolution. Almost all reported the presence of armyworms as well but indicated that they were not a new problem. In contrast to the Tigrayan farmers, no one had lost all his harvest to the worms or reported the death of cattle due to consumption of the grass by worms. It is possible that the crops in Wollo have had time to evolve a resistance to this pest or that different patterns of rainfall affect the hatching of the larvae. One farmer noted that the worm problem was not as bad before the revolution because "with Haile Selassie we had insecticides."

At this point it may seem as if Wollo farmers are justifiable candidates for resettlement. But significantly, in spite of the drought's severity, resettled Wollo farmers do not consider themselves drought victims nor do they attribute their suffering to inadequate rainfall. When Wollo farmers from different villages were asked "Did you know of any hungry people in your community?", 81 percent answered yes. When asked why people were hungry, the two reasons given were impoverishment caused by the extraction of taxes (mentioned previously) and the disruption of agriculture due to military conscription. The following are a selection of their responses:

Farmers were taken by the government, and people can't cultivate. There is a quota for each village.

The government comes to conscript us and then we have to hide in the forest. They come every six months, so we go back to the forests. Then when we are in the forest, the wild animals eat our grain.

Many people run away so they wouldn't be conscripted and then birds and pigs ate their crops. In this way the government caused hunger.

Many people were selected [for military service] in my village. When their parents cried, they were beaten. I hid myself in the forest, and my harvest was eaten by animals. When people returned [from the forest], they may find their families imprisoned and their land and cattle seized.

Our crops were growing well. Hunger was caused by high taxes. We were not free to move and sell and travel to family to get food or sell firewood.

This is why it is bad: When people go to these campaigns, we can't plant. When a person goes to war, there is no one left to protect the crops from wild animals. Or a person might get killed in the war, and then his family will starve.

A person has a family. He works hard and feeds his family. The Dergue comes and says to go fight in the Red Sea, Eritrea, Harar. His land might not be tilled. His animals may be eaten by hyenas.

I had to hide in the forest for 15 days a month until the Dergue went away. During this time, my parents and handicapped people took care of the fields, but crops suffered, eaten by wild animals and birds.

Like the Tigrayan farmers, all Wollo farmers said they disagreed with the official reason for the resettlement program ("The land of Wollo is dry and the soil poor for farming"), although there was no clear consensus as to the real motive for the program. Of 14 respondents, five said resettlement was designed to control them; two said it was a form of punishment for their rebelliousness; two said it was to mobilize them for conscription; one said it was to spread Amharic language to the south; one said the government was trying to kill them; and two said they did not know what the government's intentions were.

Table 1
Drought Severity and Frequency in Respondents' Homelands

	Tigray	Wollo
Drought Severity for All Respondents		
Never a Problem	23.5%	11.8%
A Moderate Problem	41.2%	11.8%
A Severe Problem	35.3%	76.4%
Frequency of Drought Among Respondents Reporting Inadequate Rainfall		
A Problem Last Year Only	65.0%	0%
A Problem for the Last 2-3 Years	25.0%	0%
A Problem since the Revolution	5.0%	100%
Always a Problem	0.0%	0%
An Infrequent or Sporadic Problem	5.0%	0%

Table 2
Perceived Reasons for Resettlement Among Respondents

Some people say that the people from Tigray/Wollo should be resettled to these new camps because your land is dry and your soil poor for farming. Do you agree with this?

	Tigray	Wollo
Agree	0%	0%
Disagree	100%	100%

Why do you think the government resettled you?

	Tigray	Wollo
Because We Support the TPLF	92%	7%
Because the Dergue Wants to Kill Us	6%	7%
Don't Know	2%	14%
In Order to Control Us	0%	36%
In Order to Punish Us	0%	14%
In Order to Mobilize Us for Conscription	0%	14%
In Order to Spread the Amharic Language	0%	7%

These refugees' statements certainly do not disprove the existence of chronic drought or ecological degradation in the highlands of Ethiopia. Independent evidence suggests that these factors are indeed a reality. Assefa Kura, an environmental scientist, has documented the historical deforestation of the highlands, beginning during the period of 1412–1636, when the emperors of Abyssinia and their endless retinues crisscrossed the countryside to find new locations for their capitals. Kura estimates that 40 percent of the country remained covered by forest at the turn of the twentieth century; by 1982, this area had dwindled to 3.1 percent (Kura 1985:1). Fieldwork by ecologist Ken Newcombe has shown how highland soil in some areas of Ethiopia has become less productive as economically stressed peasants sell firewood for cash and divert animal dung for use as fuel (Worldwatch Institute 1986:22-26). An agriculturist working for REST in TPLF-controlled areas said that he has observed a change in the hydrologic cycle in severely deforested areas of Tigray: blanketing fogs and fine rains, once common events, have become rare (personal communication). In addition, recent increases in the load of silt the Blue Nile River carries into Sudan testifies to the reality of accelerated soil erosion along Ethiopian watersheds.

However, the testimony of the refugees interviewed in Damazine indicates that the land of those people in Tigray and Wollo currently being seized for resettlement in Tigray and Wollo does not fit the definition of an ecological wasteland — if evidenced only by the common complaint that wild pigs, baboons and hyenas ravage crops and livestock and the fact that farmers can escape army recruitment campaigns by living for several weeks in nearby forests.

Most importantly, the testimony of these resettled farmers reveals that the resettlement program in Wollo and Tigray does not address the problems of drought or land degradation. It neither selects as its participants victims of the land's "unproductiveness" nor does it attempt to reverse the cause of ecological destruction — instead, the homelands of these people are simply conceded to drought. Thus, in no way is the resettlement program a form of rehabilitation, or are the ecological pretexts used to justify its implementation valid arguments. Indeed, it is fair to say that the Ethiopian government's policies create and perpetuate the "drought-prone," "precarious" situation that it blames on nature and therefore claims is intractable. The more taxes the Ethiopian government extracts from destitute farmers, the more trees are cut down and sold as firewood to raise cash. The more people it removes from their homes, the more unplanted, untended fields are exposed to erosion and the more topsoil is drawn into the atmosphere, preventing cloud formation and creating drought.

One farmer from Wollo eloquently described the interrelationship between the various causes of his suffering:

When there is lack of rain, there are insect problems. But the problems caused by the Dergue are very bad. First they take our sons and our brothers into the army. Then they charge us heavy taxes; when the harvest is reduced, they do not reduce the taxes. My land has decreased in size since the Dergue came into power, but my taxes have increased fivefold. All members of the family must pay these taxes — even children. So I am forced to sell my grain to get money to pay taxes.

When we don't have cereal, we are forced to cut trees and sell them in the town for firewood. If these conditions did not exist, the drought would not have caused us to be hungry. In this way the Dergue causes suffering. If I had more money, I could buy pipes for irrigation [see Appendix D for complete text].

It might be useful at this point to consider an alternative form of rehabilitation — which the Ethiopian government claims does not exist (see, for example, Ethiopian Embassy 1986:6). Such an alternative is currently being tested by the agricultural project of the TPLF in an attempt to reclaim a truly drought-devastated region in central Tigray. In 1984 in one of the most parched areas of Tambien, a small-scale terracing project was set up. At the end of the first year, according to an agriculturist from REST in an interview in Khartoum, the yield from the project site was 32 quintals (100 kg) per hectare, while the surrounding farmers were reaping only one-tenth of this. Hundreds of farmers have subsequently come to study the site.

The ultimate objective, the agriculturist said, is to create ways to "discourage people from farming heavily eroded hillsides." Thus, in addition, people are encouraged to move down to the flatter plains so that the upper slopes can then be reforested. Rather than declaring the land useless and moving people elsewhere, this agriculturist advocates the use of terraces and local resettlements to rehabilitate both the people and the land. The apparent success of this TPLF project needs to be verified by independent observers (see also Wright 1984; REST 1984, 1985; Twining 1985).

From Tigray to Gambella

"We were punished by burying the dead."

Most of the Tigrayans Niggli and Holcomb interviewed in early 1985 had been sent to resettlement camps in the Asosa area. In contrast, all Tigrayan refugees in Damazine in 1986 were settlers who had been routed to newer camps in the Gambella area — the vast majority to a settlement called Oala. These people represent the first group of escapees from these camps.[1] In October 1985, the RRC reported that 17,553 heads of families had been settled in Gambella.

However different the destination, the way resettlement is executed has changed little since it first began. The 38 farmers I spoke with were captured for resettlement between January and October 1985. None had volunteered. All said they had traveled into town for one reason or another and were subsequently abducted at gunpoint and forced into lorries by government troops. The marketplace was often the center for these roundups. One-third were captured while buying grain and salt or selling animals and produce (goats, cheese, beriberi, cattle, honey). Three had gone to town to visit family. One man was captured on his way to get treatment at the hospital.

Niggli and Cultural Survival reported that false promises of free grain were used to lure Tigrayan people into government-controlled towns and out of the TPLF-controlled areas during the resettlements of 1984. The practice of using grain as bait continues. Over half (54 percent) of those interviewed said they were captured in this manner. Responding to an announcement for a food or seed giveaway, farmers gathered in the designated place of distribution and were then surrounded by lorries and taken away. Sometimes whole families were abducted in these raids.

> First they said we would get a donation. I alone went to get the ration, but they said, "No, you must bring your whole family." When I returned with my family, they took us to the airport.

Many refugees were furious that they had been duped by this lie and referred to themselves as the people who had been fooled or tricked; they emphasized repeatedly that they had never been under the control of the Dergue until this happened to them. Some also stressed that they were not in desperate need for these handouts.

> There was a lack of cereal in our area, but we have other resources like cattle we can sell. Of course, if there is a donation, we will go there and try to get it. There was always plenty of food. Even last year we weren't so bad off. We only went to the government after repeated calls for free food. We had leftovers from the previous year and we had other [non-cereal] crops that survived.

Others indicated that their circumstances forced them to risk traveling into town:

> Yes, there was hunger. Because of the suffering we had to go to the enemy.

Because forced resettlements have been executed in much the same way since 1984, it could be expected that the rural population, having heard of these tricks, had become more suspicious and taken certain precautions. Some evidence suggests this is true. One man was captured while trying to stop his wife from going to town:

> I was out of town when my wife responded to the call to come to town and get seeds. I returned home because I was worried she might be resettled. I rushed to warn her. We were both resettled. Our children were left behind.

Others noted they responded to the call to get donations only after several calls:

> There was a call from the government to come out and get Red Cross food. After about the tenth call, we decided not to let the soldiers eat all the food, so we went to Axum.

> We only went to the government after repeated calls for free food.

Tigrayans captured for resettlement in 1985 were then transported to temporary detention camps in Mekele or Axum, as they were in 1984. Here they were held under armed guard for a period of time ranging from two weeks to as long as seven months until transport south became available. At this point, of 82 percent interviewed who were married men, 81 percent had been separated from their wives and 86 percent had left some or all of their children behind. The following account is typical.

> I left part of my family behind when the government said to come to town and get some seeds. We were captured — me, my wife and two children. We left two children behind in Tigray.

Detailed descriptions of the conditions in the holding camps were gathered from these refugees by REST in January and indicate that nothing about these camps has improved since Niggli and Holcomb first documented the systematic deprivation of human rights which took place there. I did not ask the farmers detailed questions about life in the holding camps, but those who had survived Mekele and felt I must know about the horrors they witnessed and endured there often spontaneously offered stories:

> We were fed very little. Many people died — an uncountable number. We were punished by burying the dead. There was no medical aid. Those who escaped at night were killed, sometimes as many as 100 each night. But more were brought from the village every day.

> We only saw people dying in Mekele. We never saw any dead persons in our villages. But in Mekele people are kept without food, and disease comes and people die like flies.

Those who survived the holding camps were then transported by plane to Gambella. The details of the travel conditions of this part of the journey were gathered by a representative of REST in January and, for that reason, were not documented in this study.

According to the Ethiopian government, the resettlement program, as a form of "rehabilitation," has been awarded "highest national priority." Government agencies involved in its implementation include the Ministry of Public Health, the Ministry of Agriculture, the Ministry of State Farms, the Ministry of Construction, the Water Resources Commission, the RRC, the National Committee for Cultural Planning and the Politburo itself (Ethiopian Embassy 1986). Yet the wretched conditions under which Tigrayan resettlers are held — sometimes for months — persist.

The fact that the various logistical bottlenecks that initially plagued other relief efforts have since been overcome should make us wonder if the temporary camps do not serve some function other than simply holding resettlers until transport south becomes available. Certainly people who are starved and diseased and who are witnesses to the executions and beatings of their comrades lose their powers of resistance. Are the holding camps a means to create the "volunteers" who the Ethiopian government insists are the only people being relocated? Of those farmers I interviewed, 64 percent said that they experienced either no problem with drought or only moderate problems; less than half said they knew of hungry people in their home villages; 100 percent said they were more hungry after they were seized for resettlement than before. It is not unreasonable to ask whether the holding camps are a means to *create* the famine victims the Ethiopian government insists must be resettled through this program.

From Wollo to Asosa

"We traveled by moonlight, darkness and daylight.
And then they dumped us into the grass."

The Wollo refugees Niggli and Holcomb interviewed in 1985 were among the first to be resettled. Most of them reported that they had been sent to their peasant association chairmen to receive food aid in the nearest market town. Once there, soldiers rounded them up and informed them that they were to be resettled. Niggli predicted that more forceful methods would follow once the Wollo population became aware of this deceit. By February 1985, Joseph Collins from the Institute for Food and Development Policy and members of MSF's staff observed that peasant associations were forced to supply a quota of resettlers in order to receive food rations (Niggli 1985). In April 1985, basic relief rations were being withheld from families living in

People being resettled from the north, transported by trucks and buses from Addis Ababa to Asosa.

areas of Wollo targeted for resettlement, thereby exacerbating famine conditions and undermining a supplemental feeding program set up by Oxfam UK (REST 1985a).

The Wollo refugees I interviewed were early resettlers also. Eleven of 16 were resettled in late 1984. The others were resettled at various times throughout 1985 (and therefore without regard to planting or harvesting schedules). They reported slightly different methods of capture: 81 percent said that they were resettled while attending mandatory government meetings. Some noted that they had been mobilized for this meeting by the militia. Of the remaining, one had gone to town to look for employment; one was taken while buying and selling at the market; and one was captured while at home. None had volunteered.

The resettlers from Wollo are probably not kept in holding areas as long as the Tigrayans before being taken on the next leg of the journey, which is by lorry rather than plane. However, the withholding of food to weaken resistance and encourage "voluntariness" was a common practice in Wollo as well:

> *The government called a meeting in Habro. They said they would give us food. We were hungry so we went. Then they told us there would be no food and no assistance. They said, "If you want to eat, we will take you to a place where there is food." They kept us at the meeting place without food. After three days of this we couldn't do anything, so we were taken to resettlement.*

The cadres in Wollo also engaged in more subtle forms of persuasion to convince the resettlers of the great future that lay before them. The refugees found some of this propaganda amusing in retrospect:

> *The Dergue showed us pictures of what looked like maize. He said we would get three harvests a year in the resettlement camps. When we reached Asosa, we found this plant. It is called bamboo. It looks like maize, but you cannot eat it. The Dergue lied to us.*

Overcrowded conditions were one reason given to some Wollo farmers for the need to relocate. For example,

> *Because there was a drought, I left my farm and went to town to look for work, to carry water and sacks for rich people. Because the town was saturated with people, the government pushed us into trucks. They said we should go to resettlement camps, a better place where seeds will grow.*

This is consistent with Niggli's suspicion that the government is following a systematic thinning-down policy, based on the argument of land scarcity and overuse. This argument is considered in the text that follows.

Once the Wollo farmers were sufficiently starved and force-fed promises of a better life in the new fertile lands of the south, they were loaded into lorries and driven nonstop to a place they called "Megele" in the Asosa area of Wollega province. One farmer described the whole experience:

> *There was a meeting. The Dergue said there would be cereal to distribute*

*because of the drought and bad harvest. We didn't know where we were go-
ing. For five days we traveled by moonlight, darkness and daylight. And then
they dumped us into the grass.*

Wollo refugees in Damazine were considerably younger (mean age: 29
years) than those from Tigray (mean age: 45 years), a difference also found
in 1985. This age difference probably reflects the difference in the method of
capture. Tigrayans must be lured from the TPLF-controlled countryside into what they consider to be enemy territory—under the known risk of being
captured for resettlement. Thus they are more likely to send older members
of the family to receive food aid. But because the farmers of Wollo can be
rounded up using the peasant association infrastructure and by simply calling a mandatory meeting, young vigorous members of the community can
be collected. Because of their young age, the majority (63 percent) of the
Wollo refugees were unmarried, but of those I interviewed who were married, all reported that they had been separated from their families when they
were captured. (There were, however, some Wollo farmers in the camp accompanied by their wives or children, who were not represented in my random sample.)

Considering that the removal of young men from the fields by conscription (or fear of conscription) was one of the major reasons Wollo refugees
cited for famine conditions in their homelands, the government's plan to
"thin down" the Wollo population by nine percent with the relocation of its
most vigorous members can only mean a further drop in food production in
Wollo. According to the age structure of a rapidly growing human population, approximately 24 percent will be between the ages of 20 and 35. If
resettlements are entirely targeted at this age group and a 9 percent population reduction is achieved, then 37.5 percent of the 20–35-year-olds will be
removed from Wollo. If only one-half of the resettlements involve this age
group, the population of 20–35-year-olds will still decline by nearly 19 percent. Even if one believes that land scarcity and overpopulation are legitimate problems in Wollo, it seems absurd to think that removing 19 to 37.5
percent of the best producers from the land could ever be a viable solution
to famine.

Table 3
Method of Capture for Resettlement*

Activity When Captured	Tigray	Wollo
Buying and Selling at Market	32.4%	6.3%
Responding to Call to Get Free Grain	54.1%	0.0%
Attending Mandatory Government Meeting	0.0%	81.2%
Visiting Family in Town	8.1%	0.0%
Traveling to Hospital	2.7%	0.0%
Traveling to Warn Relative About Resettlement	2.7%	0.0%
Looking for Employment	0.0%	6.3%
At Home	0.0%	6.3%

*Compare to Clay and Holcomb 1985:86.

Life in the Virgin Lands

One hundred percent of resettled farmers interviewed said they were more hungry in "fertile," "virgin" lands in Gambella than they had ever been in Tigray. One hundred percent of Wollo farmers interviewed said they were more hungry in the promised land of Asosa than they had ever been in Wollo. These two statistics alone expose the vast deception of the resettlement operation and dispel the lie that it is a form of famine relief. Lack of alternatives—the government's reason for the need to resettle—is also the reason given by resettled farmers for their starvation in the midst of supposed abundance:

> *I lost two children in Asosa. In Wollo, I knew that there was drought. But the majority of the hunger is in Asosa. I can eat my one-month ration in two*

"Where we were resettled, there was nothing to eat . . . nothing but wild beasts in the surroundings."
©S. Steingraber

The Wollo farmer on the far right carried this plastic bowl from the Asosa resettlement to Damazine. Bowls were issued by the cadres to each resettler who received five bowls of cracked corn a week as his or her only ration. ©S. Steingraber

weeks. And then I sit idly during mealtime. If I am absent from work twice, I am beaten. When we try to sell wood to buy grain, we are beaten.

In Wollo, I could carry firewood to make money, although, yes, I was very hungry. But in Asosa, there was only one stage left before my death.

There was a lack of cereal in my area, but we did have resources like cattle to sell. But in Gambella we were attacked on three sides: hunger, flies and disease.

The hunger in Gambella is unsurpassed. At home if you are hungry while you are working, you can go home and eat, but not in Gambella.

In Tigray we could sell our animals. But in Gambella, there is no market, no options.

Their hunger in Gambella is different; it is so much. At home we kept our mealtimes. No one died of hunger. But in Gambella the hunger brought disease, and we died.

Peter Niggli's description of the resettlement farms as enforced labor camps is, one year later, still accurate. Stripped of all decision making, farmers said they were organized into work brigades and spent their waking hours laboring under the command of petty cadres. In Gambella, these labors mainly involved clearing the land and building huts; only 24 percent said they were actually involved in farming (defined here to mean planting, cultivating and harvesting). In contrast, of 16 Asosa resettlers, 15 were involved in clearing, building and farming; the other was used as a medic. This difference may be due to the fact that Asosa is an older camp; the first wave of resettlers may already have finished the heavy clearing. Another reason may be simply that the Asosa resettlers stayed longer in the camp before escaping: 79 percent stayed more than one year, while the median length of stay among Tigrayan resettlers was only three months.

All descriptions from both Gambella and Asosa resettlers indicate that the forest was first simply clearcut by hand by the resettlers and then bulldozed in the most indiscriminate way:

There was no pattern to chopping the trees. We left the stumps. No, we were not shown how and what to cut. The cadres never left their tents to show us, so we cut the nearest ones.

In Asosa, resettlers were required to dig up the roots of the trees — however large — and chop all branches and roots into small chunks. They concluded that this work was assigned just to make them tired.

In preparing the new government fields for planting, the sequence of labor was reversed: the machines (tractors) came through first and the resettlers followed on foot, digging and chopping the soil with hoes. No trees were left standing in this process. One Tigrayan, who spent time in both Gambella and Asosa, compared the activities and conditions of each site:

In Asosa, I built houses and farmed corn for the government. In Gambella, I cut grass and was digging. Both places look the same. There is the same food. Both are equally bad.

Resettlement site in Wollega.

Forced to dig the soil by hand, the farmers, accustomed to plowing the ground with oxen, experienced a process of acute dehumanization. This psychological phenomenon probably cannot be appreciated fully by those of us who have seldom dug the ground at all. But it was quite real for those farmers — especially from Wollo — who repeatedly wanted to show me the calluses on their hands, the results of months of digging, and demonstrated in mime exactly how they drove their shovels into the earth. To Wollo farmers, digging with their hands was tantamount to becoming a draft animal or machine, and they often described their lives in the resettlements with these metaphors:

> The tractors plowed, but we worked like oxen following the tractor and breaking the ground. The party cadres beat us like donkeys.
>
> We did not farm. We dug the ground like animals.
>
> We became oxen in Asosa. We became tractors.
>
> The cadres told us, "If you have finished your flour, eat soil and come to work."

In contrast, the dehumanization of the people in Gambella seemed to be brought on more by the sheer wildness of their surroundings than by the nature of their work. Their camp, Oala, is located inside of what is supposed to be Gambella National Park, an area renowned for its big-game hunting. To the Anuak people, whose traditional lands these once were, the name Oala refers to a pool within the park where wild animals come to drink. It is little wonder, then, that the Tigrayan farmers described themselves in Gambella as "food for the wild animals." While clearing the forests, many had witnessed or heard of the deaths of fellow workers by snakes, hippopotamuses and elephants. "We were living with lions," said one survivor.

Contact with the indigenous people was more extensive in Asosa than in Gambella. In both cases, the resettlers were apprehensive about interacting with the people whose homelands they knew had been seized for resettlement. In Asosa, some of the Wollo inhabitants traded firewood with the Oromo for food and seeds, although this was forbidden and punishable by death. Several farmers said they witnessed the public shooting of one man whose crime was secretly selling wood, and others said they heard that seven men in a nearby camp had been executed for the same reason.

According to the Wollo inhabitants, the attitude of the Oromos toward this influx of settlers was mixed: on the one hand they bitterly resented them, and on the other they wanted to help them become strong enough to escape the camp and leave the area:

We met Oromos in Asosa. They helped us, gave us coffee. But they were not happy. The Oromos said, "We have suffered a lot for you; when you came, the sickness increased. You brought diseases from your homeland and made the Dergue compel us to work for you. So please, go home. There is the road back to your homeland."

The Oromos did not like us. They told us to go home, called us dogs. They showed us the road home, but we cannot go because of the drought in our homeland.

We saw many Oromos. Some were friendly, some not. Some people traded with them, especially firewood. But I only worked with the cadres because I was afraid.

We didn't get along with the Oromos. They said we are the people who came to bring bad times. But the government brought us there; what could we do?

Given the Oromo ancestry of the people from Wollo, Clay and Holcomb speculate that the indigenous population and the resettled colonists could unite against their perceived common enemy in a popular uprising (see Clay and Holcomb 1985:16-18). There is no evidence that this has occurred during the past year. Indeed the government has succeeded in creating and perpetuating strife and ill will between the two groups. Of course, whether such strife iscarried out fortuitously or as part of a divide-and-conquer strategy, is to the government's advantage. As has been previously reported, the Oromo are forced to build houses and relinquish resources to the newcomers. This practice continues. In addition, two farmers recalled that Wollo resettlers were forced to plow the fields of the Oromos who had been taken away to fight in the army. If they refused, they were shot.

In Gambella, most of the resettlers had no contact with the local Anuak population until their escape; interactions were limited to a few clandestine exchanges of cash and blankets for seeds. According to my translator, who left Gambella in November 1985, the Anuak people are also being forced to provide living quarters for the newcomers. But unlike the Oromo people of the Asosa region who must also relinquish food supplies and household goods to the colonists from Wollo, preparations by the Anuaks seem to be restricted to hut construction. In 1985, schools in Gambella were closed so that students and teachers could cut grass and wood to erect huts in the camps.

In contrast to the fanning of intercommunal conflict that characterizes the cadres' policies in the Asosa camp, Anuak people and Tigrayan people in Gambella are evidently encouraged to mix with each other and even inter-marry. A Tigrayan priest in Damazine told me that party cadres tried to force him to marry an Anuak woman when he arrived in the resettlement camp without his wife. The "bride" was presented to him bare-breasted, and he refused. She was presented a second time — fully clothed — and he refused again on the grounds that polygamy was against his religion. These at-tempts support Niggli's theory that one of the items on the hidden agenda of resettlement is the dissolution of tribal or national allegiances, and one of the ways of achieving this is through creation of a new breed of people — "the new man in the new Ethiopia" (Niggli 1986:34).

The OLF contends that resettlers unwittingly become instruments as well as victims of the Ethiopian regime's policies and attempts to squelch mass resistance movements in the south. It alleges that conscripts from early resettlers are deployed in fighting against the OLF and, as armed militia, in guarding the most recent newcomers. I did not ask any direct questions of the refugees that would elicit evidence for or against this assertion, but anecdotes related by those resettled to Gambella — which is near areas of OLF activity — give us reason to take the claims seriously. Several farmers told me that 300 "fat people" (meaning healthy) were selected by the party cadres and taken away and never heard from again; some refugees suspected that they were taken into the army. Another group of Gambella refugees also said that the frequent disappearance of heavy-bodied people from their camp was the factor that finally scared them into escaping. One farmer told of the brief reign of the camp militia, made up of earlier reset-tlers:

> When we were there, the government came and selected some people and trained them to be guards and watch us. When they got their weapons, they tried to fight the Dergue. Then the Dergue told them a lie and said, "Turn in your weapons and we will give you automatic weapons." In that way these new guards were disarmed.

Comparison of Settlement Conditions with Earlier Reports

The Ethiopian government officially launched the resettlement program in he fall of 1984, billing it as a "new rehabilitation approach" (RRC 1984:20-21). The government has continued to claim the program was initiated "on account of the aftermath of the current severe drought" (Ethiopian Embassy 1986). Not highly publicized is the fact that large-scale resettlements from Tigray and Wollo to areas in the southwest have been carried out under the direction of the current government for at least eight years, long before the drought of 1983-1984. According to one account, over 13,000 people from Wollo had already been moved to Wollega by early 1979 (Dines 1982). Because the receiving camps for many of these resettlers were located in Asosa, a comparison between the testimonies of those recently escaped from Asosa and the experiences of the resettlers-cum-refugees who were participants in the earlier operations might prove fruitful.

In August 1982, Dines interviewed refugees in Sudan who had left the Asosa camps over the previous 18 months. Then, as now, ecological degradation was an excuse used to justify the relocations. According to Dine's report, in Tigray peasants were told it was "scientifically" impossible for their land to accommodate them. Others were told they had to leave after the military deliberately poisoned large areas of their land with insecticides. Again, just as previously, areas targeted for resettlement in the north were described as drought-afflicted to aid-giving agencies, although the majority of people in the Wollega camps told Dines they did not come from such areas.

Likewise, Mekuria Bulcha interviewed resettlement escapees in Sudan in January 1983. The RRC again used the pretext of drought to move these people from Wollo to Asosa state farms. However, at this time, according to Bulcha, only one province in Wollo was affected by drought, and none of the respondents came from this province.

From the descriptions given to Dines and Bulcha, the methods of obtaining "volunteers" for the program seem to have changed little over the years:

Whole families and in some cases villages were rounded up by the military and put on trucks; houses and villages were surrounded, usually at night, and the inmates forced onto transports (Dines 1982:2).

People are usually rounded up in marketplaces and packed onto military trucks and directly deported to resettlement areas. . . . Many resisted deportation and were imprisoned in Wollo for four months before they were taken to Asosa (Bulcha 1983:6).

The prospective settlers are usually rounded up in a market or garrison town and then transferred to the next temporary collection camp. . . . Often the peasants did not receive anything to eat (Niggli 1985:14-15).

Because the town was saturated with people, the government pushed us into trucks (Wollo farmer 1986).

Life in the resettlement camps of Asosa seems to have been as miserable for those resettled seven years ago as it is today.

Work was backbreaking. First the "settlers" had to clear the land, chopping down trees and clearing brush, and then they built shelters from grass and sticks. Only a few shelters, which had been built by forced labor from the indigenous population of Wollega, had been put up in advance. Food in all camps was scarce and the majority of the people had to live on maize and water (Dines 1982:2-3).

In Asosa, they were settled in camps and ordered to clear the land of brush, large trees and heavy stones, work suitable for bulldozers. In spite of the arduous job, the "settlers" were given very little food — a few cups of flour, salt and pepper every week per person. Whatever is produced with their labor on the farms is shipped to Addis Ababa (Bulcha 1983:6).

One difference between refugees' descriptions of the Asosa camps then and now is found in the reports given to Dines, which indicate that men, women and children were kept in separate camps, an arrangement the refugees did not report in 1986. However, the population of the camps — 500 people each — the presence of an armed militia, and the central location of a prison compound are characteristics of the camps reported by refugees in both 1982 and 1986.

The RRC made oblique references to the earlier resettlements in its 1984 announcement of the "new approach." While claiming that 69 percent of the 83 previous resettlements had become "self-reliant," it blamed failures on the overuse of machinery and the inability of traditional peasants to "in a short time adapt to the high technology in use" (RRC 1984:20-21). As the above descriptions attest, bafflement by high technology was not among the problems escapees from the early settlements reported.

Under the new approach, according to the RRC, "assistance provided is minimal, machinery service is provided only in places where it is impossible to clear the land otherwise" (1984:21). If the new low-tech image was designed to make the resettlement scheme more palatable to outside donors, this was not an aspect of the program included in the propaganda pitches to the farmers selected for resettlement. In fact, many farmers who were captured in 1984 and 1985 were reassured they would be provided with all the equipment they needed to farm. Instead, they found themselves in the resettlement camps uprooting forests and digging the ground by hand without even the assistance of draft animals. Inquiries as to the location of the promised equipment could bring beatings or imprisonment. A group of Tigrayan refugees from the Gambella camps said that while digging the ground by hand, one of them had asked the party cadres, "You are the government; why don't you bring us tractors?" The cadres replied, "No, this is your punishment for being reactionaries."

Escape to Sudan

*"We left because we would rather be eaten by wild animals
than be beaten by the cadres like donkeys."*

All Tigrayan refugees interviewed in Damazine in 1986 said they had left ambella in October and November 1985, fleeing in groups ranging in size from 3 to 1,885. Interviews conducted by a REST representative in January

In explaining how she escaped Gambella, a Tigray mother said she was forced to plaster the walls of the cadres' houses at night and do other manual labor during her pregnancy and that her baby was born "very small" in the resettlement camp. ©S. Steingraber

documented in detail the journey of four escaping groups and revealed that only 20 percent of the original 3,000 escapees had made it to the Damazine camp. I did not attempt to document the fate of each escaping group, but descriptions of the escape attempts gathered during random interviews are consistent with the findings of the REST investigation (see REST 1986).

Hunger, thirst, disease, abuse and worry about family who had remained in Tigray were reasons cited for attempting escape from Gambella. Refugees said that October and November were auspicious months for flight because the summer flood stage of the many surrounding rivers had subsided. Many of the farmers I interviewed expressed fear of the deep swift rivers (not found in the highlands of Tigray) and recalled the drownings or captures of those who had tried to escape during the summer months. Those caught during escape attempts were imprisoned or beaten.

Mass breakouts were seen as the best escape strategy because they minimized the danger of animal attacks. Refugees who were members of these large groups could recall exactly the number of those escaping with them (such as the largest group of 1,885) because they had arranged for the Anuak people to ferry them across the rivers in canoes. This service cost E$1 per person for earlier groups escaping in October 1985 and E$3 for later groups. Potential escapees pooled their resources to raise cash for the fee—some used money they had brought from Tigray; some sold blankets or firewood.

My translator, who left Gambella in November with three other Anuaks, had not heard of this arrangement but said it was entirely likely, given the Anuak people's desire to remove the highland settlers from their lands. He also noted that many of the resettlers he had seen in Gambella could scarcely walk without assistance because their feet were so swollen and infested with chiggers.

The journey to Sudan required 15 to 30 days of walking, with one farmer reporting that he had traveled only seven days. Hunger, thirst, drownings and injuries from previous beatings were cited as causes of death during the journey. The tired and sick were abandoned along the way. All who traveled in large groups reported attacks by armed and uniformed bandits who beat and robbed them, and captured the women and children. This report is typical:

> When we came from Gambella, many people died because they drowned in the rivers and an army took our wives and children and stole our clothes and beat me.

The farmers had little knowledge about the "armies" who attacked them. According to OLF and ORA representatives, they are members of the Ethiopian-backed Sudanese People's Liberation Army (SPLA), splinter groups of which have become little more than bounty hunters, rounding up and preying upon resettlement escapees. Tigrayan women who later arrived in the Damazine camp told me they had been raped and held as slaves in SPLA camps. (See Appendix C for details about SPLA captures.)

According to Holcomb, many of those who escaped from the Asosa camps in 1984 had "hit the ground running" almost as soon as they arrived. This is no longer true for those escaping in 1985. Of 14 Wollo farmers, 11 had lived in Asosa for longer than one year and all longer than three months. Many reported previous unsuccessful escape attempts for which punishment was severe. A group of Wollo farmers who had only been in Sudan for eight days reported that

> We left Asosa because we were hungry and suffering. We tried to escape as soon as we arrived but were caught and beaten. Twice we tried to escape and were caught. We were beaten by cadres and imprisoned in a place full of dust

and insects. We were given a little water and no food for the first five days. And after that they gave us roasted grain. During the day we dug latrines. They beat us with whips, 50 lashes twice a day for one month.

Fear of drowning or being shot or captured by camp militia were reasons given for not escaping sooner. Others reported that they were warned by the cadres that "no one will help you if you run to Sudan." These security and disinformation measures are undoubtedly a response to previous escapes. To my regret now, I did not ask questions regarding the camp militia's role in preventing escapes or the relationship between the militia, who are made up of earlier resettlers, and the camp cadres. These issues warrant further investigation.

Compared to the newer camps of Gambella, the danger of being killed or caught while escaping appears to be greater at Asosa; after a successful escape, however, the journey to Sudan is less arduous. Fleeing in large groups to ward off wild animals was considered desirable here as well, although the largest group size was 73 (as compared with 1,885 from Gambella). Reaching the border from Asosa required three to eight days of walking at night and sleeping during the day. No one reported attacks or kidnappings along the way. The local Oromo did not appear to play a direct role in facilitating these escapes, although this is not a question I asked directly. Several refugees mentioned that the Oromo were encouraging Wollo settlers to return directly to their homelands through Gojam.

As refugees in the Damazine camp, both Gambella and Asosa escapees perceived themselves as survivors of a massive slaughter. Frequent mention was made of the uncounted and uncountable dead, especially in the transit camps and during the flight to Sudan.

My own expressions of sympathy during an interview with a Tigrayan woman were shrugged off. Although she had been captured and gang raped during her escape, she said she considered herself one of the fortunate ones to have survived the journey: "There are so many of us dead in the forest. Thousands. No one knows how many." (See Appendix C for complete text.)

In fact, even by conservative estimates, the carnage along the border is tremendous. Of the 3,000 resettlers the REST interviewer determined had escaped in four groups from Gambella in the fall of 1985 (REST 1986:2), only 25 percent made it to Damazine by March 1986, leaving 75 percent unaccountable. If we assume that one-half of those not accounted for are still alive (representing those who returned voluntarily or by force to Gambella, or are still held captive), then the mortality rate of those escaping is 37.5 percent. Even if we assume that three-fourths of those not accounted for are still alive, the mortality is still higher than that estimated by MSF to represent the death rate in the transit camps and during transport south (one out of every six or seven). Certainly rates of escape and deaths during escape are factors that should be figured into the kind of cost-benefit equations policy makers use to assess the value of the resettlement program — especially when the same agencies will be asked to tend to the needs of the surviving escapees across the borders.

The Wollo and Tigray escapees perceive their current situation quite differently. When asked, "Do you want to return to your homeland?" 100 percent of the Tigrayans said yes. Some were extremely impatient to do so. Three who identified their villages as under Dergue control said they would move their families to TPLF-controlled areas. Some expressed concern that they would not return to Tigray in time to plant the next season's crops. None thought that obtaining the needed materials for planting would be a significant problem. Of 32 farmers, 69 percent said they could obtain seeds from their neighborhoods or at the market; 20 percent thought the TPLF would give them seeds, and 11 percent said they had personal supplies of seeds, including one optimist who believed he could obtain seeds from the crop he had planted last spring immediately before his capture. These responses were typical:

> I am longing to see my wife and children and know that in my neighborhood I can find some seed to plant. I don't think there is anything that better suits me than the land my father gave me. We had been doing just fine.

> We feel we have been kept here too long. We have families back home. They are longing for us, and we are longing for them. We had already planted when we left and hope to find a crop in the field when we get back.

> Those along the road are dead. But the ones who are here want to go back and cultivate. We are worried about our families.

> The families we left behind may die because no one is there to farm. But the Dergue cannot take our land. If we can get back to Tigray, the Dergue will never attack us again. But our families can die now because no one is there to help them.

In contrast, only 26.3 percent of the farmers I interviewed from Wollo said that they planned to return to their homelands in the near future. Drought, fear of being resettled again, fear of punishment or persecution and general destitution were reasons cited by the majority for wanting to remain in Sudan. This reaction is quite different from that of Wollo refugees interviewed in 1985, nearly all of whom desired and planned to return home. This difference could simply reflect the fact that most Wollo refugees in 1986 had arrived in Damazine only very recently and were still quite fearful and unsure of their safety. Of those not wishing to return to Wollo, nearly 80 percent said they did not know what they would do in Sudan. The others said they planned to seek employment in Sudan or would follow the Tigrayan refugees back to Tigray. In contrast to the defiance of their Tigrayan counterparts, the Wollo often described their situation in very passive terms:

> I would like to go home, but there are two reasons why I don't. The government will lead me to resettle again. And the other reason is drought. I can't cultivate. I will suffer. My cattle died because of drought; there is no way to eat. We don't know what to do. We don't have rights. We don't have money. We are waiting for the commissioners.

"We are sick for the sky of our homelands." Refrain of a song sung by a Wollo farmer, musician and poet, Damazine, Sudan, 1986.

©S. Steingraber

The cattle are gone, we have no money, no resources, nothing. We aren't going anywhere without the Red Cross.

We will stay here as sons of the UN [the UN does not operate or have a presence in the camp]. *We are waiting for decisions. We have nowhere to go. We are worried about the children who are still in Wollo, but the man who goes to get his children will be killed or resettled again to Asosa.*

I want to go home, but my children are dead. Until the government changes, I won't go home because I will be resettled again.

We are afraid of losing our lives. We like our homeland. But because of the government, we will be resettled again. We have no money.

The five farmers who said they did plan to return to Wollo all lived together in the same tent. When asked if they feared another resettlement, they replied, "We are not afraid of the Dergue because when the Dergue comes, we will hide ourselves in the forest."

Expressing anger, the Tigrayan farmers sometimes described their life in the Damazine camp as a prison sentence: "We are in prison here now, but as soon as we are free, we will return. No one can stop us." In contrast the Wollo farmers saw the Damazine camp as refuge of safety:

At home we are like people. But in the new place [Asosa camp] we were treated like monkeys. Now we are children, babies. We were born, twice. Our mothers gave birth to us in a good place. Now we have escaped from the reset- tlement camp and we are born again.

The Tigrayan refugees perceived themselves as more fortunate than the Wollo:

The difference between us and the Wollo people is that they have more drought and no liberation front.

The Wollo people are like toys the government plays with.

The Failure of Agriculture in the Resettlement Camps

All human abuses aside, if the resettlement program is to succeed in "rehabilitating" peasant farmers, as is claimed by the RRC, then either the farmers will know how to adapt their agricultural skills to the ecological conditions in the resettlement sites or they will be taught new methods ap- propriate to the environment. Neither is happening in Gambella and Asosa. All evidence from my interviews indicates that most agricultural efforts failed in these camps during 1985.

As discussed above, most farmers in Gambella spent their days clearing brush, felling trees and digging the ground; few were directly involved in the cooperative agricultural schemes. Of those who were, all reported that the cereal crops they planted grew poorly or not at all. Sweet potato was the only crop identified as having produced any kind of harvest. Sorghum and corn were cited as particular failures.

When asked why, in their opinion as farmers, the crops did not grow in Gambella, those interviewed spent considerable time discussing the ques- tion among themselves. No clear consensus emerged. Bad timing, too much rain, not enough rain, bad soil and insects were among the reasons cited, but these seemed to be guesses which I pushed them to make. Some simply said they had no idea.

The government crops did not grow well. We don't know why.

The soil in Gambella is very warm but in our homeland it is cool. So the plants rot in Gambella.

In Tigray there is more rainfall.

The soil is too muddy and seeds rot. We planted only the straight kind of sorghum, not the bent kind. We planted it in the right kind of soil; I don't know why it wouldn't grow. The seedlings grew well at first and then died. White people came once and said this is not a good place for sorghum.

The crops I saw looked bad. All grew well at first but then died because of insects or because they dried out. Except for sweet potato.

We planted but it was the wrong time for sowing and the worm ate the crops.

The Ethiopian government has assured potential donor agencies in the West that each farmer would be allocated his own plot of land to farm in addition to participating in cooperative schemes. In December 1984, the RRC said that resettlement families who are moved to lands that have "not hitherto been put to use" are given two hectares of farm land which the government will clear and plow for them during the first two years. "The machinery service will be discontinued at the end of the second year, and in the third year, families are expected to be self-sufficient" (RRC 1984:22). By September of the following year, the amount of land the government claimed it was allocating to each family had been revised down to one-half hectare and was referred to as a "garden" (rather than as "farm land") which the resettlers would plow themselves; the self-sufficiency claim was omitted. In a radio broadcast of his speech to the Central Committee, Colonel Mengistu said, "The implementation of the resettlement plan will enable every settler head of family to clear at least half a hectare with his family in the form of a garden to *supplement his food needs* as well as being in a large cooperative farm" (Mengistu 1985, emphasis added).

The farmers I interviewed from Gambella said that they were given small backyard gardens. Some were no more than a 2 m strip around their huts; others were plots of about 10 by 15 m. Certainly, they said, the plots were not large enough to allow self-sufficiency even with a good harvest — which no one achieved.

Of 26 farmers who had lived in Gambella, 70 percent said that they planted their gardens and 30 percent did not bother. Reasons given for not planting included lack of time due to other duties and planned escapes. One man said he spent so much time in the camp prison for attempted escapes that there was no chance for personal farming. For the first resettlers, seeds for private gardens had to be obtained from the local Anuak through clandestine exchanges of cash or blankets; later resettlers were given seed by the party cadres or by their neighbors. One farmer said he could not obtain seeds but had to hoe his garden anyway under orders from the camp cadres.

Crops planted in these gardens included various combinations of corn, sorghum, sweet potatoes, sugar cane, vegetables and oilseed, depending on what seeds were available. Usually resettlers planted no more than two or three kinds of crops, a distinct contrast from the great diversity of crops maintained in their homeland farms.

Most significantly, 100 percent of those interviewed said that their gardens yielded nothing or an insufficient harvest. Since the cadres expected them to barter their garden surpluses for clothes, these failures directly affected their quality of life. Again, those interviewed reached no consensus as to the cause. Some said they did not recognize the vegetable seeds they were given and did not know how they were planted. In Tigray, they said, they were accustomed to buying vegetables on the market. Many complained about the soil in Gambella, but few agreed as to what exactly was wrong with it.

The land is new and becomes muddy very fast.

Sweet potatoes never grow well because it is a new place. We could grow it in our homeland very well. But in Gambella, the seed never grew.

In Tigray, seeds grow; in Gambella they do not. The soil is drier than in Tigray.

There is more rainfall in Gambella but the soil is bad.

The soil becomes muddy after it rains in Gambella.

The farmers interviewed also said that they were not familiar with rainfall patterns and seasonal changes and therefore did not know when to plant or harvest. Some noted that they did not know how to plant and plow with hoes since they used oxen for this work in their homelands. One farmer said he had never tried to grow sweet potatoes without irrigation before. Others said the garden seedlings that did survive were grazed by large antelope-like animals. They could not practice the labor-intensive techniques used in Tigray to keep animals away from their crops because during the day they were clearing the land for the government fields.

The story from the Wollo farmers who had escaped Asosa was much the same: both collective and backyard agricultural attempts yielded little or no harvest. These reports are especially significant because journalists and foreign nationals allowed to visit model camps in the Asosa area say they have observed fields of bountiful crops (Blaine Harden, *Washington Post*, personal communication).

Again, the farmers could not agree as to the cause of these failures: one tent cited fertility, another soil color, another insects and another rainfall.

In Wollo, the soil is red and very nice. In Asosa, it is black and things don't grow well.

The soil is not good. I don't know why. There is a problem of insects. The seedlings grew well at first and then died.

The sorghum grew well at first, but then something ate the seeds while they were still green.

Rainfall is twice in one year in Wollo. But in Asosa it is always the rainy season.

There is more rainfall in Wollo than in Mengele [camp in Asosa].

Because of insects, most plants did not grow well, but the cadres brought in the seeds and took away the harvest for storage.

Some farmers could identify — by looking at the seeds or the seedlings — the particular varieties of crops the government gave them and recognized that they were unsuitable for the climate in Asosa. For example, one farmer reported:

We planted only one kind of sorghum, the red kind. But the soil was not right for it. There are no small rocks in the soil of Asosa which this crop needs. [See Appendix D for complete text.]

One farmer recalled that he was forced to plant teff in the government fields under conditions he knew would ensure a lack of harvest. However, he could not offer his advice to the party cadres for fear of punishment.

The Dergue knows nothing about cultivating, about farming. The sacks of teff for planting contained both red and white seeds mixed together. In Wollo, we do not mix them because the seeds are of different weight. The red one is heavier; the white one needs to be planted deeper. Also, we plant them at different times. But in Asosa, they had us plant the two teffs together, white and red. So some did not ripen, and then all the harvest rotted because some seeds were too green.

Although I did not ask questions on this topic directly, some farmers mentioned the great amount of waste involved in harvesting the little crop that did reach maturity in the government fields in Asosa.

After a harvest in Wollo, they explained, a farmer would carefully spread the cereal on a cement-like threshing floor made of a hardened paste of animal dung and water. Oxen would walk around and around over the grain separating the seed from the straw. In contrast, they were appalled to see that in Asosa the cereal was simply dropped in the dirt and beaten with sticks, causing it to become mixed with impurities and scattering much of the seed. This work was mostly carried out by the cadres, who, we can assume, have little hands-on experience in farming. Farmers said the grain was then taken away to some "unknown place" for storage and was never seen by the resettlers again.

At home in Wollo we use oxen for threshing the seeds. We waste none! But in Asosa they beat the seed with sticks and threw away much seed with the husks, and stones got mixed together with the seed. When we protested, we were told we were lazy.

In our homeland, one person can produce the work of 500 in Asosa. The Dergue wastes so much cereal and so much grain. [See Appendix D for complete text.]

Backyard gardens were planted by 12 or 13 of the farmers I interviewed from Asosa. The one farmer who did not plant his garden said it was too small to be worth the effort. One-half said that although they planted a garden, they had no time to tend or cultivate it. One group of farmers said they planted only vegetables like peppers and carrots; the remainder planted some combination of corn and sorghum. No one planted a combination of crops that had the potential to be nutritionally complete — such as grain and legumes — as they did in their homeland farms. Therefore, as in Gambella, the private plots in the Asosa settlement camps do not hold the potential for self-sufficiency.

Of 11 farmers, eight obtained the seeds for their gardens from the local market and three from party cadres. Some people ate the unground corn they were given to plant. Those who purchased seeds used money they had brought from Wollo or sold firewood to the Oromos — a Catch-22 situation since such exchanges were illegal. The cadres' reasoning, one of the farmers interviewed explained, was, "Your garden is for yourself so get your own seeds." These reports are in distinct contrast to the government's repeated assertions that seed, fertilizer and pesticides are being provided to each resettled head of household.

As did the Gambella residents, 100 percent of those interviewed from Asosa said their gardens yielded nothing or a very insufficient harvest. As in Gambella, Asosa residents were expected to exchange their produce for clothes. ("The cadres said, 'You work for yourself and buy your own clothes.' ") At the same time, donated clothes went to the cadres. Without harvests, some went to work for local Oromos who would give them food as payment. This was also illegal, and some preferred to remain hungry rather than approach the Oromos — who already resented them — and risk imprisonment.

Asosa farmers offered diverse and sometimes conflicting diagnoses as to the reasons for the failure of backyard gardens. Some attributed the loss to the fact that they were not allowed to tend their own plots except at night.

We had backyards but nothing grew well. We planted maize and sorghum but got no harvest. We didn't have time to take care of it, to cultivate or plow.

Others blamed ecological factors. The disagreement among these three farmers simultaneously interviewed in one particular tent is typical: the first said the soil in Asosa lacked humus; the second said the soil was too rocky; the third said it was too new and too dry. However, all three came to the same conclusion: "There is nothing like our land in Wollo."

Seed-eating insects were also a major cause of garden failures in Asosa.

In our gardens we were given a few certain seeds to plant — white sorghum and corn — but it was only enough for children. Ants ate the seeds almost immediately. The soil is not good there; it is the soil for insects, not the soil for planting. And we were forbidden to go to the market, so we could not buy seeds. [See Appendix D for complete text.]

In our backyards the crops grew well, but then they dried up and insects ate them. The cadres gave us the seeds — corn and sorghum — but we got no harvest. The soil is not good there; there are many insects, ants and worms. The problem is not one of fertility: the ants would just come and eat the seeds as soon as they were sown. I was more hungry in Asosa than I ever was at home. [See Appendix D for complete text.]

Ecological Shock

Many ecological zones exist within the huge empire that is Ethiopia. Indeed, the country is renowned among naturalists for its great diversity of plant and animal species. Of all these different environments, one could probably choose no two more dissimilar ecological areas than the cool, dry northern highlands of Wollo or Tigray and the hot, wet lowlands in the southwestern provinces.

As part of a 1972 survey, R. L. Donahue classified soils in Ethiopia, including sites in western Tigray and the Gambella region. Soil characteristics, including nutrient content, sizes of particles, rooting depth, duration of cracking and temperature, were quite different in Tigray and in Gambella. In addition, Donahue noted that mean annual rainfall in the Gambella site was twice as high as in the site in Tigray and that rain fell in all 12 months of the year rather than only between April and November.

Thus, when a farmer from the highlands is transported to resettlement camps in areas like Gambella, he is instantly transformed from an agricultural expert to an unskilled, ignorant laborer, completely dependent for his survival on the central government. This process, multiplied by 600,000, is in essence the final result of the current resettlement program: uprooted from their homelands, 600,000 people are now utterly dependent on the government. This consideration is missing from the kinds of dollars-versus-death-rate analyses that define the current debate on the resettlement issue.

Not surprisingly, the diverse and contradictory explanations the farmers gave for the failure of agriculture in both resettlement sites contrast greatly with the precise, consistent diagnoses they provided when describing the causes of the agricultural problems in their homelands. The expertise these farmers have developed over their lifetimes — what to plant, when to plant, how to plant, cultivate and harvest — is completely bound up in a particular ecology, governed by certain seasonal changes and characterized by the specific properties of the soil and overlying vegetation. Not only their livelihoods but their entire culture — language, songs, dances, folktales — is predicated upon and has evolved within certain ecological patterns. This was emphasized to me repeatedly during the interviews. As one farmer said, "We plant and harvest according to the laws of our culture."

It is hard to exaggerate the extent to which an Ethiopian peasant farmer is tied to his land. The kinds of grasses he feeds his animals, the multiplicity of crop varieties he selects for and maintains as seed, the type of wood he uses to build with, the species of plant he uses for medicines — an entire legacy of unrecorded knowledge — are determined by a particular environment and become almost useless in another. The farmers' inability to reach a consensus about the cause of agricultural failure in the new environment illustrates the nontransferable nature of their agricultural knowledge. (Or — as in the case of the farmer who recognized that the teff was being planted incorrectly and offered his suggestion — the resettlers are punished for such knowledge.) Those who do have intimate knowledge of the new environment — the local Anuak or Oromo — are hostile to the newcomers for obvious reasons, or are forbidden contact with them, and in any case, speak a different language.

The nontransferable nature of an Ethiopian farmer's knowledge is further illustrated in the following comparison — made by the refugees themselves — between the forests of their homelands and the forests of the resettlement sites.

Of 15 Tigrayan farmers, all said they knew the names and uses of all the trees in their homelands. When asked if they knew the names of the trees in Gambella, only one claimed he recognized most of them. The remainder knew less than half; most did not know any or only knew a few. Of five Wollo farmers, all knew the trees in their homeland but none recognized the trees they were forced to cut down in Asosa; one man said he recognized only mango. Significantly, the Tigrayans claimed that the difference between the forests of Tigray and Gambella was that the trees of the Gambella forest bore no fruit to eat. One Tigrayan man further swore that the wood of the Gambella trees was useless for building.[2] For the Wollo farmers, their homeland forests represented refuges where they could hide out until the conscription campaigns passed through their villages; in contrast they described the forests of Asosa as terrifying and filled with dangerous rivers and animals.

The disgust that these farmers expressed for the soil, climate and trees of the resettlement areas is a manifestation of a syndrome I would like to call *ecological shock*. Like cultural shock, ecological shock describes a sense of disorientation one experiences in new and unfamiliar environments where native skills and behaviors are inappropriate. Ecological shock refers specifically to the psychological disorientation created when confronted by suddenly unfamiliar seasonal patterns (soil, flora, rainfall, and so on) when one's survival has always depended on an intimate understanding of these elements. It is what makes these refugees describe the supposed virgin, fertile lands onto which they were forcibly moved as barren and infertile — the same language the Dergue uses to describe the land they were moved from:

> The soil in Gambella is not a soil.
>
> In this new place we don't know the weather.
>
> Even if my family were with me, I could not stay there because I do not know the land.
>
> [Were you in Gambella during the dry season?] Yes, but it rains then. The leaves fall off the trees.

The ecological confusion the resettlers have experienced has not gone unnoticed by the Dergue. In fact, the Ethiopian government has cleverly used it as a way both to blame the victims for past failures (in those rare references to previous resettlements) and to request additional financial resources from the international community to underwrite the program. For example, to explain why the Asosa resettlement camps have not reached self-sufficiency as originally predicted, the government has claimed:

> They [the resettlers] are not yet capable of exploiting the potential of the area and of making a proper use of the natural resources that would enable them to

establish a more dependable agricultural system. The following assistance . . . is therefore needed (RRC 1985:70).

There follows a two-page list of project equipment required (with price tags) ranging from water pumps for erosion control to seed-cleaning machines to a biogas production plant designed to reduce peasant dependence on fuel wood. Why such innovations and mobilization of resources are not required for rehabilitating the lands the peasants are being moved from and whose problems they understand is a question not addressed in this appeal.

The concept of ecological shock is important for two other reasons. First, its reality calls into question the whole notion of self-sufficiency, a notion that the resettlement program is attempting ostensibly to promote. That magic word "self-sufficiency" is scattered richly throughout Mengistu's speeches and the RRC's appeals, but the term is never defined. By Mengistu's own admission, the kind of crops produced in the resettlement centers "will be based on crop specialization" (Mengistu 1985a). Thus, it is difficult to see how the cooperative farms will ever become self-sufficient, even at the level of the individual resettlement camp. As long as government-deployed "agricultural experts" dole out seeds to the resettlers for their individual gardens (assuming that the "experts" in fact do), then the central government has attained complete control over the farmers' diets—and their lives. Even if we presume these new settlements will be tremendously productive, and this is doubtful, the involuntary exchange of agricultural labor for food rations remains a form of slavery by almost any definition.

Second, the concept of ecological shock helps us evaluate the Ethiopian government's claims that the resettlement program simply mimics—in a more orderly way—the spontaneous, self-generated migrations among the Ethiopian peasantry. This is one of the most slippery justifications of the program and has been very persuasive (see, for example, Hancock 1985:110-114). According to the RRC:

Before the introduction of modern rehabilitation programs, peasants from over-populated areas and drought-prone or -affected regions have been migrating over the centuries, to places with a more promising ecology and reliable climate. . . . It is in view of this imperative need to enable the millions of drought victims to benefit from a reliable ecosystem that the RRC designed the new rehabilitation program (1984:21).

Peasant migrations are indeed occurring within the province of Tigray, as victims of drought and war move into the less populated, fertile regions in the west of the province. REST and the TPLF encourage and even orchestrate these resettlements (Wright 1984; see also Peberdy 1985:chap. 3). However, any similarity between these spontaneous movements and the Dergue's official resettlement program ends here. It is safe to wager that few Ethiopian peasants have willingly immigrated to an area where they do not recognize the plants and animals, do not speak the language or know the culture of the local inhabitants and are unable to use their skills to earn a living (the Amharic *neftanyas* [gun-carrying landlords], who colonized Oromo lands, and the Ethiopian army are, of course, exceptions).

Drinking Seawater: The Environmental Consequences

The provinces of Wollega and Illubabor, the targeted areas for most of the 1.2 million resettlers, are ecologically significant in at least three ways. They contain the largest remaining stands of Ethiopia's forests; their river systems make up a major part of the Blue and White Nile rivers; and they are the site of the evolutionary origin of the coffee plant (*Coffea arabica*). Along with Keffa and Sidamo, these two areas comprise the center of highest genetic diversity of coffee in the world. Wollega and Illubabor together supply Ethiopia with 25 percent of its coffee, the largest single source of government revenue (ILO 1982).

What will be the environmental consequences of the resettlement program? The veil of secrecy that prevents outsiders from witnessing activities except for in a few model resettlement villages has made this a difficult question to answer. However, enough indirect evidence exists to suggest that resettlements are precipitating a far-reaching environmental disaster.

In 1985, environmental scientist Assefa Kuru estimated that the resettlements would destroy 62 percent of Ethiopia's remaining forests. In these calculations, he assumed that 250,000 resettlers would each clear 10 ha of land (about 25 acres), an estimate that seems a little high but not impossible in light of the refugees' reports that they cut trees and brush from sunrise to sunset for months on end. According to Colonel Mengistu (1985a), 300,000 ha of forest would be cleared for planting in 1985-1986, which represents a loss of 7.5 percent of Ethiopia's remaining forest in that year alone; this does not include land cleared for roads, living areas or fuel supplies.

According to the RRC, the clearing of forests is being carried out in a "modern" and "scientific" way. According to the descriptions from resettlers interviewed in Damazine, the clearing is indiscriminate, wholesale and un-supervised. In Gambella, resettlers clear-cut the forest with hand tools and were followed by bulldozers, commandeered by the cadres, which pushed the slash into piles. No trees were left standing in the areas of clearing.

> There was no pattern to chopping the trees. We left the stumps. No, we were not shown how and what to cut. The cadres never left their tents to show us so we cut the nearest ones.

> We cut all the trees down. Then tractors came and cleared it out.

This same process was repeated at Asosa, except that the resettlers there also were forced to remove the stumps and dig up the roots. One man recalled that certain kinds of trees were selected for lumber, but all trees were clearcut for farmland.

> We ate the forest like a fire. There was no forest left. We pulled the stumps and cut the limbs. We thought after a year of this, it would get better, but it sent us downwards. We cleared the wilderness; our bodies became misshapen.

Some have argued that long-term concerns about forest conservation are a luxury and must be overridden when a famine of such great magnitude rages in the short term. In other words, highland farmers must be moved off their exhausted homeland soils into new areas if the cycle of hunger is to end (see, for example, Hancock 1985:110-114). Two fallacies are embedded in this argument. First, it accepts a solution that perpetuates one of the causes of the current problem. Ecologically, Ethiopia's resettlement program is analogous to alleviating thirst by drinking seawater. Second, such an argument presumes there will be at least some short-term benefit to compensate for the long-term degradation.

In fact, no evidence from my interviews suggests that the resettlement areas are suitable, even on a short-term basis, for the kind of agriculture the government is attempting there. This is especially true for Gambella, where farmers noted that corn seedlings emerged a pale yellow in color—indicating the lack of some essential nutrient in the soil (see Appendix D, intensive interview #1). Farmers also recalled that the plowed soil became slick and muddy after a rainfall and then baked in the sun, causing the seedlings to rot and die.

Anuak refugees interviewed in Khartoum were not surprised to learn of the failure of agriculture in the Gambella camps, their original homelands. They pointed out that their fathers used this land for hunting, not for agriculture. One noted that Oala, the resettlement camp where most of the Tigrayan farmers were sent, is an Anuak word that refers to a swampy area. This detail perhaps illustrates why the indigenous people had allowed these forests to remain "virgin" and "unutilized."

The Anuak of Gambella practice agriculture along the banks of the Gilo, Baro and Akobo rivers, tributaries of the White Nile. Using hand-held equipment and the rich alluvium deposited after the floods, most Anuak farmers can harvest two bountiful crops of maize and sorghum each year. Donahue's soil surveys pronounced the soil of the Baro River bank "most favorable for crop production."

It is doubtful, however, that such fertility is contained within the non-alluvial soils underlying the surrounding forests which become the settlement sites. As a rule, tropical forests are almost never good for intensive, mechanized cropping. When cleared of vegetation and exposed to the torrential rainfalls and searing heat, tropical soils are soon depleted—the vast agricultural wastelands in the tropics of Central and South America have attested to this repeatedly.

Significantly, Mengistu himself noted in his report to the Central Committee that 11 percent of the land in the resettlement areas that was plowed could not be planted last year due to the heavy rains. "In view of the fact that this same problem is still evident in many areas, it is estimated that agricultural production will not be as high as originally anticipated" (Mengistu 1985).

The sudden insertion of hundreds of thousands of people into the drainage basins of the Blue and White Nile rivers is unprecedented (see Map 1). What effect this is having on the health of the Nile, upon which millions of lives depend in Sudan and Egypt, is not known. To my knowledge, no one involved with the resettlement issue has ever been asked this question. However, data from the Ministry of Irrigation in Sudan and interviews with Sudanese engineers and hydrobiologists indicate that the siltation of the Blue Nile has increased dramatically since the resettlement operations began in southwest Ethiopia in 1979. Although this evidence is incomplete and correlative only, it strongly points to the need for a complete investigation of the possibility that the resettlement program is creating a hydrological crisis that could affect all of northern Africa.

Most of the water and silt in the Nile River come from the Ethiopian side of the border. During the flood season, 95 percent of the flow of the Nile comes from Ethiopia; the Blue Nile, with its source in Lake Tana, contributes 68 percent by itself (Imbarhim 1984:5). In addition, 80 to 90 percent of the silt in the Blue Nile comes from Ethiopia, while 75 percent of the silt in the White Nile comes from the Baro and Sobat rivers running through the Gambella area (Dr. Asim Moghraby, personal communication). Since their geologic formations — until the commencement of resettlement operations in 1979 — the catchment areas of the Sobat and Blue Nile sub-basins have been characterized by thick forests, steep slopes and low population densities. The Blue Nile sub-basin lies between 9 and 12 degrees north and covers most of Ethiopia west of Addis Ababa, including the Asosa region.

These facts make the Nile an important barometer of Ethiopian ecology: any changes in the flow or silt load of the Blue and White Niles in Sudan are a direct reflection of disturbances on the Ethiopian side of the border. Changes recorded at the Roseires Dam in Sudan are especially significant because it is only a short distance west of the Ethiopian border. For example, contaminated drinking water and electrical blackouts that plagued Khartoum in the summer of 1983 were traced to silt-plugged filters in the hydroelectric dam at Roseires, which generates 87 percent of central Sudan's power. The great influx of silt in the Blue Nile River that year was in turn traced to a road that the Ethiopian government constructed along the Blue Nile watershed from Addis Ababa to the border of Wollega. When the rains came, huge amounts of sand and silt, along with one-half of the road itself, washed into the river and plugged up the hydroelectric equipment across the border in Sudan, according to the Sudanese minister of irrigation, Hayder Yousif, and geologist O. B. Ali at the University of Khartoum.

Originally, I had hoped to compare the average silt load of the Blue and White Niles before and after 1979, the year that mass-scale resettlement operations — and the accompanying surge in resource demand and deforestation — began in the catchment areas. The amount of silt that a river system carries is a direct measure of the severity of soil erosion in its catchment area and therefore also an indirect measure of deforestation. However, baseline data collected by the Ministry of Irrigation on the Blue Nile are incomplete and were collected in different ways in different years, making comparisons over time difficult. No data on siltation rates have ever been collected for the White Nile, which historically carries little silt (its name refers to the clarity of its waters). However, the following information is known:

1) According to Kamal Tayfoor, resident engineer at the Roseires Dam, 550 million m³ of silt were deposited behind the Roseires Dam during the 10-year period between 1966 — the year the Roseires Dam began operation — and 1976. Between 1976 and 1981, a five-year period, a total of 220 million m³ were deposited. Between 1981 and 1985, a four-year period, approximately 1,000 million m³ were deposited. As of March 1986, this figure was still being revised, but it is clear, Tayfoor said, that this represents a dramatic, unexpected increase in silt deposition. Tayfoor attributes this increase to increased rates of deforestation in southwest Ethiopia. He also says that the average particle size of the silt grains has increased in recent years, but he does not know the significance of this shift.

2) Logs began appearing in the Blue Nile Reservoir at Roseires in 1980, according to Bill Campbell, a consultant engineer from Great Britain stationed at Roseires. These have increased in quantity recently. Grass, twigs and silt continue to block the screens of the dam and wear out the turbines. Dredging operations began in the reservoir in 1984 in order to clear the silt and debris away from the hydroelectric filters. The US Agency for International Development (USAID) supplied the dredging equipment at a cost of $11 million.

3) The storage capacity of the Roseires Reservoir, which supplies water for irrigation during the dry season, has decreased by one-third due to a build-up of silt during the past nine years alone, according to Dr. Asim Moghraby, hydrobiologist at the Institute for Environmental Studies at the University of Khartoum. Moghraby attributes this loss to increased rates of deforestation along the watersheds of the Blue Nile. "There has been a significant decrease in the volume of discharge of the Blue Nile in the last 10 years. . . . The high sediment loads have had a major influence on the design and operation of control works on the river" (Moghraby 1984).

When told that the Ethiopian government had moved tens of thousands of farmers into the Gambella region, Moghraby said, "Clearing of the Gambella National Park will most certainly affect the Nile." He also expressed concern for the health of the Yabuus River, which is the only source of water for the people living in the Yabuus area of Sudan and would be affected by indiscriminate forest clearing in its catchment area. (Ironically, most of the people living in the Yabuus area are Ethiopian refugees, many of them resettlement camp escapees.)

In addition to interfering with the production of hydroelectricity, increased concentration of silt in the Blue Nile caused by accelerated soil erosion in southwest Ethiopia has serious consequences for irrigated agriculture in Sudan. In an assessment of resource issues in Sudan, O. B. Ali reports:

Silt deposition has created problems for agricultural development, . . . leads to

Dredging equipment from USAID removes silt from the reservoir behind Roseires Dam, which supplies central Sudan, including Khartoum, with nearly 90 percent of its electricity. The silt is dredged in front of the hydroelectric sluices and redeposited downstream. The reservoir has lost one-third of its capacity due to siltation. March 1986.

difficulties in maintaining water quality and flow for irrigation. It increases blockages in pumps and pipes. It leads to increased vegetative growth in canals. It contributes to health problems by slowing the flow of water (Ali 1983).

Ali notes that silt has reached a depth of five meters in some irrigation canals which encourages the growth of aquatic weeds. Chemical control of these weeds was introduced at great cost — in spite of the environmental hazards — when large agricultural schemes began reporting serious decreases in yields of cotton, sorghum and groundnuts. In addition, the weed-choked canals have become the breeding grounds for water-borne diseases such as bilharzia, typhoid, infectious hepatitis and malaria, all of which have increased in spite of previous gains in public health (Moghraby 1984).

Silt deposition in the irrigation canals of the fertile Gezira triangle, watered by the Blue Nile, was investigated in a 1984 thesis by Attiyat Ahmed of the University of Khartoum. Ahmed concludes that one of the main factors for the recent drop in cotton production — one-half of Sudan's export — is the inadequate supply of water associated with silting and weed infestation in the canals. The cause of this problem, according to Ahmed, is the heavy load of suspended matter transported from Ethiopia by the Blue Nile during the flood season.

Ahmed's research was completed prior to the acceleration of resettlement into the Asosa region of the Blue Nile basin. The ongoing clearing of these remnant virgin forests can only exacerbate agricultural problems in the Sudan. Alarmingly, the Ethiopian government has reported that 10,000 ha of resettlement area forests were cleared and plowed in 1985, but remained unplanted before the rains came due to the miscalculations of overambitiousness (Mengistu 1985a). Much of the topsoil of these 10,000 ha is undoubtedly now showing up in the reservoirs and irrigation canals of Sudan.

Neither resettlement advocates nor environmental scientists are assessing the possible environmental effects of the resettlement program. In January 1986, scientists from Sudan and Ethiopia held a conference in Khartoum to discuss the ecology of the Blue and White Nile river basins and create an international task force to influence management policy. Representatives sent from the University of Addis Ababa included a land-use specialist, a geographer and the dean of the graduate college. According to professors at the Institute of Environmental Studies at the University of Khartoum who attended, the focus of this first meeting was on the carrying capacity of the river basin ecosystem (i.e., the density of human inhabitants this environment can sustain) and the famine's impact on land use along the rivers. Ethiopia's plan to resettle 1.2 million people into these areas was not even mentioned. None of the geologists, hydrologists, engineers and irrigation experts I spoke with in Khartoum knew about Ethiopia's resettlement program.

In 1982, two consultants to the International Union for the Conservation of Nature and Natural Resources (IUCN) compiled a worldwide list of ecological zones most in need of preservation. Included on the list are those zones that contain the genetic resources of the world's most economically important crop plants. Of all these zones, the coffee-growing regions of southwest Ethiopia received highest priority (Prescott-Allen 1982).

The researchers noted that *Coffea arabica*, the most valuable of the coffees and the lifeblood of many Third World economies, is native to the forests of this region where it grows wild or semiwild as an understory shrub or small tree. The protection of these forests is essential because the genetic varieties of this coffee cannot be stored in gene banks — coffee seeds cannot withstand cold storage, as can cereal grains, and therefore must be preserved *in situ*. Prescott and Allen concluded: "Conversion to cultivation is the main threat facing the forests of southwestern Ethiopia. . . . It is extremely important that a reserve be established as soon as possible to protect a viable portion of this forest" (1982).

The urgent need to preserve this habitat is underscored by Jorge Arce, the director of the seed bank at the Centro Agronomico Tropical de Investigacion y Ensenanza (CATIE) in Costa Rica. Receiving its mandate from the International Board of Plant Genetic Resources, CATIE collects and maintains the world's largest collection of coffee plants. In an interview in April 1985, Arce said that the wild varieties of coffee in Ethiopia contain important genes which offer resistance to diseases that strike Central American commercial varieties. The technology does not yet exist to hybridize the two, but recent advances in genetic engineering should make this possible. Meanwhile, CATIE carefully maintains a small field collection of coffee varieties from southwest Ethiopia — an imperfect and incomplete representation — and geneticists there hope that the natural habitat of the wild and primitive varieties of coffee will remain intact.

Needless to say, what is currently going on in southwest Ethiopia is very much the opposite of habitat preservation; agricultural schemes in the resettlement sites are succeeding simply in accelerating the conversion of forest into cropland. The possibility that the resettlement program may deliberately be targeting habitats where wild coffee grows is not being overlooked by the OLF; it contends that the Ethiopian government is attempting to wrest control of coffee production from the Oromo people. Mengistu himself has said:

> Next year's [1986] resettlement activity will focus on these parts of our country having extensive terrain among the people in areas where there are forests of coffee which are never picked from one year to the next and go to waste and on other areas with extensive terrain (1985a).

The possibility that Ethiopian government is 1) endangering the health of one of the most important river systems in the world; and 2) simultaneously ransoming one of the world's most important agricultural resources in order to fulfill a political expedient must be addressed by the international environmental community. If not, the ecological excuses used to justify Ethiopia's resettlement program will continue to be viewed as reasonable by the international community—who will also undoubtedly be called upon to aid those devastated by the environmental consequences.

Acknowledgments

This study was funded in part by the World Hunger Education/Action Committee, the Institute for the Development of Alternatives in Agriculture, and the Rackham School of Graduate Studies at the University of Michigan, Ann Arbor. In addition, I received contributions from individuals in the Ann Arbor community for which I am grateful; I especially thank Bob Heald for his support.

Jason Clay helped me adapt the interview questionnaire from one the Cultural Survival team used in Sudan, in 1985. The Sudanese Ministry of Irrigation generously provided me with their data on siltation of the Nile River. I also extend thanks to Bonnie Holcomb, Gayle Smith, Lois Swenson, Teferi Fufa and Virginia Luling for their support and advice and to the members of the Oromo Relief Association for their support during the research in Damazine and Khartoum. Finally, I extend deepest gratitude to my translator, whose reputation for honesty and generosity in the Damazine camp made our presence there a welcome one and created the possibility for open dialogue.

Notes

[1]One man from Enderta, Tigray, said he was first taken to Asosa where he stayed one week before escaping. On the advice of local Oromos, he tried to return to Tigray directly through Gojam but was arrested and returned to Asosa. He escaped again, made it as far as Mekele, where he was captured again and taken this time to Gambella, where he stayed for three months before escaping to Sudan.

[2]My translator, who grew up in Gambella, could name all the trees that grow there, and describe a dozen different edible fruits and their preparation for eating as well as the uses of each type of wood for fashioning Anuak canoes, tools, furniture and the like.

3 | Resettlement in 1986–1987

Sandra Steingraber

B etween November 1984 and March 1986, discussions of Ethiopia's resettlement program in the Western media focused on issues surrounding the manner in which the program was being implemented. The media debate was sparked by the objections voiced by relief agencies about human rights abuses and the diversion of famine aid during the relocations. Western relief agencies working in the north had witnessed the methods by which resettlers were selected and herded into trucks, planes and transit camps. As a consequence, considerable media attention was directed at the questions of whether resettlers were moved by force and whether resettlement was undermining famine relief operations in the north. Arguments about the number of people who might have died in transit to the settlement sites were at the forefront of this debate.

Significantly, however, between 1984 and 1986 the media made little attempt either to examine the appropriateness of resettlement as a form of long-term development and rehabilitation or to report the fate of the resettlers who survived the journey south. What ultimately happened to the original lands of the peasants who were resettled? And what what happened to the 800,000 after they got off the trucks? These questions never became a central part of the public debate — probably in part because the resettlement camps themselves were largely off limits to journalists and relief workers. For the most part, the media did not question the official "bottom-line" argument that resettlement was the only way to save the highland peasants from the scourge of recurrent famines created by inhospitable climate and ecology. Even journalists who emphasized that the famine was more a result of policy than of natural calamity often conceded that resettlement seemed to be necessary.

Since its resumption in March 1987, "Ethiopia's controversial resettlement program" is again in the news. The focus of the controversy, however, has changed little. As Mary Kay Megistad asserted, "It's not a question of whether it should be done but how."

The worries about the "how" of the resettlement program have been easy for Ethiopia to assuage. Taking a "mistakes were made" approach, the Relief and Rehabilitation Commission (RRC) has assured the West that the abuses that occurred during the implementation of the 1984–1986 relocations will not be repeated in the future. This is possible, contend RRC officials, because the two factors responsible for previous abuses — the ambition of party members assigned to find volunteers and the emergency conditions of the famine — have now been overcome:

> "Overzealous local officials" . . . RRC sources say, used force to meet assigned quotas and win favor with the ruling party. They are now under strict orders to only move people who want to go (*Christian Science Monitor* 18–24 May 1987).
>
> The program was suspended . . . when a furor erupted over charges by the French aid group, Doctors Without Borders, that of 600,000 people resettled between late 1984 and late 1985, 100,000 had died.
>
> The government expelled the French group but admitted that the program had been poorly planned and hurriedly executed.
>
> This spring, the program is to start again, resettling about 30,000 people a month through September — roughly half the rate as before (*New York Times* 11 March 1987).

> As to families being split up, that did happen, but you must remember that this was an emergency . . . in view of the urgency we tended to cut corners. . . . The peasants, some of them, are still illiterate, and the buses used on the resettlement convoys were mostly the same colour. Now, after they stopped for food and rest, a lot of the settlers got on the wrong bus. The results were upsetting, but the cause was a simple mistake (head of the Economic Department of the Central Committee, quoted in Glasner 1986:20).

Public assurances of reform in the manner in which resettlement is implemented are also issued by agencies that have chosen to underwrite the program.

> In a move charged with political controversy, Band Aid also has decided to fund the development of some of Ethiopia's resettlement areas. . . . [Band Aid's executive director] stresses that the projects Band Aid supports are not forced resettlement programs: "Band Aid totally disapproves of forced resettlement" (*Christian Science Monitor* 13–19 July 1987).

In short, although three years have passed since the first settlers were taken south, public consciousness has remained fixated on the question of voluntariness. This has allowed the Ethiopian government to issue apologies and promises of reform in the program's implementation, thereby deflecting criticism. Meanwhile, the question remains: What happened to the 800,000 after they got off the trucks?

Research Design and Methods

In May and June 1987, I interviewed 24 Tigray and Wollo refugees in Damazine, Sudan, who had escaped from resettlement camps in Wollega within the last few months. I also interviewed six Oromo settlers from Wollo who had escaped from Asosa a few weeks earlier and were now living in a Yabuus refugee camp administered by the Oromo Relief Association (ORA). Questions about resettlement were asked in interviews with other refugees in Yabuus who had lived in areas of Wollega near the resettlement camps. All of these refugees had been resettled in 1984 and 1985 and so had spent at least two years in the resettlements. These interviews were to determine how conditions in the camps had changed since 1985 and 1986. I was interested specifically in the role of the camp militia, an issue not investigated in the 1986 interviews, and the agricultural productivity of the private gardens and cooperative fields.

In contrast to the interviews of 1985 and 1986, the 1987 interviews in Damazine were not conducted with randomly selected respondents; rather, I sought to identify groups of refugees who had fled the resettlement camp within the last few weeks and then speak with a few members of each group. Translations were provided by members of ORA, which has no presence in the camp, as well as by two Tigray- and Amharic-speaking medical workers at the camp. (See Appendix E for statistics on Damazine refugees.)

Similarly, those Wollo Oromo refugees in Yabuus selected for interviewing were members of two refugee groups that had fled from the camps a few weeks earlier. A member of ORA not familiar to the respondents provided the translations. All interviews were taped and checked by an independent translator in the US. (See Appendix F for statistics on Yabuus refugees.)

Life in the Homelands

As in 1986, all of the refugees interviewed in 1987 said they were more hungry in the resettlement camps than they had ever been in their homelands of Tigray and Wollo. And most of those who had suffered hardships in their homelands blamed specific government policies rather than natural factors.

Of 12 farmers from Tigray with whom I spoke as a group, half said they had never experienced hunger in their homelands and half said the cause of their hunger was the war between the TPLF and the Dergue in their area. Of two Tigrayan farmers with whom I spoke individually, neither had ever been hungry before they were resettled.

Wollo refugees in Damazine and Wollo Oromo refugees in Yabuus both reported that they had been seriously hurt by the drought.[1] Most were forced to seek relief aid after all their cattle had died. Wollo respondents were told they could not receive aid unless they agreed to be resettled: "They told us we would have to be resettled if we wanted to eat." Wollo Oromo respondents said they would not have responded to the call to receive food aid had they known they would be resettled: "We would have preferred to have died back at home in Wollo." Several respondents said that food aid from abroad that had reached their villages for distribution was sold to selected people by the appointed chairman of the peasant association. Two men said they sold firewood in order to buy relief grain and milk powder from the chairman. They also witnessed secret transfers of donated grain from their kebele into surrounding towns, where they believed it was sold on the market.

Wollo Oromo farmers attributed hunger in their homelands to taxation, forced conscription and land redistribution.

> It was only the deeds of Mengistu who brought hunger to Wollo. He sold food aid to poor farmers at the same time he raised taxes and we couldn't pay. We only cried and he confiscated our land and gave it to his favorites. We lost our land to Mengistu. For 13 years Mengistu has made us hungry. Only when we met the Oromos here did we forget what hunger was. . . . Many young conscripts die at the front. . . . If I go to the military, who will farm for my poor old father? We bribed the authorities not to conscript us. We sold everything we had.

> The government would never leave us alone in Wollo. If they left us in peace for one month, they would come up with some new policy for the next. They reduced our land in size. Many people were forced into the military. I myself had to stay in the forest for one year to escape conscription. My brothers died at the front.

Abduction and Resettlement

All of my respondents had been taken from their homelands two or three years ago and were resettled to camps in Bambesi or Megele (Bambasi or Megalle, see Map 2). Their descriptions of the resettlement operation closely match those of respondents interviewed in 1986 (who were also captured in 1984 and 1985) and attest to the accuracy of refugee testimony.

Tigray farmers from areas controlled by the Dergue were abducted at gunpoint from marketplaces, homes or farmlands. Both Wollo and Wollo Oromo farmers were captured when they responded to calls to receive food aid and were held in transit camps for several days before being transferred south. During this time they were promised that they would live in tin-roofed houses in Wollega and that all their needs would be provided for — "The cadres said that we would just have to wash our hands and eat!" A group of seven Wollo farmers said that they had been assured they would just be farming in Wollega for six months and could take back what they had produced to their families in Wollo after the first harvest.

Food Rations and Austerity Measures in the Settlements

Hunger, backbreaking labor and physical abuse characterize life in the settlement camps of Bambesi and Megele.

According to my respondents, camp residents subsist on monthly food rations which, in 1987, consisted solely of 15 kg of unground grain, usually

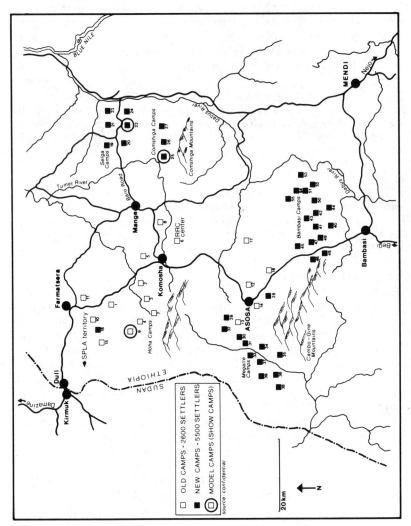

Map 2. Resettlement sites in the area of Asosa, Ethiopia.

70

maize, for each adult. Children receive half rations. This amount seems to be standard in both Bambesi and Megele. Needless to say, such an allotment hardly constitutes an adequate diet. (The recognized standard ration for famine victims is 20 kg/mo. of mixed foods.) Indeed, many of the refugees arrive in Damazine emaciated and suffering from diarrhea, according to FAR health workers; malnutrition is common among children.

The distribution of rations in the camps is controlled completely by camp officials, and food is often withheld as punishment for refusing to work. Food storage areas are guarded by militia to ensure complete control over the settlers' diet. One man who had served as a member of the camp militia said his sole responsibility was to beat anyone attempting to enter the warehouse where the grain was stored. Members of the militia, of course, receive slightly higher apportionments of food — an enticement to potential recruits. Food can also be used to create a class of informers within the camp population or to discriminate against undesirable groups. One respondent recalled, for example, that the Amhara settlers received slightly more rations than did the Oromos and were given wheat as well as maize in their apportionments.

Sometime in 1986, an announcement was made in both Megele and Asosa that settlers would now have to "economize" and eat less food. This austerity measure corresponded with the cessation of internationally donated food supplies — such as wheat and oil — which had sometimes supplemented the standard ration of maize during the first two years. Evidently, the engineers of the program had decided that these resettlements were now "self-sufficient." This proclamation enraged the settlers, already in a state of constant hunger, and often precipitated their decision to attempt escape. One man was told he should make up for the deficit in his rations by eating wild fruits.

Some settlers supplement their diets with food obtained illegally from the local Oromos. As reported by respondents in 1986, clandestine trades of firewood for grain are common. Beating or imprisonment remain the standard punishment for such offenses. Wollo Oromo settlers have the advantage of speaking the same language as the locals and thus, not surprisingly, have the most contact with indigenous peoples. No doubt because the Oromos of Asosa are viewed as potential OLF collaborators, communication between Oromo settlers and Oromo peasants meets with severe retribution. However, Oromo respondents said they continued these contacts out of hunger.

The local Oromos gave us things and cared for us. We were dying of hunger. If not for them, we would have died. When we were very, very hungry we went to them and they fed us and we talked to them. But then the cadres would beat us all night.

They kept us apart from the local people, but we contacted them underground. When the cadres found out they beat us and accused us of conspiracy to join the armed struggle.

Agricultural Productivity in the Collective Farms

At the same time settlers were "economizing" on food, agricultural production in the settlements was improving. These crops included maize, teff, sorghum, wheat, lentils, onions and peanuts. Respondents interviewed in 1986 reported poor harvests of all cereal crops in the Megele settlements. In contrast, refugees this year said the crops were growing well in both Megele and Bambesi — with the exception of teff, which yielded little harvest. They attributed this improvement to increased inputs such as fertilizer in the second year and to the fact that the land was still "too wild" in the first year of cultivation.

In answering questions about the yields of various crops, respondents always stressed that although they had spent all their days clearing, planting and cultivating the collective fields, they received none of the fruits of the harvest except for their meager rations of maize. All the harvests of all other crops produced by the settlers were stored in guarded warehouses and later trucked away. Settlers who thought their lives might finally improve when they saw how well the crops were growing in the last year were disappointed; the size of their rations remained the same after the harvest.

We planted oil seed, maize, teff and wheat for the government, but we never saw any of this except a handful.

We were working in cooperatives, but even though they called it that, we didn't get any of it. It was all taken by the government and we were given only 15 kg of grain each month. This ration was only maize in the second year. The first year were were also given salt and one tin of oil for 20 people. This was aid food. Then we were told that foreign aid was stopped and we should live in an economical way.

At first we were just thrown into the bush. We had to cut bamboo and dig the whole day. In the second year we planted for the government. By the third year the harvest was excellent but our lives did not improve and the ration did not increase.

For two years we cleared the land and were plowing. We got nothing for it. The harvest was collected by the government. We planted teff, wheat, maize, beans and oil seeds. We asked the government to give us the wheat we had harvested; they told us the food would come, but it never arrived. The harvests were transported away by trucks. We don't know what happened to it. . . . In 1985 we harvested 3,000 quintals of grain. In 1986, this increased to 4,000 quintals, but even though the harvest increased, we got nothing.

We planted maize, wheat and teff and some kind of sorghum we didn't have in Wollo. But we were given only maize to eat. We never ate what we planted. The ration for 15 days we had to eat over 30 days because we were forced to economize. The maize ration was harvested by us, but we did not eat any of the other crops. We don't know what happened to them. We were working the whole day. They transported it to somewhere else.

We were hungry in Wollo because the rains had not come for seven years. But we were more hungry in Wollega. We worked so hard and got very little food. Even though the storehouses were filled with grain and lentils and other things, we weren't allowed to eat it. . . . The production of crops increased

A new feeding center in Wollega where, despite plentiful rains, the government activities kept farmers otherwise occupied.

each year. They just stored it, and some was destroyed by insects. They preferred to store it rather than distributing it to us. Then it was trucked away.

Private Agriculture

Ethiopian officials have repeatedly deflected accusations that the resettlement program is a stepping stone to collectivization by indicating that settlers are given their own private plots of land to farm in addition to participating in cooperative agriculture.

The relationship between collective and private agriculture in the settlements has been variously portrayed at different times, as has the slippery and undefined concept of "self-sufficiency." In the early days, the professed goal of the resettlement program was to make each resettled family "self-sufficient" in three years. To achieve this end, each family was to be given 2 ha of land for private farming; as a kind of sideline, farmers would also farm on a cooperative. Later on, the goal of "self-sufficiency" was discussed in reference to the settlement site as a whole rather than at the level of the peasant family. In 1985, the amount of land each family was to receive was revised down to one-half hectare and its stated purpose was to *supplement* food needs of the settlers, whose main work would be in a large cooperative farm. Since then, both settlers and settlement farms are said to be approaching self-sufficiency.

In March 1987, President Mengistu announced that one of the lessons learned in the past two years of the program was that "settlers were able to satisfy their food needs for themselves and their families from half a hectare of land." Since settlers had thus proved they could achieve self-sufficiency through private farming, it was now

> necessary for them to produce cash crops such as sesame, groundnuts [and] peanuts . . . from the collective farms so as to satisfy their other needs through modern farming tools and technology. Hence the production of industrial products by most of the farms of settlers has not only enabled settlers to be fully self-sufficient, it also contributes to the enhancement of the country's economic development (Radio Addis Ababa 28 March).

The relative emphasis on private and collective farming in the settlements of Bambesi and Megele was portrayed quite differently by my respondents. All vehemently denied that private gardens contributed anything significant to the diets of the settlers over the last three years; they claimed that subsistence comes almost entirely from the maize rations produced in the collective fields. In contrast to the improved productivity of the collective fields, private gardens yielded very meager harvests in 1986. Respondents said they were only allowed to work in their plots at night. Additionally, some said the soil was "too new" or "too red" to produce well. Many also noted that even if their crops had grown well, the small size of the gardens — which they described as a strip of land between adjacent huts — precluded any possibility of self-sufficiency.

> *We planted some corn in the garden around our houses and were eating this. The seeds were distributed to us. We planted the garden three times but there was only enough for two to three months. The gardens were too small to be sufficient. They told us that private ownership must be discouraged so this is why they gave us such small plots. They said if we were given larger gardens we would concentrate on them and not work enough on the government cooperative farm.*

> *We had small plots of land around the huts — 10-m strip — for corn and other seeds. We fed this to our children. We could eat everything from these gardens in one day! Even if they had given us a bigger plot we had no time to work on it.*

Work Conditions in the Resettlement Sites

Clearing forested land, plowing and cultivating in the collective fields and constructing houses constitute the daily activities of settlers in Bambesi and Megele. Men and women are organized in separate work brigades and rise at dawn to begin work. Instructions are given by brigade supervisors who also mete out punishments to those who appear to be sloughing off. My respondents said the nature of their duties had changed little during the two or three years they had lived in the camps.

Forested land continues to be clearcut and prepared for agriculture. As in 1986, settlers use hand tools to dig and to remove trees and vegetation. This work is considered to be the most exhausting.

Mechanized agriculture does not seem to be common in Bambesi or Megele, although I did not ask any direct questions about this. Respondents reported that they saw all plowing and cultivation in the collective fields done by hand. As in 1986, Wollo farmers expressed their disgust at this type of farming, pointing out that where they come from plowing the ground is work for oxen, not men. As in 1986, respondents indicated they were not permitted to contribute suggestions or criticisms about methodology, even though the brigade supervisors knew less about the correct way to plow and plant than did those who had to perform the work. One man said his brigade was forced to plow a field three times more than he knew was necessary for a particular crop. Another noted, "We knew already how to plow with oxen and everything about farming, but they moved us from our land to these cooperative farms where we were treated like ignoramuses. We were forced to farm with our hands as if we knew nothing."

Women's work groups carry out many of the same duties as the men, including plowing and construction. No time off is granted for pregnancy, breastfeeding or child care. One Wollo Oromo woman described her experience in Bambesi as follows:

> We had to plow and dig, just like the men. . . . While the men were building houses, we women had to bring water to prepare the clay. Even if they had small children, the women worked equally with the men. So we left at 8 a.m. and came back at 9 p.m. even if we were breastfeeding our children. At night we had to grind our grain and cook until late in the night. We also had to build houses for the chairman and chairwoman of the camp.
>
> They appointed Amhara women to order the other women and tell us what to do. She sat in the shade and breastfed her child while ordering us to work, and we could not feed our children.

Beatings, Imprisonment and Torture

Several of my interview partners both in Damazine and Yabuus bore on their bodies the marks of beatings and torture, which they said they received in the settlements.

According to respondents, beatings by party cadres are frequent and routine. Insolence, disobedience, absence from work, refusal to work or suspicion of communicating with the local people are all punishable by beatings or lashings which can also be followed by a period of imprisonment.

Escape attempts provoke more severe punishments. The most commonly cited was beating the escapee with sticks while his hands and feet are tied together behind his back. Severe beatings on the soles of the feet ensured that the culprit would not repeat his offense in the near future. Respondents said they had seen people die during this form of torture. One group of escapees said that they were forced to leave some of their comrades behind because they were physically disabled from punishments following an aborted escape attempt two and a half months earlier. Repeated plungings into vats of water is another form of torture inflicted upon captured

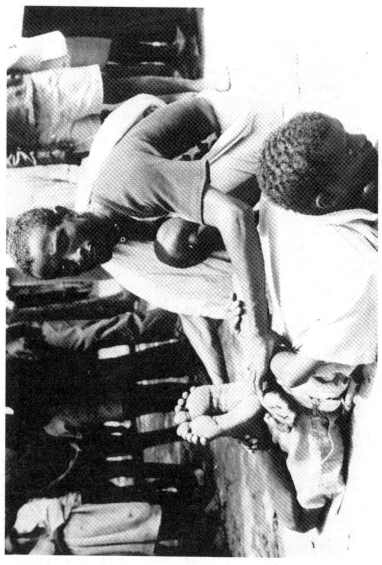

A common form of torture in resettlement sites is binding victims' hands and feet, and beating the soles of their feet with sticks. It is here demonstrated by a victim from Wollega.

©S. Steingraber

escapees and witnessed by some of my respondents. Following the physical punishment, escapees endure a prison sentence and some form of forced labor, such as digging latrines. One Wollo Oromo woman estimated she knew of 200 incidents of torture in her two-year tenure in Bambesi, 20 of which involved people whom she knew personally.

Prison compounds are present in both the Bambesi and Megele settlements. Besides housing captured escapees, the prisons also are used to detain the families of people who have disappeared. One woman said she and her baby were imprisoned after her husband left the camp in an attempt to return to Wollo. During the day she was forced to fetch water for the whole camp. After being released, she was ordered to marry another man, but she refused and moved into a house with her brother, a member of the camp militia. When her husband returned five months later, the cadres forced them to remarry. One month later they both escaped to Yabuus.

Settlers as Militia

According to my respondents, two types of militia are recruited from among the settlers: those who work inside the camp and those who are sent out into the surrounding communities. My information about the first group comes from the escaped settlers whose testimonies have been presented above. My information about the second group comes from interviews with Oromo refugees fleeing from villagization who had lived in communities near the settlement sites. Of the respondents I interviewed in Damazine, three said that they themselves had served as members of the camp militia. However, they were clearly reluctant to speak about their experience in front of the other refugees. I did not speak with anyone who claimed to have served in the "external" militia. The following discussion should be viewed with this in mind.

The main duty of the camp militia seems to be to prevent settlers from leaving the camp. Additionally, they guard machine shops and storage areas where food is kept before being transported out of the camp. Three Wollo refugees who had served in these functions said they were armed only with sticks. However, testimony from other refugees indicates that at least some of the militia guarding the camp perimeter are equipped with rifles.

The cadres select militia recruits. Two respondents said that during a meeting in their camp the cadres chose 60 young and able-bodied men from among the residents; some were taken for the army, and some for the militia. At least some militia members from all nationalities — Tigray, Oromo and Amhara — are represented among the camps (though perhaps not in any one camp). One ex-militiaman said that people who had served in militias back at home were preferentially chosen: "I had served in the militia in Wollo, so when I came to Wollega the cadres said, 'Since you have been in the militia before, you can serve here also.'"

Militiamen work closely with the cadres and have special privileges. Besides receiving more rations, they also sleep in a special place — though not inside the cadres' sleeping quarters. I regret that I did not ask whether militia members participated in the implementation of beatings and torture that were described previously.

The Oromo Liberation Front (OLF) has long alleged that highland settlers organized as militia groups are used by the Dergue as a tool to control and terrorize Oromo communities whose loyalty to the government is suspect. In 1985, Oromo refugees in Yabuus told Holcomb that groups of armed settlers, brought from Wollo in the early 1980s, were ordered to locate and punish local farmers identified as OLF supporters. Some militia groups were assigned the task of confiscating coffee supplies from "hoarders" and had been granted unlimited powers of search and seizure. According to Holcomb's respondents, both of these groups ransacked homes and granaries, raped women and destroyed property (Clay and Holcomb 1985:176–182).

According to the refugees I interviewed in Yabuus in 1987, these practices continue. In addition, Wollo settlers now appear to be used for at least two other purposes: to torture and execute political prisoners and, organized as armed security forces, to enforce the implementation of villagization.[2]

In Oromo communities that have not yet been villagized and are located near OLF operational areas, armed Wollo militia sometimes harass the families of farmers who have disappeared and are presumed to have joined the rebels. One woman from Begi whose husband fled after being pinpointed as a collaborator reported that

> the whole family was being attacked and harassed because the government thought my husband was secretly returning to the farm. Once my child's hands were tied behind his back for a whole day. This was done by armed Wollo settlers [from a nearby camp]. They didn't speak our language. They came with the government administrators. They were the same people we had built houses for.

Two Komo farmers, also from Begi, said that men are often taken from their homes by Wollo militia on the pretext that they are OLF supporters. While they are being detained, other members of the militia rape their wives. They explained that this was the second wave of suffering that the Komo people had endured because of the settlers; the first came when they refused to build houses in the resettlement camp.

> We were ordered to cut big trees to build them big houses. We cut everything down and collected the wood into one place. Those who refused were beaten or killed. They would tie his eyes and tell him to walk until he falls into a ditch. Or sometimes they put pepper powder in our eyes to torture us as a punishment for refusing to build houses. The whole village suffered.

As in 1985, rape of Oromo women by armed Wollo settlers was commonly reported by respondents. They claimed that the frequency of sexual assaults had increased in the last year. Several women with whom I spoke said they themselves had been raped but were too ashamed to discuss the circumstances. They did say that the threat of assault has created hardships for the whole community since women feel they can no longer fetch water

Komo military guides working with the OLF in Wollega, 1987.   ©A. Grilz

or firewood or travel alone to the market. They also said that gangs of armed Wollo would sometimes come into their homes under the pretext of wanting a drink of water and then proceed to rape the women after killing or beating their husbands.

According to the testimony of three different respondents, militia forces made up of Wollo settlers participate in the execution and torture of political prisoners. I spoke at length with one Oromo farmer who had been the chairman of his kebele in Gidami. In 1986 he was captured in a mass arrest and imprisoned for seven months, during which time he periodically was tortured to extract a confession that he was an OLF collaborator. He said the torture included beating the soles of his feet and his testicles, plunging his head into water and putting wax plugs that contained needles into his mouth. During the beatings he suffered broken ribs (still visible through his skin) and burst testicles. This torture was carried out by both party cadres and Wollo Oromo militia when the cadres became tired. He emphasized that the Wollo were forced to participate in this; they wore uniforms with short pants so that when they did not appear to be beating the victims severely enough, they themselves were beaten on the legs by the cadres. Other stronger prisoners were recruited to continue the beatings.

Also in 1986, in a kebele in Begi, Wollo militia were used to execute 18 prisoners suspected of supporting the OLF. I spoke with two women who witnessed the execution. The following quote is the account of one of them.

They imprisoned 18 people and moved them to Nekempt. Then they brought them back and gathered all the kebeles together and shot each man. I saw this with my own eyes. These people were merchants. They had been traveling to Kirmuk to sell coffee because their wives had no clothes and were naked. Many wives were told that their husbands were cooperating with the rebels. They used the husband and wife to inform on each other. They also used the conflicts between two wives to make them spy on each other.

The women were gathered in a place where we couldn't run away and were told to sit. They brought in the 18 people in a truck. They brought in the armed Wollo people also to shoot them. They forced them from behind to shoot these people. Slogans were shouted: "Anyone who feeds reactionaries and rebels will be shot."

Before they gathered us here, they completely disarmed us — even took away our sewing needles in a thorough security search so we couldn't react. The relatives of these people were forced to keep their eyes open and no one was allowed to cry or show any sorrow. After this, they dragged them into a single ditch like dead dogs. And the relatives had to watch.

The process of villagization in the Asosa, Gimbi and Kellem districts of Wollega is described in detail elsewhere. (See Steingraber, "Villagization in a War Zone," this volume.) Militia forces from the resettlement camps seem to be involved in the process in three ways. First, they serve as a security force for government officials, orchestrating and overseeing the move. Respondents from many different areas mentioned that the party representatives, district administrators and members of the Ministry of Agriculture arrived in their villages surrounded by armed guards "who did not speak our language." Some recognized these guards as settlers from nearby camps.

Second, in some cases, the militia oversee the seizure and collectivization of crops and animals which accompanies villagization. In one kebele in Gidami, armed men guarded the fields — which were ready for harvest — while the villagers moved their houses. People from other kebeles were brought in to harvest the crop, which was then taken to a place unknown to the villagers.

Third, the militia oversee the actual move, including the dismantling and rebuilding of houses. In this same kebele in Gidami, villagers were told the Wollo militiamen would "guard" their old houses while they labored in the new village, a three-hour walk away.

> Wollo militia were brought in with the government forces to carry out the orders for villagization while the men were building the new houses. The Wollo lived in our houses to guard them. They didn't speak our language. They raped the wives and girls, and the women began to suffer from diseases from this. This rape is common.

In one Berta (Fedhashi) community in Begi, Wollo militia were involved in all aspects of collectivization and villagization. A spokesperson in Yabuus said that harassment by Wollo settlers was one of the main reasons for his village's (800 people) flight in March 1987:

> The Wollo settlers were armed against us and supported by the government to kill us. They raided us and threatened us with guns. We didn't have anything. They asked us every day for money, but we have no money. Money is no use to us. . . .
>
> [The army] brought the Wollo and settled them all over the country. They came three years ago. Then they armed them and told them to kill us and beat us. [The settlers] told us not to work, not to use money. They said to build our villages together and then sit idly. They told us our harvest would be taken away by the government and government people would eat it. We never ate what we produced. So we ran away because they took everything from us.

Militia from the resettlement camps in Illubabor played a major role in the arrest and execution of Anuaks following a recent uprising in Gambella. The details of this incident are described in the following section of this report.

Return to Wollo and Escape to Sudan

When asked whether the quality of life in the resettlement camps had improved or worsened during their tenure, respondents either said that their lives had not changed or had become worse; no one thought life had improved. The introduction of austerity measures coincident with good harvests in the collective fields convinced many of them that their lives would never improve; this is when they began to contemplate escape seriously.

All respondents said that security in their camps had tightened in the last year, but that the number of escapes had also increased. They cited hunger, exhaustion and feelings of despair ("I just couldn't stand it there anymore") as reasons for attempting escape.

> *The second year security was stronger, but people preferred to die than stay there.*

> *There was so much work to do but so little food.*

> *My husband and I left because I couldn't manage the hard labor.*

> *In Wollo we were hungry because of famine and drought. But in the resettlement camp it was no different. This is why I decided to leave and come to Sudan.*

> *For two years we were so unhappy there. We were so isolated and we couldn't get any information. We were living in darkness. We worked the whole day and were always tired. At night we just slept. We were prisoners. We couldn't talk or move.*

Wollo Oromos also noted that they heard about the Yabuus refugee camp ("Oromos living in Sudan who were Muslim") only after two years in Bambesi. Undoubtedly stories of settlers who successfully escaped as well as information about escape routes have been filtering back to the camps and influencing the decisions of those remaining.

Strategies for escape have changed since 1986. The 1986 respondents cited physical factors, such as drowning and attacks by wild animals, as the major threats to escape attempts. They considered the dry months (September through December) when the rivers were not so formidable as the most favorable for escapes; to minimize animal attacks, most chose to flee in large numbers. In contrast to 1986 responses, refugees in Damazine in 1987 said their major problem was security, both at the camp itself and along the border regions, due to the presence of SPLA and Ethiopian armies. For this reason, most settlers now opt to flee in small groups during the rainy season when military activities are reduced. Refugees arriving in Damazine in mid-June told the Canadian medical staff that hundreds more escapees were hiding in the bush near Kirmuk waiting for the rains to resume before daring to cross the border. Respondents emphasized that many people are captured or killed along the way, although most of them also said that their particular escape group had suffered few casualties.

Some settlers now are attempting to return to Wollo directly "for a visit," something which was not reported in 1986. Respondents who had done this insisted that these visits were not officially sanctioned and that they had been warned against making the attempt. However, they also indicated that they were not dealt with as captured escapees when they returned to the camp. The purpose of these visits seemed to be to determine the likelihood of a permanent return to their homelands and to find out what had happened to their land. One Wollo farmer who returned to his kebele discovered that the chairman of the peasant association was farming his land. He was forced back to Asosa: "They told me I had no land there anymore." A Wollo Oromo who returned saw that his land had been overgrown by bush. He recruited the assistance of his peasant association chairman, who pleaded his case for him to some higher authority. However, his request to remain in Wollo was denied and he was returned to the camp. At this point, he gathered his family and they escaped to Sudan. What impressed — and angered — both of these men was how green and lush their lands in Wollo had become.

> Now when I went back to Wollo, I saw that the farmers who remained there were still suffering even though the rain had come again. Farmers are still being asked to pay high taxes, 40 birr each, husband, wife and child. In this way Mengistu brings famine.
>
> Look, I saw Wollo with my own eyes. The rains have come and it is green and beautiful and they are harvesting a lot of sorghum, but still the government is telling people they have to be resettled.

Ecological Considerations

The possibility that the resettlement program is creating the same ecological problems it ostensibly set out to solve was first raised by Clay and Holcomb in 1985 and became a focus of my research in 1986. (See "Resettlement in 1985–1986," this volume.) Of central concern is the resource demand created by the sudden insertion of hundreds of thousands of people into forested areas which historically have supported low human populations and small-scale or shifting agriculture. In some places the human population was tripled or quadrupled instantly upon the settlers' arrival. Reports from 1987 respondents indicate that brigades of settlers are continuing to clearcut forested land for collective agricultural schemes.

Ecological changes that have accompanied the resettlement program have not gone unnoticed by the indigenous people. Berta (Fedhashi) refugees were especially upset at the ongoing loss of trees in their area: "The Wollo people are cutting the dense forests every day for building houses. We don't know why the Wollo cut our trees down."

Not incidentally, forested areas targeted for resettlement form the catchments for the Blue and White Nile rivers. Deforestation and subsequent soil erosion in these areas could precipitate a far-ranging ecological problem. Evidence that this may be happening already comes from the Rosieres Dam on the Blue Nile River just on the other side of the border, where hydrobiologists and engineers have noticed increased loads of silt and logs in the river. They attribute these changes to increased deforestation in southwest Ethiopia.

After the short rains in May 1987, large numbers of logs appeared in the Yabuus River, which has its source in the resettlement areas of Asosa. ORA staff members and long-term refugees in Yabuus said they had never seen so many logs in the river in years past. (Refugees collect and use this wood for fuel.) The director of the refugee camp estimated that the quantity of logs in 1987 was at least three times what it had been any of the previous five years.

When I arrived in early June, some of these logs were still scattered along the banks and stacked in nearby piles to dry. To give a rough estimate of quantity, these logs could have filled two or three lorries. Refugees said that this represented about half the total number of logs that they had pulled out

Logs in a refugee camp in Sudan taken from the Blue Nile River. The logs are from Ethiopia, apparently resulting from the deforestation associated with the resettlement program. Some of the logs have worked surfaces, indicating that they were intended for construction. The heavy rains that washed the logs into the Blue Nile probably caused serious soil erosion as well.

©S. Steingraber

84

of the river at this particular spot; the rest already had been hauled back to their huts.

All the logs consisted of tree trunks. Some two-thirds of them showed clear signs of having been cut by hand tools; the remaining pieces were too worn by the water. Most were of a uniform size — between 3 and 6 m in length with diameters ranging from 4 to 8 cm. None were uprooted trees or branches that had snapped off. Some 5–10 percent showed clear signs of having been burned.

Clearly, deforestation is taking place along the tributaries of the Yabuus River, which are lined with resettlement camps. (The Megele camps are roughly 40–60 km upstream from Yabuus along a main tributary.) A reasonable scenario is that these logs were left lying along the riverbank after an area of forest had been clearcut and were then swept into the water with the arrival of the rains.

Summary and Conclusions

Interviews with recent arrivals in May and June 1987 reveal that little has changed about the camps since Niggli described them as forced labor camps in 1985. According to the testimony of these refugees,

1. Although the productivity of the resettlement collective farms has increased over the last two and a half years, agricultural surpluses are stored in guarded warehouses or trucked away. Residents subsist on meager rations of maize which are withheld or increased at the whim of the cadres.

2. Food rations decreased in 1986 when the supply of foreign aid ended. Settlers were told to economize and eat less.

3. Private gardens contribute only nominally to settlers' diets.

4. Work brigades continue to clearcut forested land.

5. Torture, beatings and imprisonments are routine.

6. Residents are recruited for militia groups which are used both to guard the camp and to terrorize villages of local Oromo thought to be sympathetic to the OLF. These militia also have been used to enforce the implementation of villagization in the region and to carry out executions and torture of political prisoners.

The experiences of these respondents during their years as settlers in Megele and Bambesi clearly indicate that the resettlement program does not live up to its professed goal of "the rehabilitation of famine victims." In essence, the program is turning peasant farmers — many of who had never experienced famine — into sharecroppers for government landlords subsidized by foreign aid.

What the magic buzzword "self-sufficiency" really means is keeping settlers alive on minimal rations of grain grown in collective fields and removing all other agricultural products resulting from their labor. The government achieves such "self-sufficiency" by coercion and threats of imprisonment and physical abuse. Through the achievement of such "self-sufficiency," the government has attained complete control over the settlers' diets — and therefore their lives.

Clearly, settlers have no way out of a life of regimented oppression, hunger and hard labor except by taking up arms for the government. Refugees reported the arming of settlers as militiamen to Clay and Holcomb over two years ago. Based on their interviews, they predicted that the military and political agendas of the resettlement program would grow in importance. This is evidenced in 1987 by the participation of settler militia groups in the enforcement of villagization and in campaigns of terror designed to destroy the grassroots support of a liberation army. The specific use of settler militiamen to torture and execute political prisoners has frightening implications; it warrants further investigation to determine how widespread such practices are.

At least two questions remain. First, what has happened to the land of those taken for resettlement two or three years ago? According to the two farmers who returned to Wollo to answer this, the land of one had fallen into the hands of the kebele chairman and the land of the other had reverted to brush. Other refugees said they had heard from their families that their farms were given to Ethiopian soldiers. According to President Mengistu, these lands will eventually be reforested and allowed to recover, "or, perhaps, depending on the mineral resources available, go for industrial development" (*Courier* 1986:28).

Second, what ultimately happens to the crops that are produced by the settlers in the collective farms and mysteriously trucked away? A clue might be found in President Mengistu's triumphant announcement in March 1987 that the unprecedented volume of grain stockpiled by the agricultural produce marketing organization over the last year (5 million quintals) was creating a shortage of storage space; meanwhile, over the same time period, the price of grain in Addis Ababa dropped by 32 percent (Radio Addis Ababa 18 March). The resettlement farms, he continued, are now "contributing to the enhancement of the country's economic development." Future resettlements will be "set up along this line" and "will have a greater contribution towards realizing this objective."

So, indeed, the resettlement program is a form of "development." But perhaps this is not the kind of development that aid agencies supporting resettlement have in mind. If not, then they would be wise to consider the political, military and economic agendas of the resettlement program that lie not far below the surface and have nothing to do with ecology or rehabilitation. The real intentions of these agendas are already obvious to the ex-settlers living as refugees in Sudan. As one said, "Mengistu told us to farm but not to eat. He wants us to feed him."

Acknowledgments

This study was funded jointly by the Gesellschaft für Bedrohte Völker (Society for Threatened Peoples) in Göttingen, West Germany, the Kirchlicher Entwicklungsdienst of the Evangelical Churches of Germany in Hannover and Cultural Survival in Cambridge, Massachusetts.

Jason Clay, Wolfgang Heinrich and Ulli Delius provided much advice and information during all stages of this research; their generous support has been indispensable. I also extend gratitude to Suki Allen, Brian Burt, Kulane Gudena, Gunnar Hasselblatt, Bonnie Holcomb, Virginia Luling and Peter Niggli for their assistance and advice. Members of the Oromo Relief Association supported me throughout the trip, assisting with travel permits and administrative details and providing transportation and lodging. A special thanks to those who accompanied me on the long and muddy trek between Damazine and Yabuus and who, through their kindness and generosity, transformed a difficult journey into a pleasure.

Most of all, I thank the refugees I interviewed in Sudan. Their testimonies about life inside the resettled and villagized areas of Wollega and Illubabor represent one of our only sources of information about a region of Ethiopia, off limits to outside observers, where a vast human experiment is being conducted.

Notes

[1] Settlers brought from Wollo Province to Wollega include both Amharic and Oromo speakers. To distinguish them from the Wollega Oromo and from each other, I hereafter refer to them as "Wollo" and "Wollo Oromo," respectively. These labels do not necessarily represent ethnic identity as perceived by the respondents. (Many Amharic-speaking peasants in Wollo are of Oromo ancestry, for example.) In this study, all Wollo respondents interviewed (Amharic speakers) came from Habro district and all Wollo Oromo (Oromo speakers) from the Daway area of Kalu district. For a discussion of ethnic identity in Wollo, see Clay and Holcomb 1985, pp. 6–17.

[2] These are the first reports of such incidents and derive from testimony gathered in five different interviews. How common or universal such practices are cannot be discerned from these few interviews; this issue needs to be addressed by further research. The conclusions drawn here are tentative and certainly should not be generalized to apply to other regions of Ethiopia.

Appendix A
Demography of Refugee Population
in Damazine Camp, March 1986
Including Those Captured During Their Journey

Camp Population: 1,011 people, as of 3 March 1986

Place of Origin (of 962 legible entries)*	Population	Description/Reason for Fleeing Ethiopia
Tigray	753	All Escaped Resettlement Camp, Gambella
Wollo	191	All Escaped Resettlement Camp, Asosa
Wollega	7	2 are Oromo Priest and Wife Who Fled After Dergue Destroyed Koranic Texts and School; 2 are Oromo Couple from Gidami Fleeing Conscription; 3 Unknown
Addis Ababa	5	Political Refugees: University Students and Ex-Government Workers
Illubabor	2	Anuak Students Fleeing Conscription
Eritrea	1	Merchant Who had Traveled to Tigray and was Captured for Resettlement
Kefe	1	Unknown
Shoa	1	Unknown

*Information from FAR Registration Book

A REST representative who visited the camp on January 25 reported a camp population of 630, nearly all of whom were Tigrayans. The Wollo people began arriving in small groups in early February. All the refugees were to be evacuated from this camp before the rainy season and moved to a more permanent camp in the Gedaref area in the east where the Tigrayans could be repatriated.

I was working in the camp on the evening of February 21 when 57 Tigrayans — 54 of whom were women and children — arrived in a lorry from Kurmuk. According to ORA representatives, all had been captured and held by SPLA members after escaping from the resettlement camps in Gambella. I and a Tigrayan translator registered 52 of them, which gave me the opportunity to gather more detailed information on their families' whereabouts.

These refugees arrived in miserable condition; several were so weak they could not stand, and some of the children were suffering from obvious marasmus.

**Tigrayan Refugees Who had been Held by the SPLA
and Who Arrived in Damazine on 21 February 1986**

Female Adults*	30
Male Adults	4
Female Children	9
Male Children	9

*Adult = 15 years old

There were no intact families; all either had some children or parents or spouses left in Tigray and/or had lost them since resettlement.

Of 41 heads of households (41 includes seven children who arrived without parents), 17 percent reported immediate family members still captured and held by the SPLA.

Of 41 heads of households, 51 percent said they had immediate family members who had died, had been captured or otherwise were lost on the journey from the resettlement camp.

Of this 51 percent, 48 percent reported *more than one* family member dead or unaccounted for on the journey from the resettlement camp.

By early March, at least three of the women suspected they were pregnant by their captors and asked FAR health workers about the possibility of obtaining abortions.

The above statistics should be considered *underestimates* because some arrivals reported the presence of family members in the camp whom they presumed had avoided capture and arrived months earlier but in fact had not.

A REST representative, who visited the camp in January 1986 and intensively interviewed the Gambella survivors about their escape, reported that 1,055 Tigrayan escapees were known to have been captured in Sudan. Thus the release and arrival of these 57 means that almost 1,000 of those refugees captured are still unaccounted for.

REST also estimated from interview accounts that 3,000 Tigrayans were known to have fled the Gambella camps during October and November 1985. If this figure is accurate, then only 35 percent of those made it to Damazine as of March 1986.

An interview with one of the women who had been held captive appears in Appendix D.

Appendix B
Questionnaire Used in February-March 1986 Interviews

Geographic Origin
    What is your name?
    How old are you?
    Where were you born?
    How long did you live there?
    Did your father and grandfather also live there?
    Are you from an area controlled by the government (Dergue)? (Do you
        pay taxes to the Dergue? Does the Dergue conscript people from your
        village into the army?)

Background
    What is your religion?
    Are you married?
    Where is your wife?
    Do you have children?
    Where are your children?
    Any other family with you?

Resettlement
    When did you leave Tigray/Wollo?
    Tell me about the day you left your homeland.
    Where were you taken then? What was the name of the place?
    How long did you stay there?
    What did you do there?
    Did you have any contact with the local people there?
    Tell me about the day you left for Sudan.

Farming in the Homeland
    Now I want to ask you about your farm in Tigray/Wollo:

    Did you parents/grandparents farm the same land?
    How large was your land?
    What was your source of water? And your father's?
    What was your source of firewood? And your father's?
    How did you clear the land and plant it? How did you harvest? Who
        taught you to do these things?
    How many kinds of crops did you plant? What are they?
    Was your land irrigated or rainfed?
    Did wild animals ravage your crops? What were they? What did you do
        when this happened?
    Did you have problems with insects? What were they? How bad? For
        how long?
    Was there more or less rainfall in recent years?

Was drought a problem for you?

What changed for you when the Dergue came to power (after the revolution)?

What was the biggest change between your time and your father's time?

Were there people in your community who were hungry? If so, why?

Were you forced to consume your seeds? Were your parents ever forced to do this?

Were you more hungry in Tigray/Wollo or in the resettlement camp?

Ecology

Was there forested land near your home?

What was it used for?

Is there more or less forest now as compared to when you were a child? What is the reason for this difference?

Are there more or less wild animals now? Why?

Resettlement Agriculture

Now I want to ask you about farming in Gambella/Asosa:

Is the land in Gambella/Asosa similar to the land you farmed in Tigray/Wollo?

How is it different? weather? soil? rainfall?

While in the resettlement camp, were you involved in farming for the government? If yes,
Specifically, what did you do?
Were the crops you planted or harvested the same as those you planted at home?
Were they familiar to you?
Did you know how to plant and harvest them?
Did these crops grow well? If not, why?

While in the resettlement camp, did you have a backyard garden?
How large was it?
What did you plant in it?
Where did you get the seeds?
Did the plants grow well? If not, why?

Were you involved in clearing the land at the resettlement camps? Describe how this clearing was done.

Did you know the names of the wild plants and trees in your homeland?

Did you know the names of the wild plants and trees in your resettlement area?

Assessment of the Situation

Do you want to return to your homeland?

Will you farm again if you return?

Where will you obtain your seeds for farming?

Some people say that the people from Tigray/Wollo should be resettled to these new camps because your land is dry and your soil is poor for farming. Do you agree with this?

Why do you think the government resettled you?

Appendix C
Personal Background of Farmers Selected for
Random Interviews in Damazine Camp, March 1986

	Tigray	Wollo
Total Interviewed	38	16
Sex – Male	100.0%	100.0%
Religion		
Coptic Christian	100.0%	0.0%
Moslem	0.0%	100.0%
Political Forces Controlling Home Village		
Dergue	10.5%	100.0%
TPLF	89.5%	0.0%
Marital Status		
Married	92.1%	37.5%
Single	7.9%	62.5%
Present Location of Wife		
In Damazine Camp with Respondent	10.5%	0.0%
Home Village	81.0%	100.0%
Captured	2.5%	0.0%
Arrested	2.6%	0.0%
Children		
Yes	81.6%	31.8%
No	18.4%	68.7%
Present Location of Children		
All in Damazine Camp with Respondent	0.0%	0.0%
All in Home Village	86.7%	80.0%
All in Resettlement Camp	33.0%	0.0%
Some in Damazine, Some Captured		
During Flight	3.3%	0.0%
Some in Damazine, Some Captured		
During Flight, Some at Home	3.3%	0.0%
Some Dead, Some at Home	0.0%	20.0%

Appendix D
Six Nonrandom Interviews, March 1986

Nonrandom Interview #1
Abeba, Age: c. 60
Tigray
Background Information: lived in an area never under Dergue control

I plant all kinds of crops [about 20]. I can plant 10 kinds of wheat depending on the weather. There are highland and lowland varieties. If there is a drought, I plant certain kinds, if it is cool, I plant other kinds.

There are five kinds of corn. There are six kinds of teff, each has different ripening times: three varieties of white teff, two red varieties and one that is intermediate be-

tween these. There are six kinds of sorghum, both white and red kinds. We learned from our ancestors how and when to plant all these crops.

I have all the problems with insects. Also monkeys, baboons and worms. When the worms attack, they will not eat the ripe kinds; they only attack the unripe ones. When I select seeds for next year, I choose the fast-ripening ones.

Before the revolution, there was more harvest, but in every year since then, the harvest has decreased steadily. Last year the drought came. Some parts of Tigray had been affected by drought before this irrigation. But last year the water dried up and there was no rain. We did not irrigate because it was too difficult. Also, because there were worms that ate the grass, there were no places for the cows to graze. The grass was finished. The cows died, and we ourselves had no resources. Our cereal was finished. We suffered very much. I plant one kind of wheat that can grow without water. It grew well in the drought, but then the worms finished it too. The drought came on one side and the worms came on the other side. There was no harvest last year.

Rain has decreased since the revolution. God knows why this is so, but I do not know.

There are forests near our village. We used them in the way our parents taught us. We cut down the trees in one place and use this for farming and then later we will go to another place and let the trees grow back. We use this place for hunting and beekeeping and firewood, which we can sell on the market. This is according to our parents.

When I was a boy, there was a dense forest, but this has decreased. The TPLF taught us not to cut this forest anymore because it will increase drought and bring deserts. They said, "Be careful when you use the forest. Don't cut down the trees without reason." We tried to follow this advice.

Life was worse for us before the revolution. Haile Selassie's government was more harmful to us. We had to pay five birr to the rich people just to wash our hands! We had to put down five birr just to wash, and if there was no one to put down the money, we could not wash. We might be arrested. Our hands were tied. Also, we had to divide our cattle with these rich people. It is better now. We don't have to pay these taxations. The Dergue cannot reach in our area.

Now I want to tell you how I came to be resettled. I went to visit my brother in Mekelle. When I got there, I learned he had gone to get government rations, so I went also, hoping to get free seeds. I was arrested. I tried to escape three times. Other people also tried to escape—most of them were killed. They were shot, and they died. Because I had tried to escape, they kept my hands tied—like this—and put me in the truck. Throughout the whole journey my hands were tied.

In Gambella we were made to dig the ground and mow the grass. We also cultivated corn and sweet potato for the government. In our backyard gardens we planted corn, sorghum and sweet potato. We bought the seeds from local villagers [Anuak] or we got seeds from our friends.

Even when we plowed with a tractor, we didn't get much harvest in Gambella. The soil is very dry there. In Tigray, the soil is sticky, but not in Gambella. We planted corn for the government but I never saw any corn plants. I don't know why. We tried to plant more seeds there, but they too did not grow. There was only one kind of corn they gave us to plant in Gambella. Its name is fasa—it is a red kind. In Tigray, we plant this kind of corn on wet soil. In Gambella, this corn comes up a pale color, not green.

Nonrandom Interview #2
Mahare Melis
Enderta, Tigray
Background Information: lived in contested area between Dergue and TPLF

In my farm in Tigray I use two pair of oxen to plow. It takes 16 days to plow my fields working all day.

When I select seeds for next year's crop, I look for good stems and big seeds. I choose those that ripen fast and that are free of disease.

I plant [around 15 kinds of] crops. Three kinds of teff: white, red and one that is in between. Teff is planted in July. I plant them all at the same time but in different plots. If all plots receive equal rainfall, they will ripen at the same time.

The white teff is for selling — it is in high demand. The kind that is in between red and white ripens fast; it is for eating now. All three have different protection against disease. Their taste is the same.

Sorghum is planted before teff — in March. It needs more water — would be irrigated if a tributary were nearby. I plant two kinds. One kind bends downward; the fruits are large and white. Another kinds stands up straight; I plant this kind because it needs few seeds to plant, but it gets a good harvest. I harvest sorghum in December; it takes six months for it to ripen.

Lentils I plant in July and harvest in September.

Wheat is planted in June. There are two kinds: white and red. I plant them at the same time. The white one has market value; the red one we eat at home.

Twelve years ago and last year we had a problem with black worms. Last year was the worst. The worms did not eat the corn or sorghum, but they ate the teff. The white teff suffered the least.

Drought is worse than worms. It affects all crops. I got a harvest in the lowland places because it is wetter. It would not have been sufficient, but I could have sold my cattle to make up the difference. Most of the time the worms eat the seeds in the dry season. If the rains come, the worms will die. So last year there was hunger.

In Perebong [a resettlement camp in Gambella], we planted corn in rows. Sorghum would not grow there. Sweet potatoes, oilseed and cotton grew well, but nothing else. I had no garden there — I was just sent there to work. We only planted the straight kind of sorghum, not the bent variety. We planted it in the right kind of soil; I don't know why it wouldn't grow. The seedlings grew well at first and then died. White people came once and said this is not a good place for sorghum.

Tigrayan soil is fertile. The soil in Perebong is better than Oala but not as good as Tigray.

Farming is my work. To feed my children I must farm again. I have nothing now, but when I return to Tigray, I can borrow a little seed.

When I plow, my sons follow me in the field. I say to them, "Now you try what I just did."

Nonrandom Interview #3
Issigejo, Age: c. 40
Haju, Wollo

The problems began after the revolution when the Dergue took control and reduced the size of my land. Now I do not have the same land my father farmed.

I plant [about 15 kinds of] crops. I select my seeds from the previous harvest or, if I have eaten the seeds, I can buy them on the market. Every year since the Dergue came to power, I have been forced to eat my seeds because of drought and insects. Worms, locusts and ants eat the fruits. But if I had my original land, I would have had enough to eat.

In March I plant sorghum, three kinds: red, straight and the kind that bends over that is called wansa bucase. I plant all kinds because the land is different; each soil needs a different kind. I plant corn at the same time and sow it together with the sorghum.

I also plant three kinds of teff, each according to the soil. But last year the insects ate them all. My irrigated vegetables were also consumed by insects.

I spent one year and four months in Asosa, at the place called "Megele 32." I was digging, clearing, building and harvesting. There was teff, sorghum, maize, groundnuts, peas, sweet potatoes, carrots and grapefruit. We planted only one kind of sorghum, the red kind. But the soil was not right for it. There were no small rocks in the soil of Asosa, which this crop needs. The teff grew well but never produced seeds. The sweet potato grew well at first but then became rotten. Because of insects, most plants did not grow well, but the cadres brought in the seeds and took away the harvest for storage.

The cadres gave us unground corn kernels for food. We would have to pound and grind it by hand. The cadres told us to use these seeds to plant in our backyard gardens, but I bought some seeds at the market by selling firewood illegally. When we didn't have food, we would work for the Oromos, and they would give us food as payment. But we had to be careful because this was not allowed. The Oromos did not like us coming into their land. They told us to go home and called us dogs. They showed us the way back to our homeland, but we cannot go there because of drought.

I was hungry in Wollo and hungry in Asosa. During the year I lived in Asosa, we left camp one by one to go into the forest and study it. In this way we planned our escape to Sudan. Now we are here, waiting for the Red Cross leaders to tell us what to do.

Nonrandom Interview #4
Rosa, Age: 33
Cobo, Wollo

I farmed the land as my father, but it was made small after the revolution and the Dergue took power. At first it took 30 days to harvest, then 20, then 10, then finally none. This is the fault of the government. Every year since the revolution, I had to eat my seeds.

I planted many kinds of crops. There are six kinds of sorghum I planted: two red kinds, two white kinds and two kinds that are intermediate which ripen very fast. There are also types we eat while the fruit is still green. There are five kinds of teff and three kinds of corn: red, orange and white. Each is planted according to its season, and each has its own time to plant. In September, I plant chickpeas, then in March, the first kind of sorghum, then in May, two more kinds of sorghum. June is the time to plant three kinds of teff and another kind of sorghum, and then in July I plant another teff and another sorghum, also oilseeds and peanuts. In August, I plant the last kind of teff. This is according to our laws.

When there is lack of rain, there are insect problems. But the problems caused by the Dergue are very bad. First they take our sons and our brothers into the army. Then they charge us heavy taxes; when the harvest is reduced, they do not reduce the taxes. My land has decreased in size since the Dergue came to power, but my taxes have increased fivefold. All members of the family must pay these taxes — even the children. So I am forced to sell my grain to get money to pay taxes. When we don't have cereal, we are forced to cut trees and sell them in the town for firewood. If these conditions did not exist, the drought would not have caused us to be hungry. In this way the Dergue causes suffering. If I had more money, I could buy pipes for irrigation.

In Asosa, we dug the ground by hand. We were not human beings there: We became like oxen; we became like tractors. The Dergue knows nothing about cultivating, about farming. The sacks of teff for planting contained both red and white seeds mixed together. In Wollo, we do not mix them because the seeds are of different weight. The red one is heavier; the white one needs to be planted deeper. Also, we plant them at different times. But in Asosa they had us plant the two teffs together, white and red. So some did not ripen, and then all the harvest rotted because some seeds were too green.

Also, at home in Wollo we use oxen for threshing the seeds. We waste none! But in Asosa they beat the seed with sticks and threw away much seed with the husks, and stones got mixed together with the seeds. When we protested, we were told we were lazy. In our homeland, one person can produce the work of 500 in Asosa. The Dergue wastes so much cereal and so much grain.

In our gardens we were given a few certain seeds to plant — white sorghum and corn — but it was only enough for children. Ants ate the seeds almost immediately. The soil is not good there; it is the soil for insects, not the soil for planting. And we were forbidden to go to the market, so we could not buy seeds.

We left Asosa because we would rather be eaten by wild animals in the forest than beaten by the cadres like donkeys. Now we will stay here as sons of the UN. We are waiting for decisions. We have nowhere to go.

We are worried about the children who are still in Wollo, but the man who goes to get his children will be killed or resettled again to Asosa.

Nonrandom Interview #5
Gabeze Tedessa
Wollo

I plant [15-18] crops and some vegetables. There are three kinds of teff: red, white and brown. Their planting times are different. There are four kinds of sorghum; one is a very short kind that ripens quickly. I also plant barley and wheat and two kinds of corn (red and white).

There is the problem of drought and the problem of the government, which is worse. Why? Because he increases taxes for all people, because he takes people to war and because he resettles people. If there was no taxation, I could irrigate my fields. Three times I had to escape military recruitment. I went to hide in the forest while the crops were in the field. Luckily my family could take care of the crops and we had a good harvest.

In Asosa, I was digging and planting — peanuts, teff, corn, sorghum. They all grew well, but many had no seeds. The sorghum grew well at first, but then something ate the seeds while they were still green. And the harvest is impure because it is mixed with dirt. In Wollo, we pour water and cow manure, and it becomes just like cement. Then the oxen can walk over the seeds. But in Asosa, the party cadres just swept the dirt floor, dropped the cereal on it and beat it with sticks.

In our backyards the crops grew well, but then they dried up and insects ate them. The cadres gave us the seeds — corn and sorghum — but we got no harvest. The soil is *not good there; there are many insects, ants and worms. The problem is not one of fertility: the ants would just eat the seeds as soon as they were sown. I was more hungry in Asosa than I ever was at home.*

Nonrandom Interview #6
Tigrayan woman, SPLA victim
TPLF-controlled area of Tigray

I am 27 years old. I have three children in Tigray; they are aged 11, 8 and 6 years. Last year my husband took me to the hospital in Axum because of an eye disease. There we heard an announcement from the government about donations of cereal grain. We wanted to get food for our children, so we went there. That is when we were captured and sent to Gambella. Really, except for last year, there was no drought. But in the last year my husband could not work much because he was always taking me to the hospital.

In Gambella, my husband worked for the cadres. The women roasted grain and worked in the backyard gardens, but nothing grew well there. We suffered indeed. In October, my husband and I escaped from that place with a large group—over 1,000 people—and we fled into the forest.

When we reached Sudan, we met people who at first gave us food. Then they gave us money and led us to the next village. That is when they took the children away. After that they took us, the women. I don't know why they took the children—for workers maybe, for slaves. These men had uniforms. The people who gave us food did not wear uniforms.

When they tried to take us, there was a battle. Our husbands tried to fight with them, but it was sticks against guns. Some husbands were killed, some wounded. The army was victorious. The remaining husbands ran into the forest. The army took us to their camp by a roundabout direction. We stayed there six nights, then the fighters divided us among themselves, choosing the most beautiful there were. There were 205 women who had been captured, but after this we were always kept separately. We were sent to the huts of each fighter and always guarded, even when we went to the toilet. They took us because they wanted to mate with us, because they wanted children by us. Other than this, we did not understand them because we did not speak their language.

During the day we pounded maize for them. There were other wives, women previously captured. We worked for them also. Pounding maize is unfamiliar work to us. In Tigray we use a mill for grinding, so to do this with our hands is like punishment. When we protested, they beat us. I lived in a hut with three fighters. At night they exchanged me among themselves. This went on for two months.

After our release, we walked two days on foot to Yabuus and then were taken by lorry here to Damazine. This is a good place; we are given food and are not compelled to work. But always I am worrying about my husband. I thought I might find him here, but I think now he was killed in the forest when I was captured. There are so many of us dead in the forest. Thousands. No one knows how many.

Of course, I want to go back home to Tigray, where my children are. Two of them are with my parents now, and the other is with my husband's parents. I think maybe I am pregnant now. I do not want to have the baby of these people. In Tigray, I will look for medicine to end the pregnancy. But mostly I am worrying about my husband. We here in this camp are the lucky ones.

Appendix E
Refugees in Damazine — 1987

As of 17 June 1987, 720 Ethiopian refugees were living in the Damazine holding camp. Of these, 641 (89 percent) were escapees from resettlement camps in Wollega.

Fellowship for African Relief (FAR), a Canadian-based agency, was providing medical assistance and distributing food at the camp; the Sudanese Commission for Refugees was in charge of administration. On 18 June, all 720 residents were taken by lorry to Gedaref, after which time FAR ended its presence in the camp.

Camp Population

Province of Origin	Percentage of Camp Population
Wollo	86.5
Tigray	6.8
Gojam	2.0
Wollega	1.0
Eritrea	0.3
Unknown	3.4
Time of Arrival	
10–12 mos. ago	71.0
3–6 mo. ago	12.0
Less than 3 mo. ago	17.0

Source: Collin Adams, director of FAR in Damazine.

Patterns of Flight

In contrast to 1986, refugees are fleeing the resettlement camps in small groups rather than by mass breakouts. According to FAR records, they have been arriving steadily between August 1986 and June 1987. Between my first visit to the camp on 27 May and my last visit on 17 June, another 45 refugees had arrived, some within the previous few days. Three days after the camp was evacuated, 75 more refugees arrived.

According to the FAR director in Damazine, refugees said they preferred to attempt escape in the rainy season when SPLA and Dergue activities slow down. Last year, refugees told me that they had waited for dry weather to make their escapes because they feared drowning in the rivers.

Recently arriving refugees reported to Adams that many hundred more escaped settlers were still hiding in the bush near Kirmuk, waiting for the rains to resume before crossing the border and making their way to Damazine.

Health of the Arrivals

Medical workers at FAR told me that most refugees arrive emaciated and exhausted but not in critical condition. Malaria and diarrhea are very common among newcomers. Children are often malnourished upon arrival.

Appendix F
Refugees in Yabuus — 1987

The Oromo Relief Association (ORA) established itself in Yabuus in 1982 and began systematically settling refugees there in 1984. In June 1987, ORA officials in Yabuus estimated that 5,000 refugees now live in the area of Yabuus. (This includes those both completely dependent and partially dependent on ORA assistance.) Of this total, 3,000 have arrived within the last two years (after Bonnie Holcomb's interviews at that camp in 1985), half of those within the last six months.

Refugees are settled in six different "village" areas which, to some extent, represent their time of arrival and ethnic group.

ORA officials said that since Holcomb's study in 1985, increased SPLA activities along the border region have closed many routes that refugees had been using to escape to Yabuus. For example, the route to Dega Post is now closed due to SPLA activity. Resettlement camp escapees and other displaced persons now often head for OLF-controlled areas inside Ethiopia and request assistance. OLF brings certain groups of refugees to Yabuus (some then go to Damazine or Khartoum) and resettles others inside their operational areas.

ORA said security in the resettlement camps is now very tight. They are no longer seeing any escapees from the Gambella resettlement sites. Those who do escape either do not survive the journey, are captured by the SPLA or attempt to return to their homelands through the interior of Ethiopia. (REST of Germany says some settlers in Gambella have successfully returned to Tigray by bribing their way through the interior.)

According to ORA, refugees in Yabuus came almost entirely from three of the six districts of Wollega: Kellem and Asosa (both adjacent to the border) and Gimbi.

Camp Population

Date of Refugees' Arrival	Number of Refugees	
1982–Jan. 1987	406 heads of families X 5*	= 2,030 refugees
Jan. 87–present	310 heads of families X 5	= 1,550 refugees
Total:	716 heads of families X 5	= 3,580 refugees
		+ 1,500 refugees†
		5,080 refugees

* Assuming average family composes five members.

† Refugees living in the camp's outer vicinity (partially dependent on ORA).

Thus, of those refugees living in the inner vicinity of the camp (the population I interviewed), more than 40 percent have arrived within the last six months. ORA attributes this increase to villagization and resettlement.

Resettlement Refugees in Yabuus

Beginning in April 1986, Oromos from Wollo who had been resettled into Wollega began arriving in Yabuus after hearing that a community of Oromos was living in Sudan. As of June 1987, they numbered 100 heads of families (500 refugees) and thus make up about 14 percent of the Yabuus population.

Villagization Refugees in Yabuus

ORA could not estimate what percent of the camp's population were those who had fled villagization. Several large groups of refugees, representing whole villages, fled together immediately before they were to be villagized. For example, ORA says 115 heads of families (575 people) arrived together in January 1987 after fleeing villagization in the Gaukebe subdistrict of Kellem; another group of 150 people fled from the Jarso area of Gimbi in February. And a group of 160 people fled in February from the Begi area of Asosa (Mimi village). Several large groups of villagization escapees have also been resettled inside OLF operational areas.

Non-Oromo Refugees

Berta and Komo people together represent 50 heads of families (250 refugees) in Yabuus. ORA says that the Komo have been in the camp from the beginning whereas the Berta began arriving in small groups in 1985, coinciding with SPLA activity in their area.

Part Two | Villagization

4 | Introduction

Jason W. Clay

In 1978 the Ethiopian government first began to move peasants into villages in Bale administrative region. This program was intended to restructure rural life, modernize agriculture and create agrarian socialism. The process came to be known as *villagization*. From 1978 through 1986 more than 5 million people have been relocated into more than 10,000 new villages. Current plans call for the creation of an additional 5,000 new villages in 1987. Government officials estimate that by the end of 1987, 25 percent of the rural population will have been moved to new sites.

The intensification of the program in the fall of 1984 in Hararghe and subsequently in the fall of 1985 in Arsi, Hararghe, Shoa and Wollega and to a lesser extent in four other administrative regions, at the same time as the 1984-1985 famine, struck many observers as an unwise policy choice. Furthermore, the simultaneous occurrence of the government's massive, ill-advised and inhuman resettlement program increased international skepticism about the advisability of the villagization program. Some analysts saw resettlement and villagization as the same program; however, the programs are different, but related. They represent two ends of the same stick. They are linked both in agricultural and security policies, and they are being pursued to change irrevocably life in the countryside and to create a government-directed agricultural production system.

The information presented in this part of the volume is devoted to villagization and is divided into four sections. The first section focuses on the general development of the villagization policy and its overall implementation under the present government in Ethiopia. The history of the policy is explored through a close examination of official government sources, the testimony of former government officials and Western expatriates working in the country, and the published observations and opinions of Western journalists. The first section reports the government position regarding the villagization as it has been officially presented in uncirculated documents, official press sources and on-the-record comments.

The second section explores — or rather, pieces together — the history of the villagization program in Bale administrative region. The "successful" experiences in Bale are often cited as the basis for the extension of the program to other regions. This section examines the relationship between the various settlement programs in Bale and conditions in the region of the war with Somalia, the influx of refugees to Somalia and, finally, the relationship of Western agencies such as UNICEF, Lutheran World Relief (LWR) and the Mennonite Central Committee (MCC) to the program. All the elements that subsequently have come under close scrutiny regarding villagization could have been examined in Bale if observers had cared (or dared) to look. Given that Bale is the success story of the government's villagization program, it is regrettable that, to date, no one has examined the case closely.

The third section describes the experiences reported by former residents of Hararghe administrative region during villagization in their area. As a result of the villagization program these people, along with some 40,000 others, fled to Somalia in 1986. In addition, perhaps half that many fled to Somalia in 1985 as a result of the implementation of the first phase of the program. It is ironic that no officials or agencies working in Ethiopia or Somalia had bothered to ask the refugees why they left for Somalia in 1985. Yet, now it seems clear that much of the influx resulted from villagization in Hararghe undertaken in 1984–1985.

The interviews conducted in April 1986 with refugees in Tug Wajale, the Somalia refugee camp, constitute the most methodical research, both from a sampling and interviewing point of view, ever undertaken in Somalia. They also represent the most systematic, replicable research undertaken concerning villagization in Ethiopia. However, all reports of research undertaken with refugees from Ethiopia in Tug Wajale, no matter how impressionistic, come to basically the same conclusion as those reported here: villagization in Hararghe was accomplished only through the use of threat, intimidation and, all too often, force, which resulted in massive human rights violations. Reports from inside Ethiopia increasingly support these findings.

In the fourth section, Sandra Steingraber reports on her interviews with Oromo who fled to Sudan from Ethiopian attempts to establish new villages in western Wollega. Steingraber's findings are important for a number of reasons. First, her data shift the international debate on villagization away from the Hararghe administrative region, which is hundreds of miles distant. Second, her findings echo those obtained from refugees who fled from Hararghe in Somalia: villagization was preceded by acts of terror and intimidation; armed guards forced people to participate; the construction of new villages disrupted farming; villagers were not allowed to select new village sites; no social services were provided; and villagization was accompanied by collectivization. Third, and perhaps most importantly, villagization in western Wollega, an area that is both isolated and highly militarized, offers useful insights about the possible implementation of the program in other isolated, war-torn or conflict-ridden parts of the country — for example, Wollo, Tigray and Eritrea. As with the data collected from refugees about villagization in Hararghe, Western NGOs and visitors to Wollega have not reported conditions similar to those reported by refugees from the area.

It is not surprising that research on villagization undertaken inside Ethiopia, however, has not uncovered the same level of abuses as the villagized refugees in Somalia and Sudan reported. A number of factors might account for these discrepancies. Those who elected to flee the country might have experienced extreme suffering at the hands of a few local zealots who used the program to settle old scores. Furthermore, those who fled to Somalia or Sudan might have been wealthier and have had more to lose. However, the fact that refugees, who fled two different parts of the country to two different countries of exile, report the same conditions indicates that abuses associated with the program might be far more widespread than people working inside initially believed. Only careful study inside Ethiopia can determine the representativity of the problems and abuses associated with villagization that refugees reported in Somalia and Sudan.

Unfortunately, the two studies to date, Roberts (1986) in Hararghe and Cohen and Isaksson (1987) in Arsi, were not undertaken in such a way as to dispel the concerns about those human rights violations associated with the program that were voiced by refugees in Somalia and Sudan. Although both studies include considerable useful information — and indeed were critical of the program on economic and environmental grounds — they were not undertaken in such a way that one can speak with certainty either about the voluntary nature of the program or the more general issues such as the representativity of the data collected, the respondents' freedom to speak, the areas not visited and the respondents' view of those undertaking the research.

5 | Villagization in Ethiopia

Jason W. Clay

Although [villagization] will take a certain amount of time to progress it has had an auspicious beginning. It is a basic revolutionary movement which will enable us to restructure rural life in a short period of time. Placing farmers into collective villages will enable them to promote social production in a short time. It will also change the farmer's life, his views, and his thinking and will therefore open a new chapter in the establishment of a modern society in the rural areas and bring about socialism.

While the historic land decree was one major stepping stone in a new democratic life for the farmer, the villages program is a movement that will create additional appropriate conditions for the farmer to free himself from a life of backwardness by exercising the democratic rights he has consolidated.... Forming collectives in villages has previously been going on in certain areas. It is one of the coordinated methods of rural development that has been laid down in the WPE [Workers' Party of Ethiopia] program and which has been emphasized in the 10-year development plan (Lt. Col. Mengistu to WPE, Radio Addis Ababa 10 April 1986).

For eight years Ethiopia has pursued a policy of incorporating peasant farmers into new villages to establish cooperative agricultural production. The process is known as villagization. Whether the villagization program is indeed the result of the peasant farmer "exercising these democratic rights he has consolidated," as Ethiopia's leader, Lt. Col. Mengistu Haile Mariam, claims, however, is disputed.

Moreover, although the government has clearly demonstrated its ability to create new villages, it cannot create communities. Yet it is traditional communities, unhindered by government programs, that are families' best defenses against famine. In the last three years the government has destroyed an estimated 30,000 to 40,000 traditional communities, most in areas that are known to be surplus food-producing regions.

Since 1978, government efforts aimed at restructuring rural life through villagization have been most successful and intense during periods of social and economic chaos, such as the aftermath of the war with Somalia and the 1984-1985 famine. The government appears to have used these chaotic periods as a smoke screen for forcibly moving people into villages and organizing them to work cooperatively. During chaotic times, the provision of Western assistance, first humanitarian and then developmental, was also a critical factor which permitted the government to expand the villagization program more than it could have done on its own. Western assistance appears to have been used in two ways. First, it was used as bait, luring farmers to participate in villagization programs. Second, it picked up the slack in the food production system that had been deliberately created by military and economic policies.

A close examination of the history of villagization in Ethiopia, including the role of Western assistance, offers insights into both the goals and the methods with which the program was implemented in 1985, 1986 and 1987. In the last three years, more than 15,000 new villages were created. According to Ethiopian officials, by the end of 1987, 25 percent of Ethiopia's rural population would live in new villages (*New York Times* 11 March 1987). This figure is not random; these people are primarily Oromo peasants who occupy the most fertile, agricultural surplus-producing regions of the country. Table 1 demonstrates the progress of the program, by province, from 1984 to 1987. Appendix A gives a detailed report, province by province, of villagization from 1984 through mid-1987.

Background to Villagization

In 1977 and 1978, a team of Ethiopian diplomats and officials (no development experts were included) visited Tanzania to assess the appropriateness of that country's *ujumaa* villagization program for Ethiopia. According to a member of the Ethiopian team, the delegation was impressed with the potential of the program—even though in Tanzania farmers were already abandoning the new villages due to ecological, economic and social problems.

The Ethiopian delegation concluded, however, that the Tanzanian villagization program's main problem was the insufficiency of central government control. Consequently, the team recommended that Ethiopia adopt the program but that the central government provide more direction and use more force to bring farmers into the new villages and keep them there. These recommendations were echoed subsequently in the Ethiopian government's internal, undated memo, probably from the fall of 1985, titled "Directive on Villagization" [hereafter cited as Government of Ethiopia (GOE)].

It is essential that the villagization programme be implemented, coordinated and controlled centrally in order that fundamental changes are made in the

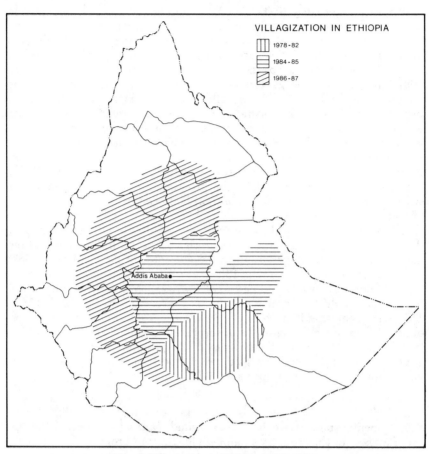

Map 3. Villagization in Ethiopia, 1978–1987.

society and that the desired results are obtained. It is on this principle that the present directive is prepared (GOE:5).

In 1979, villagization, or "settlement," as it was initially labeled, was identified publicly as a goal of the Dergue, the ruling military body. Mengistu Haile Mariam, addressing the second annual meeting of the All Ethiopia Peasant Association on 11 May 1979, said,

In so far as efforts are dispersed and livelihood is individual, the results are only hand-to-mouth existence amounting to fruitless struggle and drudgery, which cannot build a prosperous society....

The *Ethiopian Herald* goes on to editorialize that

[t]he task of eliminating the gap [between urban and rural] may be fulfilled only by [an] organized restructuring of the whole social economy, from in-

Table 1

Reports of Villagization in Ethiopia 1985–1987

Region (date studied)	9/85	2/86	3/86	4/86	1/87	2-3/87	end 3/87	4/87	5-6/87	Goal in 1987†
ARSI (1985)										
People			810,000				1,207,000	91,000		
Houses		100,508	164,449				183,500†	19,490		
Villages		69	1,009				922	140		1,095
Peasant assoc.			839							
Animal pens			25,000							
Grain stores								3,311		
PA offices								93		
Ass'bly halls								31		
Schools								16		
% completed							73%	60%		
BALE (1979)										
People							980,000			54,000
Houses							129,300†			12,000
Villages							562			
Peasant assoc.										
PA offices										53
Meeting halls										41
Storehouses										25
Silos										7,220
Kindergartens										9
Schools										21
% completed							99%			
ERITREA (villagization has not commenced at this time)										
GAMU-GOFA (1986)										
People							33,000			
Houses							6,900†			
Villages							39			
% completed							2%			
Gamo Province										
People								33,057		
Houses								6,783		
Villages								33		
Wollayta Prov.										
People								41,726		
Houses								10,464		

Table 1
Reports of Villagization in Ethiopia 1985–1987

Region (date studied)	9/85	2/86	3/86	4/86	1/87	2-3/87	end 3/87	4/87	5-6/87	Goal in 1987†
GOJJAM (1986)										
People							957,000	600,000		
Houses				30,584			208,900†	125,571		
Villages				458			921	757		
Peasant assoc.										
Schools								41		
Clinics								12		
Silos								30		
Dams								6		
Water wells								51		
% completed							29%	20%		
Motu Prov.										
People									122,000	
Houses									25,019	
Villages									197	
Metekel Prov.										
People									51,180	
Houses									10,236	
Villages									157	
Peasant assoc.									55	
GONDAR (1987)										
People							39,000	39,389	306,182	73,244
Houses							7,600†			14,649
Villages							158	179	326	72
Peasant assoc.										31
% completed							1%		11%	
Libo Prov.										
Houses						2,047				
Gondar Zuria P.										
People									123,700	
Houses									24,740	
Villages									107	
Peasant assoc.									65	
Debra Tabor P.										
People						74,945				
Houses						17,890				
Villages						86				
Peasant assoc.						34				

Table 1
Reports of Villagization in Ethiopia 1985–1987

Region (date studied)	9/85	2/86	3/86	4/86	1/87	2-3/87	end 3/87	4/87	5-6/87	Goal in 1987†
HARARGHE (1984)										
People	375,277		92,213	50,090			2,629,000	72,000,000		
Houses			19,720	16,222			416,400*			
Villages	2,115		150	707			3,441			
Peasant assoc.										
Latrines				2,197						
Garbage pits				1,200						
Elem. schools				48						
Coop. shops				10						
Parks				10						
% completed							63%	98%		
ILLUBABOR (1986)										
People						61,880	352,000			220,200
Houses						17,070	60,600*			53,490
Villages						166	757			347
Peasant assoc.										
Kitchens						868				
Latrines						1,592				
Cattle pens						328				
Garbage pits						63				
% completed						7%	36%			25%
Buno Prov.										
Houses						7.328				
Sorna Geba P.										
Houses						4,405				
Mocha Prov.										
Houses						3,317				
Gore Prov.										
Houses						2,025				

Table 1
Reports of Villagization in Ethiopia 1985–1987

Region (date studied)	9/85	2/86	3/86	4/86	1/87	2-3/87	end 3/87	4/87	5-6/87	Goal in 1987†
KEFA (1986)										
People			[14,539]			370,000	601,000			814,768
Houses			[5,432]			79,834	115,400†			159,753
Villages			[105]			925	699			1,560
% completed						35%	24%			
Limu Prov.										
Houses					54,970	38,869				
Jimma Prov.										
Houses						22,585				
Kefa Prov.										
Houses						10,971				
Kulo Prov.										
Houses						4,475				
Gimira Prov.										
Houses						1,998				
Maji Prov.										
Houses						853				
SHOA (1985)										
People		19,021			548,916		1,468,000	[790,620]		1,881,721
Houses		[78,960]			190,944		284,300†			362,380
Villages		[264]					2,682			2,903
Peasant assoc		[143]								
% completed							18%			
Haikotch-Butojira Prov.										
People										
Houses						12,182				
Peasant assoc.						144				
Tegulet-Bulga P.										
People						6,005				
Houses						2,802				
SIDAMO (1986)										
People					52,985		230,000			415,227
Houses					13,218	10,571	26,400†			81,346
Villages							83			
Peasant assoc.										
Schools										
Clinics										
Silos										
Dams										
Water wells										
% completed							6%			
TIGRAY										
Enderta Prov.									X	
Raya Azeba P.									X	

Table 1
Reports of Villagization in Ethiopia 1985–1987

Region (date studied)	9/85	2/86	3/86	4/86	1/87	2-3/87	end 3/87	4/87	5-6/87	Goal in 1987†
WOLLEGA (1986)										
People							235,000			
Houses							40,950*			
Villages							1,050			
Peasant assoc.										
% completed							9%			
Huro-Gudro P.										
Villages						631				
WOLLO (1987)										
People							21,000			
Houses							5,200†			
Villages							35			
% completed							1%			
TOTAL										
People						5,725,530	8,752,000			3,084,515
Houses						1,138,265	1,486,800			782,850
New villages						11,460	11,349			4,148
Km of road										2,240
Kitchens						42,304				
Toilets						125,655				
% completed						15.4%	24%			

Source: *The Ethiopian Herald,* numerous dates; US Department of State telegram 22 June 1987; Food and Agriculture Organization and anonymous sources.

* Estimate calculated by multiplying numbers of new villages by average number of families.

† All goals are projected figures.

[ ] Indicates announced goals.

dividual small households to a publicly owned, large-scale economy (1979 Mengistu speech cited in the *Ethiopian Herald* 11 January 1986).

In 1978, however, settling peasants in Bale was a strategic move that was part of a military strategy. Full-scale implementation of the program in Bale administrative region began when peasants were moved to shelters that subsequently became new villages (see "The Case of Bale," in this volume). Between 1978 and 1982 the government created nearly 600 new villages in Bale with a total population of more than 600,000. Although the program continued in Bale from 1982 to 1984, most people were moved during the first three years. The reduction in numbers related partly to the tapering of foreign assistance and to the inhospitable areas, both ecologically and politically, that remained to be villagized. By 1984, however, officials announced that Bale was villagized and on the road to cooperative farming. Local officials bragged to visitors that in terms of the organization of socialist production, Bale was the most advanced administrative region in all of Ethiopia.

Meanwhile, by the end of 1980, the RRC (Relief and Rehabilitation Commission, the government agency with sole responsibility for villagization until 1984) had also established 14* new villages containing 46,000 families in Sidamo administrative region (Fikre and Manzoor 1980:25), involving approximately 250,000 people. If these figures are accurate, new villages in Sidamo are far larger than those in other regions.

By 1982, villagization was being implemented in the Arba Guuga district of neighboring Arsi administrative region. Some sources indicate that between 1982 and 1986, 600,000 people were moved into new villages in Arsi.

By mid-1984, officials announced the extension of the program into Hararghe administrative region (see Villagization in Hararghe). Implementation was intensified in spring 1985 and again in the fall. By summer 1986, according to government figures, about 50 percent of Hararghe's rural population (out of a total of 4 million) had been moved into new villages. The program in Hararghe has continued, with minor interruptions, into 1987.

In addition to these four massive programs just described, between 1979 and 1985 villagization was also implemented selectively in a number of communities and relatively restricted areas. Beginning in late 1984 the program became a government priority and was extended from early 1985 through 1986 to eight provinces where new villages were created, often virtually overnight. (See Appendix A for the limited official details available on these programs.)

By August 1986 reports indicated that new village sites had been pinpointed on maps in district and subdistrict offices in Wollo administrative region. In November 1986, in an interview with the BBC (British Broad-

---

*Perhaps this figure was a typographical error. These villages would average more than 3,000 families each. It is more likely that 140 new villages were created.

casting Corporation), the representative of World Vision – UK indicated that the villagization program had begun in Wollo. Villagization had also begun "officially" in Wollega and Illubabor administrative regions. The term *officially* is used because in some areas of these administrative regions, as well as in Kefa, another administrative region in the southwest, the Ethiopian government has been moving local residents into new villages since 1979, when it began colonizing lands of peoples indigenous to the southwest of Ethiopia by resettling peoples from the north.

Ethiopia's official position through public pronouncements regarding its villagization program, as well as the record of the first massive implementation of the program undertaken in Bale administrative region from 1979 to 1984 (see the case of Bale), clearly link villagization to the creation of producers' cooperatives. Yet many Western diplomats and assistance agencies cling, in some cases desperately, to the belief that although villagization has proceeded at a rapid pace with coercion playing a large role in the program, no evidence exists of the creation of producers' cooperatives during the villagization program's intensification in 1985 and 1986. To clarify disputed aspects of the program, therefore, it is important first to reproduce official statements concerning the goals of the villagization program from the government's directive on villagization and from the government-run newspaper and radio, the *Ethiopian Herald* and Radio Addis Ababa.

The Government's Goals for Villagization

The government's stated purposes of the villagization program are many-sided. However, villagization should also be seen as the third phase in the government's strategy to create rural socialism. The first phase of this program occurred in nationalizing all land. The second phase entailed creating peasant associations. Thus, the most important goal of villagization is to create a "modern," state-directed agricultural production system such as those based on producers' cooperatives. Increasingly, labor is to be organized communally and directed by local officials. Finally, villagization is intended to enhance both collective projects and political education.

Villagization and Producers' Cooperatives

Throughout 1986 and 1987 the tandem creation of new villages and producers' cooperatives was stated directly by government officials and in official publications. The following quotations leave little doubt about the relationship of villagization and producers' cooperatives in Ethiopia. On 11 January 1986, the *Ethiopian Herald* noted that "[i]n 1979, it was proposed to group small dispersed rural settlements. This important measure is directly linked with plans for creating a broad network of producers' cooperatives." Three months later, the paper reported that Legesse Asfaw, the architect and the person responsible for the 1986 expanded villagization program, was reported to have maintained that

the satisfactory results in the villagization programme alongside the cooperative development and [Legesse Asfaw] said that producers' cooperatives not only contribute to the enhancement of the productivity of peasants but also facilitate the scientific utilization of the land. He pointed out that the villagization program should be based on the cooperative model of development (*Ethiopian Herald* 5 March 1986).

Additional published official comments include the following.

> The rapid development of the agricultural sector . . . is imperative. No doubt, the introduction of the villagization programme and the collective undertaking of agricultural activities have a tremendous role to play in this regard (*Ethiopian Herald* 26 January 1986).

> The establishment of producers' cooperatives . . . attest to the commitment of the WPE and the revolutionary government to raise the standard of living of the peasant masses. . . . The villagization scheme has a great deal to contribute towards the improvement of agricultural production (*Ethiopian Herald* 26 January 1986).

> In the search for increased agricultural productivity and for a fuller life to the rural population, the villagization and resettlement schemes currently being undertaken with vigour play a significant part. Under these schemes, the peasants who had lived a scattered life in the past, very often in unproductive areas, are now being moved to more fertile areas of the country in newly sprouting and well-organized villages with a number of amenities which the rural population hadn't enjoyed before. One of the significant aspects of the new re-settlement scheme is cooperation. The peasants are learning a new meaning to the word cooperation in their collective effort to increase agricultural productivity through cooperatives, peasant associations, producers' cooperatives and the like (*Ethiopian Herald* 13 May 1987).

> That is why the revolutionary leadership issued successive proclamations and a number of directives for the progressive socialization of agriculture in line with the declared policy of the country. The measures have subsequently given an impetus for the establishment of peasants' producers cooperatives. . . . This is the basic rationale for increasing the number of peasant associations farming their own cooperatives. The idea behind the villagization programme is not basically different from the quest for the socialization process going on in [the] rural sector. . . . The villagization process is therefore both a natural response to the drought situation and a strategy for boosting rural productivity on the basis of long-term socialization of production (*Ethiopian Herald* 5 June 1987).

> The Deputy Chairman of the NCCP urged all comrades concerned to intensify efforts to organize the peasant farmers under producers' cooperatives in accordance with the decision of the third plenum of the Central Committee of the WPE (*Ethiopian Herald* 28 January 1986).

These decisions were adopted at the September 1985 annual meeting of the Workers' Party of Ethiopia (WPE). Announced on the radio, the text and resolutions confirmed the government's intended role of villagization leading to cooperative farming.

> In regard to facilitating the provision of various services for the proper utilization of land so that the agricultural sector of the economy contributes its share to national construction, and in general to organizing the countryside in the spirit of the construction of the new society, it [the WPE] called for the ongo-

ing activity of collectivizing the farmers in the villages to be strengthened and continued. . . .

3. That the work to collectivize the farmers in villages to make the agricultural economic sector contribute its share in the country's development, through the proper use of land, the provision of various services, and the building of the villages in the spirit of building the new society be further strengthened (Radio Addis Ababa 4 September 1985).

Later, the *Ethiopian Herald* also reported the approved resolutions, which clearly link the producers' cooperatives with the villagization program.

The Ethiopian peasantry having secured its organization[al] status thanks to the revolution has been made ready for the next struggle awaiting it by adapting resolutions calling for its strong reorganization along new lines that will be suitable to the implementation of the programs of the WPE.

He [Legesse Asfaw] reminded them to watch out so that *kulaks* or new private property owners will not exploit them and to continue their support for the mushrooming of more and more producers' cooperatives which are the basis for the growth of a rural socialist economy (*Ethiopian Herald* 3 July 1986).

In its directive on villagization distributed by the National Committee for Villagization to all administrative region and district villagization committees, the government's intended relationship between villagization and producers' cooperatives is also explicit.

From the inception of the great popular revolution, the bringing together of the rural population was one of the major considerations being undertaken. The changing of the lifestyle of the farmer, the organization and expansion of the peasant cooperatives were matters of utmost consideration in order to provide better lives for the farmers. The establishment of cooperatives and associations which were essential for greater productivity and better utilization of land and the implementation of villagization was a vital strategy along with the earlier decisions. The efforts of the establishment of producers' cooperatives along with the villagization programme implemented in the last years cannot be underestimated. However, the organization and increase of peasants into producers cooperatives has not instilled in them the sense of communality. The struggle to eradicate the sense of personal gain is a long and hard one (GOE:4).

As the directive explains, however:

Thus, the organization of cooperative and producer associations must go together with the villagization programme so that production increases are not adversely affected in the short term. It is thus that the 3rd regular session of the Central Committee of WPE, in order to increase the agricultural production in the short term and to change the social life of the peasant, decided that the villagization programme ensure individual holding during the implementation of the project and directives to this effect have been made (GOE:4).

The same document explains further on:

In the short term villagization will provide opportunity for the expansion of economic and social services, the growth of productivity and social security of the community. In the long term villagization will promote communal productivity, expanded exchange of goods and gradually bridge the existing gap between urban and rural relationships (GOE:8).

The short-term and long-term plans of villagization parallel those for peasant associations, linking both to the eventual creation of producers' cooperatives. The overall percentage of farmers in producers' cooperatives has doubled to 4 percent in recent years. In Hararghe province, where villagization has been most intense during the last three years, a World Bank official estimates that 8 percent of all farmers belong to producers' cooperatives.

Villagization, as the government directive states, was orchestrated from the top. Whereas the precise timing of the program appears to be left to the discretion of regional and local officials, guidelines were established at the national level and were to be complied with locally.

In some areas the creation of new villages and producers' cooperatives have occurred simultaneously. In others villagization has proceeded rapidly while the creation of producers' cooperatives has lagged behind. Without more information it is difficult to see a consistent pattern in the creation of producers' cooperatives. Variables that should be examined closely are: nationality and religion of those villagized, soil quality and topography of the villagized area, cash crops presently grown or with high potential to grow in the area, relative portion of agriculture and/or livestock to subsistence production or income, and finally, distance of the area from areas controlled by or sympathetic to liberation fronts, or *shiftas* ("bandits," usually a euphemism for national liberation front fighters).

Creation of Communal Labor Systems

Official Ethiopian press reports, as well as Western newspaper articles and refugee testimony, indicate that labor in the new villages is being organized and deployed along government-directed "communal" lines. For example, in some cases new village construction was undertaken by a nearby producers' cooperative (see *Ethiopian Herald* 25 April 1986) or peasant or youth association. Other reports (e.g., *Ethiopian Herald* 16 February 1986) indicate that whereas "it took a peasant family six months to build a house in the past now it takes only five days with peasant association members."

Although Western diplomats and humanitarian agency officials claim not to have seen systems of cooperative labor, former government officials indicate that villagization has led to the creation of communal labor systems. As the *Ethiopian Herald* reported, "Collective efforts helped them [villagized peasant farmers] to harvest their crops in time and provide them with marketing facilities" (25 February 1986).

The government's intent to create communal, cooperative labor systems is spelled out clearly in its directive on villagization.

The farmer can be directed to farm methodically and produce in accordance with set plans.... By being together the farmers also solve their problems in common, use common resources and have common goals. Otherwise, it might have been difficult if they went individually their way and their individual efforts certainly would not have great impact. Hence, villagization has created for them [an] opportunity to work together, discuss common issues and find common solutions to their problems.

Living in common villages will enable the peasantry to construct feeder roads, plan irrigation development and undertake construction projects, which, in scattered situations, he [sic] would not have been able to do (GOE:8).

When implementing villagization, use the population of the village in teams for constructing houses, bringing needed material, others for supervision, some for control. Such operation reflects socialist work ethics and competition (GOE:12).

The population in an area can provide collective labour (GOE:35).

Other sources echo these statements:

Labor for road building was provided by the peasant associations although the Ministry of Highways did, on occasion, provide equipment. The peasant associations are also required to maintain the roads (Anonymous 1987:19).

The refugees [from Hararghe in Somalia] talk of long hours of forced labor at the new sites — building houses, digging latrines and constructing roads (Community Aid Abroad — Australia 1986:2).

Political Education

Local peasant association officials reported to the government press that villagization made both collective projects and political education possible. Such officals were reported to have said that

when they were living in isolated communities it took them one or two days to mobilize members to carry out joint development activities. Now that they are together, they said, they can, after daily chores, easily gather together and discuss issues of common interest and concern, their future programmes, their achievements and problems and their desires and aspirations (*Ethiopian Herald* 26 April 1986).

Security in the Countryside

The majority of the rural population live far from accessible road and ... are also scattered [too] far and wide for them to have proper security services (GOE:3).

The government directive on villagization instructed officials to "use the population of the village ... some for control" (GOE:12). Yet apparently without noting the contradiction, the government report indicates that "[i]n the past, when there were tribal and feudal clashes, these [remote] areas were also easily protected and could be easily defended from enemies" (GOE:5). From whom do these isolated people now need to be protected? If such areas are so easily defended, why do people need to be moved?

Administration of the Program

According to the government directive on villagization and keeping with the recommendations of the team that visited Tanzania, villagization in Ethiopia is a highly centralized and structured program. Directives have been issued that guide officials from the top down, including local peasant associations.

During the initial villagization programs, primarily in Bale, Sidamo and Arsi, the Relief and Rehabilitation Commission oversaw the program. Now it appears the task is too important for the RRC. The deputy chairman of the Council of Ministers is chairman of the National Committee on Villagization; the vice-chair of the committee is the Minister of Agriculture.

From the outset, the government realized that it would take considerable "propaganda and agitation" to induce people to move, as the following guidelines from the directive indicate.

> It is not an easy task to move families from areas in which they have lived for years. Their consciousness and social awareness is backward. Therefore it becomes essential to use concentrated propaganda and agitation to assist in such an operation (GOE:10).

> The implementation of villagization requires care and caution — therefore convincing agitation must be made by the party, government, mass organization organs and by individuals who may have some weight in a given area, so that the peasantry is convinced of the program and that villagization is implemented with [the] least obstacle (GOE:10-11).

> Implement effective agitation and propaganda measures so that the community is convinced of the value of villagization and that villagization is implemented with conviction (GOE:31).

> It [the peasant association committee on villagization] shall undertake effective propaganda within its area of operation so that the population is fully convinced of the value of villagization and that it will participate with willingness and enthusiasm in the implementation of villagization (GOE:39).

If propaganda and agitation for the program do not convince farmers to move, the government directive also includes guidelines for establishing subcommittees on security whose responsibilities include eliminating opposition to the program. Each subcommittee is to ensure "that [its] force is effective."

> The Sub-Committee is responsible to the Regional Coordinating Committee for Villagization and shall have the following duties and responsibilities:
>
> 1. It will ensure adequate guardianship and complete security so that forces inimical to villagization will not put obstacles in the implementation of villagization.
>
> 2. It shall bring to the higher organs for proper action against persons who may attempt to render ineffective the villagization program.
>
> 3. It shall give directives for covert and overt security measures and ensures the effectiveness thereof . . . (GOE:35).

The district coordinating committees are instructed to

> create effective security force so that inimical forces of villagization will not

render ineffective the project. It shall ensure that the force is effective ... (GOE:38) and ... organiz[e] strong security so that the villagization is not hindered by anti-revolutionary forces (GOE:31).

After the new villages have been established, village administrative committees are to be created "to establish ... order and to determine relationships among the inhabitants" (GOE:39). These committees report to the peasant association. Among other things their functions include

> settling disputes, sanitation and initiating ideas for the improvement of their locality. If, however, the Kebele Peasant Association is all located in one village, the function of the Kebele Administrative Committee shall be taken by the Kebele Peasant Association (GOE:40).

Prior to villagization, the kebele peasant association was the lowest level of the government administrative apparatus. Now villagization administrative committees exist in each new village so that more than one can, but need not, exist in each kebele peasant association.

Implementation Guidelines

Site Selection for New Villages

> The sites for villagization are selected on the basis of specific criteria. As far as possible the area should be flat, should have in the immediate vicinity water and should be adequate not only to accommodate members who would settle there but also to build such facilities as roads, water supplies, [a] school, clinic and market place as well as warehouse to store farm products. Land for cultivation of various crops is, of course, the main prerequisite (*Ethiopian Herald* 25 February 1986).

> The establishment of villages, depending on the local topography may follow a circular, straight or semicircular road, and should have common service centers. However, in the present situation, the new villages should have straight roads and similar type of houses (GOE:23).

New villages are to be situated in a "locality where primary development services are available" (GOE:17). The areas selected are not to be those already designated as state farms, or areas identified for other state development projects or to be converted to state farms. "Irrigation projects must not be curtailed" (GOE:17). Village sites are to be selected by the authorities; villagers have little say in site selection ["choice for them (peasants) should be made with care" (GOE:17)].

According to government officials quoted in the Western press, however, peasants are allowed to select new village sites and to construct their new homes. Old houses are dismantled, providing nearly all the materials for new house construction. The new houses "are generally constructed with the materials from former [demolished] houses" (GOE:24).

The government directive on villagization indicates that at least 30 families will be in each new village. However, partly due to experiences with resettlement, authorities now cite 500 as an optimal number of families in the new villages. In general, the government stipulates that the maximum

Newly villagized area in Shoa.   ©ALEM/PHOTO

number of families possible should be brought together. As stated in the directive, "[u]nless . . . there should be major obstacles, creating small, scattered villages should be avoided" (GOE:18).

The government directive on villagization also specifies that new villages, ideally of 500 families, could contain two peasant associations.

> In a kebele peasant association the number of families on the average is 250. Thus, to create a village of a kebele peasant association, it requires two kebele associations to bring up the number to the minimum of 500 families. Thus, it should be realized that bringing two kebele peasant associations in one village should not create difficulties in providing the services they require and administering the locality. All other criteria being the same, it would also be useful to bring together people who are familiar with one another in a given village (GOE:18-19).

Reports in the Western press as well as those from relief agencies and refugees indicate that the new villages contain from 50 to 1,000 houses (one family per house) and that these houses are lined up in parallel rows, approximately 30 m apart (*Washington Post* 17 December 1986).

According to the government directive on villagization, villages were to be reasonably close to the fields so that peasants would not have to travel far and thereby grow discouraged and sabotage the program. Eventually modern technology (both regarding agriculture and transportation) intends to allow new villages to be located further from the areas under cultivation. It appears that smaller villages will be further consolidated at a later date. "In the present circumstances the average distance between the village and the farms should not exceed 5 km" (GOE:20).

In Hararghe, farmers now have to walk considerably further than before to tend their crops. For example, a group of French agricultural researchers in Hararghe region found that in a survey of six farmers, the average distance to farmers' plots was increased fourfold as a result of villagization (Wibaux 1986:11).

Another observer in Hararghe notes that

> new villages make it further for farmers to walk to their fields and difficult for their wives to bring them their mid-day meal. In addition, livestock must be fed every day, they can no longer be allowed merely to graze near the new villages. Some farmers find it easier to bring fodder to their animals, but that, too, takes considerable time. Manure, if it is to be used as fertilizer, must now be carried from the houses where the animals are tethered at night (Anonymous 1987:10).

The directive on villagization also expresses concern about the possible outbreak of epidemics in the new villages.

> It should also be recognized that bringing people together in villages could also create situations in which if an outbreak of epidemic [occurs], an uncontrollable situation could arise. So this factor should be taken into consideration when establishing villages. To prevent such a situation, safeguarding the hygienic condition is important. If possible, each household should have a lavatory — pits — if that is not possible, common pits should be available (GOE:24).

Voluntariness of the Program

The government has long claimed that the villagization program is voluntary and that, in fact, it is the voluntary nature of the program that has allowed it to move ahead quickly. However, Blaine Harden, a writer for the *Washington Post*, reported in December 1985 that "one agency disputes the claim — most of the farmers said that they did not want to move and that they were forced to do so by [armed] party cadre.... Party cadre have quotas of 'villagized' that they must meet" (*Washington Post* 17 December 1986). Harden also wrote that one farmer told him that his house had been torn down on order from political cadre of the ruling WPE. The farmer then had to carry his house on his back for 5 mi to the new village site. Numerous other reports and firsthand observations (see photo) indicate that if people did not willingly dismantle their houses and move them, the thatched roofs were either removed or set afire.

According to relief workers in Hararghe, residents were told to destroy the planted cactus fences that encircle their houses and serve as livestock corrals. After the homes have been moved, the fences cannot remain even to shelter animals pasturing in the area.

Relief workers in Hararghe in 1987 indicated that in some areas water in highland areas is being channeled to irrigation projects for new villages located in the lowlands. Many Western agencies are involved in bringing the water to the new sites. In some cases, at least, if people want water for their crops they must move. Many if not most farmers from the highlands of Hararghe used traditional irrigation systems prior to villagization.

Timing of the Program

The government of Ethiopia reported that the implementation of the villagization program would take into account the peak agricultural labor needs in each region and be adjusted accordingly. However,

[I]n a given month there are [x number of] working days. But the whole day is not devoted to harvesting the crop. If we take teff for example, it is usually harvested on cool days and early in the morning and late afternoons leaving considerable time for the construction of new villages even during the harvest (GOE:20).

The government directive does not indicate whether the harvest of such crops as teff traditionally complements or is coordinated with the harvest of other crops.

In theory, at least, the government appears to have intended that villagization take place after the harvest.

After harvesting the crop the farmer has to take his produce to market and buy the foods for his needs. He does this after completing his harvest and prior to starting preparation for the next season. It is this period that is intended for the implementation of villagization (GOE:21).

The report later states that "[i]f this period is fully used for villagization, it could negatively produce unnecessary or unwanted situation on the market

A house in Wollega that was burned in order to force the couple to move into a new village during the rainy season. Instead, the couple chose to move into an OLF area 40 km away.

exchange aspect" (GOE:21). In other words, peasants would not have time to sell their crops. To circumvent this problem, officials not only implemented the program during the growing and harvesting periods but also often registered total production at the time of harvest. This process of inventorying was assisted by the records kept by communal harvesting teams, as well as by door-to-door surveys. "Surpluses," in some cases at least, appear to have been "extracted" at that time. A relief worker reported that in Arsi, in March and April of 1986, livestock were also being "nationalized" during the villagization and inventorying process. Refugees in Somalia also reported that this was a common occurrence in Hararghe (see Villagization in Hararghe). Nationalization of livestock, or forced sales of animals to reduce herd sizes, also could explain how in 1985 and 1986, during the height of the famine, Ethiopia exported four times as many animals as in 1984.

Land Rights

Publicly, government officials insist that land rights are respected and that villagers can keep former lands if they so desire.

As a result of the revolution every peasant was given 10 hectares of land. That right is still fully respected. Every peasant continues to own his own 10 hectares of cultivable land, in case he or she abandons unproductive land on the hill top where he or she used to live, alternative productive land is provided (*Ethiopian Herald* 17 December 1986).

The secretary of the WPE reiterated this point for Hararghe in an interview cited in the *Washington Post*: "farmers will be allowed to farm their own plots of land and . . . their crops will not be collectivized" (*Washington Post* 17 December 1986).

Evaluating the validity of contradictory information regarding "official" land policy in Ethiopia is difficult. *New York Times* reporter Sheila Rule was told that as a result of villagization the amount of land available to each farmer had almost doubled.

Many peasants must return to their former home areas to keep tending their fields, but officials say that is no more than a few miles. And by bringing together scattered settlers and, freeing large amounts of land for cultivation, the land holding of each peasant here has doubled, to just under four acres, the government says (*New York Times* 22 June 1986).

No one has attempted to explain the contradiction between the 10 ha (25 acres) of land the government claims each farmer owns and Rule's finding that land available to peasants had doubled, as a result of villagization, to just under 1.6 ha (4 acres). For her own part, Rule fails to indicate how moving people frees large amounts of land for redistribution. Eliminating people or moving them on to the land of others might accomplish this task however.

One observer, a former official in Hararghe in 1975, indicated that at that time peasants were lucky to receive 2 ha; they certainly didn't get 10. Many, in fact, in the cash crop producing areas, received less than one hectare. Furthermore, this former official indicates, distribution was not undertaken in an equitable manner.

The government reports that every village is allotted land for communal tree plots, and that "a special plot of land is also reserved for pasture so that the livestock will graze only in special pastures" (*Ethiopian Herald* 25 February 1986). Pasture, then, is communal, but what of the herds of livestock? According to the directive on villagization each farmer is to receive 2,000 m² (.2 ha) of land that is to be used for gardening *and* raising domestic livestock. Gardening aside, this amount of land is insufficient to maintain even one cow, sheep and goat on a yearly basis.

In contrast to its public statements, the government's directive on villagization indicates that in new villages, farmers are to stop cultivating their former lands. The government decided that land should be allocated evenly; agricultural land is not to be distributed on the basis of former ownership because that would create ill feeling (GOE:22). The directive warns against the allocation of too much land to individuals because "it would conflict with the aim in general and create an obstacle for the main goal" (GOE:22), that is, to coerce people into joining producers' cooperatives. The document also cautions: "In particular, when we are trying to induce and encourage the planned use of land along with villagization, the allocation of big farm[s] . . . at this stage could create further problems and complicate our task even more" (GOE:22).

The government directive on villagization also makes clear how much land should be set aside for individual cultivation.

Cultivating [a] backyard garden and using his own labour, the farmer can satisfy his needs in regard to vegetables and domestic animals such as cows, sheep, goats and poultry. It should be kept in mind that the settlers should have and cultivate backyard gardens. Depending on the particular area and its peculiarity, each settler family should be given up to 2,000 m² of land for backyard gardens. If this is not feasible in some area, then 500 m² should be given to each family adjoining its house and the remaining 1,500 m² a little further apart. This could be in a common area for all the villagers (GOE:24-25).

However, the directive cautions that

[c]areful steps must be taken to eliminate long distance between the farmer's house and his land for cultivation, so that his will to work is not adversely affected. Sufficient area for his vegetable garden and pastureland for his cattle, sheep and goats must be allocated close to his home. Sufficient and equitable land must be allocated to those farmers that owned such land previous to their moving to new villages. . . . This, of course, must be done without creating irregularity in the whole set-up (GOE:13).

Religion

The government directive on villagization makes it clear that the issue of religion might cause villagers to oppose the villagization program. Local officials were directed to make the program "palatable" through the inclusion of religious institutions "as much as possible" in the new villages. As can be seen from the following quote the entire discussion about religion in the new villages begins with the premise that the goal of the revolution is "the emancipation of the population from spiritual influence."

When considering implementation of villages, one of the concerns that is frequently raised is the question of a place for worship. The existence of such a place of worship in the area of these villages becomes essential. The longterm aim of our revolution is, of course, the emancipation of the population from spiritual influence to enhance their belief in materialism. But we have learned from . . . socialist experience in other countries that this will take a long time.

To build a people or a society free of spiritualism and strong in scientific materialistic concept, the society must have strong social awareness and developed cultural and material conception. The Ethiopian people are least developed in this regard and their . . . religious beliefs . . . [are] strong and of long standing. In order to change this situation, our effort should concentrate in teaching, agitating and propagating the new concept of materialism and developing the consciousness of the people. It is therefore essential that the question of religious belief be handled with extreme caution. . . . It is beneficial, therefore, that religious institutions be allowed to exist, as much as possible, in the villages that are being established. It would be in order that when the community raises the question of religious institution, that plots be indicated in the village and encouraged to build. This would make villagization palatable (GOE:25).

According to Western relief workers who visit and work in new villages in Hararghe, religion is not an issue. The design of the new villages allows no room for mosques.

Provision of Goods and Services

The government acknowledged in its directive on villagization that it would be unable to provide all the goods and services needed in new villages. But it expected that "peasants would be able to coordinate their inputs by bringing their collective effort — be it finance or labour — and establish development services" (GOE:22).

As anyone can observe, one of the objectives of the villages program is to facilitate conditions whereby peasants who have been living on widely scattered farms can help each other in eliminating their social problems and where they can jointly obtain government support (Radio Addis Ababa 2 May 1986).

The government made it clear that the provision of new services, henceforth, would be *limited* to new villages.

We should make certain that the schools and clinics we build and the water wells we bore, from now on must follow the villagization program. If this is not done, the founding of villages will lose the material support it requires; the program will lose impetus. As a result, it will be difficult not only to build new villages but also to maintain the existing ones. The founding of the villages is part and parcel of the class struggle and the building of new social order that we are waging to bring about (GOE:26).

Various economic and social projects being implemented in the rural areas will serve to strengthen and enhance the implementaton of villagization (GOE:28).

We have planned in our annual plan to provide firstly the farmers collectivized in villages with educational facilities, health care and running water (*Ethiopian Herald* 23 March 1987).

This programme creates conditions favorable for direct contact of peasants with agricultural experts deployed by the Ministry of Agriculture — through peasants' cooperatives (*Ethiopian Herald* 19 April 1987).

Central Committee member Sileshi Mengeshe was quoted in the *Ethiopian Herald* as saying that "the peasants will be provided with education, health, communications, mills, shops, water, roads, electric and telephone services if they volunteer for new settlement under the villagization program" (US Department of State telegram 22 June 1987). For example, according to the *Ethiopian Herald* (6 June 1987) Shoa has 48 surplus-producing districts, one-third of all those in Ethiopia. Fertilizers and selected seeds were distributed only in surplus-producing districts, and more than 80 percent of the assistance was channeled through producers' cooperatives.

Thus, peasants living in new villages in surplus-producing regions are able to obtain what little government assistance is available. In addition, Western relief and development agencies can only expand their programs into new areas if those areas have been villagized. Therefore, the promise of foreign assistance coerces farmers to take part in a program that they might otherwise have opposed. As with famine assistance in the resettlement program, the government's offer of *allowing* development assistance from the West is being used as a carrot, and its withholding or directing away from areas as a stick. If the Western agencies do not provide "enough" assistance, the government can blame them, as it did with the famine in 1984, for the inadequate supply of development inputs.

Villagization and Agricultural Production

According to the directive on villagization, the program is essential in order to rationalize agricultural production and to ensure that rural producers pay their fair share in the modernization of Ethiopia (90 percent of Ethiopia's *earned* foreign exchange comes from the agricultural sector). Toward this end, bringing the peasants together into common villages has become an essential step, allowing the government to educate the farmer as to which land is for cultivation, pasture or forestry, and to successfully control and plan agricultural production (GOE:7).

According to Mengistu, in a speech to the WPE, "the timing of the program is conducted in all regions such that it will not disrupt harvest" (Radio Addis Ababa 10 April 1986; see "Timing of the Program" earlier, however). Western reporters in Hararghe insist that the program does adversely affect agricultural production. Blaine Harden, for example, indicated that after villagization, peasants

> walked five miles to tend sorghum. . . . Agencies operating here say the mass relocation [villagization], as it has been carried out so far, is likely to create more famine.
>
> "Why create turbulence in one of the few productive areas of the country, especially now that the country's need for food is so great?" [said an] agricultural specialist. . . . Many said they were transporting houses when they should have been tending crops. . . . Hararghe has food shortages for 1.3 million people. Bad weather is part of the problem but rapid implementation of the [villagization] program is another (*Washington Post* 17 December 1985).

Writing in the *Observer* (26 January 1986), Madeley states that the RRC said crops in 22 of 39 cropping regions of Hararghe "have almost totally failed." In most other regions harvest will not last more than a few months. Madeley then concluded that "in Hararghe, villagization seems to have reduced food output seriously." He goes on to describe how this takes place.

> A field worker with an aid agency, who asked not to be named, said: "A million people in Hararghe were moved by zealous members of the ruling party at the very time when they were planting seeds. People hated it. Instead of growing crops they were forced to build new houses."

Villagization is being implemented by members of the ruling Workers' Party of Ethiopia. Ignoring pleas from the Ministry of Agriculture to delay the move until after the harvest, the party ran a competition among districts in Hararghe with prizes for those which could complete villagization the fastest.

Some party members refused to join in, believing they could not disrupt agriculture for ideological reasons.

In some villages eyewitnesses claim that people who refuse to move have their houses burnt down at night, leaving them no option but to move.

A party official admitted to aid workers that there were military reasons for Hararghe's choice as the first province for villagization. . . .

Seeds supplied to farmers in Hararghe by voluntary agencies and the UN's International Fund for Agricultural Development are producing additional food and offsetting the worst aspects of the famine.

Relief agencies in the province believe that now the famine threat has been identified, action can be taken to prevent it leading to widespread deaths. But they say success will depend on sustained support from abroad. Some 240,000 tons of food will be needed in Hararghe this year (*Observer* 26 January 1986).

And, as four other Western reports noted:

Government officials say that the process of relocation was carefully planned so that the taking down and rebuilding of homes would not cut into vital agricultural seasons. Critics dispute this and say that people have been busy relocating instead of tending their fields, a situation that could lead to more famine (*New York Times* 22 June 1986).

Villagization contributed to a sharp drop in food production (*Inquiry* June 1986).

The process of villagization is apparently now continuing throughout the country. It affects ethnic groups with a range of settlement and subsistence patterns, and will have somewhat different consequences in each case. The built-in inefficiency of moving farmers away from their farms will surely be a negative factor everywhere (Anonymous 1987:15).

A senior UN official estimates that this year's harvest will decrease by 30 percent because of villagization. Time is lost both in having to move and hiking every day to and from distant fields — back where farmers old homes used to be (Magistad 1987:62).

The government directive acknowledges the potentially negative impact of villagization on agricultural production. Yet, although the government apparently accepts the drops in production levels of food crops as consequences of the program, it is concerned about decreased cash crop production and the resultant drop in foreign exchange earnings. Such losses, the government maintains, are to be avoided at all costs.

It is therefore absolutely important that a drastic step of implementation should not affect the production and picking of coffee. Utmost caution must prevail in these areas. In other words, at the moment when we are making every effort to encourage the coffee farmers to take every care for their plantation and bring to the market their produce, the establishment of villages should not affect coffee production. It must indeed be realized that coffee is

Newly villagized area. In this village, as in 15,000 other new villages, intensive land use in the immediate vicinity of the village will lead to a decline in soil fertility and production unless expensive inputs can be provided to farmers. ©ALEM/PHOTO

the biggest foreign exchange earner for Ethiopia. It is thus essential that the implementation of the establishment of villages in areas of coffee production should be delayed until opportune moment . . . establishment of villages in areas of coffee, fruits and vegetables must wait for a second phase — until then these areas are excluded from the programme of villagization (GOE:16).

It appears that the government's lack of similar concern for food crop production is linked to its belief that the West will provide famine assistance and its desire for increased crop specialization; the goal in the new villages is crop specialization rather than self-sufficiency.

The habit of each individual trying to produce only for his own needs is one type of behavior in a backward production system. So, in order to be freed from this situation and strengthen agricultural productivity, each area should concentrate on the product which it can best produce. The gathering of peasants into villages is one of the principal conditions necessary in order to study and plan each area's production focus . . . (Radio Addis Ababa 2 May 1986).

Such specialization is a dangerous experiment that could have dire consequences for peasant farmers. First, it takes the power of deciding what to plant out of the hands of producers and makes it the responsibility of, for the most part, urban-based politicians who have been traditionally and are now increasingly more concerned about feeding soldiers and urban residents than farmers. Such specialization, and its inevitable periodic failures, also certainly has implications for Western donors who have been asked to step in and feed those who are no longer responsible for or even allowed to feed themselves.

Official Justifications for Villagization

The numerous justifications for villagization included nation-building, security, political education, the creation of socialism and even the creation of "communities" (or rather, cooperative labor systems), as the following quotes indicate.

Build a Nation

Peasant masses of Shoa fully endorsed the scheme as part of the nation building process (*Ethiopian Herald* 16 February 1986).
[Villagization is] to improve their livelihood and contribute to the nation-building endeavor (*Ethiopian Herald* 1 April 1986).

Improve the Organizational Capability of Peasants

[T]he villagization programme [is] devised to consolidate organizational capability of peasants (*Ethiopian Herald* 4 March 1986).

Improve National Security

. . . the collectivization of farmers in villages means pooling their joint energy to ensure their security and that of the area (Radio Addis Ababa 5 September 1985).

The program adds to security (*Washington Post* 17 December 1986).

Assist Political Education

... facilitates teaching Marxism/Leninism to farmers (*Washington Post* 17 December 1986).

The "ideological advantage," as one member of the Workers Party of Ethiopia put it, is education in Marxism-Leninism, cultural expansion and the creation of good conditions for a "working relationship among peasants" (*New York Times* 22 June 1986).

Create Socialism and Carry Out Government Programs

A resident father of 15 children is reported to have been very emphatic on the fact that the villagization scheme was elemental in helping build a new socialist order and in executing party and government programs (*Ethiopian Herald* 16 February 1986).

Create Community

Perhaps the most ironic (certainly the most self-serving) official justification for the villagization program is that it is needed to create a sense of community. Although this is the most oft-stated goal of the program, it perhaps most reflects the urban bias of the politicians planning the program. No one knows the exact figures, but reconstructed from the government's own reports collaborated with numerous other sources, at least 30,000 traditional villages and perhaps as many as 40,000 were destroyed in the process of creating the 15,000 new villages during two and a half years from late 1984 through 1987. Much of the world and most of the international human rights community was justifiably outraged when government troops destroyed 400 villages in a similar villagization program in Guatemala. Why then do people remain silent about government abuses in Ethiopia?

At government direction, an even greater number of local, kin and communal work groups have been destroyed in the process of creating the new communities. The difference is that the government is in charge of the new cooperative labor systems. Traditional religious, cultural and social values that once held peoples together, even in the face of previous invasions, have fallen to this onslaught. The government's public pronouncements specify this aspect of the program clearly.

The whole idea of the villagization programme is to bring the peasants closer in order to enable them to enjoy a community life ... [rather] than live in a scattered village where he [peasant] used to live on the top of an inaccessible hill (*Ethiopian Herald* 25 February 1986).

... Introduced a villagization programme so as to enable the peasantry to benefit from a communal mode of living (*Ethiopian Herald* 26 January 1986).

"We cannot give our people social services and economic assistance when they are all scattered around the countryside," said Kassaye Aragaw, first secretary of the WPE in Hararghe. "Basically, man likes to live collectively" (*Washington Post* 17 December 1986).

[The] villagization scheme [is] aimed at collectivizing the scattered way of living of the peasantry (*Ethiopian Herald* 31 May 1986).

. . . [peasants were] without neighbors for miles around (*New York Times* 22 June 1986).

The government's publicly announced justifications for villagization shifted in 1986, perhaps both to make the program more palatable to Western governments and humanitarian agencies as well as to give the same Western players a key role in the process. Recently, the two most popular justifications for the villagization program, for international consumption at least, have been that it is essential for providing social services and for increasing agricultural production. The following quotes explicitly specify these justifications.

[I]f the present way of living continues it will be difficult to construct either [a] school, health center or a hospital or set up a market place or a bank within easy reach of each peasant, difficult to build [a] road leading to the abode of each peasant or provide it with electricity, water supply or telephone lines (*Ethiopian Herald* 11 January 1986).

Among other benefits, officials say that villagers have been organized to use spring water for irrigation and build dams, easing their dependence on annual rains (*New York Times* 22 June 1986).

The policy of villagization, or grouping of farmers, was adopted in order to solve man-made and natural problems faced by farmers and to create conditions through which they can be provided with basic services and assistance. The aim is to increase their production, thereby improving their standard of living. . . .
Unless we increase the productivity of the agricultural sector, become self-sufficient in food and provide the raw materials needed by other sectors of the economy, we cannot create the strong material base needed to speed up the building of a new society. But they have tried to hinder the villagization program by placing a false interpretation upon it. . . . However our efforts are based on improving the lives of farmers and providing for their needs (*Serto Ader* editorial broadcast on Radio Addis Ababa 22 May 1986).

The main objective of the villagization program is to provide basic social facilities like schools, health centers, drinking water, electricity and infrastructures in road and communications (*Ethiopian Herald* 25 February 1986).

Comrade Mengistu explained to the peasants the advantage of living in an integrated community neighborhood instead of living in isolated and scattered villages which were exposed to natural and man-made calamities and backward social and economic practices. Comrade Mengistu noted that there is no alternative for peasants to extricate themselves from backwardness, to increase productivity and to improve their overall standard of living other than regrouping themselves (*Ethiopian Herald* 1 April 1986).

The villagization scheme is being stepped up in order to arrest wastage of natural resources, overcome backwardness and expand modern technology (*Ethiopian Herald* 5 March 1986).

[R]egrouping peasants was very essential in order to apply modern agricultural and mechanized system and to provide peasants with selected seeds and fertilizers (*Ethiopian Herald* 28 January 1986).

Although one of the government's stated goals of the villagization program is to provide social services, neither government reports nor foreign observers indicate that this goal has been realized.

New villages do not have permanent water, health clinics or schools. . . . [T]he program is designed to improve social services, but none of the new villages have social services. The only building is the party office, draped with flags (*Washington Post* 17 December 1986).

According to Mr. Kasaye, secretary of the WPE in Hararghe, "Nothing was given by the party and the government except knowledge. No other help was given" (*Washington Post* 17 December 1986).

As in Bale from 1978 to 1984 (see The Case of Bale), the government expected Western agencies to provide their promised services; once again, Western agencies were willing to comply. After an April 1986 tour of villagization sites, the representative in Ethiopia for the humanitarian agency Save the Children said, "We will help Ethiopian children wherever they are. Villagization has an advantage in that it provides an easier access in establishing health stations, schools and other social services" (*Ethiopian Herald* 26 April 1986). Save the Children did not bother to ask about the costs of villagization. How many of the new villages will Western agencies ever be able to work in?

While officials attempt to give priority to the productivity and social service goals of the villagization program, the official government position — that the villagization and producers' cooperatives are linked directly — continues as officials address rallies and speak in official publications and radio broadcasts. As Mengistu Haile Mariam pointed out in his address to the annual convention of the WPE,

essential for increasing productivity and improving the economic and social life of the farmers is to collectivize farmers in villages. The collectivization of farmers will create favorable conditions for extending political, economic and social services to the farmers in the villages. He said that the collectivization of farmers in villages means pooling their joint energy to ensure their security and that of the area (Radio Addis Ababa 5 September 1985).

Thus, the government's goals for villagization are political, economic and social, in that order. And as usual the Ethiopian government did not undertake cost-benefit analyses, social or environmental impact assessments or even projections of population growth and their implications in the new village sites.

6 | The Case of Bale

Jason W. Clay

Ethiopia's villagization program was first implemented extensively in the Bale administrative region beginning in late 1978. Most people in Bale are Oromo, although there is a "sprinkling of Somali-speaking nomads in the south" (Matheson 1981:20). In 1978 Bale had an estimated population of between 800,000 and 1,000,000. Between 600,000 and 650,000 people were moved into new villages during the first three years of the program. People living in isolated and rugged terrain or in OLF-controlled areas were subsequently villagized.

The experiences in Bale served as a model for the subsequent extension and intensification of the villagization program in other administrative regions. According to Alastair Matheson, writing in *UNICEF News*, Bale was chosen as "a bold experiment."

> As they huddled in the makeshift shelters during the miserable aftermath of the fighting [Ethiopian-Somali war of 1977-1978], with the relentless sun scorching the parched countryside, the people of Bale could have hardly imagined that out of this disaster to their lives and livelihoods could spring a bold experiment, in which they would be the pioneers. The Ethiopian government chose to introduce into Bale a programme of "integrated basic services," a programme which would provide data and a tried model for the introduction of similar services into most of rural Ethiopia, where 90 percent of the population lives.
>
> The decision to introduce the project into Bale first was taken because the combination of hostilities and drought had meant that virtually all Government services had come to a standstill. . . .
>
> With the Ethiopian Relief and Rehabilitation Commission (RRC) in sole charge of supervising emergency assistance in Bale, the scene was set for the introduction of services that dovetailed with each other. . . . [and i]n accor-

136

dance with the principles laid down by the Government when it launched its National Revolutionary Development Campaign in Bale in 1978 (Matheson 1981:20-21).

Bale has been labeled "a more successful experiment" in villagization by people who have (apparently) not visited the area, such as Blaine Harden (*Washington Post* 17 December 1985). Harden, following numerous other journalists as well as diplomats and relief officials, accepted the official Ethiopian position on the Bale program. He reported that the "program provided homes for people whose cattle and lands had been destroyed by the Ethiopian-Somali war" of 1977-1978 (*Washington Post* 17 December 1985).

Although people were moved into shelters in Bale beginning in 1978, it appears that most "displacement" occurred *after* the Somali army withdrew in April 1978 (see Tables 1 and 2) and as a direct result of Ethiopian — *not* Somali — military activities. In fact, displacement and subsequent villagization occurred in northern and western Bale, Arsi and parts of Sidamo that were untouched by invading forces from Somalia. As a result of these military and security operations villagization was not officially completed until the end of 1982; in the more isolated areas of these administrative regions it still continues.

Table 1

Displacement in Bale

	# Displaced in Shelters (RRC)	Number of Shelters	Estimated # Displaced Not in Shelters
Sept. 1978	250,000	139	
March 1979	400,000	unknown	
May 1980	600,000	281	>65,000*

*According to the MCC (Mennonite Central Committee, a Western humanitarian agency), 65,000 is the number of "persons fleeing from the *present conflict* and drought; the number is expected to triple by the end of the year" (MCC News Service 30 May 1980, emphasis added).

Table 2

Refugee Arrivals in Somalia from Southwestern Ethiopia
(Somali withdrawal from 9 March through April 1978)

	Cahill in camps	NY Times	Melander in camps	US State Dept. and Senate reports
mid-1978	80,000		85,000	85,000
1/1979				103,159
mid-1979	220,000		220,000	
10/1979			350,000	331,000
11/1979	300,000		391,000	390,904
12/1979			475,000	441,853
1/1980	500,000			474,286
8/1980				650,000
10/1980		848,000		

None of the relief agencies or Western governments assisting the displaced people in Bale or the newly arrived refugees in Somalia asked the obvious question: Why was the number of displaced people continuing to increase three years after the Somali army had withdrawn from Ethiopia? Or a corollary question: Why were so many refugees continuing to flee from Ethiopia to Somalia well into the 1980s? Or the related question: Why did so many Oromo refugees travel to Somalia between 1979 and 1982, *after* that country had withdrawn from the area? If people were going to leave wouldn't they have attempted to accompany the departing army, or at least have left during the same year? War and drought are the answers the government most often gives for displacement in Bale. Such explanations may be partially correct but they do not tell the whole story.

Source: Adapted from Melander 1980:23.

Map 4. Ethiopian refugee centers in Somalia, 1978–1980.

The idea that there was a relationship between the deliberate relocation of rural Oromo and Somali populations in Bale on the one hand and the massive refugee flow into Somalia in the early 1980s on the other hand was proposed in 1982 by an independent group of scholars called the Joint African/American Research Committee for Refugees in Northeast Africa. My research has enabled me to document hypotheses put forth by that group and uncover many aspects of the situation in Bale that had hitherto been ignored.

After the revolution, according to expatriate observers, the new government did not trust Oromos in southern Ethiopia. In Bale, government troops disarmed the rural Oromo population in the areas that it controlled. According to one source, after being disarmed the Oromo could not protect themselves or their crops. By contrast, the government allowed Amharic-speaking peoples in the area to keep their arms. The government did not trust the Oromo even before the Somali invasion of the area.

Somali troops invaded most of eastern Ethiopia, including Hararghe, Bale and Sidamo, in July and August of 1977; they were forced to withdraw beginning on 9 March and through the end of April, 1978. During the 1977 invasion, retreating Ethiopian forces reportedly attempted to destroy anything valuable that they left behind. The Somali army occupied the region for six months and then, in turn, destroyed or carried away property and belongings during its retreat.

Undoubtedly people were displaced during the war with Somalia. According to Western observers in the area at the time, *some* villages were destroyed, but not all of those in Bale; the invading army did not reach many northern and western areas. The MCC reported in September 1978, for example, that "the war also resulted in extensive destruction of many villages in the area" (22 September 1978). The MCC first had access to the villages along the roads in the area. It is likely that these villages would have been most affected both by the invasion and the recapture of the area. The fact that they were not all destroyed leads one to speculate about how many of the allegedly destroyed villages, off the road, were relatively untouched.

According to former RRC officials, the government used war, famine and general chaos in Bale, and subsequently to a lesser extent in Sidamo and Arsi, as a cover for the forcible transfer of people into villages where they could be watched and organized into peasant associations and producers' cooperatives. Not as well understood are the postretreat military activities in the region. According to some Western observers the Oromo in the area were sympathetic to the Oromo Liberation Front (OLF), which continued to be active in Arsi, Bale, Hararghe and Sidamo after the "official" invading forces withdrew. Few stories reached the West concerning the process of active displacement pursued by the Ethiopian military. Three accounts describing the Ethiopian army's attack on civilians in Sidamo in March 1981 (see Appendix B) indicate that the attacks followed a classic, high-tech counterinsurgency strategy. Air support located in Awasa and ground forces located in regional cities coordinated attacks on isolated regions suspected of harboring or at least sympathizing with the OLF or the Sidamo Liberation Movement (SLM). Helicopters served to "soften" a region through gunfire and incendiary devices, followed by jets that strafed the region.

In addition, a chemical weapon was used in Sidamo which appears to be similar to CBU 55. First developed and deployed by the US government in Vietnam, CBU 55 works in two stages. First, canisters of ethylene are released from helicopters. Upon impact the ethylene spreads over the ground like a fine mist or fog — it stays at ground level because it is heavier than air. Next a plane fires an incendiary device that causes the ethylene to explode. Highly flammable material, such as roof thatch, might catch fire during the resulting explosion, but most of the damage appears to result from the explosion itself. US military tests on the affects of the weapon are classified, but according to American scientists who have viewed the film of the deployment of the weapon in Vietnam, it could have two impacts. First, the force of the explosion could cause concussions to all animal life in the immediate vicinity. Second, the explosion could deplete the oxygen in the area so that all animal life would be asphyxiated. CBU 55 is considered a chemical weapon because it is indiscriminate, killing all animal life in the affected region.

The March 1981 attack in Sidamo lasted three days. An estimated 2,000–3,000 people died out of a total population of 20,000. Homes, animals and crops were destroyed. The former residents of Huavea fled to Somalia as refugees or became displaced. The Ethiopian Red Cross soon arrived on the scene and established a tent shelter, and a new village was created. The West was then asked by the Ethiopian government to provide food to those "displaced" people remaining in Sidamo, those left destitute by "the war" — which war was not specified.

Additional reports indicate similar military sweeps in Arsi, Bale and Hararghe. According to an OLF Military Communique dated 11 May 1981, from February 1981 onward the Ethiopian government deployed more than 5,000 troops and an equal number of militia in a military offensive against OLF forces in eastern Hararghe and central Arsi. According to the OLF report troops began by terrorizing the local population. The communique indicated that OLF efforts forced the troops to retreat to fortified camps. From those camps government forces launched scorched-earth attacks "in certain areas using aircraft and destroying villages, crops and vegetation." Aerial bombardments reportedly occurred in mid-April 1981 in the Guggu mountains of Arsi's Arba Guggu Warreda.

According to Wolde Emmanuel Dubale of the Sidamo Liberation Movement, Ethiopian government forces called villagers together in Sidamo administrative region to discuss security problems. Troops then reportedly surrounded the group and killed 615 civilians, allegedly in retaliation for a guerrilla attack on a military convoy (AP, "Ethiopia Death Claim," *Boston Globe* 9 November 1981).

According to an internal report prepared by the Mennonite Mission in

Ethiopia for the Catholic Relief Services, as late as July 1985 Westerners were not permitted to travel in Beltu Wareda of Bale administrative region. Only small military convoys could move into the area.

In a 1983 speech, Dawit Wolde Giorges, head of the RRC, stated that refugees and displaced people "are two sides of the same coin," and that permanent solutions must be sought for both.

> We fear that if today's displaced persons are not given the assistance they so urgently need and deserve, nothing can stop them from becoming tomorrow's refugees. The problem of displaced persons is rather a time bomb on the international community whose explosion will have much more serious consequences than the legal distinction that has forced us to close our eyes to their plight (1983:14).

In another speech in 1983 before the UN, Dawit stated that the Ethiopian law declaring it illegal to be a refugee had been suspended for two years and that the suspension had subsequently been extended for two more years, making it possible for refugees from Ethiopia to return without fear of punishment. However, refugees would not be allowed to return to their former homes and live with relatives and friends, for among other rights refugees could expect "resettlement and rehabilitation."

Referring to the refugees in Somalia, Dawit went a step further, denying that political refugees lived in Somalia and insisting that there could not possibly be 700,000 refugees in Somalia since there were only 500,000 Somalis in Ethiopia.

> The objective reality is that there are no genuine Ethiopian political refugees in Somalia. The false assumption that there are 700,000 refugees in the territory of Somalia continues to be disseminated, while a recently published document, prepared by an independent fact-finding committee composed of members from internationally recognized NGOs, indicates that the total population of this particular ethnic group [Somali] in Ogaden is around 500,000. In the light of this the astronomical figure that appears in the [UNHCR] document is ridiculous and misleading, because it suggests that the alleged number of refugees in Somalia is more than the total population of the supposed place of origin....
>
> This however, should not be understood as denying the presence of Ethiopian nationals forcefully taken or attracted by free distribution of food across the border. We can easily attract these same people to our side of the border if we were to start a programme of free distribution of food inside Ethiopian territory.

For internal reasons, both Ethiopia and Somalia were determined to depict the Ethiopian refugees in Somalia as ethnic Somalis. Who, then, were the displaced people referred to by Dawit? Who were the refugees who fled to Somalia? As observed in *STORM*:

> There [are] said to be 750,000 of them. Yet the war with Somalia took place largely in the area generally referred to as "the Ogaden" ... a region sparsely inhabited by nomadic herdsmen. No one surely is arguing that these Somali herdsmen have fled to Ethiopian towns and now have to be resettled in safe and peaceful areas outside the Ogaden? (p.3)

According to the RPCV's (Returned Peace Corps Volunteers) *Somalia Newsletter* II (2) 1980:6, Oromos were also displaced.

> Somalis aren't the only people who are fleeing Ethiopia in great numbers. The Oromos are too. In February and March of this year, when the population of Somalia's refugee camps was passing the 600,000 mark, Somali and international officials in Mogadisho estimated that out of that number at least 200,000 — one-third — were Oromo. Now one American scholar who recently returned from Somalia has estimated that up to one million Oromos may have entered Somalia as refugees, whether into camps or otherwise. Others add that the flow into Somalia is now mostly Oromo (65-70 percent) and that these people are coming from the central plateau of Ethiopia....
>
> Why are the Oromos leaving Ethiopia in such great numbers? Explanations which invoke drought and famine — while undoubtedly true this year *in the arid regions* — hardly seem adequate. They would be fleeing from frying pan to fire, over long distances, and to a country with whom their only tie is shared religion.
>
> An Amnesty International official recently told me, "It looks as though the Ethiopian government is trying to practice genocide in those areas." The WSLF, the OLF refugees and Somali officials all say that the Ethiopian military slaughters animals as well as people, destroys crops and wells and in general terrorizes the areas in question. It's probably also true that vicious circles of violence involving both guerrillas and government forces ... are occurring in the "catchment area" from which Somali and Oromo refugees are coming.

For whatever reasons, Ethiopia had become uninhabitable for more people than just the Western Somali.

These interpretations of events that led to villagization in Bale and subsequently in Sidamo, Arsi and Hararghe differ from the official interpretation and, consequently, the one reported by journalists who were not allowed free movement and by Western agency officials who supported the villagization program.

Blaine Harden, writing well after the fact, reconstructed the process by which people came into the new villages as follows: "According to the UN Children's Fund which helped organize the Bale program, roads, wells, clinics, schools, and vocational training were provided to lure 650,000 people into villages in Bale" (*Washington Post* 17 December 1985). Harden did not ask how more than half a million people lived for an average of 18 months without cattle or cultivable land. Nor did he explain why people in such desperate conditions needed to be "lured" to the new villages.

Harden is not alone in this rather simplistic interpretation of the Bale villagization program. A Canadian newspaper account in November 1984 described the program as follows.

> In 1979, after the Ethiopian-Somali war, 640,000 refugees were resettled in 230 communities, most of them instant creations, in Bale province....
>
> There was no safe water supply in 132 of these communities. Only five had first-aid clinics, and these were without adequate staffing or technical supervision. Bringing the people together in villages led to a rage of communicable diseases.

The refugees [displaced people], most of them semi-nomadic, had inadequate agricultural skills and, in any case, lacked basic agricultural tools (in fact, all they had were their bare hands, bereft of pots, plates, grain pounders and grain grinders).

The choices were simple: they could become permanent charity recipients (and eventually emergency aid would end), they could die in the thousands, or, with minimal assistance (which is all that was available) and a lot of thought, they could be brought to the point of looking after themselves (*Toronto Globe and Mail* 26 November 1984).

In an article in *UNICEF News*, Fikre Menkir and Manzoor Ahmed attributed the displacement to a continuation of man-made causes.

Another important cause of the displacement of large numbers of people in Ethiopia is the man-made conflict and violence. In the wake of the 1977-78 war in the Ogaden, a large number of people in the southern part of the country — in the regions of Bale, Sidamo and Hararghe — found themselves uprooted from their homes and livelihood and were obliged to move in thousands in search of food and shelter. The plight of these people has been aggravated by continuing guerrilla activities and banditry, as well as unusually low rainfall during the past two years. . . .

The RRC's response to meet immediate relief needs and to provide permanent rehabilitation for the victims was . . . to establish settlement communities. There are 251 settlements in the northwestern part of Bale for 120,000 families . . . (1980:24-25).

The settlement sites for displaced Bale residents were less well prepared than those for colonists resettled from Wollo to Bale beginning in 1978 on the heels of the departing army. As Menkir and Ahmed reported:

Forced upon the authorities by events, these settlements for the Bale people are less planned and prepared than those for the settlers from Wollo. They sprang up as the droves of homeless people arrived, in places where there was no adequate study of the sites or of the availability of water. . . .

Only about 25 [out of 251] of these new settlements have an adequate water supply, and schools do not exist at distances within the reach of most of the people. Agriculture has been hampered by the shortage of animals and ploughing implements as well as the poor rain and pests (1980:25).

It is curious, however, that the government would spend more time identifying settlement sites for people from Wollo who were moved hundreds of miles and installed within months of the departure of a retreating enemy army than it would in creating those new villages for local residents over a period of two and a half years after the retreat.

In a subsequent issue of *UNICEF News*, Matheson described the armed conflict and subsequent chaos in a slightly different way.

Swooping across the ill-defined border from Somalia in July 1977, well-armed invaders struck at Bale with a startling suddenness, over-running most of the region in days, just as they did with the neighboring regions of Hararghe and Sidamo.

A year of bitter fighting followed before the invaders were finally driven out. Then as if the civilian population had not endured a sufficient ordeal, Bale was hit by a severe drought. This prolonged drought retained its grip on the region until early this year, with vast numbers of livestock dying, as did some of the farmers and their wives and children, who were unable to get food in the remoter regions.

In the early days of the invasion, large herds of cattle had already been driven across the border into Somalia. The subsequent drought decimated the rest, as well as most of the sheep, goats and even the camels. . . . The uprooted peasant farmers of the [northern Bale] highlands could not plant food crops, while the nomads in the south had lost their livestock, the mainstay of their livelihood.

Only by accommodating most of the population in temporary shelters (almost one million at the peak period) was mass starvation prevented (1981:20).

Matheson wrote that in 1981 280 settlements existed with around 500 families in each (1981:21).

The Ethiopian government invited Western agencies to assist the displaced people in Bale almost immediately. According to the MCC, "malnutrition and illness claimed many lives" (News Service 11 March 1983). The previously cited *Toronto Globe and Mail* article indicated that "bringing the people together in villages led to a rage of communicable diseases" (26 November 1984).

Regardless of the invitations from officials in Addis Ababa, the government took several months to give Western agencies the required permits to work in the area. Furthermore, the government only allowed Western agencies to work in certain places at certain times. As Matheson wrote: "With the most urgent emergency feeding needs met, the Ethiopian Government, with the help of various organizations including UNICEF, began work on the [basic service] project in January this year" (1981:21).

The MCC News Service reported:

[In] Bale province . . . crops have been destroyed as a result of the war with Somalia, and . . . loss of oxen, plows and seeds has prevented food production in quantities sufficient to meet even local requirements. . . . The war has also resulted in extensive destruction of many villages in the area.

The war drove many villagers into hiding, as warring armies alternately gained control of the area. Now that relative security has returned to the area, people are returning and setting up temporary shelters to replace their destroyed homes. In early September 280,000 displaced and destitute people had crowded into 139 shelters in the general area of Goba, Bale (MCC News Service 22 September 1978).

Western agencies were not permitted into the primarily Oromo agricultural areas until tent villages had been established at government-selected locations. Most Western agencies did not begin to provide services to the new villages until January 1981 (Matheson 1981:21), nearly three years after Somalia's withdrawal from Bale.

From the available material, it appears that few assisting agencies knew anything about the Oromo population. Interaction was made possible by government interpreters who seem to have promoted basic misconceptions about Oromos' agricultural skills and background. According to the same *Toronto Globe and Mail* article, based on UNICEF information, "the refugees [displaced people], most of them semi-nomadic, had inadequate agricultural skills and, in any case, lacked basic agricultural tools (26 November 1984). The MCC reported that "After the 1977-1978 Ethiopian-Somali war, which also ravaged the region, the Oromo tribe, traditionally cattle herders, were settled into villages. In 1979, the Oromo villagers were hungry and had few agricultural skills" (MCC News Service 11 March 1983).

It is interesting to note that traditionally agricultural and livestock surpluses in Ethiopia have been extracted from Oromo populations. Perhaps new types of agriculture (e.g., irrigated) were being taught or new crops (i.e., vegetables) were to be grown. It is equally plausible that Ethiopia, via the RRC, was attempting to raise international funds by claiming the need to offer courses in agriculture to people who were already farmers. It is clear, however, that in most cases individuals were not allowed to farm their own lands.

Vast tracts of flat, fertile land, which had been cultivated by peasant farmers, were subsequently incorporated into the capital-intensive (e.g. mechanized production, including airplane-sprayed pesticides) state farms on which wheat and barley were cultivated (see photo). Labor on these state farms was supplied by conscripts from urban centers and during peak periods by men drafted from neighboring peasant associations. Land was

Burned land used for state farm agriculture on the Goba road in Bale province. In this area, villagization allowed the government to increase the size of state farms by confiscating the land of peasant agriculturalists.   ©ALEM/PHOTO

also taken from former cultivators and set aside, either directly or after having been used as a state farm for a few years, for people who were resettled from Wollo (see below). Local residents were not allowed access to their former lands. According to a Mennonite Mission report prepared for CRS (Catholic Relief Service) in July 1985, some of the most fertile land in Bale is located in Gololcha where the government has established two state farms.

According to an expatriate ecologist visiting the area, the government often set up new villages outside the best farming areas, at the edges of valleys on hilly uncultivated land that was unsuitable for farming. "A whole network of new settlements has sprung up in the cool climate of the Bale highlands, many of them on virgin land" (Matheson 1981:21). Some deforestation resulted. Because these lands were not flat the government deemed them unsuitable for mechanized agriculture and therefore appropriate for new villages.

While people in the towns in Bale had adequate food supplies during this period, "the people in the temporary shelters built in the countryside were hungry" (*Mennonite Reporter* 19 February 1979). Leaving aside the important questions of who produced the grain that was available in the towns and how the government obtained it, it appears that grain was available locally but that the government was not distributing it to those in rural areas who needed it. Yet the government released grain when international agencies or nongovernmental organizations (NGOs) agreed to purchase it for distribution. For example, the MCC traded Canadian wheat for corn produced in Bale and Arsi to distribute as relief food in Bale.

According to one Western observer present during the early stages of villagization in Bale, food (in many instances from the West) provided the incentive for starving people to travel to the new settlements. In 1979, in the southern and eastern part of Bale the agencies, like their counterparts during the 1984-1985 famine, did not ask why people were starving. Rather, as the same observer continued,

> people were coming because food was available in the Ethiopian settlement sites. I'm quite certain that had the Somalis and associated Oromo rebels been able to offer food rations as well, many people coming to the Ethiopian side may well have gone to the other side.

The same observer went on to note that relief was also a carrot used in villagization in the northern and western part of Bale. The RRC in that area of Bale told the people, "If you move into these settlements, you will be given water, clinics and schools, if you stay where you are [i.e., in your homes, which implies that many of these people were not yet displaced] you won't get these things."

An Ethiopian visiting the US in 1980 indicated that his family was from Bale and had not been displaced by the war with Somalia. Rather, he said, local cadre had told them to move to new village sites. They had been given five months to make the move and were told that after that date they would be considered *shiftas* [Bonnie K. Holcomb (BKH) Interview 1980]. In 1983 an Oromo farmer from Bale living in a Somali refugee camp said that local cadre had told them the same thing (BKH Interview 1983).

Most of the new villages in Bale contained 1,000–2,500 people. In the southern and eastern part of Bale new villages and new peasant associations were created simultaneously; in the northern and eastern part of the area, peasant associations remained intact. New villages in the north and west tended to be larger than those in the areas directly affected by the war with Somalia. In the south and east some of the smaller new villages combined to form one peasant association. Throughout Bale, however, the construction of the new villages allowed the government to organize or reorganize peasants—from the top down—into peasant associations and incipient producers' cooperatives. Peasant association leaders were handpicked by government officials and subsequently "elected" by the local association. Peasant association leaders had to speak Amharic.

Publicly, the government claimed that the purpose of the villagization program was to secure and organize the population so that the effects of war and drought-induced famine could be more easily alleviated through the central distribution of assistance. In fact, the Dergue established the new villages in Bale in order to keep the population under surveillance and secure the area under central government control. A willing partner, UNICEF helped implement the settlement and distribution program; Western humanitarian agencies such as the Mennonite Central Committee and the Lutheran World Federation (LWF) also supported parts of the program.

Expatriates observed that troublesome or even "rebellious" new villages were slow to receive services; their schools and clinics were "a little slow getting started." The government prohibited Westerners from traveling or working in these settlements until it deemed them "untroublesome." The government's position was clear: regardless of local need, it would not permit Western agencies to work until it was "ready" for them to be in the area. Such conditions may be similar to those imposed by many governments throughout the world, but they have serious consequences in a country such as Ethiopia.

The Lutheran World Federation described the context in which it implemented its programs in Genale District of Bale as follows. The displaced Oromos

> are returned to the same districts from which they were displaced in 1977/78, but not necessarily to the same spot where they lived before. Most are being settled along the main communication line [road] and in units [villages] of reasonable size, so that there is a foundation for having a school, a clinic and a market place (LWF 1983:14).

According to LWF, 600,000 people were displaced in 1977 and 1978. Both LWF and Norwegian Church Aid provided emergency assistance to displaced people at that time. By 1980 the Ethiopian government had asked LWF to continue its program in the area, but to shift the focus from emergency assistance to development activities in the new settlements; LWF agreed to the proposal.

LWF later described its goals as "to assist the people in establishing or reestablishing even new villages to become self-sufficient in food production and build a self-reliant community" (LWF 1984:6). According to LWF, its programs for new settlements were limited to the area on the main road in Bale between the towns of Dodola and Adaba. This 15-by-75-km area of highland plateau was the site of eight new villages (Keta, Mudemtu, Harohunte, Baka, Gedira Racha, Ketta, Berissa and Burachelle) with an estimated population of 20,000–30,000 people. But it was not until September 1980, after more than a six-month delay, that LWF reported that the government approved its new program. By this time, village sites had already been identified and construction of most houses completed. Settlers continued to be added to the new villages.

Most of the existing new villages in which LWF had permission to work were located either on or near major roads. In addition to work in agriculture, the agency's programs included road building and improvement, provision of social services and, most important, extension of new villages. LWF undertook credit, marketing and small-scale industry projects on a cooperative basis through local organizations (e.g., peasant or women's associations). Donkeys for hauling water were donated to local cooperative organizations.

By the end of 1982, LWF reported (based on information from the government) that 463,000 people in Bale were still considered "displaced," that is, not living in new villages. However, at that time, LWF wrote that in the seven villages in Genale District where it was working, most farmers were self-sufficient food producers; only widows with many children were not. In accounting for the large number of widows, LWF asserted, "the husbands have been killed or *got lost* during the Somali invasion" (1983:16; emphasis added).

LWF reported that "the project was handed over to the government on 17 April 1984" (1984:7). John Cohen and Nils-Ivar Isaksson visited an LWF-supported village in 1986. They described it as follows (1987:190–191).

Bura Chele . . . gives every sign of decay and lack of community spirit. The *tukuls* [houses] are in a bad state of repair. Many need new thatching and caulking. No improvements have been made, such as the doors and windows the government promises the current campaign will lead to . . . .

In 1983 the Lutheran Church bulldozed a road into the village. But it is now deeply rutted and not being kept up. So, too, the diesel-based well and water system built by the church is also in disrepair. Bura Chele's people are back to using water from the area's streams.

The Mennonite Central Committee's experience in Bale was similar. The Ethiopian government also asked MCC to provide famine relief for displaced people in the area. Its first program, however, was to provide emergency medical assistance to Amharic-speaking farmers who had been resettled in the area from Wollo province. Eventually the RRC took over the medical treatment of the Wollo settlements, and MCC's work shifted to the new villages in the vicinity of Ginnir, where its medical teams visited 16 of 25 local peasant associations and later held weekly or biweekly clinics in seven of 60 settlements. The government created about 100 new villages in Ginnir between 1979 and 1984.

The MCC claimed it "anticipated the present food shortages almost a year ago" (News Service 9 February 1979) and wanted to prevent a disastrous famine. The same report went on to note that "we want to keep the people out of shelters where they are removed from their fields and their work." This well-founded concern appears to have run counter to the government's intent. From this statement, it seems that the agency still believed, as much as two years after it had begun work in the area, that the new settlements were temporary and would eventually be abandoned so that peasants could return to their own lands. It did not realize that the reorganization of land use and villagization in Bale made this impossible.

The issue of land, always an important one to farmers, became a crucial part of the postrevolutionary government's stategy. In Bale as in other parts of Ethiopia, all lands were nationalized after the revolution in 1974. Many peasant farmers in southern Ethiopia assumed they would receive the lands from which their families had been separated since the invasions by Menelik in the late nineteenth century. Yet large estates usually were turned into state farms immediately. At the time of the land decree, government officials also wrongly assumed that most peasant farmers would immediately form producers' cooperatives in order to farm collectively. After a decade, only about 2 percent of cultivated lands in Ethiopia were in producers' cooperatives. By 1988, World Bank officials estimated that 4 percent of all farmers in Ethiopia were members of producers' cooperatives. Recently villagized Hararghe, at 8 percent, has the highest proportion of its farmers in producers' cooperatives. In the late 1970s, as a result of the slow voluntary move toward collectivization, the government began to identify for future state farms flat, fertile areas for mechanized agriculture. The clearing of residents off such areas so that they could be used to produce directly for the state appears to be a primary reason for villagization in Bale.

In the area around Ginnir, for example, newly organized peasant associations, to which all farmers were required to belong, abutted one another and accounted for all land not incorporated into or reserved for state farms, resettlement sites or government-controlled forest areas. It was impossible for cultivators to return to their former lands. In the new settlements, areas closest to the houses were cultivated intensively; more distant areas were grazed.

To the west nearer Goba as well as in the area around Dodola, the villagization program was implemented simultaneously with government military sweeps that "displaced" people — in many cases from relatively flat, fertile lands that the government subsequently turned into state farms. The creation of state farms on such recently "uninhabited" areas began in 1978 during the postwar chaos, when they could be cleared of people.

According to expatriates living in Ethiopia as well as former RRC officials, new villages in Bale were always intended to be producers' cooperatives. According to the MCC:

> [I]n five settlements where springs and rivers are available for irrigation, . . . [MCC staff] are working with the settlers in planting, watering, cultivating and harvesting cooperative vegetable gardens. . . . At four settlements, the people have harvested their first crop of vegetables. The women gathered the vegetables, collected pots and knives, carried water, built fires in their traditional method using three stones and wood, cooked the vegetables, and called the village together for eating. . . .
>
> As we watched the children gulping down handfuls of swiss chard, saw strange shapes protruding from under the women's clothes where a big round tomato was hidden or discovered young fellows' pockets bulging with carrots, we did not question whether they like the food.
>
> For the second planting one settlement has taken seeds provided by the Ministry of Agriculture and has started a large cooperative garden without assistance, thus moving toward the goal of self-reliance.
>
> The school director at another settlement has asked for help with a school garden. Seventy-five first graders, ages 8 to 18, worked together digging, planting and watering the seedlings. Their enthusiasm provides an incentive for their elders (*Mennonite Reporter* 19 February 1979).

During the initial phases of villagization in Bale, however, individual cultivation was tolerated. According to the MCC, "the settlers' [individual] plots were small ones dug right behind their houses" (*Mennonite Reporter* 19 February 1979). As late as 1984, although some land, in addition to the household garden plots, was farmed privately, each village had cooperatively farmed land that was given priority; only local peasant association officials and militia were excluded from working on it. Foreign assistance for economic programs went through the peasant association and was destined for cooperative, not individual, efforts.

At times the chairman or other officers of the peasant association benefited personally from international economic assistance. For example, in one peasant association in Bale, the only farmer who benefited individually from a foreign-financed irrigation scheme was the peasant association chairman, who grew chili peppers on his own irrigated plot of some of the best land in the area. For the most part, however, traditional peasant production was financed individually or through kinship and communal groups that predated the new villages. Lands cultivated by individuals were not the best lands; they did not receive the new services (e.g., irrigation) and were farther from the houses than the collective plots.

According to MCC *News Service* reports, the number of displaced people in Bale continued to grow well after Somalia's withdrawal from the region. On 30 April 1979, the *Mennonite Reporter* reported that

> the Bale province settlement camps are improving rapidly. . . . Six months ago displaced persons were sheltered by plastic sheets stretched over stick frames. Approximately 250,000 were located then in 139 different shelters. Each shelter housed several thousand persons. Today displaced persons number about 400,000 but they live in mud huts neatly arranged in straight rows which form a village.

By 30 May 1980, two years after Somalia's troops withdrew from the region, the MCC reported that

> currently 281 settlements are in Bale province with 600,000 persons in them. The area now also has a rapid expansion of temporary shelters for some 65,000 persons fleeing the present conflict and drought; the number is expected to triple by the end of the year.

The same MCC *News Service* report clearly described the conflict referred to above: "During the last five months, the Ethiopian army has mounted a strong offensive to drive out or defeat the 'internal saboteurs' " (30 May 1980).

According to Western newspaper articles in 1981 (see Appendix B) coordinated military campaigns occurred in Bale in the autumn of 1980 and in neighboring Sidamo in early 1981. Reports on UNICEF-funded activities in Bale indicate that all assistance went through the RRC in Addis Ababa, which implemented the programs. According to first-hand accounts, "displaced" peasants were not only organized into new villages, but also into community development, farmers' and women's associations before UNICEF started its assistance programs. UNICEF provided draft animals and looms that were owned and used collectively in the local peasant associations.

Most relief and development agencies provided seeds and equipment to peasant associations for communally cultivated plots. It seems, from the MCC quote cited above, that residents felt they had to steal produce from such plots in order to receive it. The agencies do not report what happened to the produce from such plots, although in 1985 expatriates observed produce being trucked away from peasant associations in Bale against the wishes of local residents.

In 1981 the government claimed that almost 100 percent of Bale's rural population had been moved into new villages; yet military and government personnel continued to travel regularly into regions off the main road where they claimed shiftas were active. As a result of these military activities, between 1981 and 1984 the settlement program expanded into the more remote areas of Bale, where only army and government personnel were allowed. Expatriates heard that government teams were going into the more insecure districts and forming new villages long after the withdrawal of Somali troops from the area. The government restricted access to new villages in such areas until it deemed them secure; in the northern and northeastern parts of Bale —particularly by the region of El Keyere, where OLF positions were strong—access was denied. Only the city by that name could be reached by air.

For the first few years after the government permitted agency assistance, it often provided its own translators for expatriate workers. Foreign workers could visit, but not live in, the new villages. Many international organizations, such as UNICEF, channeled their money directly through the RRC and did not have foreign workers stationed in Bale to monitor their programs. Even when agencies visited newly opened areas, government officials accompanied them. Travel time limited the amount of contact that could be maintained. The MCC reported that the Oromo settlements their nurses serviced "are a one and a half-hour drive from where the nurses [were required to] live in Ginnir" (MCC *News Service* 11 March 1983). Consequently, as mentioned above, the MCC visited only seven of 60 settlements in the area, and these on only a biweekly basis.

As recently as 1983 and 1984, World Vision, a Western humanitarian agency, was reported to have flown grain into famine-affected, remote regions of Bale precisely where government troops had launched a number of campaigns against local shiftas. According to expatriates in Bale at the time, no one from World Vision had assessed the causes of the famine or monitored the distribution of the food in the area. World Vision officials, reportedly on hand when their grain was flown into the area, left before it was even distributed. They did not see what was happening in the area and seemed unconcerned about the correllation between the movement of government troops against peasant populations and the creation of famine victims.

Ethiopia actively courted Western agencies, both public and private, to provide assistance in Bale. The government often led visits to the sites of activities for groups such as UNICEF, MCC and LWF as a way of gaining additional funding for similar projects either in the same area or in different regions. For example, in 1980 two UN teams visited Ethiopia to evaluate the problems of displaced people resulting from war with Somalia and from drought. A mission from UNDRO visited Ethiopia from 27 May–7 June and a mission headed by Faruk Birkel, coordinator of the UN Disaster Relief Organization, visited the country from 6–15 June.

In their report "Assistance to Displaced Persons in Ethiopia" (E/1980/104, 18 July), the UNDRO team made far-reaching recommendations for project funding despite the brevity of their visit (ten days). The report, which included recommendations not even requested by Ethiopian officials, was subsequently adopted with minor changes by the 1980 session of the UN General Assembly.

Much of the information contained in the report was provided by the Ethiopian officials who accompanied the team during their stay. It does not appear that the team adequately evaluated the information provided, for in one instance the team recommended aid to a Soviet military base.

According to *STORM* (1982:9), Ethiopian officials were encouraged by the response of the UN missions to the information they had been presented. As a result the RRC was instructed to organize similar tours to raise financial support for the displaced people in southern and southeastern Ethiopia.

In April 1981, in an attempt to increase the international assistance available for its villagization program, the RRC asked the International Council of Voluntary Agencies (ICVA) in Geneva to visit and evaluate a number of its programs with displaced people. Between 16 and 30 January

1982, an ICVA team, which included members from CRS (Catholic Relief Services), Oxfam-UK, World ORT Union and the CRDA, visited southern and southeastern Ethiopia.

The ICVA team visited shelters and settlements; its 1982 report is filled with statistics provided by the RRC. The mission attempted to verify some of the figures by checking camp registers, but the RRC could have prepared these, too. They did not interview, systematically or otherwise, residents of either shelters or settlements. A critique of the ICVA report appeared in *STORM* (1982), a London-based human rights publication on the Horn of Africa (see Appendix C). Many of the criticisms *STORM* raised regarding villagization in Bale in 1982 have proven prophetic.

The ICVA team, however, was somewhat more critical of the conditions they saw than were the UN missions. The ICVA noted, for example, irregular food deliveries, lack of water, lack of economic opportunities, bare minimum living conditions and tight security around the shelters and settlements. What is equally clear from the ICVA report, however, is that team members were woefully unprepared to evaluate critically the living conditions or their causes. They had little background information on the regions visited or on the nature or duration of the war with Somalia. Team members assumed that the programs were voluntary. Two examples illustrate the type of information that the ICVA team reported as fact.

The team was told that residents of the Babile shelter in Hararghe had been displaced by drought. This was not the case. Babile is located 32 km from Harar. The OLF had been active in the area in the late 1970s and early 1980s. For this reason the government launched a coordinated attack on the region using troops from both the air force and the army. The bombings and ground attacks left many houses, buildings and crops destroyed and many people and animals dead. Residents of Harar even reported hearing these nearby attacks.

Residents of Bale told the team that the Oromo population of northern Bale was scattered during the war and returned to find their property destroyed. Yet, the Somali-backed invaders did not reach the most heavily populated areas of northern and northwestern Bale, where new villages were being constructed. Rather, the Ethiopian government gave residents as much as five months to voluntarily move and then proceeded to attack them.

What the ICVA team failed to note was the active role the Ethiopian military played in creating displaced people in southern Ethiopia. Many survivors of the attacks moved into government-guarded shelters, others fled to Somalia as refugees and still others fled to inaccessible areas in the mountains. Many of this latter group were eventually rounded up by the military and put in shelters. It is at least a debatable question as to whether the "tight security measures" noted by the ICVA team were necessary to prevent shiftas from attacking the camp, as the government claimed, or to prevent the residents from escaping to return to their home areas or neighboring areas out of the control of the government.

A few new villages in Bale were located on the sites in the center of previous dispersed settlements. Most villages, however, were constructed along roads to enable easy access and to clear large areas of land. About 500 families made up each new settlement, far more than traditional villages in the area. Residents of new villages were not necessarily related to people in the new site or even to people from the area. Newcomers were added who reportedly came "from the bush" and arrived in an extremely malnourished state. People brought to the sites by Ethiopian security forces had "lost" all their livestock. Expatriate workers in the area were told by Ethiopian officials that the Somalis had either killed or taken them.

According to foreigners who have visited a number of new villages in Bale, the ones that are successful — at least economically — are situated in fertile areas where abundant water allows for irrigated agriculture. However, these areas contained prosperous communities, using irrigated agriculture, that had existed there prior to villagization. In other words, even the few cases of prosperous villages do not appear to have resulted from the government's villagization program.

Resettlement in Bale

In 1978, 7,500 people were resettled from Wollo administrative region to sites in the Harawa Valley in Bale. Between 1979 and 1982 some 15,000 people were trucked from Wollo and resettled along a river at Melka Oda in Bale. According to two journalists who visited the area, the colonists were installed "where land for new settlements is available (Fikre and Manzoor 1980:24). They were settled in villages on land that had been turned into state farms; men were brought first.

> The settlement plan calls for the heads of the families to travel first to the new sites, and with the assistance of the RRC, to build the family *tukuls* [dwellings], prepare and plough the land or embark on other productive activities, and establish the rudiments of a community life. Only then do the wives and children follow (Fikre and Manzoor 1980:24).

In Melka Oda women and families followed as much as two years later. Militia were recruited from among the Wollo colonists who, according to observers, "outranked" local militia. According to Shemelis Adugna, head of the RRC at the time, some of the settlers received six weeks of military training and were armed (STORM 1982:2,10). The Wollo militia manned the security check, which consisted of road blocks along the main road in Bale. Thus, settlers from Wollo were brought to Bale almost immediately after the cessation of armed conflict in the area. The settlers themselves were armed and used for security in the area.

Colonists from Wollo were organized into communal production systems; private cultivation was prohibited. At Melka Oda, they were settled along a river on the assumption that this was the most fertile soil. No preliminary studies were done to determine the best locations for resettlement sites. The colonists built houses, cleared land and planted teff. The first crop failed, so women and children were not brought to join the men.

The second crop also failed. While these were dry years in the area as a whole, the sites selected for resettlement were also poor. UNICEF provided food during this period: "A grain ration and a supplementary feeding programme for children and mothers supported by UNICEF are helping the families tide over the period until crops are adequate (Fikre and Manzoor 1980:24). But, by 1980, Fikre and Manzoor reported:

> The families still depend on the RRC for a part of their food because the rain has been unseasonably irregular and scarce during the past two years. Moreover, ploughing implements, seeds and pesticides have not been available in adequate quantities, and there are few other avenues of earning an income. Life in Harawa is not exactly prosperous (1980:24).

The MCC, by contrast, began to provide medical assistance to the settlers in December 1978.

The Harawa settlements received approximately 7,500 heads of families in 1978. However, two years later in 1980, after one-quarter of the families had been reunited, only 5,500 settlers lived in the area (Fikre and Manzoor 1980:24). The decline in the settler population can probably be attributed to high death rates ("this is the first time [Wollo] people have encountered . . . malaria" [Fikre and Manzoor 1980:24]) and an abandonment of the program by many people, perhaps those who had not volunteered in the first place. If we calculate that the quarter of the family heads reunited with their families (1,875 in all) had on average four people per family, a conservative estimate, then a total of 13,125 settlers should live in the area. However, only 5,500 people were in the Harawa sites in 1980. This means that the missing 7,625 people constituted three-quarters of the original group and more than one-third of all the families moved in 1980.

Yet, according to local observers, the Harawa settlements proved to be more successful for agriculture; gradually, the Wollo people from the Melka Oda settlements were moved there. It is possible, however, that the turnover of colonists, through death or desertion, left a number of places vacant for others. By 1982, nearly all the colonists at Melka Oda had moved to Harawa. At that time, lands from a neighboring state farm were incorporated into the Harawa settlement. Only a few Wollo farmers who depended on river-fed, irrigated agriculture remained at Melka Oda.

During the initial period of resettlement, the Wollo colonists strained the resources of the neighboring Oromo population who, it should be remembered, were only recovering from their own displacement and resettlement. Certainly, considerable produce flowed from the new Oromo villages to the resettlement sites. This produce probably came from the communal plots planted and cultivated with seeds and other assistance from the West. Resentment against the settlers was considerable; it was further heightened as a result of conflicts over local women, which increased when the Wollo women and children were not allowed to come when expected.

In addition, conflicts arose over resources. Wollo colonists put considerable pressure on wood and animal supplies. For example, in one area local Oromo residents were required to pay for such resources as sand and gravel and the labor it took to extract them, while Wollo colonists received the goods for free. In other instances, local residents were required to cut poles for the houses of the Wollo settlers from their own wooded areas. According to local residents they were paid for the poles, but below the value of the resources and their labor.

After two years in the sites, some of the women and children were bused from Wollo to join the men. For the most part, the reunions were joyous. However, in some instances, wives had not known what happened to their husbands and had remarried and borne additional children. In some instances, irate former husbands killed the children from the new marriages. These unfortunate events indicate, at least in some cases, that husbands did not have a chance to tell their wives where they were going when they were relocated. This suggests that not everyone volunteered for the program.

Agricultural production in the Wollo resettlement sites in Bale was highly mechanized and subsidized. Not only were tractors used for plowing, but combines were used for harvesting and airplanes for spraying crops. Between 1982 and 1984, however, government policies appear to have been changing. Officials began to explore the possibilities of using draught animals. The FAO (Food and Agriculture Organization of the United Nations) assisted with the design of an improved two-oxen plow that was tested on these sites. In general, observers agree, the resettlement sites received far more assistance than the local population in the new villages.

While the Wollo resettlement sites in Bale were to have substantial services, they were slow in coming. In 1980, according to Fikre and Manzoor, "The children in Harawa still do not go to school, because no school exists ..."(1980:24).

7 | The Case of Hararghe: The Testimony of Refugees in Somalia

Jason W. Clay

The Late 1984–Early 1985 Influx

There is considerable confusion about the relationship of the 1984–1985 influx of refugees from Ethiopia into Somalia to the 1985–1986 influx. After a two-week visit to Somalia, including a trip to Tug Wajale refugee camp, one observer made the following report.

> Initial reports of the present influx mistakenly described it as a continuation of the influx which took place in 1984–1985. Thus, UNHCR's initial emergency appeal included aid for Tug Wajale along with aid to the camps created for the 1984–1985 influx. This misperception continue[s] at the international level for some time (even up to the present in some cases).

> In fact, the two influxes are rather distinct. The 1984–1985 influx was 75 percent or so ethnic Somalis, and those who arrived in the northwest were primarily people from the Ogaden. While reasons for leaving still remain unclear, there is agreement that famine played a major role. The present influx is essentially one of Oromo farmers, not Somali nomads; and represents villages in the higher elevations of Hararghe province, most heavily those in the area of Harar. The tendency to lump these two distinct influxes together confuses the reasons for coming, and therefore the implications for what is happening inside Ethiopia. Famine is not noted as a current problem by the refugees (although continued villagization could change that); active persecution by the government is. The solution therefore is not food aid, but rather pressure to alter government policies (Clark 1986:16–17).

157

Contrary to this assessment, we know very little about the people who fled to Somalia in the 1984–1985 influx. They were never systematically interviewed by representatives of the UNHCR or NGOs working in the camp, or other visitors or reporters. For example, we do not *know* that "75 percent were Somalis," that they "were primarily people from the Ogaden," that "famine played a major role" in their flight or that most were "Somali nomads." Clark reports that there is *agreement* on these issues, nothing more. Who is agreeing? On what basis do they agree?

How can the accepted explanations concerning who those refugees were or the causes of their flight from Ethiopia be considered accurate when the careful calculations of numbers of refugees in Somalia in the 1984–1985 influx were so far off the mark? Clark, for example, points out (1986:10) that while 60,000 people were registered in Gannett B camp, the location of most of the 1984–1985 influx to Somalia, when the camp was moved and someone bothered to undertake a count there were only 26,000. (Incidentally, in 1986, a mere count of the tents in Tug Wajale indicated that there were no more than 40,000 people in the camp rather than the nearly 70,000 that were officially registered.) If Somali nationals or refugees from other camps swelled the ranks of ration receivers in 1984–1985, then the number of actual refugees in the camp might even have been mostly Oromo. But we will never know the truth about that refugee population.

My research in early 1986, however, indicated that the two refugee populations — i.e. those who came in 1984–1985 — were probably in large part in Somalia for the same reason. Refugees I interviewed in April 1986 had had family members flee Ethiopia during the beginning of the villagization program in late 1984 and early 1985. A UNHCR interviewer who worked with both populations indicated that many, if not most, of the earlier arrivals had fled persecution, confiscation of property and the beginnings of villagization. Unfortunately, no one knew what villagization was at that time because the Western agencies inside Ethiopia weren't even aware that it was going on until almost a year later. The only interviews that were recorded and published in early 1985 with this earlier influx were in the *Philadelphia Inquirer*. Those interviews sound remarkably similar to the findings of interviews conducted by a half dozen researchers with the 1985–1986 influx. Excerpts from the *Inquirer* piece (Rosenthal 1985) include the following:

> The refugees who have come to Gannet came from the Harer province in eastern Ethiopia and are members of the Oromo tribe or ethnic Somali. In recent interviews, the refugees said much more than drought and famine had pushed tens of thousands eastward into Somalia in the last six months.
>
> Ethiopian authorities and military forces have in recent months accelerated a campaign against the Oromo people and the ethnic Somalis in their villages and home areas, the refugees said. They have denied refugees food sent by international relief agencies, forced conscription of young men, nationalized farms and property, and blocked people from practicing their religion, which for nearly all of them is Islam.

Wadiye said that he came from a village called Aubelet, near Harer in Ethiopia. He said that since mid-February, the Ethiopian army . . . had been harassing the people and that he had finally decided to leave after seven men had been shot dead in front of him after they refused to join the army.

"They are taking things and doing everything by force," Wadiye said. "We cannot defend ourselves. They said we must change our culture. It is not the drought that did this but the Ethiopians. They blocked my water and took my farm. Then I saw them kill men in my village and we fled."

Omar was a tall thin man. . . . He said he had come . . . in mid-January from his village of Fedhacad near Jijiga in Ethiopia.

"Because of the socialist policy, I left," Omar said. "I used to have farm and animals. And the government people came and said they would take all and make it that of the government. They wanted me to change my religion, and when this happened we must move and find a place where we can live as we please.

"They had said to me," Omar continued, " 'If you are going to follow your religion, then go, you can no longer farm.' For some months we argued, talked and argued. We were told if we came back to the farm they would shoot me. Many were killed. We were told the government owned all the land, the religion, the animals, the women, everything."

Omar . . . said that it was true there was a famine in Harer but that he could have survived that. . . .

"Before there was famine and drought in the time of my father and grandfather," Omar said. "But my family stayed and came out of the famine. But in my father's and grandfather's time, the people did not have to face guns. After the famines in the past we could fill our stomachs and there would be plenty. This time the guns made us leave, not our hunger. The hunger itself is nothing. It is normal for us. We can defeat hunger but not oppression. . . .

"What has happened to me happened to everyone," he said. He said that he had farmed wheat, sorghum, maize and beans and that he had a good crop last year— so good that he still could be feeding his large extended family with it, except the Ethiopian army had taken all his stores and burned his house and two storehouses (Rosenthal 1985).

In addition to those explanations recorded in 1985, a number of refugees explained to me in April 1986 that there had been an intense conflict over land in the Jarso area between the Jarso Oromo and Giri Somali. This conflict, between groups that had been living together peacefully and even intermarrying since just after the turn of the century, centered on rights to land. Government officials eventually became involved, but the conflict seemed largely outside of their control. The conflict resulted—in some villages but not all—in a number of the Somali being burned out of their homes and being forced to flee the area. Likewise, some Oromo were displaced. However, the Somalis living in the Jarso area were agriculturalists with herds of cattle, not nomads. Further, they were not from the Ogaden. It is not known if villagization intensified conflicts over land between Oromo and Somali in the Jarso area.

According to one translator who had worked for the UNHCR, neither famine nor drought was the primary cause of the 1984-1985 influx of refugees into Somalia. The conflict in Jarso was probably the most important cause, followed by persecution and confiscation of property associated with the first stages of villagization, and only finally by drought and famine, of which a small segment of the refugee population complained. This interviewer expressed regrets that neither he nor any of the UNHCR or NGO personnel in Somalia knew about the villagization program that was being implemented in Hararghe. He said that many of the refugees did not know what the program was called at that time although they described the same processes that refugees did in 1985–1986. No one knew what to make of their testimony.

The December 1985 Influx

In December 1985 refugees began to arrive, once again, in the northwest region of Somalia. According to UNHCR Site Report No. 1 the new refugees cited the following factors for their flight: "political, economic and religious persecution. If the causes continue, the influx is likely to go on despite the weather and crop conditions." By mid-March of 1986, 46,000 new refugees had been registered. From January through April the rate averaged 500 or more new refugees per day, reaching a peak of 700 per day during March. By May the number of registered refugees exceeded 70,000.

Initially about 3,000 of the new arrivals were put in Darbi Hare, 200 km northwest of Hargeisa; the majority were sent to Tug Wajale "B" reception center approximately 80 km northwest of Hargeisa and 7 km from the border. Later all newly arrived refugees were registered at the border and sent to Tug Wajale "B" reception center.

Tug Wajale "B" was intended only as an initial reception center for a few thousand people maximum. Established in 1985 as a temporary holding camp, the center was to hold arrivals from the 1984-1985 influx before they were transferred to more "permanent" camps. The site did not have its own water supply. Moreover, no all-weather road linked it to paved roads from which supplies could be received. In addition, the area was flat and poorly drained.

The government decision to keep all the 1986 refugees in Tug Wajale posed serious problems for providing water, food and health care during the wet season and protection during the dry season. After March 1986, with the onset of the rains, the conditions deteriorated accordingly.

According to National Refugee Commission (NRC, cited in UNHCR Site Report No. 1) people in Tug Wajale were mostly Oromo (60 percent) and Somali (25 percent). Approximately one-quarter were children and more than two-thirds of the refugees were female. The average family size was just over three people — probably a result of the separate registration of multiple wives and the high number (perhaps 15 percent) of students who also registered separately.

Table 1

NRC Profile of Refugees in Tug Wajale

Oromo	60%
Somali	25%
Others	15%†
Children under age five	24%
Ratio of women to men	7:3
Average family size	3.2

†Amharic, Tigrean and Eritrean students

On 10 March UNHCR Site Report No. 1 indicates that a number of health problems had been reported in Tug Wajale.

Table 2

Reported Health Problems in Tug Wajale

Health Problem	Number of Cases
Diarrhea	1,150
Malnutrition	642
Eye infection	507
Pneumonia	369
Fevers	338
Anemia	288
Skin disease	268
Ear infection	256
Cough and fever	198
Injuries/wounds	32

A survey of the camp population in early March indicated that 14.5 percent of children under age five were less than 80 percent of the recommended weight for height; 6 percent were less than 70 percent of the recommended weight for height. Two percent of women in the camp were pregnant and 4 percent were lactating.

Refugees in the camp in early March were supposed to receive rations of 490 g/day, but since the anticipated supplies did not arrive, the actual rations were only 335 g/day. By April the rations rose to 435 g/day. In late March and April there were sufficient supplies to provide the new refugees with an adequate diet. At that time, however, the Somali government refused to allow the new arrivals higher rations than other refugees in the country. Many refugees in older camps have two or more ration cards, so the low rations do not pose undue hardships. Likewise Somali citizens who receive refugee rations (illegally) use them as a supplemental feeding program. New arrivals in 1986, however, did not appear to have multiple ration cards, perhaps because their Oromo identity made it more difficult to obtain extra cards.

Table 3

Daily Ration Levels in Tug Wajale

late February	335 g/day
10 March	415 g/day
27 March	350 g/day
2 April	350 g/day
9 April	435 g/day
16 April	435 g/day

Source: UNHCR Site Reports

Table 4 lists the foods included in the 350 g/day ration of late March 1986.

Table 4

Composition of the Daily Ration

Cereal	150
Wheat flour	50
Oil	30
DSM	30
CSM	30
Sugar	30
Beans	30
Total	350 g/day or 1,400-1,500 calories

The low levels of rations received by mid-March caused a general deterioration of health in the camp and a rising mortality rate, as shown in Table 5.

Table 5

Mortality Rates in Tug Wajale — 1986
(reported deaths per 10,000 camp residents per day)

10 March	.10/10,000/day
20 March	.26/10,000/day
27 March	.35/10,000/day
2 April	.72/10,000/day

The rising mortality rate in the camp was no doubt affected by the dearth of available blankets after April 1986, and that some materials essential to maintaining the camp population's health "disappeared." For example, each of the more than 4,000 tents distributed by April 1986 was to have had a ground cloth, but none of the cloths were distributed. The ground cloths, however, could be purchased in local markets. Refugees in the 1986 influx claimed that the same thing happened with refugees who entered Somalia during 1984-1985. At that time ground cloths, which were to be distributed to refugees in Somalia, could be purchased in the market in Dire Dawa, a major Ethiopian town in the administrative region from which refugees had fled. Similarly, in 1986 cooking sets for refugees were in short supply — supposedly 1,000 were "missing" — yet sets intended for refugees could be purchased in nearby villages in Somalia.

Another major problem faced by refugees in Tug Wajale was the availability of firewood. Because refugees did not receive adequate supplies in the camp, they spent many hours searching for firewood. Some refugees collected firewood to sell in order to purchase additional supplies of food. By April, however, the wooded areas around the camp had been depleted and the owners of nearby forests told people not to take their wood. When the warnings went unheeded, refugees — including women and children — were reportedly beaten.

The Interviews

The data presented in this chapter were collected from individuals who fled from the Ethiopian government's villagization program in Hararghe administrative region, eastern Ethiopia, to Somalia between December 1985 and April 1986. They were interviewed in Tug Wajale "B" Camp (hereafter referred to as Tug Wajale) in April 1986. The refugees were interviewed about their personal backgrounds, general conditions in their village during the last five years, specific events and conditions associated with villagization in their areas and their trip to Somalia and reception in that country.

Forty refugees randomly selected in the camp were interviewed — 20 of the earliest arrivals (those who arrived in Somalia before February 1986) and 20 of the latest arrivals (those who arrived after February 1986). The camp is divided into 32 sections, roughly equal in size, which were occupied sequentially. Two individuals were selected from each section 1 through 10 (the earliest arrivals) and from 23 through 32 (the latest arrivals). Dividing the sample between early and late arrivals permitted investigation into possible changes in Ethiopia which forced the refugees to flee. The data in this chapter are presented so that early and late arrivals can be compared: the statistical tables refer to the "Early Arrivals," the "Late Arrivals" and the combined "Total."

In addition, 10 nonrandomly selected refugees who were active supporters of the OLF or from OLF areas were interviewed. Given the likely relationship of villagization to OLF activities and the clear implications of villagization for future OLF activities, such interviews seemed essential to predict the full range of implications the villagization program poses. Information gained from these interviews is not included with that collected from randomly selected respondents.

All of the interviews were conducted with one Oromo translator present. Interviews with native Somali speakers were conducted with the additional assistance of a translator found in or near the tent of the person being interviewed. All interviews were tape recorded; a random selection was translated independently in the US to determine the accuracy of the translation and clarify ambiguous or subtle details. The translator in the camp did not select any of the individuals to be interviewed, nor were any self-selected. No one — either refugee or Somali national — followed us through the camp to listen to each interview. All interviews were conducted inside the respondents' tents; in some cases, people from neighboring tents listened to the interviews. However, no one other than the translator and myself listened to more than one interview.

The two individuals chosen from each section where interviews were conducted were from opposite corners of the section, for example, the third or fourth tent of the third or fourth row from diagonally opposite corners of the section. No one who listened to an interview was later interviewed; nor were people attending interviews allowed to interrupt an interview to make their own comments. Rather, at the end of interviews, those present were allowed to recount their own experiences and account for the differences. Although none of the comments from people outside the random sample are included in the percentages presented here, many provided useful insights that have been incorporated into the analysis of the data and are quoted to highlight specific findings.

In late 1985 refugees arrived between Booramo and Faraweine along the border. Later, apparently at the direction of Somali nomads, refugees learned that they had to be registered by Somalia's National Security Service (NSS) at Tug Wajale town, so most traveled directly to that village. Once the refugees were screened by the NSS at the border and certified to be refugees by the NSS official in charge, their names were placed on a list that was sent to Tug Wajale camp where they were registered and, only then, issued ration cards, tents and other equipment.

Neither at the initial border screening nor in the refugee camp did legitimate refugees appear to have been denied refugee status or discriminated against in any meaningful way. A number of nonrefugees, however, have acquired refugee status — perhaps as many as 30-40 percent of all registered "refugees" fall into this category (see Reception and Conditions in Somalia).

Place of Origin

By April 1986, five different surveys had been conducted among refugees who were either in, or subsequently transferred, to Tug Wajale camp (see Table 6). These surveys each indicate that 80 percent or more of the refugees come from villages in the highland areas of Harar, Gersum or Jijiga districts in Hararghe Province. With few exceptions, those refugees from whom precise village of origin information was collected came from highland agricultural areas (see map for precise village locations of refugees Cultural Survival interviewed).

The Cultural Survival survey indicates that the refugees' areas of origin appear to have shifted slightly to the west over the course of the influx. Data from the 10 other nonrandom interviews do not entirely support this interpretation (see notes for Table 11 for possible explanation). In the absence of free access to all areas of Ethiopia where villagization is taking place, systematic checks at the border and in the new sections of the camp

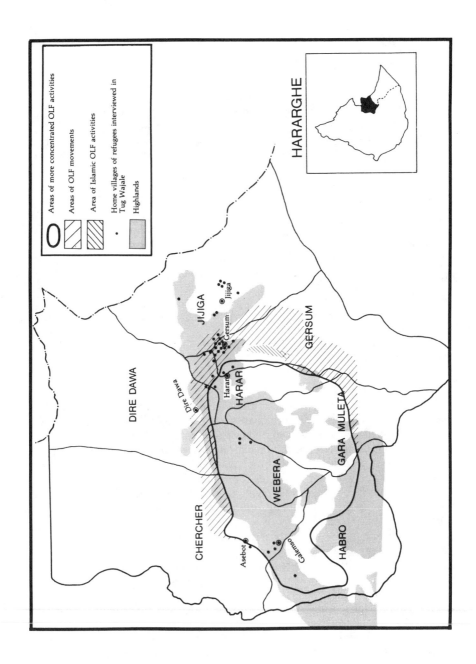

would allow observers to predict more accurately the origin, if not the size, of future refugee populations.

Table 6

District of Origin of Refugees in Tug Wajale Camp
According to 5 Surveys Conducted between 12/85 and 4/86

District of Origin	Somali NSS Count 12/85	CS Early Arrivals 12/85-1/86	UNHCR Survey 2/86	Somali RHU* 3/86	RPG† Survey 4/86	CS Late Arrivals 2-3/86	Average All Surveys
	(%)	(%)	(%)	(%)	(%)	(%)	(%)
Harar	43.2	20	22.9	44.8	40.9	30	33.6
Gersum	40.7	40	40.0	11.7	13.6	40	31.0
Jijiga	12.3	25	25.7	24.6	31.8	10	21.6
Habro	1.2	0	0	8.1	0	15	4.0
Dire Dawa	0	5	2.9	1.1	0	0	1.5
Charchar	0	5	2.9	0	0	0	1.3
Obbora	0	5	2.9	0	0	0	1.3
Awash	2.5	0	0	0	4.5	0	1.2
Garamulata	0	0	0	0	0	5	.8
Dhegahbur	0	0	0	.4	4.5	0	.8
Other	0	0	0	7.7	0	0	1.3
Sample Size		20				20	

*RHU = Refugee Health Unit (Somalia)
†RPG = Refugee Policy Group

Personal Background

More than half of the refugees interviewed were female (see Table 7). Because men were primary informants when both spouses were present, however, it is likely that an even higher proportion of women existed in the total adult population in the camp than the sample indicates (57.5 percent). The average age of those interviewed was 39.3 years, with the earliest arrivals being nearly 7 years younger than later arrivals.

Only 5 percent of the earlier arrivals reported any change of residence for themselves or for their parents or grandparents; more than one-third of the later arrivals indicated changes of residence.

Forty percent of the earlier arrivals were from Gersum and 25 percent were from Jijiga, the Ethiopian region nearest Tug Wajale. Whereas 40 percent of the later arrivals were also from Gersum, 30 percent were from Harar, a district farther from the border (see Map 1 for home villages of those interviewed). However, all those interviewed in both samples were from highland agricultural areas. Although most had livestock, none were nomads.

Nearly 70 percent of all those interviewed identified themselves as Oromo ("Oromo," "Jarso," "Warrahume" or "Kottu"); the remainder said that they were Somali (identifying themselves as "Somali," "Western Somali" or

"Giri"). An average of 10 percent reported that one parent was of a different nationality.

Nearly 70 percent spoke Oromo as their first language; the remainder spoke Somali first. However, 77.5 percent spoke Oromo fluently and 5 percent spoke some Oromo; 42.5 percent spoke Somali fluently and 10 percent spoke some Somali. About one-third of those interviewed spoke both languages (35 percent).

All those interviewed were Moslems.

Only 15 percent of those interviewed had any education; 17.5 percent of their children had some schooling.

Table 7

Profile of Refugees

	Early Arrivals (%)	Late Arrivals (%)	Total (%)
Sample number	20	20	40
Sex			
Female	60.0	55.0	57.5
Male	40.0	45.0	42.5
Age	35.9	42.8	39.4
District of origin			
Gersum	40	40	40.0
Jijiga	25	10	17.5
Harar	20	30	25.0
Habro	5	15	10.0
Dire Dawa	5	0	2.5
Webera	5	0	2.5
Garamulata	0	5	2.5
Had ever moved	5	35	20.0
Nationality			
Oromo	65	62.5	63.8
Somali	10	17.5	13.8
Western Somali	5	5.0	5.0
Wara Humi	0	5.0	2.5
Giri	15	0	7.5
Jarso	5	10.0	7.5
Had parent of different nationality	15	5.0	10.0
First language			
Oromo	70	65	67.5
Somali	30	35	32.5
Second language			
Oromo	0	30	15.0
Somali	20	20	20.0
English	5	0	2.5
Three or more languages	0	10	5.0
Moslem	100	100	100
Education			
Self	15	15	15.0
Children	25	10	17.5

Family History

All of the refugees interviewed had been married at least once. Some 22.5 percent had been married, on average, 2.5 times each (see Table 8). The earlier arrivals had been married an average of 6 years less (14.6 years) than their later counterparts. Sixty percent of those interviewed said that their spouses were with them in Tug Wajale. About 17.5 percent were widowed.

More than 90 percent of those interviewed had children — on average, 5.1 children per couple with children. More than one-quarter reported that they had had children die. More than 80 percent reported that their children were with them in Tug Wajale, but 25 percent reported that their children were elsewhere.

Of those interviewed, 92.5 percent reported that they had an average of 5.7 siblings. More than 20 percent reported that some of their siblings were with them in Tug Wajale. Twenty-five percent of the earlier arrivals reported that their siblings were somewhere else in Somalia, but none of the later arrivals had siblings in Somalia other than at Tug Wajale. In addition, 20 percent of the earlier arrivals reported that one or both parents were in Somalia, whereas none of the later arrivals had parents in the country. Although the early arrivals clearly had more relatives living in Somalia for a longer time, there was no significant ethnic correlation. More Oromos had siblings in Somalia than did ethnic Somalis.

Economic Background

Nearly all of those interviewed in Tug Wajale were farmers (97.5 percent) and had owned livestock (90 percent) before escaping from the government's villagization program in Ethiopia (see Table 9). Nearly half also had used gravity-fed irrigation for limited areas, usually 1-3 ha, devoted to cash crops.

Whereas the average nuclear family comprised 6.9 people, the average number of dependents in the extended family who farmed as a unit and consumed produce from family supplies was 8.7.

Most of the refugees interviewed (60 percent) indicated that they were worse off than their fathers were at their same age (about 40 years old). Ten percent reported that their fathers had died before reaching their present age. Only 12.5 percent reported that they were better off than their fathers had been. This is significant given that historical accounts from the area indicate that under Ethiopia's previous regime most producers in the area were tenant farmers who paid taxes and contributions to landlords and officials that ranged from 50 to 90 percent of their total harvests. Even with the land reform undertaken by the military government after the revolution, those interviewed thought that their fathers were by and large better off, a telling statement from people, as seen below, who did not have problems feeding their families and generating cash income.

Table 8

Family History of Refugees

	Early Arrivals	Late Arrivals	Total
Marital status			
Single	0%	0%	0.0%
Married	100%	100%	100.0%
Married once	20%	25%	22.5%
Average no. of years married	14.6	20.7	17.7 (longest marriage)
Widowed	20%	15%	17.5%
Divorced	5%	5%	5.0%
Location of spouses			
Tug Wajale	65%	55%	60.0%
Ethiopia	10%	15%	12.5%
Tug Wajale and other Somalia	10%	5%	7.5%
Tug Wajale and Ethiopia	0%	5%	2.5%
Not specified	10%	10%	10.0%
Children			
Had children	90%	95%	92.5%
Average no. of children	4.0	5.8	4.9
Average no. in Tug Wajale	3.7	3.4	3.6
Had children die	25%	30%	27.5%
Location of children			
Tug Wajale	75%	90%	82.5%
Ethiopia	20%	20%	20.0%
Other Somalia location	10%	5%	7.5%
Siblings			
Average no. of siblings	6.1	5.3	5.7
With brothers	90%	100%	95.0%
With sisters	95%	85%	90.0%
Deceased	15%	30%	22.5%
Location of siblings			
Tug Wajale	45%	50%	47.5%
Ethiopia	70%	85%	77.5%
Other Somalia location	25%	5%	15.0%
Location of parents			
Tug Wajale	20%	0%	10%

Agriculture

The refugees interviewed reported impressive agricultural yields of both subsistence and cash crops before the government imposed villagization. The cereals and grains they produced included sorghum, corn, wheat, barley and teff (see Table 10). Most families also grew several varieties of pulses (e.g., peas, beans, lentils). On average, producers recorded yields for 1985 of 670 kg/person in the extended family that consumed their produce. This figure is more than three times the level of production (200 kg/person) needed to meet basic subsistence needs.

Table 9

Economic Background of Refugees

	Early Arrivals (%)	Late Arrivals (%)	Total (%)
Farmers	100	95	97.5
Used irrigation	40	50	45.0
Had livestock	90	90	90.0
Nomads	0	0	0
Other occupations	35	20	27.5
Sold charcoal or wood	15	10	12.5
Traded	5	0	2.5
Sold milk and/or butter	10	5	7.5
Sold prepared food	5	0	2.5
Black market activities	5	5	2.5
Wove baskets	0	5	2.5
Wealth compared to father			
Better off	15	10	12.5
Worse off	65	55	60.0
Same	5	0	2.5
Father dead	0	20	10.0
No comment	15	15	15.0

In spite of impressive production of cereals and legumes, 70 percent of the refugees interviewed reported that they relied on a variety of sweet potato (*mitatesa/dinicha oromo*) as their basic food staple. Those who reported specific areas for farming indicated that they planted this tuber with a variety of crops, usually on more than 3 ha of land. This crop was not correlated with ethnicity; both Somalis and Oromos cultivated it. In some cases, it was marketed.

In addition to the subsistence crops the farmers sold or traded in excess of food needs (the one exception was sweet potatoes, which reportedly were never sold), 90 percent of those interviewed cultivated cash crops. The most commonly grown cash crop was *chat*, a locally grown shrub whose leaves are chewed as a stimulant. More than three-quarters of the refugees interviewed produced and sold chat; in 1985 they earned, on average, more than E$4,100 (US$2,050) from sales.

In addition most of the farmers interviewed cultivated English potatoes and red onions; more than 40 percent cultivated coffee or peanuts. Half of those interviewed also grew one or more of the following cash crops: garlic, cabbage, tomatoes, leeks, lettuce, carrots, beets, sugarcane, hot peppers, tobacco, cotton or various fruits. Twenty percent of all those interviewed reported that in 1985 they earned, on average, E$5,300 (US$2,650) from the sale of fruit and vegetables alone. Although a slightly larger percentage of Oromos than Somalis produced vegetables, there was no significant correlation between ethnicity and any cash crop.

Table 10

1985 Agricultural Production of Refugees

	Early Arrivals	Late Arrivals	Total
Cultivated subsistence crops	100%	95%	97.5%
Sorghum			
Farmers who cultivated	95%	95%	95.0%
Average yield	1,874kg	2,680kg	2,277kg
Corn			
Farmers who cultivated	100%	90%	95%
Average yield	1,240kg	1,790kg	1,515kg
Wheat			
Farmers who cultivated	70%	60%	65%
Average yield	736kg	750kg	743kg
Barley			
Farmers who cultivated	80%	65%	72.5%
Average yield	670kg	1060kg	865kg
Teff			
Farmers who cultivated	45%	60%	52.5%
Average yield	430kg	310kg	370kg
Pulses			
Farmers who cultivated	80%	85%	82.5%
Average yield	586kg	1080kg	833kg
Sweet potatoes			
Farmers who cultivated	75%	65%	70%
Area cultivated	3.04ha	3.15ha	3.1ha
Cultivated cash crops			90.0%
Chat			
Farmers who cultivated	75%	80%	77.5%
Average earnings	E$3,762	E$4,520	E$4,141
	(US$1,881)	(US$2,260)	(US$2,070.50)
Peanuts			
Farmers who cultivated	50%	35%	42.5%
Average yield	1,082kg	825kg	953.5kg
Coffee			
Farmers who cultivated	35%	50%	42.5%
Average yield	1,286kg	3,520kg	2,403kg
English potatoes			
Farmers who cultivated	55%	70%	62.5%
Average yield	1,630kg	1,800kg	1,715kg
Red onions			
Farmers who cultivated	55%	60%	57.5%
Average yield	913kg	1,080kg	996.5kg
Other cash crops			
Farmers who cultivated	45%	55%	50.0%

The farmers interviewed insisted that in a good year they produced everything they ate with only one exception — salt — which they purchased after it was brought from the coast by nomads. Some farmers even grew cotton which they used locally to make material rather than selling it as a cash crop.

Livestock

Virtually all of the refugees interviewed reported that they had owned livestock before escaping villagization (see Table 11). Two of the exceptions, however, are worth noting. One widow had fled her peasant association, leaving her animals behind, after the police had arrested and tortured her husband to death on suspicion of black market activities. Another man reported that he had not owned animals since 1973: "At the end of Haile Selassie's rule I had to contribute all my animals for the starving. I haven't had any animals since then."

Some 87 percent of those interviewed reported that they had owned oxen in Ethiopia. On average, each had five oxen, two of which were needed to pull the type of plow used in the area. One-quarter of all those interviewed did not have the two oxen necessary to plow their own fields. Most people interviewed reported that one-fourth to one-third of the people in their peasant associations did not have a pair of oxen, indicating that the sample of refugees interviewed in Somalia were slightly more wealthy than their former neighbors. Those people who did not have oxen to plow their fields said that they borrowed animals from friends or relatives or, more often, that they worked in groups of five to 40 people (relatives, friends or neighbors, or a combination) who helped each other farm. Some farmers reported hiring others to plow their land and commented about labor exchange and oxen shortages as follows:

My brother has oxen and I can use his. We exchange labor.

Sometimes I hire laborers—they receive E$3 [US$1.50] per day, and sometimes I exchange labor with family members or friends.

We ask people to help us through labor exchange. If a person brings oxen and plows your land you have to work one day for him. Sometimes people lend oxen and let you use them to plow.

We mostly farm by ourselves. Sometimes we exchange labor with two or three neighbors.

There are about 20 of us who exchange labor. Mostly we are Somali, but some are Oromo who speak only Somali. The Oromo live nearby in Jarso.

I don't have oxen. I have to hire them. I pay E$20 [US$10] per day and I need about 12 days total. Sometimes I give some of the grain or the fodder to the owner of the oxen for his animals.

Work groups were common, even among individuals who had oxen. None of the refugees interviewed, however, saw any similarities between and certainly did not equate their traditional, communal work groups with the new producer's cooperatives the state was imposing. Traditional work groups were organized to share labor, *not* to produce!

Most of the refugees interviewed also had owned cattle, donkeys and goats before their escape. Nearly 40 percent had owned sheep, 17.5 percent camels, 12.5 percent mules and 5 percent horses. Although few of the refugees owned mules and horses (less than 13 percent), or reported that they were common in the area near their former homes, they did note that camels represented vast wealth and were extremely important possessions for their owners. Camels allowed owners who occupied the drier areas to trade and engage in market activities.

Half of all the refugees interviewed had, on average, more than seven beehives each. This ownership was strongly correlated with Oromos, for only one Somali reported having bees.

The refugees also reported that they had owned more animals five years before they left their homeland than they had the year before they left. Half of those interviewed reported that their animals had died; two-thirds reported that they had sold animals to pay taxes and contributions and, in a few cases, to meet household expenses. More than half of all those interviewed indicated that the militia and peasant association officials had stolen, on average, 9.6 large animals (oxen, cattle and camels) from them over the past five years—nearly two per year. Those interviewed also reported that the number of smaller animals (goats, sheep and chickens) stolen by the militia and peasant association officials was too numerous to mention. The refugees reported that the state had "nationalized" many of the animals before they had been able to escape.

Other Occupations

Nearly 30 percent of the refugees interviewed indicated that they had earned income from occupations in addition to farming or herding. More than 10 percent reported that they sold charcoal or wood to earn money, although the government has forbidden this practice in some areas. As two refugees reported:

We sell wood, but now the government tries to stop us.

We sold charcoal and wood to help make money. We could still cut wood in the forests because we lived so far from the government.

In addition, of those interviewed, 7.5 percent sold milk or butter, 2.5 percent sold prepared food, 2.5 percent worked as traders, 2.5 percent traded on the black market and 2.5 percent made and sold woven baskets.

Such activities supplemented family income. Only the trader who bought and sold goods on the black market had derived most of his income from that source rather than from farming or herding. The basket maker, for example, reported that "for baskets that sell for E$7 [US$3.50] to E$25 [US$12.50], I have costs of E$4 [US$2] to E$10 [US$5]."

Some of the refugees interviewed said that they were discriminated against by local officials or that new policies had prevented them from earning a living as they had previously. As two respondents indicated:

This year they stopped me from teaching because I am an Oromo.

Under Haile Selassie I traded livestock between villages. But now traders are not allowed to move between the different peasant associations. You must bribe the chairman to trade in his area. This is what merchants do.

Table 11

Livestock Owned by Refugees in Ethiopia

	Early Arrivals	Late Arrivals	Total
Livestock owners	90%	95%	92.5%
Oxen			
Owners	85%	90%	87.5%
Average number	4.2	5.8	5
Cows			
Owners	85%	95%	90%
Average number	11.1	14.7	12.9
Sheep			
Owners	40%	35%	37.5%
Average number	25.9	37.1	31.5
Goats			
Owners	50%	70%	60%
Average number	22.3	28.6	25.4
Donkeys			
Owners	60%	65%	62.5%
Average number	3.7	3.2	3.5
Mules			
Owners	10%	15%	12.5%
Average number	1	1	1
Camels			
Owners	15%	20%	17.5%
Average number	15.7	6	10.8
Horses			
Owners	0%	10%	5%
Average number	0	7	7
Beehives			
Owners	50%	50%	50%
Average number	5.3	9.1	7.2
Number of animals owned compared to 5 years ago			
More	60%	15%	37.5%
Less	10%	0%	5.0%
No change	25%	0%	12.5%
Not Asked	5%	85%	45.0%
Owners whose animals died	45%	55%	50.0%
Owners who sold animals	75%	50%	62.5%
Owners whose animals were stolen	55%	50%	52.5%
Owners whose animals were killed	0%	5%	2.5%

The latter individual reported that as a result of this system, one or a few merchants have trading monopolies in many of the more isolated peasant associations. This former trader also reported that the impediments to trade, even between neighboring peasant associations, cause artificial scarcities, which in 1985 and 1986 pushed the price of wheat to E$300 (US$150) per quintal (100 kg) and corn to E$200 (US$100) per quintal when surpluses existed in nearby associations.

Causes of Production Declines

Among those refugees interviewed, there was no consensus as to which year under the present government had been the most financially lucrative (for best years regarding agricultural production see Table 12). More than 25 percent said 1982 was the best year, but from 10 to 20 percent reported that 1981, 1983, 1984 or 1985 were the best years.

Table 12

Best Year for Agriculture

Best Year	Early Arrivals (%)	Late Arrivals (%)	Total (%)
Before 1978	0	5	5.0
1979	0	0	2.5
1980	15	0	7.5
1981	15	10	12.5
1982	35	20	27.5
1983	5	30	17.5
1984	5	25	15.0
1985	10	10	10.0
No difference	10	0	5.0
Don't know	5	5	5.0

Those interviewed indicated that forced labor and drought were the major causes of declining agricultural yields. Some 17.5 percent reported that drought was a major factor in declining yields, although 30 percent reported that it was a minor factor; some 35 percent did not report drought as a specific cause of production declines because they said the fluctuations were minor, the kind one would expect from one year to the next.

When asked directly if drought had caused recent production declines, 47 percent said no, 30 percent said some, 12.5 percent said in 1985 and 5 percent said in 1984. Even those who reported production declines related to drought insisted that they were not significant. Indeed the agricultural production levels described earlier indicate that production levels reported by these refugees are extremely high.

Of those interviewed, 85 percent indicated that insects were not a major cause of declining yields in their village.

When asked specifically why production had declined, 30 percent reported forced labor as the major cause. Their observations included the following comments.

Because of the method of ordering people to work together [on peasant association communal plots] our crops are not worked when they should be.

For the last five years we have not been able to work regularly on our land. Instead we have to work on the peasant association plot. We give 10 days each for plowing, planting, weeding, harvesting and threshing.

When they [peasant association officials] forbid us to work for ourselves, we had no food so we had to leave.

We can't go regularly to our farms. They [peasant association officials] order us to work on the farms of the chairman, officials and militia. We also work on the 10-ha peasant association plot where we grow teff, corn, potatoes, onions and garlic.

There are 25 peasant association officials and militia in our village. We work for all those people, mostly on their farms. We have little time to work on our own land.

If you are sick one day, but don't get a paper to excuse you from work, two militia will be sent to beat you.

We had to work 25 days per month for these people [militia and chairman] and the government during the agricultural season.

After the new village was built, it took us two hours to walk to our fields. They gave us five days per month to work our land. We weren't even allowed to stay overnight; we had to walk back and forth each day.

Every time we should plant they [militia] didn't allow us. We have to work for them. When our young men refused, they were put in prison.

For five years every local peasant association has had its own government farm. The members have to work on this farm. The farms are called "Le Matt Irsha." Every year we plant 10,000 coffee trees. We only had two days per week to work on our own land.

Since the peasant association was started we got less produce each year. They [militia] order us to work for the peasant association and the officials most of the time.

In Habro there is a government plot where we had to plant coffee; we have planted 77,000 trees in all. The first ones are already producing.

Thirty or 40 peasant associations in the woreda *[subdistrict] helped on this property—"Le Matt Irsha." There are five or six woredas that have similar coffee farms with the same name.*

We had to work six to 10 days on each task [plowing, planting, weeding, harvesting] on the peasant association plots or the plots of the chairman or militia. If we didn't, we were beaten with sticks.

One international observer, who wished to remain anonymous (hereafter referred to as Anonymous 1986), reported that people indicated that they often had to work "from 7 to 5 and 7 to 9 on cooperative coffee farms."

Why Did You Leave Your Homeland?

The open-ended question, "Why did you leave your homeland?" elicited responses that identified multiple factors (see Table 14). Certain reasons (homes destroyed, animals and crops taken, socialism, villagization) directly reflected changes associated with villagization and the creation of producers' cooperatives. In Hararghe, forced labor and religious persecution

Table 13

Causes of Production Declines

Causes of Decline	Early Arrivals (%)	Late Arrivals (%)	Total (%)
Forced labor	15	45	30.0
Drought	0	35	17.5
1985	0	25	12.5
1984	0	10	5.0
Some	40	30	35.0
Insects	0	30	15.0
1985 yes	0	15	7.5
1984 yes	0	5	2.5
1984 some	0	5	2.5
Some	10	5	7.5
"The government"	15	0	7.5

were associated with the creation of a new social and economic order. Specific responses to the question included the following:

The Amharas destroyed our house, registered our livestock and stole our crops. This year they even cut our chat.

They [government officials] finished [took] all our crops and cattle and we stayed, but finally they took our children [one of the speaker's children was taken] and we couldn't stay anymore.

The Amharas destroyed our houses, and beginning with the new village site they forced us to work together. Next year everyone would have to work together. All our cattle and crops were registered. They wouldn't even let us use the milk from our cows. The land was to be taken.

My husband was arrested in November 1985 because he didn't help enough with the new village. We had to pay E$100 [US$50] to get him out. Then we left.

They [government officials] always asked us to give or pay something. Then they destroyed our houses and took our livestock and crops. We came here to save only ourselves.

They destroyed our house and burned the Koran. I have beautiful daughters that were raped. The Amharas did this.

We were fed up being told to bring things to the government all the time. We were tired of working for them. They destroyed our culture, houses and religion.

They [government officials] ask for what we don't have and destroy our houses. Baboons and wild pigs eat our crops. We can't watch our crops and we don't have guns to protect them.

We had to tear down our house. I had to work with my husband to tear down the roof and beams. There was no place to sleep.

They [government officials] destroyed our house and took coffee and livestock. Then I left for Somalia.

Table 14

Reasons for Leaving Homeland

Reasons for Leaving	Early Arrivals (%)	Late Arrivals (%)	Total (%)
Homes destroyed	45	65	55.0
Forced labor	50	30	40.0
Religious persecution	40	40	40.0
Animals taken	25	45	35.0
Crops taken	10	45	27.5
Socialism	50	0	25.0
Villagization	10	15	12.5
Taxes and contributions	10	15	12.5
Cultural persecution	0	25	12.5
Women raped	5	10	7.5
Children taken	0	10	5.0
Amharas killed people	0	5	2.5

Human Rights Violations Against Villages and Families

When asked about specific government-related activities directed at their villages, *most* of the refugees interviewed reported that in the last few years:
- the village was attacked by the Dergue
- people were killed in the village
- animals were stolen by the militia or government representatives
- men were forcibly conscripted into the militia
- crops were stolen by government representatives
- farm and household equipment was stolen by the militia or government representatives
- people were imprisoned at the local or subdistrict level
- women were raped by militia in the village
- people were beaten in the village
- people or animals were held by peasant association officials until their families/owners paid taxes or "voluntary" contributions
- crops and fodder were burned by the militia
- the village was bombed by government troops

More than half of all the refugees interviewed reported that these abuses had been committed against them or their family (see Table 15). The only category listed above that they did not report as frequently was the burning of fodder — only reported by 45 percent of those interviewed.

The following comments from people who had fled many different areas of Hararghe illustrate a wide range of shared experiences.

Village Attacked/Bombed by the Dergue

The Amhara came from town to attack our village.

Cows and even baboons in the forest were killed by the bombs two years ago.

Our village was bombed this year [1986] because people refused to work on the new village site.

Table 15

Human Rights Violations Against Villages and Families

Human Rights Violations	Early Arrivals		Late Arrivals		Total	
	Village (%)	Family (%)	Village (%)	Family (%)	Village (%)	Family (%)
Village attacked by Dergue	N.A.	90	N.A.	90.0	N.A.	
People killed	85	65	75	55	80.0	60.0
Animals stolen	85	65	75	60	80.0	62.5
Conscription	90	75	100	90	95.0	82.5
Crops stolen	85	70	85	85	85.0	77.5
Farm or household equipment stolen	85	70	80	80	82.5	75.0
People imprisoned	85	70	95	95	90.0	82.5
Women raped	75	30	85	65	80.0	47.5
People beaten or tortured	85	70	100	90	92.5	80.0
People held for taxes	55	70	50	85	52.5	77.5
Crops burned	70	60	65	50	67.5	55.0
Fodder burned	55	45	55	45	55.0	45.0
Village bombed	60	N.A.	55	N.A.	57.5	N.A.

Because the people refused to work regularly for the peasant association and because the OLF was in the nearby forests, they [the military] bombed our village.

The district political cadre called all the local peasant associations together in the end of January [1986] and proceeded to select and kill 12 people because the villages were accused of supporting the OLF.

Two other times they have killed 20 people in a neighboring woreda.

My cousin was also accused of supporting the OLF and was killed.

Troops sometimes destroy our villages and then leave, but most of the time when they try to come into our area even to take taxes, etc., they can't.

The OLF is not really in our area, it is a little farther away. But the government comes to the village, burns houses, imprisons people and even kills some.

Three years ago the militia asked for contributions. We refused so they bombed the village and killed some livestock.

Three years ago we were bombed because we were suspected of supporting the OLF. Before that we were bombed because we were suspected of supporting the Somalis.

People Killed

The military attacks at planting time. Last year they killed many people in our village.

The militia suspected one man in our village of supporting the OLF so they locked him in his house and burned him alive.

The holes we dig to store our sorghum in, they [government officials] fill with dead bodies. In 1984, 50 people were killed like this in my village. They were accused of helping the OLF.

They also dig up the sorghum and steal it.

My brother went to Somalia and then returned. For that he was killed.

The soldiers tie people's hands behind their back and shoot them, both men and women.

Those who fled from the village after us said that there were reprisal killings in the village because so many had left.

The Dergue accused us of supporting the OLF. Last year a cousin of mine and another man were put in a house and burned. It was an example for us. We lived about 6 km from the OLF.

In April 1985, 130 in my area were killed by the government and 700 were imprisoned. They were accused of supporting the OLF.

Animals Stolen by Government Representatives

I have no guns so I cannot protect my animals from the army.

The militia came about once a month. They always take an animal. Giving money wasn't enough.

The Amharas hear the OLF is in the village in one day and they come and take livestock the next.

Conscription into Army and Militia

Twenty-two were taken for the militia in two years from my village [Haramaya/Alemaya].

In my village it costs E$100 [US$50] to keep someone from being conscripted.

I paid the chairman of the peasant association E$1,000 [US$500] to make sure my son wouldn't be taken for the militia. He took the money and took my son anyway.

My father paid the chairman of the peasant association E$3,000 [US$2,500] to keep three of my brothers from being drafted. Still they took them.

In 1985 they [government officials] took my son for the militia, so I went to the chairman to give him money so that my son wouldn't be taken. He took E$5,000 [US$2,500] and then the army shot him in front of the village. We all had to watch the execution. The military shot him.

My uncle paid the chairman E$500 [US$250] to keep my cousin out of the militia, but my father didn't have any money so my brother had to go.

Crops Stolen by the Militia

They [government officials] have taken our crops—they have dug it up [from where we store it] and have taken it for the military.

The government comes sometimes and refuses to allow merchants to purchase coffee. Twice the government has stolen my coffee. In 1982, for example, they stole 10 sacks. The militia and the peasant association chairman took it.

The militia always comes during April when we dig up our grain to get seed to plant. They come and steal it.

We give one quintal of whatever we have [harvested crops] when they ask. We also give food, goats, honey and work their [the militia's] land.

Equipment Stolen by the Militia or Peasant Association Officials

The militia stole my plow in 1985. They sold it so that they could buy alcohol.

The militia steal our household utensils and plows and sell them to buy clothes and drink.

The militia stole my cooking utensils, everything made of leather and farming equipment, an ox and a plow.

They [the militia] would take farming equipment, cups, kettles — anything for the kitchen, leather and lumber.

People Imprisoned by Local Officials

This year [1986] my brother was put in prison because he hadn't paid his land tax. All his livestock were registered so he couldn't sell any of them to pay the tax. He is still in prison.

My son was put in prison this year because he refused to tear down our homes to create the new village.

I have been in prison five times. The last time was for two months when I told the militia not to attack our women. Finally I paid E$80 [US$40] and was released.

In 1983 I was put in prison for one year for not working enough on the peasant association. Finally I paid E$1,500 [US$750] to get out.

My husband told the militia not to attack the women. My family sold livestock and paid E$1,000 [US$50] to get him out of prison.

My husband was in prison in Harar. We paid E$7,000 [US$3,500] to get him released.

During the beginning of villagization I was sick and didn't work so they put me in prison for three months.

My husband didn't work on the new village site so they put him in prison. We had to pay E$400 [US$200] to get him out.

I was put in prison for eight months for refusing to do communal work. They also accused me of being with [supporting] the Somali government. My wife sold two ox and 15 cows to get me out. In all she paid E$9,000 [US$4,500].

Women Raped by the Militia

The militia told the men to go to someplace and the women to another. No Moslem men were allowed to be with their wives. Then five militia took each woman.

The militia are Oromos, but not Moslems. They're from Wollo and Wollega.

When my wife's sister was raped she hid in the forests. We were split up. I don't know where she is.

Women are raped by the militia when they go to the forest to get wood.

I saw my cousin raped, but I was a woman. What could I do?

The militia are told to attack the women. Only the old women and the wives of the other militia are left alone.

The militia speak in Amharic when they attack the women. Men who try to protect their women are killed; they're not put in prison.

They sent two militia to sleep with a pregnant lady and she miscarried. The husband was stabbed with a bayonet when he tried to stop them and the peasant association chairman had to take him to the hospital.

Usually five militia go to a house to find women. They do this two times a week. They order the husbands to go sleep in the fields and watch the crops.

The militia tell the men to go to a meeting and then they rape the women.

The militia raped my daughter. That's why I left.

People Beaten/Tortured by Local Officials, Militia or Political Cadre

When my husband demanded to know why militia had attacked his sister, he was beaten.

They [local officials and militia] have captured people and taken them to the peasant association where they dunk them in water, beat them up to get information about the OLF. Once they have the information they kill them.

My husband was arrested and taken to the police station in Funyanbira [Amharic name is Gersum]. He was accused of working on the black market and taking things to Somalia. He was killed in the station.

When I told them [the militia] not to touch the women they arrested me. That was last year. In prison they beat me and now I can't see out of one eye.

In 1985 the militia said I wasn't working enough on the new village site. It was during planting season and I wanted to plant our crop. The militia beat me. I had to sell two oxen to pay for my treatment in the hospital. Later, when I had no food, I received a ration [from CARE].

Because the OLF sometimes comes to our area, the army often comes to the area and beats people up. They break their bones and some even die as a result of the beatings.

I was beaten for refusing to give the militia sorghum.

People or Animals Held by Peasant Association Officials Until Contributions Are Paid

Every time they [local officials] ask for something we have to sell animals and give them money.

Sometimes local militia take all the animals and hold them until there is payment. If we don't pay that day they will kill the fattest animals and eat them.

They [peasant association officials] took our livestock in 1985 and held them until we paid them E$200 [US$100].

Crops and Fodder Burned

The army attacked [1985] while we were threshing our sorghum; they burned it.

For the last two years the militia have taken sorghum and burned corn in the field.

This year [1985] the government stole food from us and burned some of our crops.

The militia came to our village and burned some of my corn and sorghum and took barley that was already harvested.

Peasant Associations

All but one of the refugees interviewed in the random sample were from government-held areas — one individual was from an OLF village — and belonged to peasant associations. Most peasant associations were started in 1976, although some were started after the Ethiopia-Somalia war (see Table 16). The refugees reported that each association comprised an average of nearly 600 families, or about 3,000-4,500 individuals. The number of families, however, varied tremendously from 100 to 2,000. Although there were exceptions, Oromos tended to belong to peasant associations with more members than did Somalis, but Somalis tended to belong to associations that had more land.

Table 16

Year Peasant Association Started

Year Started	% of Peasant Associations Started Each Year
1976	30.0
1977	7.5
1978	5.0
1979	10.0
No PA (OLF area)	2.5
Not allowed to join	2.5
Not asked	42.5

As mentioned earlier, one woman indicated that she was not allowed to join the peasant association in the village where she moved because she had left the old one without permission after her husband had been killed. "I fled Finyambira [Gersum] and went to live with my daughter after my husband was killed by the police. Because I didn't have any authorization to leave I could not join the peasant association at my daughter's." Displaced people in similar positions appear to be tolerated, that is, allowed to live in a peasant association, although they are not eligible to join it or to receive either land or other government assistance or assistance from international relief agencies. It is unclear how many displaced people are able to live as "nonentities" in government-held areas. It is clear, however, that they place an added burden on the families that take them in.

All of the refugees interviewed specifically about peasant associations indicated that they had originally elected the peasant association officials, but that since the late 1970s they had been required to "elect" government-identified individuals. Those interviewed commented on this situation and its implications.

The early officials were elected, but now everyone is appointed. The earlier people are around but they aren't active [in the peasant association] anymore.

Before, all the officials were elected. But all those officials have been tortured and killed, and the new officials are appointed at the district level.

The former peasant association officials were elected. But they are all in prison now. Now the woreda officials appoint the officials.

The chairman is appointed by the government. It "elects" him for us. The chairman leads the government's attacks against the village.

Many of those interviewed indicated that their loss of control over the election of local officials paralleled their lack of support for the peasant association and reflected a general deterioration of their situation. As two men reported:

For four years, yields were good under the new government.... We didn't have to contribute as much [to the government] as our parents. Then things began to deteriorate. Now, we have to contribute as much as 100 kg of each crop to the peasant association. The officials decide who is taken to prison when there is a bad harvest.

The chairman collects cattle and crops. He, himself, we are afraid of because he is like the Amharas. We give him money, plow his land and pay him to attend meetings.

Others echoed this sentiment, indicating the alienation of local leadership from the people it claims to represent. Many of those interviewed stated that the chairman's loyalty is no longer to the village even though in all cases he is from one of the villages in the area. Rather, he is loyal to the state. As one man explained, "The peasant association chairman is the only party member in our village."

In the administrative region of Hararghe, refugees reported, peasant associations often contain different nationalities or peoples. In the past this was not threatening to any particular group because people were able to maintain their close relationships with friends and relatives. In some areas Oromos and Somalis had interacted frequently, even exchanging labor or marrying, but all this was done on their own terms. Villagization is seen as a threat to these separate identities, because it destroys communities as well as the networks and reciprocal relationships that allow families, villages and even regions to endure adversity, whether political, economic or climatic. With the creation of new villages, people and peoples who had carefully regulated contact in the past are now being forced to live and work together. Although the villagization program has demonstrated that the government can create settlements, whether it can create communities remains to be seen. The refugees interviewed indicated that they believed the deliberate mixing of cultures in the new villages was a direct attack on their cultures. As one reported:

There are both Oromo and Somali in our peasant association. Oromos are the majority. They live in the higher areas where they grow coffee and chat.

Somalis live lower down. The new village for our peasant association is built on the Somali land; it is lower, flatter land with a road. This will allow the military to easily come into the area.

Both cultures are mixed up [in the new village], that is the goal.

Nearly 90 percent of those interviewed reported that they were required to perform unpaid labor on the fields of the chairman of the peasant association, the fields of other officials and the militia, and designated plots in or near peasant associations where all produce went to the government.

The chairman of the peasant association had 18 ha. The militia had 40 ha of special land and the youth association had 30 ha of land. We cultivated all this land before our own. We were not paid anything.

The peasant association in my area is using some of the better land to plant coffee for the government. Last year it took 3 ha of my land. Every year we plant 10,000 coffee plants. We plow all the land; then dig holes every 2 m by 4.5 m and add fertilizer and the seedlings. The oldest ones [plants] are bearing fruit. We must hoe between all the trees once per month and we're not allowed to plant other crops between the plants.

They [the peasant association officials] bring people to estimate the harvest [to prevent the residents from stealing it], and others come to help us pick it. We add fertilizer each year.

All in all we work four days per week on the coffee and one day per week on the land of the chairman and militia. We have only two days to grow our own food.

There is no communal plot in my peasant association, but we go to one nearby and work three days each on plowing, planting, weeding and harvesting.

There is a 100-ha state farm near our peasant association. Each of the six near-by peasant associations has to go work on the farm. They grow sorghum and corn there.

In Habro if you have two sons, one must go to work on the government farm six days per week.

Producer's cooperatives in our area expanded gradually. Some of my land was taken so I had some in the producer cooperative and some I could farm for myself. At the end of November 1985, all my land was taken.

I couldn't work on the land properly because I had to work for the government. The government scattered my children so there were fewer to help.

Since last year [1985] the government doesn't allow us to sell charcoal.

We plant wheat and beans on the peasant association plot. And the chairman and militia have chat that we have to cultivate. They make us take our oxen and work on their land. Three days for each [government plot, chairman and militia] we have to give for plowing, planting, weeding and harvesting.

The government is the major cause of production declines. Sometimes we can work our land, but most of the time we work for the [peasant association] officials or dig roads for the government. During the peak agricultural periods we have to work four days per week for the government or the officials.

The Oromos interviewed were required to perform more days of un-compensated labor than the Somalis. This resulted perhaps from the fact that they appear to live in more densely settled areas where social control is easier. Furthermore, Somalis tend to live in regions closer to Somalia, or at least had Somalia as an escape hatch if the burdens the state placed on them were too great.

Of those refugees who indicated that they were required to perform un-paid labor, the least amount reported was 12 days/year (one day/month) for the chairman. The most required labor reported was five days/week on either peasant association plots or nearby state farms and one day/week on the land of the chairman. One individual reported 25 days/month during peak periods of agricultural labor. The most arduous weekly labor re-quirements were reported by people from the western parts of Hararghe Province, in particular the Habro area, where people were required to work on expanding the government's coffee farms.

Some of the refugees interviewed indicated that rather than being re-quired to work on a weekly basis, they were required to contribute a set number of days of labor per each of four agricultural tasks (plowing, plan-ting, weeding, harvesting) during the agricultural season and additional days, as required, throughout the year. The per agricultural task labor re-quirements ranged from one to 19 during each of the farm tasks, for exam-ple, or four to 76 days/year not including other required labor such as road building or maintenance or the building or maintenance of houses or offices for the peasant association or officials.

Refugees reported that in the past 18 months before they escaped to Somalia, they were increasingly organized into small labor gangs, and their work was directed by an overseer.

The government told 10 of us to work together to bring in the harvest.

The government told us to work together in groups of 10.

Only 20 percent of the sample was asked how much land they were able to use in their peasant association. The average amount officially allocated was reported to be 12 ha, which was divided more or less as follows:

Agricultural land   5 ha, often including 1-2 ha of irrigated land
Pasture land   7 ha. In some associations most pasture was in communal grazing areas.

Although the refugees interviewed reported that the amount of land allot-ted to the chairman of their peasant association is not huge, they indicated that the chairmen receive both more and better land than average farmers. The refugees indicated that their chairman received, on average, 18 ha, whereas other farmers received only 12 ha. In addition, they said that as much as 40 ha was cultivated for the militia and 30 ha for the youth associa-tions. Those interviewed also explained that in some areas, small peasant association, militia or youth association plots were scattered throughout the area rather than concentrated in one large field.

Fifteen percent of the refugees interviewed said that communal work groups (usually 10 people) had been instituted in their areas before they left. Such groups helped to construct the new villages and harvest the 1985 crop. Most of those interviewed indicated that uncompensated, required labor had increased during the past few years and that the land they were allowed to use privately had been reduced. One man reported:

> I had 20 ha of land, 15 ha of pasture and dry cultivation and 5 ha of irrigated land. Five hectares of my land has already been taken (1 ha of irrigated land and 4 ha of other land). It was to be cultivated in common (communally) through the chairman for the government ... now the land is all under the control of the government.

A few other refugees said that areas within their peasant association had been taken over by the government and turned into producers' cooperatives. Farmers who formerly had land in the areas were required to join the producers' cooperatives or move to distant regions where they were given inferior land and were isolated from friends and family. According to those interviewed, producers' cooperatives existed within the peasant association; they were not a separate entity.

Other Associations

In addition to the peasant association, refugees indicated that all women must join the women's association and all young people between the ages of 14 or 15 and 30 must join the youth association. Each of these associations has a variety of obligations. Most women's associations meet on Sundays. The frequency of meeting depends on the season and the location, from once a week to once a month, from 9 am to 1 or 2 pm. These meetings are used mainly for political education. In addition, women's associations are required to work when men in the peasant associations do. As one woman put it, "The women's association has to help whenever the peasant association members are working. We cook, carry water and do other things." In addition, each member must pay a monthly fee (see below) and make other contributions in cash and kind.

Youth associations also have either weekly or monthly meetings that focus on political education. All young people in a village, whether single or married, must belong to the association and pay monthly membership fees. In addition, refugees report that members are required to cultivate a 4- to 30-ha plot. None of those interviewed reported what happened to the produce from the youth association plot.

The Literacy Campaign

According to the refugees interviewed, the literacy campaign is run by the local peasant association. In some areas, they said people paid monthly fees (E$10/month, or US$5) whereas in other areas they cultivated a plot, the proceeds of which paid part of the program's costs. One man reported that prisoners were forced to cultivate these plots. "There is a farm for supporting the literacy campaign. Prisoners have to work on this farm. Sometimes the peasant associations are called to work on these farms too."

Another man indicated that the literacy program was not only eroding local language and culture but was also limiting production.

The government had a three-month literacy campaign [for adults] each year. It met every morning from 7 to 9 from May through July. We were forced to go or else we would be punished—one absence cost E$5 [US$2.50]. Only old men and women didn't have to go. They teach in Oromo with Amharic letters.

This further limited the land that we could cultivate.

One refugee interviewed indicated that political education campaigns were now being run by non-Oromos, explaining, "There were too many problems when Oromos did it."

Taxes and "Voluntary" Contributions

The refugees interviewed reported paying seven general types of taxes and contributions in 1985 (see Table 17): All Ethiopia Peasant Association fee; National Land-Use tax; drought contribution; Women's Association fee; Youth Association (for all between the ages of 15 and 30 regardless of marital status) fee; local peasant association fee; and contributions in cash and kind to the chairman of the peasant association, political cadre and militia. One person reported paying a E$10 (US$5) monthly school tax.

Table 17

Average Taxes and Contributions Paid in 1985

Taxes and Contributions	Average E$(US$)	Range E$(US$)
All Ethiopia Peasant Association	12.75 (6.38)	10-30 (5-15)
Land use	37.60 (18.80)	20-80 (10-40)
Drought contribution	151.60 (75.80)	40-2,000 (28-1,000)
Women's Association	3.0/mo (1.50)	1-8/mo (.5-4)
Youth Association	3.17/mo (1.59)	1-7/mo (.5-3.5)
Local peasant association	4.49/mo (2.25)	1-20/mo (.5-10)
Money to chairman/militia/cadres	217.05 (108.53)	30-1,000 (15-500)
Total	546.92 (273.46)	103-3,145 (51.5-1,572.50)

Note: Figures in parentheses are US dollar equivalents; mo = month.

All of those interviewed indicated that taxes and "voluntary" contributions were a heavy financial burden. Indeed, the average figure cited above (E$546.92, or US$273.46) is more than twice the estimated per capita GDP in Ethiopia of US$140 in 1982. Half of the refugees indicated that they had to sell livestock to make these payments. Some of their comments indicate clearly their feelings about such payments.

I have sold five oxen per year to pay my taxes and contributions. I have had cattle die, too, but not that many.

When chat and other crops are cheap, I have to sell animals to pay taxes and contributions.

Every year we sell one ox to buy clothes and to pay taxes.

Three years ago we had 12 cows and 14 goats. I had to sell five cows and 12 goats to pay our contributions. Two cows and two goats died.

In five years I have sold four oxen and two cows to pay taxes and contributions.

Last year I sold an ox and a mule to pay my taxes and contributions.

I sold four cows to pay taxes and contributions. In addition I gave money, goats and other things for the [peasant association] chairman, including things for his house.

The chairman of the peasant association collects taxes and contributions and always adds more for himself. In addition we work on his farm. We also have to work on the land of the militia, build their houses, buy their soap, clothes, shoes, etc.

We give one quintal of whatever we have when they ask. We also give food, goats, honey and work their land.

They [the militia] ask for money a lot. Every time they ask we have to pay.

In addition to the regular taxes and contributions, the refugees reported that they also had to pay taxes to buy or sell certain produce. In 1985, they said the tax to buy a cow was E$20 (US$10). The average tax to sell chat in a public market was reportedly about 30–40 percent of the market price. In addition, the farmers reported that the chat is also taxed in the field each year. Although some chat was taxed, much was not. The farther from a village a farmer was, the more likely he was to sell the chat outside official market channels where it was not taxed. Taxes on vegetables vary. In most cases, people reported that they tried to sell part or all of their crops to merchants or neighbors, even for lower prices, so that they would not have to deal with the government officials or be taxed when selling in the market. One man explained that in his area sellers were taxed before they started to sell. Even if they did not sell any produce, the officials kept the tax.

Villagization

More than 90 percent of all the refugees interviewed reported that villagization had begun in their area before they left. For most the program began in 1985, but in only 25 percent of the cases had the program been completed (see Table 18). In *every* instance where villagization was reported to have begun all animals were registered by government officials. In all but one instance, all crops and personal belongings were registered as well.

The refugees interviewed indicated that, on average, more than seven old villages were moved together into the new villages. Each new village reportedly contained about 300 families. In addition, they said the new villages are, with few exceptions, comprised of populations in existing peas-

Table 18
Villagization Measures Taken 1985-1986

	Early Arrivals (%)	Late Arrivals (%)	Total (%)
Villagization not started	10	5	7.5
Villagization started	90	95	92.5
1985	30	15	22.5
3-4/1985	0	15	7.5
10-11/1985	40	40	40.0
1986	15	0	7.5
Not specified	0	40	20.0
Villagization completed	15	35	25.0
Villagization almost completed	15	15	15.0
Old houses moved	75	65	70.0
Animals registered	90	95	92.5
Animals confiscated	20	50	35.0
Crops registered	90	90	90.0
Crops taken	15	40	27.5
Belongings registered	90	90	90.0

ant associations. In cases where the populations were too large, more than one village was created. The following quotes best describe the villagization process as the escapees saw it.

Building the New Village

All new villages are called "Safaratabia." They will each have a number eventually.

All day we worked; we had to have others work for us so we could harvest our crops. It took one hour to walk to our fields from the new village.

We worked from 8 in the morning until sunset. We had to do this until the site was finished. They [peasant association officials] allowed us to plant some crops, but then the cadres came again and forced us to work on the village. Within two months it was finished. Then it took us one hour to walk to our fields.

Villagization started in our area in April or May of 1985. We were allowed to take time off to plant our crops and then we were forced to continue building the new village.

We had to walk 30 minutes to our fields. We were allowed to harvest our crops, but the government noted the amount produced. We were told we couldn't sell the crops.

If you want to sell anything you have to have a paper, otherwise the government confiscates whatever you want to sell. You can buy a paper from the secretary of the [peasant association]. A paper for a goat costs E$1 [US$.50]; for a cow E$2 [US$1].

I think the government will take our land and crops.

People had three choices. They could stay, join the OLF or go to Somalia. I came here.

We work from the early morning until sunset. Women bring food every day. We worked on the site every day when we weren't harvesting. It took us three months to build 500 houses.

The new village had a central square. There was a peasant association office in the center and a state-run store. The peasant association chairman and the other officials had houses closest to the center.

There was no mosque in the new village.

Our animals were registered in October 1985 just after construction on the new village site had begun. Later the animals and the crops were taken. We left before seeing what else would happen.

We worked early morning until the sun set. Even at night we often worked by lamps. Women worked too. We worked seven days per week.

People in the same peasant association are moved into new villages.

Each house in the new village has a number.

Villagization is a step in making socialism, to take over everything. The villages allow the government to control the movement of the people. There are no fences around the new villages, but the militia will patrol them.

The chairman announced the program. We couldn't say anything. He announced it in September. For three months we had to work on the village every day. We couldn't go anywhere. The members of the youth association harvested and threshed our crops. The government registered them.

Villagization is the Dergue's attempt to control the OLF.

It was a two-hour walk to [cultivate] our old lands. We were told that we could return to [cultivate] them until the new village was finished.

We started our village site some months ago. It will take a year to finish.

Villagization has been undertaken to control the OLF, make it easier to watch the people and form producers' cooperatives.

There will be a school in the new village, but only Amharic will be taught. Oromo culture will be destroyed. If I had said any of this in Ethiopia I would have been killed.

The place where I used to grow coffee was taken over for the new village site. All the land in that area is used for coffee and chat. The chat is cut. They give us coffee to plant there.

In the new site it is easy to control people, see who tries to leave. If a woman goes to market, she must leave her baby behind so she won't try to escape.

Villagization and Harvest

Sometimes they give us permission to work on our crops, but it is not enough time, and the baboons and pigs eat the crops.

While the monkeys, pigs and birds were eating our crops, the officials ordered us to go build a new village.

The women from the family harvested the crop and at night the men would help. The men were forbidden to help harvest; they had to work on the new village.

We women collected the harvest, the men were not allowed to do this. The youth association had to work on the village site and didn't have time to help.

Because the government was taking everything I didn't even bother to dig my [English] potatoes. I just left them.

I left before my harvest. They would have taken it anyway.

Registration of Belongings

All our animals are registered, even chickens. They registered crops, too; the only thing they didn't register was our clothes.

They took all our property, our livestock and our crops. They registered everything and they told us not to work alone. They said, "What you produce we will take."

All animals are registered, but only those with sufficient crops have them registered and taken.

They registered the livestock and then took them away. Then they registered everything in our houses.

They registered our animals in January 1985 and told us we couldn't sell them. They came again in November and registered our animals again. They registered our crops both times. Later, they took our animals before I came [to Somalia].

After threshing our crop, the government registered it and told us we could not sell it. They told us to bury it in the ground and not touch it. The militia was to come back and distribute what was needed.

They [political cadre and militia] first registered [our animals] and then left. Later they came and took my cattle and put them under a government-appointed herder to watch them on our communal grazing area. They also took our crops. They registered our animals and sprayed paint on them so that they couldn't be sold. Later they took them and we left.

They registered our animals, but I sold one to a local farmer anyway.

The government gave us permission to thresh our crop and then they registered it. They registered everything in our house too — pans, bowls, even eggs.

They registered all our animals and crops. They didn't take them, they just told us we couldn't sell them. They even counted our chat bushes and how many clothes we had. Those that came later told me that they have taken the land.

A man in my peasant association was imprisoned when he tried to sell animals after they were registered. They [government] registered coffee bushes, chickens — they counted everything.

Resettlement

Only 5 percent of the refugees interviewed indicated that people had been brought to or taken from their areas as part of resettlement programs. Although many indicated that much land would be taken out of cultivation as a result of the creation of producers' cooperatives, they did not speculate that this land was vacated so that resettlement by outsiders could occur in the region.

Sixty-seven people were moved from the village to Haramaya; 90 people were moved into Umar (near Jijiga). They were Harari [Adare] and Amharic speakers.

As discussed in Part II, villagization in Bale administrative region, which began in 1978, was accompanied by resettlement programs. Observers have speculated that the Bale experiences served as a model for Hararghe. There are striking similarities between the two regions. For example, Bale is inhabited by both Oromo and Somali who are also agriculturalists and pastoralists. Both areas are fertile and considered part of Ethiopia's "bread basket" and actively supported liberation fronts. Large parts of the two area's highlands also are suited to the cultivation of coffee. Bale, too, is Moslem, but in Bale religious persecution did not appear to accompany villagization. Perhaps the government has come to oppose religion increasingly, because, ironically, religious groups across the board have increased their followings under this government.

Clearly government moves to resettle loyal populations, probably Amharic speakers, into the fertile, recently vacated areas of Hararghe must be closely monitored. As a member of an international agency working in the area commented, "It would make a logical one-two push." Such a strategy would allow the government to increase security in the area — individuals who have been resettled are frequently harmed and used for surveillance and special security forces — and speed up the assimilation of peoples who have consistently opted to retain their cultures, languages and religion.

Religious Persecution

Two-thirds of all those interviewed reported that religious persecution had been common in their area. Although not asked to elaborate this point, many offered specific examples of religious persecution. Because respondents were not asked systematically about these incidents, however, the list in Table 19 must be considered partial and only an indicator of the types of religious persecution that occurred rather than a reliable indicator of the frequency of such events.

Some specific observations include:

The government doesn't want Moslems. So the sheiks are accused of agitating villages and are imprisoned. Five were imprisoned in my village.

The new village will not have a mosque; the old ones have been destroyed.

In our village we were forbidden to pray. They took all the sheiks to prison.

I was praying and they said I had another meeting to go to so I couldn't pray. I refused and was taken to jail. I had to pay E$300 [US$150] to get out.

They destroyed our mosques, jailed the sheiks and forced the Koranic students to build roads.

Table 19

Types of Religious Persecution

	Early and Late Arrivals (%)
Mosques destroyed	30.0
Mosque materials desecrated	20.0
Sheiks imprisoned	30.0
Sheiks killed	17.5
Korans burned	10.0
Prayer forbidden	17.5
Koranic schools closed	7.5

The sheiks were imprisoned and some were killed. Forty people in my village were killed while they were praying. My father was a sheik. He escaped to Harar.

They destroyed our mosque and used the tin roof to make a store.

The peasant association chairman came with the militia and started arresting the sheiks and religious leaders and taking them to prison. I asked why they just imprisoned and killed people without trial. The reason, of course, is that the Oromo sheiks are agitating for the Oromo Liberation Front.

After I raised my voice they tried to force me to kill the sheiks but I refused. They took me to prison. There they put a pole under my knees and then tied my arms under the pole. Then they beat me, particularly the bottom of my feet. I couldn't eat for 15 days.

Most refugees in the Tug Wajale camp reported that villagization began with the arrest and imprisonment or even public execution of religious sheiks, such as this man, as the government attempted to eliminate local leadership and potential opponents to the program.   ©J. Clay

Sheiks are imprisoned and people who pray are killed.

Beginning last year many sheiks were killed; others were imprisoned. I'll tell you what happened. They told me that the person who reads the book [the Koran] can't live here [Ethiopia]. Those who pray will be killed.

They killed sheiks and destroyed their houses and the mosques and their Korans. I had another house where I taught Koranic school. Later they came and scattered us. I escaped to Somalia with about 20 of my students. I don't know where my wife and three children are.

This last year I was told to stop teaching [Koranic school]. They destroyed our houses, mosques — they used the tin roofs for latrines — the Koran was torn up and thrown into the latrine. They told us, "If we see this book again we will shoot the person who has it."

Ethnic Persecution

Three-quarters of all the refugees interviewed indicated that there was ethnic persecution in their area. One-quarter said that the government wanted to destroy their culture. These reports came equally from both Oromos and Somalis.

They would kill me for saying, "I'm a Somali," or "I'm an Oromo."

They attacked us because we are Oromo. If I said I was an Oromo I would be hanged. If I said I were an Amhara nothing would happen to me.

They are trying to destroy the culture of the Oromos.

Those who don't speak Amharic are doomed.

There is a problem, Oromos are killed.

Those who know the history of the Oromos [elders] are killed.

The Journey to Somalia

More than 80 percent of those interviewed walked from their homes to Somalia. The entire journey took, on average, 10 days. Fifteen percent went part of the way by car and walked the rest. One person took a train part of the way before walking the rest of the way. Some left their villages in organized groups, others left amid considerable chaos and confusion. Specific descriptions of their escape follow:

I changed my clothes and dressed like a Somali so if we ran into the military they wouldn't think anything about it.

My husband was sick and could not walk well enough to make the journey.

I was split from my wife and a son in the confusion as we left our village.

I escaped from prison where they had put me for not working enough on the new village site. It was night and I came alone. I couldn't go get either of my wives because they might have caught us all. One wife and our children came later.

When I left we were forced to split up. We couldn't all leave the village at the same time.

The Amhara military were in front of us and scattered us. I haven't seen my husband since then.

Even coming here [to Somalia] the military stole three oxen.

The government has all the land and animals now. It doesn't even allow us to give things away before we leave.

I left Ethiopia in May 1985 and went to Borema town. About 1,000 people came together. Most were from my village. The [Ethiopian] government [had] registered all our cattle and three sheiks were killed at that time. That's why we left.

There were 140 in our group. Fifty were captured by the militia. Three men were killed and eight donkeys too. This was five months ago.

More will come. Many stayed behind; we couldn't all leave the village at the same time. Many from our village arrived here yesterday.

My father came earlier. He came with all my uncles a year ago. Two of my brothers were also already in Somalia. One was taken for the militia so he left with the other to escape.

At the beginning we paid what was legally asked. But then they asked [for] contributions and taxes for things we don't get. When we see this we had to leave.

I dressed like a Somali so they wouldn't know I was an Oromo. Everybody does this.

The PA leaders stay behind because they work for the government.

Those interviewed said that people left their homes in groups of 20, on average, and joined others along the way so that by the time they arrived at the border their groups were about twice the size. Some people brought animals with them, usually beasts of burden, but this was more common among the earlier arrivals then the later. As one refugee explained:

We left with 10 other families. On the way we met a lot of other families and traveled together. The local Ethiopian militia stole everything from us on the way.

About half of the people interviewed encountered trouble on the way. Ten percent reported that the Ethiopian military or militia scattered their groups. A slightly smaller percent reported Ethiopians killing members of their group; 12.5 percent reported that Ethiopians captured members of the group. One-quarter reported being robbed — in nearly every instance, by the Ethiopian military or militia. Reports included the following:

I escaped from prison and got my wife and seven children. When we got closer to the border the Ethiopian army attacked and killed my wife and children. Some of them caught me and robbed me.

At the border I was attacked by two men, one spoke Amharic and one Somali. They stole my shirt and the money I had.

Reception in Somalia

The people who had arrived first in the camp had been there, on average, 3.3 months; the later arrivals had been in the camp less than 2 months. Many of the refugees had to be encouraged to discuss their problems in Somalia. One even said, "I would be shot for talking about things like this in Ethiopia." It was often the other occupants of the tent who forced the person being interviewed to mention problems.

The most common complaint was the shortage of rations (see Table 20). Although plenty of food was available at the time of the interviews, the UNHCR was only allowed to give each refugee less than 400 g of all foods daily. The Somali government did not want refugees in Tug Wajale to receive more rations than refugees in other camps. Another complicating factor was that at the time of the interviews, approximately 35 percent (25,000) of all the people receiving rations did not live in the camp. These people were either not refugees, were refugees from other camps or were refugees in Tug Wajale who had more than one ration card each.

Table 20

Problems in Tug Wajale

	Early and Late Arrivals (%)
Insufficient rations	67.5
Lack of cooking equipment	42.5
Lack of ground clothes	42.5
Too many people/families per tent	30.0
Insufficient health care	7.5
Lack of schools for children	2.5

Possibility of Returning

At first, none of the refugees interviewed said that they would go back to Ethiopia. As some of those interviewed explained:

I wouldn't go back even if you gave me gold. You can't trust the Ethiopians; things can change in a few days.

My father sent word [to Somalia] that I should not go back because I would be killed or taken to prison.

I would like to go back, but the government would say I came from Somalia and kill me.

Only when pushed on this point did the refugees say they would return — but only under certain conditions (see Table 21). Thirty-three percent reported that they would return, "When we have freedom from the Amharas"; 15 percent said when there is a change; 7.5 percent said only with a new government. One person said he would return only if forced to by Somalia and the UNHCR. Another man, a 70-year-old Oromo, said, "I am expecting to get a gun and go back." Other specific responses included:

Somali guard at Tug Wajale overseeing refugee registration. ©J. Clay

I will return only if the Amhara leave our country.

I won't go back unless we (Giri Somali) get freedom and the Amharas leave.

Unless I get freedom and the Amharas leave my country I won't go home.

Not until there is freedom; not until the Dergue is overthrown.

If the government changed I would return. Our land is fertile. We have fruit and vegetables. Would anyone want to remain away from such fertile land?

Table 21

Conditions Required to Return to Ethiopia

	Early and Late Arrivals (%)
When there is freedom from the Amharas	37.5
When there is a change	15.0
When there is a new government	7.5
If forced by Somalia and UNHCR	2.5

Some people do move back and forth between Ethiopia and the refugee camp. Men who have established their families in the camp often return to Ethiopia to find other family members and gather or sell some of their property so that they can bring the cash to Somalia. In other cases family members of those interviewed were away from the camp in Somalia collecting firewood, or trying to buy or sell materials that could generate additional income for the rest of the family. As two wives explained:

My husband came with me, but then he returned to our village to try to sell some of our things.

My husband returned to Ethiopia to bring some things here.

None of the people interviewed in Tug Wajale wanted to be in Somalia. Two examples illustrate this point. One man asked, "Who would want to leave our beautiful, fertile land to sit in a tent here?" Another put it more bluntly: "If there wasn't an ocean, I would have walked further."

8 | Villagization in a War Zone: Refugee Reports from Western Wollega

Sandra Steingraber

There is no clinic, health service or schools. But they have built prisons there, and in those prisons they put pepper powder in our eyes so we live in darkness. They just want to concentrate us to destroy our souls.
— Oromo farmer in Yabuus

Ethiopia's Wollega Province is a significant area in several respects. Ecologically it is extremely diverse, ranging from dense bamboo forests to temperate woodlands to open savannas. It is watered by several major tributaries of the Blue Nile River; wild and cultivated coffee grow in great abundance in the highlands. Resource use and land allocation changed dramatically in 1984 when Wollega, together with Illubabor, became one of the major receiving grounds for the more than 800,000 settlers who have been removed from the northern provinces under the current resettlement program. As the western stronghold of the Oromo Liberation Front, Wollega is also a region of active armed opposition to the central government. Since 1982, the OLF has been building guerrilla forces from among the Oromo peasants as well as from among groups of other indigenous peoples in Wollega. (For an eyewitness account of OLF activities in Wollega, see Grilz 1987.)

Villagization in Wollega began in late 1985 as part of the nationwide campaign. At this writing, little information is available on the pace at which it has proceeded there. By January 1986, however, groups of refugees fleeing villagization in Wollega's western districts — Gimbi, Kellem and Asosa — began arriving in ORA's refugee camp in Yabuus, swelling its population (see Appendix F, in Part One). According to the OLF, which operates in all three of these districts, villagization has also produced many internal refugees who are now living in OLF-controlled zones or remote areas inside Wollega.

Interviews in Yabuus

In June 1987, I interviewed 30 of the 5,000 refugees in Yabuus who recently had fled areas of Wollega that were in the process of being villagized. I attempted to locate a few members of each of the large groups of refugees — each representing an entire community — that had fled immediately before they were to be actually transferred to their new village but after they had constructed much of it. Many had witnessed and participated in the

Map 6. Administrative regions of Ethiopia. Shaded area indicates districts where 1987 interviewees escaped villagization.

villagization of neighboring communities as well. In most cases, new villages were formed by merging several communities in the surrounding area.

It is important to emphasize that the areas where all of my respondents lived are OLF recruiting grounds. All respondents reported frequent guerrilla activity in and around their communities and had experienced some form of harassment by government forces suspecting them of aiding the rebels. Conclusions about villagization based on these reports should be considered as specific to these districts. The situation in other areas of Ethiopia — or even in other districts in Wollega where the government more firmly controls the population — may well be different.

Nevertheless, these testimonies tell us much about the nature of villagization in an area of active government opposition and the possible use of this program as a political and military tool. Conclusions reached in this report are tentative and should be thought of as hypotheses for future research, which, given the swift implementation of the villagization program, is urgently needed.

Information from the camp registration book helped me identify potential groups for interviews. I was assisted in locating these groups by ORA staff members and by leaders of the refugee organization in Yabuus (which acts as a liaison between ORA and the refugee population). In most cases, I was directed to the various neighborhoods where these groups had set up living quarters and was introduced to whomever happened to be at home at the time. From among these people, I randomly selected a few to be interviewed. Sometimes I spoke with refugees alone; at other times I interviewed a few together.

The period of interviewing corresponded with an all-camp grain distribution. When no one from a particular group could be found at home, I asked refugee leaders to arrange a time for me to meet with a few members of that group. These respondents usually came later to speak with me at the central compound in the camp. Interviews with seven of the eight women respondents were arranged in this way and took place in the late evening after they had finished their daily chores. I also deliberately sought out interview partners who were known to be particularly knowledgeable about villagization; my respondents included five members of the refugee organization and one man who had been the chairman of his kebele and was in charge of orchestrating the villagization of several communities. In total, I interviewed twenty-six people who identified themselves as Oromo, three who said they were Komo and one Berta.

This method of selecting interview partners was in no way random and is subject to several sources of bias. However, my goal was not to assemble a representative picture of refugees in Yabuus through statistical sampling, as was Bonnie Holcomb's in 1985. Rather, I sought to obtain as much information about villagization in as many different areas of Wollega as possible. I did not notice any qualitative differences in the testimonies of the refugees I chose and those of refugees sent to me (some of whom had been residents of the same villages in Wollega). ORA staff members who had traveled with me from Khartoum provided translation from Oromiffa to English. Secondary translators were recruited during interviews with Komo refugees. All interviews were taped and were checked by an independent translator in the US.

It should be kept in mind that rebel activities in Wollega both cause and channel population movements (Luling 1986). The groups of refugees to which all of my respondents belonged had arrived in Yabuus with the direct assistance of the OLF. Young members of many of the groups had chosen to become fighters and had remained in OLF training camps inside Wollega. Thus, most of my respondents were older men and women with children. The OLF has resettled other groups fleeing villagization within its operational areas. Thus, the experiences of my respondents may not necessarily be representative of the whole population of people who are being villagized in western Wollega.

The refugees I interviewed were about evenly divided between those who had been actual supporters of and sympathizers with the OLF and those who sought OLF assistance only after being continually victimized. Suspicion of aiding the OLF had caused all of my respondents to suffer various forms of harassment at the hands of the government even before villagization.

Reasons for Flight

For most of my respondents, villagization was the immediate and direct cause of their flight. As mentioned previously, these people usually fled once the new village was almost complete but before they were actually to be moved in:

Everybody in Gidami was ordered to be settled in a village along the main road. We were told to destroy our houses and to build new houses used from the materials of our old houses. After everybody built their houses at the new site, I didn't want to move there.

We don't know the reason for why we had to move, but I was suspicious. . . . We finished everything and the night before we were to move in I ran away with the others.

Respondents gave different reasons for not wanting to live in the new villages. Many were convinced they would lose all control over their lives once they were moved.

We decided to move to OLF shelter because we didn't know what was going to happen to us in the new village. We would be completely under control of the Dergue then.

My husband decided it was no use to join the new village because they took all of our animals. He said we would have no independence.

Some said they would rather become refugees than live on food rations in the new village.

We were promised two cups of grain every day. We used to be independent farmers. So how could we live on a ration?

Others were wary of the location or design of the new village.

All the houses were lined along the left and right of the road. This allowed them better control of us and allows them to take our boys to war more easily.

The government built a road for the SPLA through our area. The new village was being built between two roads, one of which served the SPLA and the other the Ethiopian government.

One feared that living in the new villages would allow the government to enforce even higher taxation.

We discussed this among ourselves and decided that someday we would not be able to pay [the taxes] and they would probably shoot us.

Another said he finally decided that "if I am going to lose all my property anyway, I might as well move into an OLF-controlled area." Another recalled that "they told us we would be moved to Wollo after six months in the new village and this frightened us into leaving."

An act of terror committed against their community by the government was identified as the direct cause of flight by the remainder of my respondents. This occurred in four of the 12 villages from which my respondents came and which were slated for or in the beginning stages of villagization.

Respondents cited the following violations in Asosa district.

When we came back from the forest, our wives were in prison and we were accused of working with the rebels. They put us all in a big ditch as a prison and many died there. Many are still there. Then we fled and came here [four months ago]. (Komo village)

The Dergue army burned down 16 houses, shot people and raided corn and coffee harvests. We were on the edge of the village, so we were sometimes accused of feeding and cooperating with the rebels. . . . The decision to leave [three months ago] came after we witnessed the shootings.

The following incidents were reported in Kellem district.

My village borders on the forest where the OLF operates. Because of this, government forces came and killed people by bullets and bayonets and burned the village. First they came and searched and then they came and burned everything down and everyone left in a state of panic. We found OLF and asked for shelter [eight months ago].

They shot 18 people in front of our houses and took the corpses apart with their guns. Some people were running away when they were shot. Everyone ran off and became dispersed in both the highlands and the lowlands. Others took their children and ran.

My own house was looted and the 18 people who were killed were my neighbors. The Dergue people who were armed searched and looted each house. Before they got to my house, I collected my children and ran and hid into a maize field. After seeing that my own house had been searched and burned, I ran into the forest. After two days in the forest, an OLF unit came into the area and took us along. The whole village left — everybody who could run away.

Some of the 18 people who were shot didn't even want to run away and were just trying to explain that they were peaceful people and had paid their taxes regularly and had executed all the duties they had been asked to do. But no one listened to them. They were just shot and their bodies torn apart and their houses looted. The Dergue accused us of cooperating with the rebels and feeding them, but the whole village never failed in paying taxes.

Once we were in the forest, we even still hoped to go back to our village and rebuild it, but they raided everything. . . . Our cattle were slaughtered in the field and some just shot and left to die — just like the men. We never hoped to get this life. After seeing people dying and being tortured inhumanly, we ran away hoping to save our lives for one more day [seven months ago].

In a fifth village, also in Kellem, some 90 persons were arrested together and imprisoned for six or seven months on charges of OLF collaboration. The order to villagize came soon after their release. I interviewed two men separately who were arrested in this sweep. The testimony of one, who claimed he was tortured by Wollo militia, is included in the following section of this report. Following is the account of the other.

I was in prison for six months. They asked us if we saw OLF fighters and we said we didn't. They asked us if we saw shiftas, which to us means people who destroy houses and burn things. Of course, we had seen the people fighting for us, but they didn't do any of these things, so we told the government we didn't see any shiftas! Then they accused us of feeding OLF. We can't even feed our hens, how can we feed an army?

In the prison, they tied my feet and hanged me upside down and beat me and put me in a container and beat the soles of my feet. About 90 people were arrested at the same time as me and tortured. Some of their wounds became infected. Our families were dispersed when we came out of the prison and our land ruined.

We tried to collect our families and clear the land again, but then we were ordered to build the new village.

Life Before Villagization

Most of my respondents described villagization as only the last in a series of repressive measures which they believed were designed to weaken their resistance to government control. They referred to villagization as "the final blow," also emphasizing that other practices and policies enacted before the villagization decree had been making life in their communities increasingly intolerable.

When male respondents were asked to compare their lives with those of their fathers, all said that their fathers had enjoyed a higher quality of life. In explaining the reasons for their current hardships, respondents mentioned the following factors in various combinations: prohibitively high taxes and contributions, military conscription, resettlement of highland farmers onto their lands, harassment by Dergue or SPLA forces and frequent imprisonment.

Taxes and other compulsory payments to the state were mentioned almost universally as a cause of impoverishment and decreased agricultural productivity in pre-villagized communities. Like Holcomb's respondents in

Not-yet-villagized community in Gimbi district, Wollega.

1985, these refugees could itemize many kinds of taxes that had been levied in recent years and said that both the diversity and the amount demanded increased annually. (Perhaps the most creative addition to Holcomb's list of 17 types of taxes is the "uniform tax": women and men in one village in Begi are required to contribute 15 and 50 birr, respectively, for the uniforms of the militia.) Rates of taxation do not seem to be standard throughout the districts. In Gidami area, taxes increased threefold over a period of six years; in Jarso, taxes since the revolution increased from 3 birr to 100 birr per person; in a village in Begi, taxes rose from 25 birr to 40. All respondents emphasized that taxes were not adjusted to family income, were levied capriciously and had to be paid on demand. People who failed to pay were imprisoned.

Taxes and contributions contributed to hunger in these communities in at least two ways. First, residents were forced to sell livestock, honey and surplus grain to meet their payments. Second, many were forced to find outside employment in order to raise cash, causing declines in agricultural productivity.

> We experienced hunger in the last six years because of high taxation. We had to sell our crops and food surpluses and find paid labor. There was no hunger before this.

> We sold our clothes and the doors of our houses to pay taxes. Then they asked us for oxen as a call to the motherland.

> Before this villagization we had many problems — constant contributions. I

served other people to make money to pay taxes. I had nothing to eat at that time. They took away all that I had earned and threatened me with imprisonment.

Last year my husband sold the entire coffee harvest to pay our taxes . . . so our money for buying food and clothes ran out. I distilled arake to be able to buy the clothes I am wearing now.

We used to store our teff to sell at higher prices. But now in order to meet our tax payments, we have to sell it at a lower price.

Those respondents living in villages in Asosa district had been most directly affected by the resettlement program. I was interested specifically in the role of the settlers as militia (discussed below and in the next section of this report); I did not ask systematic questions of my respondents about the various obligations of the indigenous people to support the settlers, as did Holcomb in 1985. However, their testimonies indicate that at least in some areas, direct contributions of cash and household goods from local villagers to the resettlements are still being demanded. Following is the account of one woman who left Asosa 13 months ago.

The women's contribution alone was four cups of maize and six cups of teff. Also, 7 birr from each family member and 70 birr by each household to buy utensils for the settlers. Also, one day there would be a call for plates and another day for containers and it goes on like this — never ending. . . . We hear from those remaining that they are still contributing.

Many of Holcomb's respondents in Yabuus reported that they were required to clear land and build houses in the settlement sites, labors also mentioned by many of my respondents. In some areas, respondents reported that they had cleared forest and constructed hundreds of houses but, as of the time they left, no resettlers had arrived. Men who had to devote most of their time to this work said that wild animals devoured the crops on their untended fields.

As in 1985, imprisonment was cited by many as a cause of impoverishment.

We were accused of feeding the rebels, forced to join cooperatives . . . and also put in prison. Even if we were late for a meeting, the whole family was put in prison. We are from the lowland areas, so a lot of wild animals ate our crops while we were sitting in prison. . . . And if we try to tell them our problems — that we don't have any money — we will just get beaten and sent to prison. . . . In the prison, my husband had to lie in the dust, both day and night, and was never given food. We didn't even have any food to bring him.

Harassment and intimidation campaigns by army and militia groups have already been mentioned, but it should be emphasized that, apart from violating civil rights, these actions also have undercut local economies and destroyed resources in these communities. Women, who traditionally do much of the marketing, reported they were afraid to walk alone for fear of sexual assault; men were afraid to leave their homes to travel to trading posts. Looting of houses, raiding of granaries and impoundment of draught animals were frequent occurrences in the villages of my respondents.

Respondents from two villages in Begi reported raidings and rapings by SPLA troops as well. Women whose husbands joined the OLF — or were inexplicably absent from their villages — often suffered great losses.

In September 1986 my husband left for Sudan in order to earn money to pay taxes. The peasant association said that he joined the rebels and, because of this, they would build a house for me and control me and that I would remarry. They built the house but I refused to move there, and then they accused me of planning to join the rebels. . . . They checked on me even in the middle of the night, encircled my house at one a.m. to check for rebels. . . . One day my house and all my grain stores were burned down and I lost everything. . . .

It is common for them to remarry a wife when the husband is gone and build her a house in the center of the village.

The Dergue also raped women, but we are ashamed of talking about this.

Implementation of Villagization

The villages about which I have information were villagized in slightly different ways. In almost all cases, however, villagization involved (1) the construction of houses along two sides of a road, (2) the presence of armed soldiers, (3) the collectivization of agriculture and (4) strictly enforced construction deadlines.

Kellem

The Gidami subdistrict has now been almost entirely villagized, according to respondents. In one Gidami village the order to begin villagization was given soon before the harvest last year, with a completion deadline of four months. Fields and granaries were guarded by Amharic-speaking militia believed to be Wollo settlers; villagers from neighboring kebeles were brought in to harvest crops that were subsequently transported away. One respondent said he was told that everyone would now be "farming together in a new place"; another reported hearing that they would farm in some place away from the village. Others said they did not know how they would be expected to farm after villagization; they were sure they would never be allowed to return to their old fields.

The new village site was located along a road near a military base that for some was a three-hour walk from their old farm sites and for others an hour and a half. Respondents thought that the village was planned for about 600 people. Families were required to pay 50 birr for designated plots of land on which they were to build. These plots were described variously as "very small" and "not big enough to build a house on." (One respondent estimated the size of his plot at 20 by 20 m; another estimated his at 40 sq. cubits.) At the beginning of the villagization project, people with houses in good condition transported materials from old houses to build new houses, and poorer residents cut new materials from the surrounding forests. As the completion deadline neared, however, transporting materials became too time-consuming, so "we all just cut the trees from the surrounding forest." In principle, the houses could be of any design the builder preferred; in reality, however, the time limit allowed only for *en masse* construction with inferior materials.

Builders labored under the eyes of the militia and party representatives from Gidami. In January 1987, after constructing 100 huts at the new site, 90 residents of this village chose to flee together. They decided to come to Sudan after meeting Komo people in the forest who told them about the Oromo community in Yabuus. (One of my respondents from this village fled alone a few months later.)

I spoke with three Oromo farmers from a village in the Gaukebe district of Kellem who were in a group of 190 villagers that had fled in November 1986. In their village, animals had already been registered and collectivized before the villagization decree:

> They had told us that our cattle were not our own, nor the calves — everything belonged to the government. We had to give up some of our harvest too. We could sell our cattle only with permission and you have to explain why you wanted to sell them.

Because villagization was implemented shortly before the harvest, villagers were convinced that they would not be allowed to return to their fields. Respondents said they had seen neighboring villages become completely collectivized after villagization.

> We saw people in other new villages suffering. These people had to come every day for rations. And we saw this. These people would have nothing to eat for one day and then they would give out rations. If a woman gave birth, they wouldn't give her a ration until she started work again. If a man was late for work or goes to visit his relatives, he won't get his ration. . . .
>
> The ration was one cup of maize or wheat per person which came from the cooperative farm. There was no teff. The cooperative farm grew teff and sorghum but this was transported away.

The process of dismantling and reconstructing houses, similar to that described previously, was carried out under the eyes of both army and militia forces. The new village site was about a two-hour walk from the old one. The haste in which houses had to be dismantled created great clouds of dust, causing many people to become sick. However, even sick people were forced to work and were fined 25 birr for being absent.

Other respondents from Gaukebe reported that men were forced to participate in the dismantling and reconstruction of houses for the villagization of neighboring communities. One man said the work site was a four-hour walk from his own house; his absence left his crops to the mercy of wild animals. One woman, who daily carried food to her husband who worked on a villagization project in another town, said that houses were dismantled suddenly, often without warning. Some houses were pulled down even while women inside were giving birth; the women were forced out before they could even wash themselves. This woman also reported that because of the subsequent smoke and dust, many people became sick and vomited blood. She said that some people died from this labor, including men from her own village.

Gimbi

I spoke with five Oromo refugees from two villages, both in Jarso subdistrict of Gimbi. Four respondents were part of a group of 150 people who fled together at the end of February 1987 immediately before being villagized. They said their group represented about one-quarter of the total village population.

As in Gidami, villagers in Gimbi were told they would farm and raise livestock cooperatively after the move to the new village. Respondents said after they visited the new sites selected for cattle grazing and for the cooperative farm in order to assess their quality, they decided that the land was not fertile. They said this land was being farmed at the time by some of the people with whom they were to be villagized.

These respondents also stressed that the imposed deadline forced them to construct very shoddy dwellings: "Don't even call them houses — that is not the word for them. They were temporary." Unlike those from Gidami and Gaukebe, these respondents said they constructed their living quarters mostly from virgin materials collected from a river area and a nearby forest. They were quite insulted at the idea of living in them — their old houses, they said, were made of cement and had tin roofs. Space provided for the new houses was very small, and plots were arranged in two rows on either side of a feeder road. They estimated that the new village would consist of 1,000 houses and said they already had finished about 350 when they chose to flee.

District administrators, cadres and officials from the Ministry of Agriculture were present during construction; militia served as overseers. Anyone who missed a day's work was fined 80 birr. One respondent said that a friend of his had hanged himself because he was unable to pay the fine.

Asosa

All of my respondents from Asosa originally came from various villages in the subdistrict of Begi. With the exception of one village, collectivization of livestock and agriculture began before the actual villagization work. Some respondents reported they were also placed on rations.

They registered the hens and goats before they registered the people. And they said these would now belong to the cooperative. This announcement came right before we were to be moved. All the fields remained behind.

Before this [construction of the new village], we were dispossessed of our coffee plantations and our fields and our peace. But the cooperative farm was not successful. Also the OLF destroyed it.

We were promised private plots of land after villagization, but we heard later on that the government had already burned down our coffee plantations.

They took away our goats and separated our chickens. They took *everything from us. Later on we were told to put the harvest and fruits in one place and everyone was given a ration of 17 kg every month.*

Collective farming started in the last dry season [beginning of 1986]. They told us to forget our old fields, that the rebels would attack us. This was short-ly before the harvest. They told us to store everything in one place and gave us a ration of corn and sorghum. If a family has three children they received 10 cups of grain for two days for the whole family. Many people died of hunger. This never happened before.

[The animals] were registered for the cooperative. This happened just before villagization. The fields we once had were to be included in the new farm.

In the one village in which farms and animals were not seized before villagization actually began, women were told to harvest the crops while the men constructed houses.

The houses of the new villages, in all cases, were situated along either side of a road and were constructed out of the materials from the old houses, in the manner previously described. In one village, residents were ordered specifically not to cut down trees for construction. When residents com-plained, saying that the materials of the houses were too old to build the new houses and that their children would be eaten by animals if they destroyed the old houses before building the new ones, officials responded, "there is no solution for that." Female respondents were quick to point out that all houses were the same size no matter how many wives or children the family had.

One respondent said that no time limit was set for completion in her village, but that they were expected to spend four days of the week working on the new village and two days in the fields. In this particular village, as in some others mentioned previously, the period of construction corresponded with the harvest of wheat.

In one strange variation, a village of Komo people were also put to work constructing underground bunkers for the Ethiopian army.

Then they [Dergue] told us to dig holes into the earth and put down big pieces of wood and savanna grass on top of that and then earth on top of that, and just to leave a hole for them to come in and out. These were army bunkers.

The Various Raisons d'Etre of Villagization

The various justifications for the villagization program fall into three categories: (1) those packaged for outside consumption, such as for interna-tional agencies and the Western press; (2) those given to the participants of the program, namely the peasants; and (3) those promoted by the engineers of the program, which circulate internally. Jason Clay has compared at length categories 1 and 3 (see Clay, this volume). I would like now to con-sider categories 1 and 2 and compare both of these to what my respondents think is the real rationale for villagization.

One obvious item on any possible political agenda for villagization in a war zone is the isolation of the peasants from the rebel groups that depend on them for support. Such a rationale was admitted openly to several of my respondents, sometimes in the form of a threat ("Anyone who does not want to move into the new village only desires to feed the rebels"), sometimes in the form of a reassurance ("Living in the new village will protect you from rebel attacks").

Most of my respondents were given no official explanation for why they had to move. I presented them each with a version of category 1 by asking them the following question.

In my country we hear that the reason for villagization in Ethiopia is to bring scattered people together to provide them with better social services, like clinics and clean water. Is this what you were told also, and did you see any evidence that this is true?

The following represents a selection of their responses.

Look, this government makes every individual pay the same high taxes regardless of income. . . . We have seen people shot and imprisoned without charge. Do you think such a government is trying to improve the lives of the people? There is no development in these new villages. They just want us to work under their control. There are no services there. Even the streams have dried up since they started this program.

They just want to make us dependent. Either to make us perish or dependent.

No, nothing like this. People live on rations in the new villages. It is a one-day's walk to get medical treatment. If you can't manage this, you just have to die. They just want to make farmers dependent on the government.

The Dergue forced us to move because it wants to control us.

No, they just want to push us around. There are no services in any of the villages we saw. They don't even have land to grow their food on. Many of those who are villagized kill themselves or run away.

No. We even saw people die of thirst in the new village from last year because they were so far away from water in the village. Water became scarce there because too many people are living on one area.

After people are dispossessed of their property, they are being used as labor to collect the harvest for the government.

People in our area have said they want to finish us off systematically and slowly by making us dependent on them and feeding our children very little ration so they don't grow properly and so we are always hungry.

We have seen other new villages where people have lived for one year. There are no social services there. But they did build a big prison there.

There is no clinic, health service or schools. But they have built prisons there, and in those prisons they put pepper powder into our eyes so we live in darkness. They just want to concentrate us to destroy our souls.

Summary and Conclusions

1. Villagization in the Kellem, Asosa and Gimbi districts of Wollega has been accompanied by collectivization. Respondents were sure they would never be allowed to return to their old fields once they had been transferred

to the new villages. Some said that neighboring communities already villagized were organized as collectives and that the people living there were subsisting on food rations.

2. There was no evidence that new villages would provide social services such as clinics, schools and wells. Most respondents had not heard that provision of such services was the stated purpose of the villagization program.

3. Villagers did not participate in selecting the site for the new village. In all cases, the houses in the new village were constructed in a line on two sides of a road. In most cases, all the doors of the houses faced the road.

4. In principle, houses in the new villages were constructed using the materials from houses dismantled at the old dwelling sites. The new houses were invariably smaller and inferior in quality because (a) the allocated plots of land were very small and (b) the completion deadline for the new village prohibited careful construction. Some respondents built their dwellings entirely out of virgin materials gathered near the new village site because they had no time to dismantle, transport and reassemble their old houses.

5. The implementation of villagization occurred at various points in the planting and harvesting season. Men who were forced to assist in the villagization of neighboring communities reported that their crops suffered as a result.

6. The implementation of villagization was enforced in all cases by armed security forces, which included, in at least some cases, militia groups made up of highland settlers. (The use of settlers as militia is discussed in detail in the next two sections of this report.) Participation in the process of villagization was compulsory, and stiff fines were levied against anyone absent from work at the construction site.

7. Villagization was preceded by acts of terror directed against suspected rebel sympathizers in four of the 12 villages from which my respondents came. These involved executions, search and seizures and mass arrests.

According to the US Department of State, "To date, villagization is not associated with collectivization" (June 1987). This was also the conclusion of a task force from the Swedish International Development Authority (SIDA) that in December 1986 visited new villages in Arsi Province. SIDA also emphasized, however, that the reconstruction of rural society brought about by villagization gives the government the political control needed to establish agricultural collectives and ensure agrarian socialism is achieved (Cohen and Isaksson 1987:7-8).

The testimony of refugees interviewed in Sudan indicates that collectivization in western Wollega is part and parcel of the villagization process — or follows very closely on its heels. The certainty that their land and livestock would be confiscated during villagization was one of the major reasons for flight among my respondents.

State Department officials and SIDA task force members have reported no evidence of active coercion during the process of villagization in areas that are firmly under government control. The SIDA team predicted that the process would meet with more resistance in areas where "cultural ties" to the land were stronger or government control weaker. The testimonies of my respondents make clear that brutal coercion and massive human rights violations are distinguishing features of the villagization campaign in western Wollega. Especially alarming is the fact that public executions and other acts of violence committed by government forces against an unarmed populace preceded the implementation of villagization in four of the 12 villages from which I have information. The Oromo Liberation Front has reported similar atrocities in Hararghe and contends that such actions have been part of a deliberate strategy of intimidation.

> An atmosphere reminiscent of the "Red Terror" period now gripped the rural dwellers. Peasants were completely stunned. The army and other government agents pushed the peasants to comply with the programme before the shock wore off (1986:7).

The imposition of strict construction deadlines, the haste with which the old homesteads were dismantled and the punishments meted out to those absent from work — features reported by all of my respondents — only make sense in light of the government's political and military objectives for the villagization program. Kept in a state of continual fear and panic and forced to comply with a dawn-to-dusk work schedule, the villagers have little time or energy to protest or resist, to contact the opposition forces or even discuss among themselves the implications of what is happening to them. (Ironically, one of the stated purposes of villagization is that it will allow rural dwellers to discuss and solve common problems.) The nightmarish quality of life during the villagization process was emphasized repeatedly by my respondents.

Further research into the role of villagization in areas of active government opposition in Ethiopia is urgently needed, especially as international agencies begin to look toward the new villages as convenient conduits for their development programs. The SIDA team is right to emphasize that the role that villagization plays and the manner in which it is implemented in one particular region should not be extrapolated to other regions. However, any analysis of villagization must be seen in the context of Ethiopia's political and military objectives for that region. It is understandable, and indeed admirable, that those engaged in development work want nothing to do with the bloody military campaigns conducted by the Ethiopian government. Unfortunately, those affected by villagization are not afforded such a luxury.

Appendix A

Notes on Villagization in Ethiopia by Province

Sources on villagization in Ethiopia are scarce. The information included in this appendix has been gleaned mostly from official sources and compiled here so that it can be more easily used as a point of departure by researchers. Much of the information is significant and has implications for future research and development assistance efforts in Ethiopia. The information is organized alphabetically by province. In some cases the information presented is contradictory, possibly the result of typographical errors in the sources cited. There has been no attempt to reconcile even the obvious errors.

Ethiopian head of state Mengistu Haile Mariam announced on Radio Addis Ababa (23 March 1987) that 11,460 new villages had been started (5,116 completed) by 7 February 1987. The villages contained 1,138,265 houses and 1,082,466 heads of families with a total population of 5,725,530, or 15.4 percent of the rural population. Mengistu also stated at that time that the new villages contained 42,304 kitchens and 125,655 latrines.

The 1986/1987 villagization goal for all of Ethiopia was the completion of an additional 782,850 houses in 4,148 new villages. More than 3,000,000 people were to have been moved into new villages during the period (*Ethiopian Herald* 28 February 1987). According to the same article, peasants were faced "with the even more demanding task of clearing forests [and] building access roads" as a part of the villagization program in 1986/1987. Some of the road building is being undertaken as a part of Western-funded food-for-work programs. The remainder is completed with labor, largely uncompensated, that each peasant is required to donate to his peasant association.

Arsi

The villagization program in Arsi (population 1,660,000) intensified at the end of 1985 and early 1986. By February 1986, the government claimed that 100,508 houses in 69 villages in three provinces had been completed. Another 1,009 villages in 839 peasant kebele organizations were under construction (*Ethiopian Herald* 20 February 1986).

By mid-March, 81 percent of the villagization program in Arsi was completed. Between 10 December 1985 and 9 March 1986, 1,009 villages were completed, containing a total of 164,449 houses. Some 810,000 people lived in these houses. In addition, 25,000 animal pens were constructed in the new village sites (*Ethiopian Herald* 18 March 1986).

According to the *Ethiopian Herald*, organizers were told to "ensure that peasant farmers were involved in the scheme while at the same time attending to ploughing the land before the rains are over" (20 February 1986). Such an admission in the official state newspaper raises yet again the issues of voluntary participation and declining production as a result of villagization.

From September 1986 through March 1987, some 91,000 people were moved into 140 new villages (*Ethiopian Herald* 10 April 1987). These villages reportedly contained 19,490 houses, 16 schools, 31 assembly halls, 93 offices and 3,311 grain stores.

Cohen and Isaksson (1987:xi) write:

> The process and effects of the 1985-1986 villagization campaign on the people of Arsi cannot be fully understood unless they are seen in the light of the region's history of conquest, settlement and development.... In brief, the region is marked by a history of constant resettlement. Many of Arsi's peasants are newcomers to the area and lack the deep generational ties to the land that mark the heartland areas of Abyssinia. Importantly the region has always been strongly governed.

Contrary to this report, *most* Arsi peasants are not newcomers to the area, or at least their primarily Oromo ancestors arrived before the Abyssinian conquest that began late in the last century. Peasants in Arsi have, without doubt, been moved around by successive Abyssinian rulers, including the present state. Such moves, however, spawned a number of uprisings and guerrilla movements under previous rulers and even in the late 1970s under the present government. Furthermore, it would be impossible to prove the statement that Arsi residents did not have "deep generational ties" to the land, especially so since none of the research team spoke Oromo and they used local translators whose translations were never independently verified for accuracy. Such statements about ties to the land are tantamount to saying that blacks in South Africa do not have deep ties to the land, or that Jews or Palestinians do not have deep ties to Israel or Palestine.

Mass evictions of Arsi peasant cultivators in the 1960s to make way for mechanized agricultural estates (subsequently turned into state farms by the present government) was funded, in part, by Western development agencies such as the Swedish International Development Agency (SIDA), a principal funder of the Chilalo Agricultural Development Unit (CADU). In 1986, SIDA also funded the Cohen and Isaksson research which made the claim that Arsi peasants had been colonized and moved so many times that they did not have deep ties to the land.

According to a telegram sent from the US Embassy (#2675 on 26 June 1987) to the US Department of State, between December 1985 and April 1987 some 900,000 people had been moved into new villages in Arsi, representing 60 percent of the target population.

Bale

Most villagization in Bale took place from 1979 to 1984. By 1984, official estimates indicate that as many as 650,000 people were living in 300 new villages in Bale. Unofficial reports indicate that as many as 600 villages had been set up in the administrative region.

Villagization, however, has taken place recently in Bale, in particular in the Genale area where state farm pressure on land is high and in Beltu province where, since the Somali invasion, travel has not been allowed except in small military convoys.

According to the US State Department telegram on villagization, the government planned to build more than 12,000 new houses for some 54,000 people in 1987. In addition, 53 offices, 41 meeting halls, 25 storehouses, 7,220 silos, nine kindergartens and 21 schools were also to be constructed.

Expatriates in Bale reported that resettlement sites occupied by people from Wollo were villagized in 1985.

Eritrea
As of early 1988, there were no reports of villagization in Eritrea.

Gamu-Gofu
The government announced that 93 percent of the villagization goal for 1986/1987 had been completed in the six-month period September 1986 to March 1987 (*Ethiopian Herald* 9 April 1987). In Gamo province, 33 villages were completed, containing 6,783 houses and 33,057 people. In Wollayta province, 41,726 people had moved into 10,464 houses that had been built in seven districts.

Addis Zemen claimed that

for the most part, the sites chosen for new villages [in Gamu-Gofu] are close to the existing schools and clinics and the villagers do not have to walk long distances to get the services. . . . all-weather feeder roads are also being built by the farmers (4 September 1987).

Gojjam
By 8 April 1986 the government reported that some 458 villages in all the region's provinces had been completed. These villages contained 30,584 dwellings (*Ethiopian Herald* 25 April 1986).

Gojjam has a population of approximately 3,250,000 people living on 64,000 km² (*Ethiopian Herald* 27 March 1987). Villagization began in 1986 and is scheduled to be completed over a four-year span. The US State Department telegram on villagization reported that by April 1987, 600,000 people (20 percent of all those to be moved) were living in new villages. The new villages contained 41 schools, 12 clinics, 30 silos, six dams and 51 water wells.

The second phase of villagization in Gojjam began in February 1987 and was to end at the beginning of May. The goal was to build 125,571 houses and complete 757 new villages (*Ethiopian Herald* 27 March 1987).

The *Ethiopian Herald* (9 June 1987) reported that 157 new villages had been completed in 55 peasant associations in Metekal province. These villages contained 10,236 houses and 51,180 people. On 27 June, the *Ethiopian Herald* reported that during the first and second round of villagization in Gojjam, 197 new villages had been completed in the four districts of Motta province. These villages contained 122,000 people living in 20,462 houses with straw roofs and 4,557 houses with corrugated metal roofs.

Gondar
The villagization program in Gondar did not begin until 1987. In early

January, the villagization coordinating committee of Gondar approved a plan to create 268 new villages by September and to move 306,282 families into them (*Ethiopian Herald* 10 January 1987). According to the US State Department telegram on villagization there were numerous reports of violent resistance to the program, particularly in Gayint province. Even so, the government's goal was to move 306,182 people (11 percent of all those expected to be moved) into 326 new villages by May.

The *Ethiopian Herald* (25 March 1987) reported that 2,047 new homes had been built by residents of Addis Zemen and Yisag towns and that 1,300 families had moved into them. By the end of May 1987, 39,389 people had been moved into 179 new villages in the provinces of Zemen, Wogera and Gondar Zuria. In the last province alone, 107 new villages had been built in 65 peasant associations. These villages contained 24,740 families and about 123,700 people (*Ethiopian Herald* 28 May 1987). In three districts of Wogera and Zemen provinces an additional 72 villages are to be built in 31 peasant associations. These villages are scheduled to contain 14,649 families with 73,244 people.

The villagization goal for 1987 in Debra Tabor province included the construction of 17,890 new houses in 86 villages located in 34 peasant associations. These villages were to contain 74,945 people (*Ethiopian Herald* 6 March 1987).

By May, the government reported that 328 new villages had been completed in seven provinces.

Hararghe

The latest villagization efforts in Hararghe began in 1984. Speaking before the WPE in September 1985, Mengistu claimed that 375,277 people had been moved into 2,115 new villages. Mengistu explained that what had been learned in Hararghe could be applied easily to all regions.

> The work carried out in the region under the leadership of the region's WPE committee and through the coordination of relevant government and mass organizations, to collectivize 375,277 people in 2,115 new villages is ideal [applause]. The task of establishing villages in Hararghe Region is exemplary not only in its vast work but also in view of the fact that the houses built within a short time were mostly built using material from houses which had fallen down, thereby saving our natural wealth.
>
> On the basis of the experience gained in Hararghe we realize that as long as the collectivization of farmers in villages is carried out in a proper manner the task will not be as complicated as expected. The main issue is to explain clearly to the farmers the benefits of collectivization and get them involved in the planning and implementation process... In the work to be carried out next year and in the coming years in respect of hastening agricultural growth, the collectivization of farmers in villages is essential and hence coordinated efforts are expected from all regions to show full results within a short time (Radio Addis Ababa 5 September 1985).

On 8 March 1986, the *Ethiopian Herald* announced the accomplishments of the four-month long, "second round" villagization campaign. In this campaign 150 new villages were completed in the Gersum district of Hararghe. The villages were reported to contain 19,720 heads of families and 92,213 people.

On 15 April 1986, the *Ethiopian Herald* announced that 707 villages in Habro province of Hararghe region had been completed. Some 50,090 people appear [the text is unfortunately garbled] to be living in 16,222 dwellings. In addition there were 2,197 latrines and 1,200 garbage pits. Some 48 elementary schools, 10 cooperative shops and 10 parks had been constructed in the 707 new villages. The report indicated that "drilling water wells for settlers was well under way."

In November 1986, in a message written to the annual conference of Oromos in the United States, ORA indicated that villagization in Hararghe had begun in July 1984 in the district of Daro Billiqa. The program, ORA reported, began when army units surrounded a village. On the first day 52 peasants who refused to participate were shot and their homes burned. Three days later, 38 people were killed in front of peasants assembled in a nearby village. By the end of the first week 102 people had been killed. For weeks in early 1985 OLF units on the Arsi-Hararghe border reported seeing black smoke which they claimed was from burning peasant homes. The OLF estimated that thousands of homes in Hararghe alone must have been burned.

According to ORA, rumors were spread deliberately by the government to create fear and compliance while the program was pushed ahead. ORA reported that peasant association leaders were given timetables for completion in their area. Dozens were shot for failure to meet their deadlines. Even so, by the end of 1985, 60 percent of the eight Oromo-occupied highland provinces had been villagized.

The ORA statement also reports that the government villagization program in Hararghe often involved

one peasant association in the dismantling and moving of homes in a neighboring one. Those villagized in this manner are subsequently given the chance to avenge themselves by villagizing their neighbors in turn. The state agents of course present this as a new level of solidarity among the masses.

One of the few researchers to investigate the situation in newly villagized areas of the Hararghe highlands wrote:

In the worst cases I encountered, overzealous local officials dictated the entire process in what was perceived by informants to be an arbitrary fashion, and totally ignored the labor requirements of the agricultural cycle when scheduling the move. In these cases, a few days after officials gave the order to move, they reappeared with armed men. Families that had not torn down their houses were ordered at gunpoint to do so. The entire process of disassembling, manually moving house parts to the new village, and reassembling was backed by a show of force. The process was carried out in a matter of weeks. Since it demanded exhausting full-time effort, agricultural labor was impossible. In the worst case, villagization occurred during the sowing season (Anonymous 1987:7 fn11).

Footnote 11 goes on to state that

> In these worst cases, farmers stated that they lost part of their 1985-86 crops due to the time requirements of villagization. This was not the case everywhere, and I had no means to confirm or disconfirm their statements. If they did lose crops, famine relief helped minimize the effects (1987:18).

The report goes on to state that

> In every area visited, people spoke of the great difficulty in bringing about the move, especially those who were already weakened by continuing food scarcity. (Even in the summer of 1986, twice-weekly food distribution was occurring and was greatly needed.) According to informants, in some areas numbers of people died due to weakness and disease. Particularly in areas where the move was abrupt and forced, many people left the peasant associations and either moved in with relatives (temporarily) who had not yet been villagized, or left the area altogether. Rumors that villagization was to be followed by forced collectivization of land and livestock no doubt were partially responsible for people taking their livestock and leaving. Of those who remained, some sold livestock thinking that they would be confiscated during collectivization (1987:8).

According to this author, in Hararghe at least, "it is clear, both from informant statements and from direct observations, that villagization has made agriculture and livestock tending more difficult."

French agricultural researchers, in Kombolcha Awraja since 1983, found that in a sample of six farmers cultivating 17 fields that the average distance to the fields had increased nearly fourfold (Wibaux 1986:11). While their sample was small, it warrants further investigation. Such increases in the distances to plots would adversely affect production.

According to the 1987 US State Department telegram on villagization, by April officials estimate that more than two million people in Hararghe's highlands, or some 98 percent of the targeted population, had been moved. The population affected lived mostly in the predominantly Oromo-occupied highland areas.

Illubabor

Between June 1986 and March 1987, 166 new villages were constructed containing 17,070 houses and 61,888 people, 7 percent of all those to be moved (*Ethiopian Herald* 31 March 1987). In addition, these villages reportedly contained 868 kitchens, 1,592 latrines, 328 cattle pens and 63 garbage pits. House construction was also broken down by province: Buno — 7,328, Sorna Geba — 4,405, Mocha — 3,317 and Gore — 2,025.

The 1987 goals for Illubabor were 347 completed villages, 70 villages under construction and 53,490 families containing 220,200 people, or 25 percent of all those to be moved under the program.

Kefa

On 8 March 1986, the *Ethiopian Herald* announced that 105 new villages were to be constructed in eight districts of Kefa. These villages would hold some 5,432 houses and 14,539 family members. This implies that the average family in these villages contains only 2.7 people, which is highly unlikely. However, Kefa is the recipient of many people being resettled from Wollo and Tigray. Our research in 1985 and 1986 indicates that half of those resettled from the north were not accompanied by any family members, and only 13 percent were resettled with their entire family. The government data on villagization in Kefa indicates that either local families have been forcibly split up or have voluntarily separated in order to avoid the new villages, or that the new villages are really integrated settlements (i.e., new villages containing local villagers as well as people resettled from the north) that the government has misidentified in order to make them more attractive recipients of funds from Western agencies.

Kefa administrative region received that name because it is the primary coffee producing area of the region. Limu province, in particular, ranks first in coffee production. In 1986/1987, for example, Kefu produced 203,021 quintals of coffee for export from the region, 91 percent of its quota (*Ethiopian Herald* 1 July 1987). According to the government's directives on villagization, areas of permanent crop production were supposed to be avoided in the villagization program at this time. In Kefa, however, as in coffee producing areas of Hararghe, villagization has proceeded apace, with new villages and houses in Limu province equaling all other provinces combined.

When the first phase of villagization in Kefa ended in March 1987, 925 new villages had been built which contained 79,834 houses and 370,000 people, some 35 percent of the target population (*Ethiopian Herald* 22 March 1987). House construction, by province, was listed as follows: Limu — 38,869, Jimma — 22,585, Kefa — 10,971, Kulo — 4,475, Gimira — 1,998 and Maji — 853. According to the same report the goal for the second phase of villagization, which will end in early 1988, is 1,560 new villages and 159,753 houses with 814,768 people.

Shoa

The villagization program in Shoa was undertaken throughout the administrative region (*Ethiopian Herald* 18 February 1986). From August 1985 through January 1986, 35,908 dwellings were built and 84,110 peasant families began "receiving services" through the new villages (*Ethiopian Herald* 30 January 1986). In late January a government official claimed that 26,945 homes had been completed and that families had moved into 17,710 of them (*Ethiopian Herald* 28 January 1986). By mid-February 1986, another 3,506 houses for 19,021 people had been completed and 7,000 additional houses were nearing completion. An additional 264 new villages in 143 kebele peasant associations were planned which would contain 78,960 houses.

Two Shoan provinces, Chebo Gurage and Jibat-Mecha, have received considerable attention. By the end of 1985, about one-quarter of the plan to build 349 new villages containing 50,000 houses had been completed (*Ethio-*

pian Herald 7 January 1986). By the end of January 1986, 2,002 houses in the two provinces had been completed while 3,707 were under construction and 6,040 were planned in Jibat-Mecha (Ethiopian Herald 26 January 1986). Jibat-Mecha was to have 342 villages with 24,000 houses.

By March 1986, 380 houses in four new villages had been completed in Kolendatiti district. Four more new villages were planned (Ethiopian Herald 4 March 1986).

Villagization in Shoa is also taking place in a E$50- (US$25-) million fuelwood project jointly funded by the African Development Bank and the World Food Program (Ethiopian Herald 28 January 1986). The fuelwood project, which is designed to extend the present 40,000-ha plantation by another 15,000 ha, includes the establishment of three nurseries to provide 10 million seedlings. According to the Ethiopian Herald, the project includes plans to establish six new peasant villages, presumably to provide labor in the fuelwood plantation and nursery. By late January, two villages with 508 houses had been completed.

The Ethiopian Herald accounts of villagization in Shoa indicated that sites were selected because of their proximity to existing service centers. Furthermore, priority for the villagization program is at the same time being given to parts of the province which had not been adequately cultivated (18 February 1986).

In Shoa, armed WPE cadres were used to convince comrades to enter their new homes. When this failed, 1,120 "agitation teams" with 4,040 members encouraged the peasants to move to their new villages (Ethiopian Herald 30 January 1986).

On 16 February 1986, the Ethiopian Herald announced that 7,074 REYA members from Shoa had built 402 houses in new village sites, "as part of their effort to encourage mass participation in the villagization program." The same article mentioned that REYA youth had built 88 houses in three districts. In another report (4 March 1986) the paper indicated that 1,000 REYA youth, in five teams, helped in villagization; they "dismantled dilapidated peasant houses and prepared ground for new dwelling units." According to the same report, "similar campaigns will be conducted in the future."

The Ethiopian Herald reported that every peasant who is moved to a new village will be "given 3 to 4 hectares of farm land" (1 April 1986), implying that the peasants will not continue to cultivate lands they had farmed previously.

According to the US State Department telegram on villagization, 548,916 people had been moved by September 1986 and 790,620 by April 1987. The goal for September 1987 was 1,519,341 people moved, reduced from an earlier goal of 1,887,341.

The Ethiopian Herald (14 January 1987) announced that 190,944 new homes had been built in 1986 and that the goal for 1987 was the completion of 2,903 villages with 362,380 houses accommodating a total of 1,881,721 people.

Not all of the peasants built their own homes. The *Ethiopian Herald* (14 February 1987) reported that REYA youth associations in 11 provinces in Shoa planned to build 7,242 houses in six days.

On 13 March 1987, the *Ethiopian Herald* reported that villagization was proceeding on schedule in Haikotch-Butajira province with new villages established in 144 peasant associations in 13 districts. Some 12,182 houses had been completed with 26,084 families living in them. The same report noted that over the last eight months, 2,802 new houses had been built in Tegulet-Bulga province. These houses were for 1,471 families with a total of 6,005 people.

Sidamo

Much of Sidamo's population is nomadic and those people, for the time being, are exempt from villagization. Therefore, villagization, to date, has been confined to the northernmost areas.

By 31 May 1986, seven new villages had been completed in Gedeo province. These villages included 1,386 homes. According to government officials, "The villagization scheme is being conducted with good planning in such a way that it does not affect the production period of the peasantry" (*Ethiopian Herald* 31 May 1986).

In 1986, 13,218 homes were constructed in 22 woredas which accommodated 11,579 families or some 52,985 people (*Ethiopian Herald* 21 March 1987). However, the *Herald* (31 March 1987) reported 10 days later that 10,571 houses had been completed and that 1,895 were nearing completion. Some 9,106 families were reportedly living in the houses. The goal for 1987 was reported to be 81,346 homes which would accommodate 70,616 families or 415,227 people.

Tigray

According to the US State Department telegram on villagization, Ethiopian press reports indicated that villagization had begun in two of eight provinces (Enderta and Rayana Azeba) in May 1987.

Wollega

By January 1987, the government announced the completion of 631 villages in 10 districts of Huro-Gudro province (*Ethiopian Herald* 30 January 1987). The same article reported that 12,083 people had been engaged in constructing the villages. There have been no reports of the progress of the program in the entire region.

One report from ORA (1986) indicated that when government agents attempted to villagize the area of Mocha, the entire population fled. Other reports indicate that as many as 5,000 people have fled from Wollega to Sudan as refugees. Even more are thought to be living in the OLF-dominated isolated hills along the border with Sudan.

Wollo

According to eyewitnesses, villagization in Wollo is proceeding slowly, no doubt in part due to the fact that a large number of people who live in relatively accessible areas were taken for resettlement in 1984 and 1985. Reports from the area indicate that most villagization that has taken place has been near the Shoa border or along the primary and some secondary roads, areas where a number of Western agencies are presently working.

Appendix B

Coverage of Ethiopian Military Attacks Against Civilians in Sidamo: The Use of Chemical Weapons Against the Oromo
By Helge Kjollestad
(Reuter, Mogadishu, 27 April 1981)

In a massive assault on Oromo guerrillas, the Ethiopian army, supported by Soviet helicopters and jet fighters, has devastated a whole valley in southern Ethiopia.

Reliable sources informed *Vart Land* that helicopters sprayed their load over the entire valley. They were followed by jet fighters firing rockets throughout the same area. All human life, animals, crops and vegetation were reduced to ashes in the attack.

One of the most fertile areas of the region, this large valley formerly supported a population of 20,000–30,000. While rumors of an imminent attack caused many inhabitants to flee, it is believed that many people remained and were killed.

Experts consulted by *Vart Land* could not decide whether this constituted chemical warfare. There is no doubt, however, that the inflammable chemicals employed were devastatingly effective, and it is scarcely credible that their use can be tolerated by international convention.

After an extensive autumn offensive by the guerrillas, 10 Soviet-made helicopters were stationed in Awasa town. They made several raids before the final assault.

After the attack, Ethiopian Red Cross ambulances came to the area — an empty gesture, observers say, since all people in the valley at the time of the attack had been wiped out.

In the last few months, the guerrillas have moved south from Bale province. The great majority of the population supports the rebels, and this has angered the authorities. Throughout the autumn, there were nightly attacks on villages and brief occupations of roads and villages.

Earlier, the Gata mission — financed by contributions from the readers of *Vart Land* — had to be evacuated. It was in the area of Gata that the government, armed with Russian weapons, attacked the guerrillas. It is said that the government soldiers received a shock when they discovered that the guerrillas possessed modern weapons.

In this region of Ethiopia, the government has forced young men from nearly all the villages to form a militia to oppose the Oromo movement. The latter are fighting for liberation from Amhara rule. With its attack by means of chemicals, the government obviously intended to teach a lesson to both guerrilla and civilian populations.

Chemicals are known to have been used in Afghanistan, but this is the first time that their use in Ethiopia has been reported. Observers believe that the Ethiopian military government and the Russians feel they can safely use their entire military arsenal because so little is known outside Ethiopia of the conflict between the Oromo people and the ruling Amhara (*Vart Land* March 1981, translated from Norwegian).

Firebombs Kill 1,000 in Ethiopia

More than 1,000 civilians are estimated to have been killed when a "wall of flames" was ignited in a phosphorous bomb attack by gunship helicopters on Sidamo province in southern Ethiopia.

Eyewitness reports of the raid filtering out of Addis Ababa and reaching European relief agencies in the last few days say that crops were set afire over several square miles at Gata Waranchar, and civilians were machine-gunned.

The 10 Soviet-built helicopters of the Ethiopian Air Force taking part in the strike are believed to have been piloted by Ethiopians.

The operation was the latest and most drastic in a campaign by the country's military leadership to crush resistance among the Moslem Oromo population of southern Ethiopia following several rebellions.

Western defense experts estimate that Ethiopia has received 220 attack and troop-carrying helicopters from Moscow so far, more than half of them during the last 18 months.

Independent Norwegian witnesses of the Sidamo air raid said that after phosphorous had been dropped, the helicopters opened fire to create high flames. In addition to the deaths, many villagers were injured and left homeless (*St. Paul Pioneer Press*, St. Paul, MN, 12 April 1981, reprinted from the *Daily Telegraph*, London).

Reuter Report

A spokesman for guerrillas fighting in southern Ethiopia today quoted refugees as saying that between 2,000 and 3,000 people were killed or injured last month in three days of air strikes by Ethiopian fighter-bombers.

Norwegian missionaries arriving here said they had been forced to evacuate the area near the South Ethiopian village of Gata Warancha because of Ethiopian attacks.

The spokesman for the Oromo Liberation Front (OLF) said that according to refugees the air attacks were launched from 19 to 21 March after clashes between Ethiopian ground forces and various opposition groups linked with the OLF.

He said two squadrons from the Ethiopian air force used bombs, napalm and other chemicals in the attacks and that most of those killed or injured were women, children or elderly.

The spokesman told reporters that livestock, crops and houses were destroyed, leaving thousands homeless. He said this was the first time the government had used its air power against the Oromo guerrillas.

The OLF spokesman said the Ethiopian forces were now in control of the region which had been deserted by most of the 20,000 residents.

He said refugees fleeing the attacks had begun to arrive in Somalia.

The OLF is one of the least well-known guerrilla groups opposing Ethiopian rule. There have been reports of sporadic fighting in south Ethiopia but the largest secessionist movements are in the East Ogaden region, Eritrea and Tigray in the north.

The Oromos are Ethiopia's largest single ethnic group constituting about 40 percent of the population. They have traditionally resisted domination by the central Amhara tribe.

Appendix C
Regrouping and Rehabilitation:
The Junta's Latest Effort to Extract Money from
International Voluntary Agencies
(reprinted from STORM 2 [September 1982], No. 3:9-12)

The ICVA mission, whilst praising the efforts of the Relief and Rehabilitation Commission, was slightly more critical than the UNDRO mission.

In general, [the ICVA mission] noted irregular deliveries of food, the distance of some shelters from water supplies and the "lack of any organised meaningful or productive activity for the residents, with the exception of literacy classes at some sites." "Living conditions," they commented, "varied from place to place but were generally at a bare minimum compared to similar camps visited by some members of the team in Sahelian countries during the mid-1970s drought."

The ICVA also noticed "tight security dispositions prevailing in some areas of Hararghe, southern Bale and Sidamo." [It] saw settlers who were armed in some areas, but accepted the officials' explanation that this was to protect themselves from shiftas ... wh[o] operate widely in the areas visited. There is no indication as to whether the Mission [was] aware of this state of affairs.

The report does not say whether the Mission [was] able to check out the information given to them about the origins of the people in the various "shelters," who are variously described as Somalis, Borana (Oromo), Oromos and Haweias. [The team] visited one settlement at Harawa, apparently established in 1979, where there are reputed to be 14,227 settlers from Wollo; the RRC said that [it] hoped to expand this settlement to take 35,000 people. These details about the population could only be checked by people with an intimate knowledge of the many languages of the Horn of Africa.

The whole report, however, is deficient in background information and the team seems to have been deliberately misled both about why people in the various areas were displaced in the first instance and the Ethiopian government's real intentions in putting them into "shelters." In these circumstances, any assessment of needs, services or future development programmes must also be deficient. There is obviously a vast difference between a voluntary settlement, where residents are committed to a programme of self-reliance and have a positive attitude to their situation and an enforced settlement, such as we know many of those mentioned in the report to be.

At the same time, the Ethiopian government's intentions, linked with the truth about the original causes of displacement, are crucial to any realistic judgement about the camps themselves. The unfavourable comparison between the camps set up following the Sahelian drought — where the governments concerned were motivated by a desire to save the lives of the local population — and those in Ethiopia, where the government has no interest in saving lives, in fact contains the real clue to the real situation. The lack of meaningful occupation in most of the camps is yet another indication. . . .

The Mission [was] told that the Oromo population in northern Bale [was] scattered "during the war" and returned to find their property destroyed. This area was devastated by the Ethiopian army itself and its Oromo inhabitants driven away from their homes or killed. The RRC failed to tell the Mission which war [it was] talking about (indicating thereby that it was what [it] calls the Somali invasion), but we know that it is the war that the junta are waging against the Oromo people in the area, who are believed to be supporters of the Oromo Liberation Front.

The Mission [was] told that the people in the area were being "re-grouped" and that 470,806 people are being "established" in 256 "agricultural settlements."

No doubt we shall hear a lot more about "re-grouping" in the future and this interpretation of the military junta's policy of herding "unreliable populations" into camps and organising forced labour programmes will become accepted by those Western and other agencies who are unwilling to face the truth behind the junta's claims to be solving poverty through scientific socialism. Evidence from northern Bale indicates that the Oromo population, which is dispersed over a wide area, is being rounded up and taken to settlements, where they are being confined along the same lines as those who were held in "keeps" set up in Zimbabwe during the latter years of the Smith regime.

The junta told the Mission that there were a further 106 settlements, comprising 357,847 people in southern Bale. This means that over three quarters of a million people are being enslaved in Bale alone.

If the Mission pressed for more specific explanations about the nature of the people in the settlements, their origins and the precise details of the war, the report gives no indication of what they thought about such explanations. The vague references to war, as if it were some peculiar natural disaster visited on Ethiopia periodically and, therefore, totally beyond the control of the junta, also seem to have gone unchallenged by the Mission. Statistics were thrown at them like hailstones and, as many referred to past situations, the team could not have had any means of checking them. Again, if the report is a correct interpretation of what [it was] told by the RRC—and there is no reason to believe that it is not—the team could not possibly have checked them. In general the descriptions of the local population are also completely vague.

Almost every programme visited by the Mission was in the disaster area created by the Ethiopian army, supported by 15,000 Cubans, when they launched their offensive against the WSLF [Western Somali Liberation Front] in 1977/78. It is unfortunate that, as a result of the junta's propaganda, many people seem to believe that this offensive was carried out against the forces of the Somali government only; in fact, it was an attack on the Somali-speaking people of Ethiopian Somaliland and the Oromos in the south and southeast as a whole.

Ethiopian government representatives, moreover, seem to indicate that the war is now over. Ethiopian planes and army units still attack Oromo villages throughout the south, burning houses, killing people and livestock and driving the survivors from their homes. Some flee to inaccessible areas in the mountains, where they are safe from the junta's marauding soldiers; others are pursued by the authorities and eventually rounded up and put in the "shelters" where they can be kept under army control. Hence the "tight security dispositions" the ICVA team observed and seem to have interpreted as a response to an unnamed external threat.

Finally, there is no information in the report about the major agricultural settlements proposed in the areas [the team] visited. [It has], therefore, been unable to make any assessment about their practicality or purpose....

In the next few years the Ethiopian Government will step up its demands for assistance to keep people alive in these shelters, settlements and camps. It is important that their true nature be understood before agencies commit themselves. How much of the money they receive and what percentage of relief aid obtained will actually benefit the people concerned is very debatable. It is possible to argue that any aid at all is detrimental to the interests of both local people and settlers. As long as the army is involved, moreover, the pretence that the settlements have any social purpose must be rejected. Whether the junta call their programmes "re-grouping" or "resettlement" is immaterial. The settlements and shelters have been set up as part of the junta's overall plans for controlling populations in areas where there is opposition or suspected opposition to their minority rule from Addis Ababa....

Part Three | Integrated Settlement

9 | Integrated Settlement in Gambella: Armed Uprisings and Government Reprisals

Sandra Steingraber

Over the last two years, the rain forests of Gambella, Illubabor, have become the scene of increasingly violent dramas which eyewitnesses say are the direct result of oppressive conditions, diminishing resources and interethnic conflicts created by integrated settlement schemes.

By 1985, 70,000 highland peasants had been resettled into three large areas of virgin forest in Gambella, the traditional hunting and fishing grounds of the indigenous Anuak people. In the same year, villagization was initiated in Illubabor Province and by March 1987 had affected 7 percent of the rural population (62,000 people); by September 1988, the government plans to have villagized one-quarter of a million peasants — 25 percent of the rural population (US State Department 1987).

The distinction between villagization and resettlement in Gambella has blurred as the local Anuak, who were used as unpaid laborers to construct the resettlement camps, are now being villagized into these same camps as a part of a program of "integrated settlement."[1] Some of their original villages and surrounding gardens have been destroyed to make way for collective agricultural schemes. At the same time, some of the highland settlers have been organized into armed militia and security forces to control the Anuak population and squelch resistance.

231

In 1987, partisans of a newly formed resistance group, the Gambella People's Liberation Movement (GPLM), orchestrated armed attacks in Gambella against the Ethiopian military in general, and the settlement camp infrastructure in specific. Reprisals were severe and included mass arrests of Anuaks suspected of collaboration.

Accounts by 14 refugees of life in two of the Gambella settlement camps and of the retaliations that followed the recent uprisings are presented here.

Map 7. Resettlement and integrated settlement areas from which 1987 interviewees escaped or had firsthand information.

History of the Present Situation

The dense rain forests in the Gambella lowlands of Illubabor Province form what is undoubtedly the largest remaining tract of forest in Ethiopia. This area is also the homeland of the Anuak, a Nilotic people whose villages are distributed along the banks of the many rivers that water the region. Traditionally, the Anuak fish from the rivers, hunt in the surrounding forests and practice a form of shifting horticulture in the alluvial soils along the riverbanks.

By 1979, the Gambella rain forests had become the target of one of the Dergue's early resettlement schemes. In this year, Anuak farmers were violently evicted from their villages when Amhara settlers were brought from Wollo to serve as unpaid workers in a large-scale irrigation project along the Baro River. The clearance of Anuaks away from the rivers coincided with a mass conscription campaign as Ethiopian troops swept through Anuak villages. The uprisings that followed resulted in the deaths of hundreds of Anuaks (Cultural Survival 1981, 1984). Hundreds of other displaced Anuak moved deep into the forests and tried to begin new homesteads. By 1980, some of the survivors who had fled to Sudan as refugees founded the Gambella Liberation Front (GLF was reorganized as the GPLM in 1985) and began attacking units of the Ethiopian army occupying Gambella.

In 1984 – the same year Cultural Survival declared the Anuak an endangered people – the Ethiopian government began resettling into Gambella 70,000 highland peasants who they claimed were victims of drought. The Anuak, who number between 20,000 and 30,000, soon become a minority in their own homelands. The government closed the Anuak's schools and organized Anuak students into work brigades to clear land and build huts for the incoming settlers.

Members of these brigades, as well as settlers who escaped the Gambella camps, began showing up as refugees in Sudan in 1985. In interviews in March 1986, Anuak refugees said that they believed the resettlement program in Gambella was part of a larger government policy to exterminate the Anuak people and seize their lands (Steingraber 1986). Refugee farmers from Tigray described the Gambella settlements from which they had fled as forced labor camps. They said that they had been rounded up for resettlement at gunpoint, were more hungry in Gambella than they had ever been in Tigray and had been largely unsuccessful in producing crops on the muddy and unfamiliar soils in Gambella. (See Steingraber, "Resettlement in 1985–1986," this volume.)

Between March 1986 and June 1987, no escapees from the Gambella settlements arrived in the Damazine refugee camp, according to camp officials there, although hundreds of other settlers arrived after successfully escaping from resettlement camps in Wollega. Oromo Liberation Front (OLF) and Tigrayan People's Liberation Front (TPLF) sources say they believe that increased security and Sudanese People's Liberation Army (SPLA) activity in the Gambella region have now blocked previously used escape routes to

Sudan. A Relief Society of Tigray (REST) task force traveling in the TPLF-controlled areas of Tigray in January 1987 discovered a few Tigray settlers who had successfully escaped from Gambella and returned home by bribing their way through the interior of Ethiopia, but this seemed a rare stroke of luck rather than a common pattern of migration (Yohannes Mebrahtu, REST Germany, pers. comm.).

Thus, the only current sources of information about life in the integrated settlements in Gambella are Anuak refugees in Sudan who have recently escaped. Concerted efforts to villagize Anuak peasants en masse into these settlements seem to have begun in late 1985 and early 1986, although refugee reports indicate that Anuaks from several villages had been relocated into integrated settlements in southern Illubabor previously.

The Flight of Anuaks to Sudan

Since the Anuak people span both sides of the Ethiopia-Sudan border (about 25 percent live in Sudan), it is impossible to estimate their rate of flight from Gambella. Their physical resemblance to the Nilotic Sudanese tribes sympathetic to the SPLA has made their security in Sudan precarious at best and their chances of obtaining official refugee status almost nil. Thus, Anuak refugees fleeing alone or in small groups keep a very low profile in Sudan—many pass themselves off as southern Sudanese and try to obtain employment or educational opportunities.

However, there are indications that the increasingly oppressive conditions in Gambella have accelerated refugee flight in the past year. In March 1986, members of the Anuak community in Khartoum estimated that 40 or 50 Anuaks were living in the city, most in a poor neighborhood on the outskirts. In June 1987, Anuak leaders said they believed that there were now about 200 refugees in Khartoum, with many of the recent arrivals scattered in various neighborhoods.[2] Furthermore, the Oromo Relief Association (ORA) says that in recent months nearly 100 Anuak, including women and children, have arrived in ORA's refugee transit camp inside Wollega. (Regretfully, heavy rains prevented me from traveling to Wollega to interview these internal refugees.) Additionally, OLF sources claim that the current situation in Gambella has swelled the ranks of GPLM whose training camp lies within OLF's operational area. Italian journalist Almerigo Grilz, who interviewed Anuaks in the OLF areas of Wollega in January 1987, reported that villagization is one of the major reasons Anuaks become GPLM partisans.

Interviews with Anuak Refugees

In May and June 1987, I interviewed 14 Anuak refugees living in Khartoum who had fled Gambella within the last 18 months. All were men between the ages of 19 and 25 who had migrated to Khartoum alone or in small groups. Most had been secondary school students at the time of their flight. None had ever been fighters with the GPLM although most were clearly sympathizers. The respondents were introduced to me by two

Anuak refugees who had served as my interpreters in the Damazine refugee camp the previous year. Although these 14 respondents' backgrounds are probably representative of the Anuak refugee community in Khartoum as a whole, these interviews should not be viewed as a random sample nor the variety of their responses as statistically significant. Because most Anuak refugees in Khartoum are living without the protection of refugee identification, many are not willing to risk attracting the attention of the Sudanese police by meeting with foreign nationals. And of course, the Anuaks who did agree to speak with me are those who are on friendly terms with my interpreters, introducing another source of possible bias. All interviews are taped and conducted in English, with certain questions translated into Anuak when, at infrequent points, something wasn't clear.

Reasons for Flight Among Respondents

Seven of the 14 refugees interviewed fled together in one group in January 1986 and identified forced villagization as the direct cause of their flight. One, an engineer with the Ethiopian Air Force who arrived in Sudan in June 1987, fled after witnessing executions and mass arrests of Anuaks in Gambella town. The remainder cited resettlement, villagization and forced conscription as reasons for their flight; conscription was the immediate cause. They noted that military recruitment of secondary school students usually follows a stint of forced labor in the settlement camps. Most believed that military conscription is tantamount to a death sentence for an Anuak. As one explained:

> In Gambella most of the young men are recruited and sent to the war either in the north or east. As they recruit mostly young and middle-aged Anuaks, most are the only breadwinner for the family. While he is away, the family is "theoretically" supposed to get support from the farmer's association, which normally does not even care.
>
> In most cases, since the military took power in 1974, and in particular since 1978, no one went back home from the war except the very few who were sent back because they have lost certain parts of their bodies — eyes, legs or arms — and have become unproductive to the families and society. Since the people who are sent to war have no idea how to fight or did not get enough training in this field, many of them never returned, and nobody cares about them or their family. Furthermore, to send a peasant farmer to fight a guerrilla war without enough training is just to send him to die. What does a farmer know about guerrilla war? Basically, Anuaks depend on subsistence agriculture.

Life in the Settlements

According to the refugees interviewed, settlement camps in Gambella are located in at least three distinct areas (see Map 7). Two settlements, Oala and Perbongo, are situated in the center of Gambella National Park between the Baro and Gilo rivers (Area 1). (Tigray refugees interviewed in Damazine in 1986 had escaped from one of these two sites.) Three camps are located in a heavily forested area along the eastern edge of the national park between the villages of Pinyuda and Abwobo (Area 2). And two camps are located near the Baro River between the villages of Pinykew and Itang, approximately 18 km west of Gambella town (Area 3). Wollo and Tigray settlers began arriving into each of these three areas in 1984. By the end of 1985, Anuak began to be villagized into the five camps in Areas 2 and 3.

My respondents witnessed the formation of the two camps in Area 3, which Anuaks call Pinykew and Abol. Between 1984 and 1985, Anuak villagers living along the river as well as students from the Gambella secondary school were organized into work brigades and forced to cut trees from the forest and erect huts in these settlement sites. Their labors were overseen by militia groups who beat anyone who appeared to not be working hard enough. The refugees interviewed stressed that this period represented the first introduction of hunger into the Anuak community as their crops were lost to wild animals and neglect.

> My mother and father were hungry for two years before this [villagization] because they were being forced to cut grass and trees and had no time to cultivate — even before they were moved. I was never hungry as a young child. And my parents were never hungry before the resettlement program.
>
> We were only hungry since the highland people came because cutting trees and mowing grass leaves no time to cultivate.
>
> They came and took me and my father and mother to the forest to cut the woods. And then we came back from the forest and started digging holes for huts and fixing the wood. You are not allowed to do your own work. We used to cultivate to get our own food near the river.

Anuaks who had been farming land that was slated to become part of the settlement camp of Abol were expelled from the area once the settlers arrived. Thus dispossessed, these farmers fled into forests and began homesteading.

> We were told to go to the forest and leave the place for these new people. If you refuse to go, they will put you in prison. My father and mother are hungry now. They were not hungry before the resettlers came. Our garden became the place for these new people. Now they [mother and father] have gone far from these new people and cut the woods to get food. Their place is not good because it is too new and they don't have the right tools for it — our tools are good for the previous place because it was fertile. But we don't have the good tools for breaking the soil in the forest and digging out the roots.

According to my respondents, Anuaks were evicted from Abol, Pinykew and Opanya, three adjacent villages along the Baro River, in December 1985 and January 1986. One-half of the residents of Nyikwo, a village on the other side of the river, were expelled from their houses by February. Anuaks from these four villages were moved by militia units — some members were highland settlers — into the two settlement camps of Abol and Pinykew.

> Those who were brought from the highlands were mixed with Anuaks by force. They told us, "All of you, you have to move and mix together." They

tried to take us there [to Abol] by force but we refused. I saw their activity. Some of the Anuak were turned into militia to bring the other Anuak to the resettlement areas.

The farmers refused in my village [Pinykew] to go into the resettlement area. The militia hit people with sticks to make them leave. They hit them with sticks and stones and bound their hands. I saw the resettlement camp. I came back from Gambella and saw my father forced to cut trees for the new village and my mother and Anuak women carrying posts under the eyes of the militia. It was a heavy guard. Anuak and Abish people are both in the militia. Most people tried to escape this village. Two people were killed because they were deemed agitators by the Abish militia. I went during the night and escaped to Gambella. I used to come frequently to the resettlement camp to see people being moved.

Anuaks are taken a few at a time to the new village. Those left behind, whose turn had not yet come, are also forced to work there because if they were not forced, they would run away.

In some cases, the militia confiscated the Anuak's gardens along the Baro River and destroyed their crops. In other cases, the crops were left to wither or be consumed by wild animals. All respondents indicated that in no way were villagized Anuaks to be allowed to return to their old fields. In Pinykew, these riverbank lands were transformed into an irrigated state farm and planted in rice. According to one respondent, some of the villagized Anuaks were forced to work as laborers in the scheme; the rice harvests were trucked away to government storage areas.

Most of the Anuaks villagized into the integrated settlements worked with the highland settlers on collective farms which, in both Abol and Pinykew, were planted in sorghum and maize and cultivated with tractors. In addition, brigades of Anuak and highland settlers were put to work clearing forests and constructing police stations, houses for the militia, meeting houses and clinics. One respondent, who had lived for one week in the Pinykew settlement, said that work began at 6 a.m. and continued until 6 p.m. with a two-hour break at noon. Refusal to work brought lashings or imprisonments. Another respondent said he saw one Anuak in the Abol settlement lashed until he died after protesting that he was too tired to work.

In short, the refugees' descriptions of the integrated settlements of Abol and Pinykew are those of forced labor camps. As in the resettlement camps of Wollega, party cadres and armed militia guard the perimeter; anyone attempting escape is imprisoned or shot; all crops produced on the collective fields are transported away and stored while residents receive rations of grain distributed by the cadres.

People lived on rations of wheat and sorghum brought in from relief agencies. I think the wheat was from the EEC [European Economic Community] and Canada. They got 15 kg for 15 days. Also oil and some salt. There was no sugar except for children. The houses were very small and were built in rows with a road in between. The doors all faced the road. In between the huts were spaces for vegetable planting.

The harvest is taken away by lorry. It is forbidden to eat. They send other

Traditional Anuak village alaong the Baro River prior to villagization. Note the extensive corn crop. This area is now being used for capital-intensive sharecropping agriculture, with half of the crop going to the USSR.

©J.F.E. Bloss

food there — wheat. Wheat is strange to Anuaks; we cannot pound it. Anuaks usually eat sorghum and maize.

Two respondents said that fishing in the Baro River is now forbidden for the residents of Pinykew and Abol, except for small children. The official reason for this prohibition is that "there is time only for government work." One respondent said that his mother and father, residents of Pinykew, secretly go to the river to fish anyway, although they risk being beaten if they are caught.

Inside the settlements, relations between highland settlers and Anuak residents are tense. Lack of a common language prevents direct communication. One respondent said that he thought the highland people were treated better by the cadres and received more rations than the Anuaks. In some cases the refugees interviewed had seen Anuak and highland settlers forced to live together in the same hut, although none had witnessed marriages between Anuak and highland settlers. Forced intermarriages were reported in 1986 by a Tigrayan priest who had been resettled to Oala.

Higher levels of resentment are probably found outside the settlements in Anuak communities not yet villagized. Here militia groups of highland settlers have begun to harass the residents and help themselves to local resources.

Our people don't like these highlanders and clash with them. They are brought from a far place and rob the food of the peasants. They rob the mangos planted by the area people. They say, "The government brought us here, so we stay and eat together." But they rob us! If you go to the government and complain, they will say, "Oh, you don't like these people? You want to be alone?" And this will put you in a political case, so you just stay quiet so they don't put you in prison. . . . We ask ourselves, "Why do we have to live with these people?" If you see the situation, it can make you sick.

As in 1986, Anuak refugees interviewed in 1987 perceived that resettlement and villagization in Gambella were part of a larger campaign to exterminate their language and culture and make the Anuak people dependent on the government. Most emphasized the deceit of the programs and the helplessness of the Anuak people in the face of the programs' implementation. As one observed, "First they settled the highland people into the burial grounds of our ancestors. And then they took the land of our ancestors away from us and moved us into the graveyard also." One respondent said he thought the government specifically targeted Anuak areas for resettlement because it knew the Anuak people were powerless to protest the invasion.

When the highland people came, there was a misunderstanding between them and the Anuak since we don't have the same language. The government focused on us because our people know nothing about political ways; they knew they could dominate us. . . . Maybe if we had education and could understand the language and explain to people, we would get our rights and this would not be happening to us. But our fathers and sisters and girls know nothing about what's going on — some of them still walk naked.

Traditional Anuak fishing party on Nile tributary. Anuak now are prohibited from fishing and forced to live away from the rivers upon which their lives depend.
©J.F.E. Bloss

240

1987 Uprisings and Reprisals

The recent resurgence of the armed resistance movement in Gambella and its reorganization as the Gambella People's Liberation Movement are a direct response to the oppressive conditions created by the resettlement and villagization programs. According to OLF sources, GPLM guerrillas have clashed with Dergue forces in Gambella several times over the last six months. A GPLM spokesperson in Khartoum said that the government has been continuously arresting Anuak students and farmers on suspicion of GPLM collaboration.

One of my Anuak respondents was a flight engineer with the Ethiopian Air Force. Flying almost weekly into the town of Gambella for the last 18 months, he had witnessed the reign of terror that followed the GPLM uprisings. He was last in Gambella on 7 June and, on the day of the interview, had been in Sudan for only 11 days, having arrived in Khartoum by plane via Nairobi. According to his testimony, GPLM attacks included the burning of a clinic in the settlement camp of Abol. Following this attack Ethiopian authorities arrested Anuak workers at a German fisheries project near Abol and confiscated their vehicle. As the flight engineer explained:

[In the last one-and-a-half years] I flew from Addis to Gambella nearly every week as part of my job and was staying one or two days. I started seeing increasing problems. Near the end I began seeing that the situation in Gambella is very hard for our people, so I quit the job. I had known there were problems before, but then at the end I began to see every day worse things. . . .

Two months ago [end of April] there was a clash between the government and the people in the area of Gambella. Following this clash, conditions became very, very bad — much worse. Now we haven't any freedom at all in the area. The government captured one of the guys from GPLM during this clash. I arrived one week after the clash and saw that they were arresting many other people also — one of my friends who was with me and other workers in the town. They said, "You are cooperating with GPLM." I saw the conditions for Anuaks had reached the danger point.

The Dergue ground force was sent in. No one could be out in the street after 3 p.m. in Gambella town or they would be killed immediately. The Dergue brought in their militia with them — Wollo people from the settlement camps and those called Kambote Adiya from Shoa. They gave them guns and they were moving through the town of Gambella from 3 p.m. to the early morning, 6 a.m. At that time if they meet you and you are Anuak, you will be killed. They said, "You Anuaks are the ones who disturbed Gambella. Since this is Ethiopia, you will be killed." So there were many people killed at this time — and in very bad ways, ways people should not be killed. For example, sometimes they rope a man's arms behind his back and leave him for 24 hours like this. When they untie him, the man dies because of the blood coming, the circulation.

At the same time, unknown Anuak people and workers in Gambella were put in prison along with many government employees. They said, "You know the case, you are collaborators." They put 85 people in prison, including some peasants. I myself saw one guy shot. He was a student and knew nothing about this. During the daytime he was walking from his school and carrying his books and they shot him. When they reported it, they said he was running from the bush – this was their reason.

When they put these guys in the prison, they torture them very badly. We know this because they were taken to a special house they use for torturing people. And when their wives would go to bring them food, they saw they could not eat or talk and were paralyzed. Of course they were not allowed to talk to them. This torturing place used to be a home but it was made into a torturing place in 1982. It is far from the prison so they bring people there in cars to question them. We know one from GPLM was tortured. Even my friends from Addis saw him and said he was paralyzed. I myself was afraid. You wouldn't say anything or they would put you in prison. . . .

There is an Anuak fisherman working with the church and the car he was given by the Germans was taken by the government. They said, "This is the car used by the GPLM for transport." Even they wanted to put him in prison, but the guy escaped and went to Addis. There are a lot of Anuaks working in the fisheries department with the church. They had a big project planned on the river in Abol, the place where they have now brought the Kombate Adiya people. The Germans gave materials through the church in Gambella. Some of these Anuaks are now arrested.

During the clash between GPLM and the Dergue, GPLM burned the clinic in Abol because they wanted to kill the party cadres who brought the resettled highland people. These cadres are the ones who dominate us. Also the ones from Wollo. . . .

On this most recent trip, I returned to Addis after one day in Gambella, after seeing the situation and how people are living. At night, there was fire on every corner and guns; the people were very much in danger. I felt something and took my decision to leave the place. It was better to leave – I didn't want to see those things; maybe I will become mad. When I saw how my tribe was in danger, I didn't want to be in that place; I wanted to forget. So I took my decision to leave [for Sudan]. . . .

Even when I left [Gambella town], things were leveling off. In the months before that [end of April through May 1987], the beatings were increasing daily. The Anuak people from the villages had to leave the town by the afternoon. This is when the killings would happen. They would be asked, "Where is your ID card?" Most of the time they didn't know the Amharic language, our people. So most of the time they just wouldn't answer, unless there is a student who will translate for them. So they will kill him and say,"Oh, he escaped from the bush," if you ask them why. But even you won't ask this because you are afraid of being put in the prison. So you just stay quiet.

The killing of the student was the only one I saw with my eyes, but in the mornings you would see the bodies in the streets. Sometimes they killed them and took them to the hospital. They don't do this in public because they are afraid the people will refuse to leave the wounded or throw spears. We haven't any guns.

Summary and Conclusions
According to the testimony of these refugees,

1. Within the last year, Anuaks have been evicted from their homes and herded by armed militia into two integrated settlement camps along the Baro River.

2. Anuaks and highland settlers in these camps are organized into work brigades which clear forested land and cultivate collective fields. Produce from these fields is trucked away; residents live on rations of grain, largely wheat, which are trucked in.

3. Anuaks villagized into these settlements are prohibited from fishing in the river.

4. Beatings of residents by camp cadres are routine.

5. Highland settlers, sometimes armed, routinely help themselves to the food supplies of surrounding Anuak villages.

6. Many Anuaks threatened with villagization are fleeing their homes and are trying to homestead in remote areas.

The dovetailing of villagization and resettlement in Gambella to create integrated settlements has introduced hunger into a land of abundance and initiated an escalating spiral of violence, threatening to destroy one of Ethiopia's last remaining virgin forests, as well as the cultural autonomy of its inhabitants.

As more Anuaks are dispossessed of their land and the resource base of Gambella is further diminished, more violent uprisings will occur. The violence will undoubtedly spawn even more preemptive and retaliatory actions on the part of the Dergue as it intensifies its campaign of terror and intimidation. Unless immediate steps are taken to check the forces driving this cycle, the prognosis for the Anuak people can only be regarded as extremely grave. Pressure must be brought by the international community upon the Ethiopian government to end further resettlements in Gambella. Obviously, internationally donated grain is playing a significant role in the creation and maintenance of the new societies brought about by integrated settlement. Those aid agencies that believe they are acting wisely and benignly by refusing to support resettlement *per se* but agreeing to send food aid to settlement camps that have already been established need to rethink the consequences of their actions. Finally, the well-being of Anuak refugees in the Sudan must be safeguarded. (Currently the only organization acting on their behalf is the Sudan Interior Mission, which offers Christian services in the Anuak language every Sunday.) The desire of the Anuak people in Khartoum to organize themselves and speak out against the atrocities they have witnessed will only be realized once their security is guaranteed and the miserable circumstances under which they currently live alleviated.

Notes

1. My respondents often referred to the insertion of local Anuaks into previously established resettlement camps as "villagization." In this report, however, I refer to this type of relocation as "integrated settlement," which is the term used by the Ethiopian government. I use the term "villagization" in its literal sense to refer specifically to the formation of new villages in rural areas. For a review of the distinctions between resettlement and villagization in Ethiopia and other African nations, see J. Cohen and N. Isaksson, "Villagization in the Arsi Region of Ethiopia," International Rural Development Center, Swedish University of Agricultural Sciences, Uppsala, February 1987, *Rural Development Studies* 19, pp. 105-114.

2. Frank Moss, refugee affairs coordinator at the US Embassy in Khartoum, also estimates the population of Anuaks in the city at 200.

Part Four | State Policy and Agriculture

10 | On the Destruction of Peasant Agriculture, Famine Policy and "Development"

Peter Niggli

In January 1986, at the beginning of the dry season, several hundred Tigray refugees arrived in the Sudanese town of Damazine in Blue Nile Province. They had succeeded in escaping from the settlement area of Gambella in Ethiopia's Illubabor Province after a voyage of several weeks. Wollo refugees, who had fled from the resettlement area of Asosa close to the Sudanese border, later joined them. At the end of March 1986, 1,100 people were living in the transit camp at Damazine, supported by the Sudanese commissioner for refugees and the Fellowship for African Relief, a Canadian aid organization. In April, 200 more refugees arrived in Damazine and Sudanese police sources reported that over 1,000 additional refugees were on their way to the Sudan. Beginning in April, the refugees were moved temporarily to refugee camps in eastern Sudan, from where most of them returned to their home country, Tigray, with the help of the Tigray People's Liberation Front (TPLF).

The information presented in the following section is based on a random sample of interviews with refugees in the Damazine camp, conducted in March 1986 by Sandra Steingraber. Of the 54 refugees she interviewed, 38 were from Tigray and 16 from Wollo. Her findings are supplemented by the results of nonrandom intensive interviews collected by the author in April 1986 in Damazine. To provide a comparative source, interviews conducted by the Relief Society of Tigray (REST) in January 1986 in Damazine are also included (REST 1986).

247

Resettlement site in southwestern Ethiopia, 1986. Note the lack of available firewood, and the existence of farms (top right) prior to the creation of the new village.

Flight from the Resettlement Areas in Ethiopia

From January 1985 until April 1986, about 3,800 people from the resettlement areas in southwest Ethiopia reached Sudan. An unknown number have attempted unsuccessfully to escape. The following calculations show the dimension of refugee movement: according to the reports of the refugees questioned during our first series of interviews in the spring of 1985, 70 percent of the escapees reached the Sudan. Almost all of them had fled from the area of Asosa, which is only 80 to 120 km from the Sudanese border. To escape from Gambella is much more dangerous: only 23 percent of the Tigrayan groups who started together in Gambella reached Damazine (REST). If we assume that half of the refugees who arrived in Damazine came from Asosa and half from Gambella, then 2,700 people attempted to escape from Asosa and 8,300 from Gambella; of the total of 11,000 people, 7,000 either gave up in exhaustion, were recaptured, were held in southern Sudan or died.

In addition, many refugees had attempted to flee several times before they finally succeeded. Among the Tigray refugees we interviewed in March 1986, about 30 percent had tried previously to escape before succeeding; among the Wollo refugees, the same was true among only 6 percent. This information supports the refugees' reports that the Tigray resist settlement much more determinedly and actively than the Wollo.

Apart from those refugees visible to outsiders, an unknown number of resettlement victims try to flee back to their home areas within Ethiopia. We only know of individual cases. For example, when the TPLF freed 1,800 prisoners from the provincial prison in Mekelle in Tigray on February 8 1986, several peasants among the prisoners had managed to escape from the resettlement areas back to Tigray. In Tigray, they had been recaptured by police, forced to "confess" and imprisoned without trial (Lyou et al., 1986:12). Such incidents undermine the government's assertions that peasant resettle only on a volunteer basis; in these cases, the peasants made their desire to stay in Tigray absolutely clear.

One of the refugees interviewed had been resettled originally in Asosa, from where he escaped to Gojjam. There he was captured again and returned to Asosa. His second escape brought him to Mekelle, where he was arrested again. This time the resettlement authorities transported him to Gambella. There he joined a group with whom he tried once again to escape. His case indicates that the Ethiopian authorities seem to regard Gambella as a more secure place than Asosa. According to a rule of thumb of the RRC, Ethiopia's Relief and Rehabilitation Commission, the inclination of resettled people to escape dwindles as the distance they have to cover grows larger. We can assume that more people try to return to their home areas within Ethiopia from Asosa than from Gambella. This rule also could explain why fewer people arrive in Sudan from Asosa than from Gambella.

Preventing mass escapes may be the main reason for the authorities' practice of transplanting particularly troublesome groups of settlers to certain areas. This is particularly obvious in the case of the most refractory

Tigrayans. While in the beginning of the resettlement campaign of 1984-1985 many thousands of Tigrayans were moved to Asosa, later on the Tigrayans almost exclusively ended up farther south in Gambella or in Kefa. Out of the 89,716 Tigrayans resettled at the beginning of 1986, 51 percent are settled in Illubabor, 25.2 percent in Kefa and only the remaining 23.8 percent in Wollega. The authorities did not bring any Tigrayans to the resettlement areas of Gojjam, which are the nearest to the region of Tigray. The main group of resettlers in Wollega are the Wollo. Out of the 370,193 Wollo resettled at the beginning of 1986, 59.6 percent are in Wollega and most of the rest are farther south in Illubabor and Kefa. But only 8.1 percent of the Wollo have been pushed into the neighboring region of Gojjam. The authorities seemed to believe that the settlers from Shoa were the most reliable for that region. Out of the 107,075 resettled peasants of Shoa, 51.2 percent have been transported to neighboring Gojjam.[1]

In their escape from the resettlement areas to the safety of Sudan, the refugees face a number of problems. The militia controls the area between the Sudanese border and the resettlements around Asosa. Since December 1985, about 1,000 SPLA (Sudanese People's Liberation Army) guerrillas have camped near Asosa in order to catch and return fleeing settlers for the Ethiopian government. The same situation exists on a much larger scale in Gambella, where SPLA forces are stronger than the Ethiopian army and operate nearer to the Sudanese border. Since the SPLA is dependent on the Ethiopian government for its arms, ammunition and, to some extent, food, it can hardly turn down the Ethiopian government's request. The safest escape routes are through the area between Asosa and Gambella where the OLF (Oromo Liberation Front) operates.

The local peasant associations, composed of Bertha in the resettlement area of Asosa or Anuak in Gambella, also are obliged to catch escapees and hand them over to the authorities. If refugees from Gambella finally reached southern Sudan, they risked being captured and robbed by south Sudanese bandits, who have increased in number during the civil war in Sudan, or by the Anya-Nya II guerrillas, who are hostile to the SPLA. In this no-man's-land in the Upper Nile Province of the Sudan, women and children are kept primarily as work and sex slaves. A 16-year-old woman from Tigray said she felt like she was reborn after escaping this panoply of horror.

One October night in 1985, we fled from the Finyada camp in Gambella. We had received our food rations on this day, which we hoped would last us until we reached the Sudan. We were 450 people. The first three days we did not find water and we suffered terribly. When we found water on the fourth day, we weren't lucky either. Now we had to cross a vast swamp area. For 12 days we had to work our way through this mush which at some places reached up to our breast. Hundreds of mosquitoes swarmed around us. Then we reached dry land. Our ragged clothes dried stiff and were cut to pieces by the sharp, tall grass. About 40 people broke down because of these hardships. We could not help them anymore, and so we had to leave them to die. On the banks of a tributary of the Sobat River we were stopped by some unknown armed men who said that we had reached the Sudan and they would help us to cross the river. For this purpose they collected one birr per person and then disappeared. When our men went ahead across the river, a large group of armed men appeared. They began to seize women and children and drove them away from the river while our men came back screaming and shouting to help us. They attacked the unknown men with bare fists and sticks, but the men shot at them and smashed their rifle butts on their heads and backs. In this turmoil everyone ran away. After some hours we managed to find each other again in this grass jungle. I do not know how many of us had to be left behind, shot dead or wounded. Finally we came to a village which was in the Sudan, as the inhabitants said. After we had given them money, they brought us to the next police station. There we received food and we had to wait for 12 days. Then local guides offered to take us to northern Sudan. Again we paid and walked until we reached a camp where the situation changed abruptly. We were surrounded by armed men and they separated the men from the women and children. My brother said I was his younger male relative and managed to pull me over to the side where the men stood. Then some of the armed men went for women, pulled them into the center of the place and raped them before our eyes. Others grabbed young boys and raped them like the women — I cried for horror. Everyone shouted and cried, our men wrestled with the armed men to free us, then ran away. After several days of running in panic we were again 200 people. We did not know where we were and finally ran into the hands of SPLA guerrillas. They said they would bring us back to Gambella and when we resisted and protested, they told us to shut up. Each word was punished with beatings. The next day we broke out and ran in all directions. The SPLA shot after us but followed us only halfheartedly; finally they gave it up. As we later found out, they did not follow us because we ran in the direction of OLF territory. There we finally found peace, we were supplied with all necessary items and then we were led to freedom into the Sudan.

Famine Aid Opened Tigray for Resettlement

At the time of our interviews in March 1986, the majority of the refugees were male. About 1,200 women and children were caught and captured during their flight, either in Ethiopia or in Sudan. At the end of February the first groups of women and children arrived in Damazine. They had been freed from various armed southern Sudanese groups by OLF units which some TPLF fighters had joined through an exchange agreement concluded in 1985. By the middle of April 1986, when the author left Damazine, about 200 women and children were freed.

Three-quarters of the camp population in Damazine were refugees from Tigray. Most of the rest were from Wollo and a small number came from other provinces. Most of the Tigray refugees were caught for resettlement between January and July 1985. After waiting in the central holding camp of Zabandaero near Mekelle for several months, they were transported to the resettlement area of Gambella. Most of the Wollo refugees, however, were resettlement victims of the first campaign in November and December 1984, and had lived in Asosa for more than one year before fleeing to the Sudan.

A comparison of our 1986 findings with our findings from interviews in the spring of 1985 indicates that little has changed in the ethnic background, family situation and economic conditions of the resettled peasants. The main points of our analysis of last year (Niggli 1986; Clay and Holcomb 1985:69-119) are verified. As in 1985, settlers from Tigray are considerably older than those from Wollo. This age difference most likely results from the fact that young men in Tigray help their families in the fields only during the day, rarely dare to go to the market and garrison towns and take cover at night outside the villages. Thousands also have joined the TPLF or were forced to serve in the Ethiopian army. All Wollo settlers we interviewed were Muslim and spoke Amharic — originally they were Oromo.

Most families we interviewed had been separated during the resettlement operation. A few who had managed to stay together during resettlement were separated during their flight to Sudan. One peasant from Wollo told us, "Most of the families I know were separated by the government. One member of the family is being resettled, another is put into the army, the others run to all directions. Our families are simply destroyed."

The methods applied to force the peasants into "voluntary resettlement" changed little from 1984 to 1985. In Tigray, operations to round up peasants continue to concentrate on the garrison and market towns still under government control along the main roads. But our findings indicate one interesting change: during the first resettlement campaign at the end of 1984, more than one-third of the peasants we interviewed were dragged away from the villages that were in the immediate vicinity of army garrisons. In our second series of interviews in 1986, peasants rarely mentioned village raids. Instead, more than three times as many people were rounded up during food aid distributions. This change in recruitment tactics probably reflects not only that the villages along the main roads were already emptied by the beginning of 1985 — that is, they were already resettled — but also that a wide network of food aid distribution centers was established in Tigray by the spring of 1985, after Western governments and aid organizations had criticized the fact that famine aid had not reached the largest part of the affected population in the rebel areas in northern Ethiopia.

Many peasants ignored the TPLF's warnings that food aid distribution often was nothing but a means to lure people into government-controlled places, because they heard repeatedly of lucky people who brought home a two-week's or a month's ration of food. "We only dared to go and get 'Red Cross rations' after we heard of many proclamations of the government," said one farmer interviewed. Another added, "There was a call from the government to come out and get Red Cross food. After about the tenth call, we decided not to let the soldiers eat all the food, so we went to Axum."

Those who talked of "Red Cross distributions" seemed to use that term to describe all distributions organized by Western aid organizations. But in fact, only the International Committee of the Red Cross (ICRC) was permitted to set up a wide network of distribution centers in Tigray where food aid was distributed in cooperation with the Ethiopian Red Cross Society (ERCS). In the spring of 1985, ICRC/ERCS centers existed in Axum, Rama,

Adigrat, Idaga Hamus, Adua, Wikro, Mekelle, Adi Gudom, Ambalage and Maichew. We spoke to peasants from almost all of these places who were lured to these centers with promises that they would be given food, but who instead were resettled. In February 1985, armed men surrounded the ICRC distribution center near Mekelle and abducted 250 men. When the ICRC protested, the government only declared that it did not know who was responsible for this action, but that it would have the matter investigated (*Neue Zurcher Zeitung* 12 February 1985). In October 1985, a similar incident occurred in Mekelle.

The presence of ICRC delegates at the distribution centers protects the peasants from being resettled to some extent. Yet government officials normally try to bypass such obstacles with tricks. They round up peasants before they reach the centers as they come into town from the countryside, or they search the markets where the peasants often have tried to procure some necessary items before or after receiving food aid. Only a few of the distribution centers were turned into long-term feeding camps for famine victims: namely, the camps at Mekelle, Adua, Axum and Maichew (Mehony). In all these camps, the local party committee had taken over the administration in the spring of 1985. The ICRC no longer was permitted to decide who was to be admitted to the camp or who was to be dismissed. Anything that happened to the arriving famine victims outside the camp, in town, was not only beyond the ICRC's control, but could not be witnessed by the ICRC.

At the same time, when the government extended its network of distribution centers in Tigray, an extensive army offensive against the TPLF caused a decline of food supplies from Sudan into the rebel areas in April and May 1985. Additionally, the long-smoldering conflict between the EPLF (Eritrean People's Liberation Front) and the TPLF broke out openly at this time. The EPLF blocked all transports of famine aid into TPLF areas from Sudan via western Eritrea. This increased pressure on Tigrayan peasants to seek help in government-controlled areas; the consequences were immediately obvious. In June 1986, for example, 18,000 additional people registered in Wikro to get food aid, and in July another 20,000 people arrived. The decline of supplies and the bad harvest in 1984 coincided with the reorientation of the flow of grain aid to Tigray (see *Neue Zurcher Zeitung* 26 August 1985).

The Ethiopian government wanted to take advantage of the military offensive. It called upon the aid organizations to distribute food aid in the newly conquered areas under the army's protection. The Ethiopian government assured the American government, which had threatened to start a large famine relief operation in TPLF areas in northern Ethiopia in February 1985, that it also would permit famine relief operations into rebel areas (*International Herald Tribune* 3 June 1985). The American aid organization World Vision had already been waiting to start relief operations as close as possible to TPLF and EPLF areas. Other organizations, among them the ICRC, did not react to the government's appeal because they clearly saw this as a political and military initiative. In July the ICRC announced that no famine aid could be distributed in Tigray and Eritrea that was not strictly controlled by the Ethiopian government (*Le Monde* 19 July 1985). World Vision has become actively engaged in several well-known camps in Wollo and Tigray, near outposts of the Ethiopian army.

Naturally, the Ethiopian government was interested not only in opening up new areas in Tigray in order to recruit people for resettlement via food aid operations, but also in strengthening its control in the province's rural areas. In line with these interests, the government installed a regional radio station for Tigray at Mekelle in November 1985 (Radio Addis Ababa 28 December 1985).

Because most of the Wollo refugees were resettled during the end of 1984, data received from them present the same picture that we received from our first investigation in the spring of 1985. Moreover, resettlement in Wollo was organized through the peasant associations, which had to fill quotas of "voluntary" resettlers. In December 1985, the French aid organization Medecins Sans Frontieres presented a report describing the Ethiopian government's systematic pressure put on the large feeding camps in Wollo, exerted in order to get more victims for the resettlement operations (*MSF* 1985).

Holding Camp Zebandaero

From the beginning, the Ethiopian government's resettlement campaign evoked widespread criticism. Even those organizations that basically approved of resettlement as a necessary action caused by the ecological crisis criticized "unnecessary brutalities" and miserable "conditions of life" that occurred during the operation's long periods of waiting in the central holding camps and during the transport to the "promised land." The government accused lower officials of being "too eager," but it had in fact had an opportunity to stop these "overzealous" functionaries and introduce better conditions in the resettlement operation in the beginning of 1985. That, however, did not happen, at least not in Tigray. The holding camp at Mekelle proved to be "the waiting room to hell." In general, most of the farmers we interviewed had to wait for two months in the camp of Zebandaero. In some cases, those rounded up for resettlement in May and June 1985 had to fight for their lives in that camp during the entire rainy season, a period of almost six months. According to several reports, the camp was crowded with 12,000 people before transports by plane to the south commenced. According to one farmer, the army guarded the camp backed by 13 tanks and 10 heavy guns.

At the beginning of the rainy season, the officials finally had some shelters built. Between 300 and 500 people crowded under the corrugated iron roofs. Since the shelters had no walls, the peasants still got wet. The rain poured in from the sides and the floors turned to mud. The peasants' clothes deteriorated to filthy rags that grew stiff in the sun. Said one young woman: "We were covered with lice. We just stared and moaned and scratched our aching bodies all day long—I no longer felt like I was a human being."

The peasants received food and water daily. Every morning cadres in trucks dumped sacks filled with bread on the ground, shouting "breakfast, breakfast," while they put selected candidates for resettlement in charge of the distribution. Two little buns per person, "the size of a package of cigarettes," were handed out to the young men, who fought among themselves for rations for their relatives. One farmer reported: "We demanded *injera* [an Ethiopian pancake] for our sick people and said they needed better food to recover. But the cadres only laughed and said bread is medicine."

Water was scarce, despite a great deal of rain. One woman who was in Zebandaero for five months during the entire rainy season explained:

> Sometimes we did not get water for drinking for two or three days until we drank from the mud puddles in the camp. Although we were almost choked and it turned our stomachs, we drank that dirt that was mixed with excrement and urine.... We ourselves stank terribly. We could not wash ourselves, we could not clean ourselves after defecation, and when I got my menses, I had to let it run down my legs and couldn't do anything about it. I only could crouch and hope nobody noticed.

In April 1986, in Sudan, this young woman still suffered from indigestion, terrible headaches, pain in the chest and legs and dizziness. She coughed blood and complained that she could no longer remember the little things she had just done or wanted to do. The Sudanese doctors could not diagnose any known illness.

"People die like flies in the camp." Every morning the corpses were separated from the other bodies crouched to the ground. One person reported that two trucks were loaded every day with corpses, which the survivors had to lay on top of each other "like bamboo sticks." The reported numbers of corpses varied. One woman reported 20 to 30 dead every day in her group of about 300 people; an older priest talked of 370 deaths within one and a half months in his neighborhood. Once in a while dressers (townspeople) walked through the camp, "often laughed and joked," and accused many famine victims of being malingerers. A person had to be brought to the dressers on a stretcher to finally receive a few tablets. Many peasants feared the clinic was a "final station." One person reported that as long as one was able, one tried to look indifferent whenever the dresser came around. But those who still felt healthy feared their constant proximity to the dying.

Reports concerning the conditions of truck or plane transport to the south in our second series of interviews in 1986 were similar to those we heard in the spring of 1985. Nothing has changed yet.

The refugees from Wollo we interviewed all had been resettled to Asosa. Those from Tigray had fled from different places around Gambella. Most of the Wollo refugees had lived in the Asosa area for more than one year before they fled to Sudan, and thus had experienced one full cycle of agricultural production there. In addition to their reports, we also considered information obtained from a dresser, a party cadre and an agronomist from the Ministry of Coffee and Tea who had been working in the area.[2]

"Show" Settlement at Asosa

A Permanent State of Malnutrition . . .

At Asosa, the settlers had to work six and a half days per week. After the first clearing of the forest, the hard soil was torn up by tractors. The peasants had to run after the tractors to break the lumps of soil with shovels and hoes. "Although the tractors plowed, we had to do the work of oxen," said one peasant.

The resettlement victims planted maize, sorghum, teff, sweet potatoes, pepper, oilseeds and horse beans. Resettlement authorities handed out the seeds; planting techniques and the speed and time of work were dictated by the cadre. In Wollo the settlers received occasional breaks, but in Asosa the militia refused breaks to the laborers on the collective farms.

All of the refugees we interviewed complained that they were unfamiliar with the conditions of agricultural production in Asosa. "We did not know the weather" was a typical comment. One peasant said it was too wet in comparison to Wollo; another, too dry. In Asosa the soil was dark and heavy, in Wollo it was red and light. In Asosa the soil lacked the small stones like those that covered the fields in Wollo and preserved moisture. Instead, the soil in Asosa was crowded with ants and unfamiliar insects which destroyed the seeds. In Wollo the soil was cool, in Asosa it was warm, which is perhaps why the seeds rotted away in many places. All in all, those interviewed said that the 1985 harvest was bad and the yields of the various crops extremely low. One peasant said that in Asosa 500 people had to toil to achieve what one person produced in Wollo. (See Steingraber's discussion of ecological shock in "Resettlement in Ethiopia," this volume.)

The agronomist Ashenake, from the Ministry of Coffee and Tea, said that the new cooperative farms' yields were "unexpectedly low."[3] The technical cadres were convinced that the peasants did not show enough enthusiasm for collective work. The lack of experience in the conditions of agricultural production in Asosa undoubtedly caused additional limits on productivity. The knowledge of the agricultural experts of the Ministry of Agriculture in Addis Ababa, drawn entirely from books, was not of much help either. In addition, a seemingly permanent dispute between agricultural experts and party functionaries about the "correct methods" significantly affected the situation. Usually the party cadres made agricultural decisions. The dresser we interviewed reported, for example, that the party cadres ordered the peasants to build an irrigation system in his settlement against the advice of the agricultural experts. The peasants spent a lot of hard labor and time, and in the end not one single drop of water flowed through the drains. A peasant reported that his work squad was forced to sow red and white teff seeds, which had been delivered mixed together. Although they had protested, since everybody knew that red and white teff are grown on different soils and planted at different times, the peasants had to carry out this order. Such advice was not the kind of education they needed to compensate for their lack of familiarity with the conditions in the new area.

In return for their labor the settlers received food rations that the RRC supplied from its store of famine aid grains. According to the ex-party cadre member Simon, who was responsible for the distribution of food rations in Asosa and who fled to Sudan in January 1986, grain from Australia, Canada and the US was distributed along with donations from European aid organizations, World Vision and Save the Children Fund (US). According to the original plans, each person received 750 grams per day until the party commission responsible reduced this ration to 500 grams. When Simon fled to Sudan, his office was able to hand out only 450 grams each day. Thus it is not surprising that all the people interviewed complained about permanent hunger. Five hundred grams of grain per day simply is not enough, especially if the recipient is forced to toil hard. One refugee explained: "I ate my monthly rations within two or three weeks and still had to labor away. When I was exhausted and stayed away from work twice, I was beaten." When the settlers complained that they did not receive enough food, the cadres simply said, "If you have finished your flour, eat soil and come to work."

That these food rations are insufficient in every regard is well known to the RRC. When the RRC began to demand humanitarian aid for settlements in the early 1980s, it calculated a food ration of 778 grams per head per day, 15 percent of which consisted of pulses, in order to get the necessary minimum protein allowance. This ration was calculated on the understanding that the settlers have to work especially hard for clearing, plowing virgin soil and building the settlements five days per week, and not six and a half as has become the rule in Asosa since 1984 (RRC 1980: Annex I, 2).

Most patients treated at the resettlement area clinics consequently suffered from malnutrition and a lack of vitamins and minerals. The dresser Gebreselassie told us that the settlers received little oil and salt. Gebreselassie was ordered to go to Megele near Asosa for six months; then, in early 1986, he fled to Sudan.

All of the intensively interviewed refugees said that they had suffered from hunger in Asosa more than in Wollo, where most of them had been afflicted by the drought in 1983-1984. In Asosa, they were given no opportunity to change their situation. During resettlement, the peasants lost those few animals they had managed to save from the drought, thereby losing one last possible source of income. Although the peasants had been able to make a living during droughts by trading and sporadic wage labor in Wollo, resettlement authorities prohibited such initiatives in Asosa. If the peasants tried to sell firewood in Asosa, they were punished severely. Those interviewed reported that about eight peasants were publicly executed because they had sold firewood illegally. In this case the authorities could argue that they had to protect the region from deforestation. But another restriction prohibiting the settlers' search for wage labor at the local Oromo peasant associations can be understood only if one takes into account the change of social status of the Wollo peasants after resettlement. The Wollo peasants, who were themselves responsible for their families' lives, were turned into dependent food-for-work slaves on the cooperative farms in Asosa. Since the RRC was unable to supply the settlers with everything they needed, the amount of grain distributed should have been calculated to allow for a small surplus that could be sold or bartered. But this was not the case.

Moreover, as the RRC well knows, basic needs do not only consist of food. In its old cost calculations for settlements, the RRC included cash needs as a matter of course into the subsistence needs. In 1980, the RRC specified 290 birr per year as the minimum cash requirement for a family to buy clothes, (edible) oil, sugar, salt, kerosene (for light) and medicines, and to pay for marriages, burials and schooling. Because oil, salt and medicines, if available, are distributed gratis in Asosa, the amount can be reduced to perhaps 180 or 200 birr, without considering inflation (RRC 1980: Annex I, 3). The prohibition of marketeering and wage labor keeps the settlers from earning even one cent of this sum legally. Nonetheless, the cadres told the peasants to use their own money to get necessary items, such as seeds for their gardens. One refugee reported a cadre telling the settlers that since they owned a garden, they should buy their own clothes. This cadre had just confiscated a donation of clothes that had been sent to the settlement. A few lucky peasants had brought some money from Wollo, but after a few months they faced the same problems as all the others. Consequently, despite all prohibitions a flourishing black market developed in the resettlements near Asosa.[4]

... But a Lot of Political Services

The infrastructure in Asosa has been extended considerably since 1985. At the center of the organizational structure are settlements containing 500 families each. Several settlements together form one *amba*, basically a village that is supposed to have basic institutions, such as a clinic and school. According to the refugees interviewed, clinics and garages for tractors were built during the last year in most *ambas*. For example, Amba Megele, which consists of settlements 36 to 39, includes about 2,000 families or 5,000 to 6,000 people. In settlement 37, a garage large enough to hold 30 tractors was used by 20 settlements in the vicinity. About half of the tractors were in working repair.

Settlement 37 also contains a clinic for Megele in which three dressers worked. All three were ordered to work in the resettlement area by the Ministry of Health, and came from different clinics and hospitals across the country. They were forced to go to the resettlement camps in July 1985, together with high school and university students whom the government ordered to dig latrines and to build huts. Gebreselassie said he was sent to Megele for three months. Since this was interpreted as an extraordinary mission for the revolution, he received no payment. Instead the ministry promised to pay expenses of eight birr per day. In Megele this amount was reduced to four birr. At the end of the three months Gebreselassie was told his term was extended by another three months.

The clinic's meager equipment included some medicines and a few bandages. A large amount of medicine was donated by the USSR, but the labels were in Russian and, with no other specification, were unusable. Those medicines they could use were produced by the Ethiopian pharmaceutical enterprise Epharm. Medicines from Western countries that were sent as humanitarian aid, according to Gebreselassie, normally are sold on the market by the Ethiopian government.

A settler needed a permit from a cadre to visit the clinic. The 100 to 120 patients per day often could not be treated due to the lack of bandages and medicine: Apart from malnutrition (due to underfeeding), the most common illnesses were fevers of unknown origin, intestinal infection and diarrhea, malaria, open wounds and tropical ulcers. In the summer of 1985, about eight to ten people per settlement (2,000 people) died each month. The situation improved slightly in January 1986, when two to three people per settlement died each month. In a six month period, on three occasions Gebreselassie had to treat settlers who had been punished by being beaten severely by the militia or party cadres.

In critical cases the clinic could ask for permission to transfer a patient to the new hospital in Asosa, just built by the USSR. But the hospital was often overcrowded, so the Russian doctors sent the patients back to the clinic with a receipt for some medicine. Soldiers, militia and party cadres enjoyed priority of treatment in the hospital.

Efforts in Asosa to build a political organization are more impressive than achievements in the establishment of technical and social services. The town of Asosa is the center of a threefold power structure. Since Asosa is the "capital" of Asosa-awraja district, the awraja committee of the Workers' Party of Ethiopia (WPE) has its residence there. This committee takes care of the local subjects, the Bertha and the Oromo. Parallel to this committee is the Resettlement District Party Committee, which is in charge of the 16 old settlements and 39 new settlements built since the end of 1984. By the end of 1985, this committee governed 81,000 people. Several technical services, delegated by the various ministries, cooperate with the Resettlement District Party Committee. Together with the party committee they constitute a joint committee; such joint committees exist on district, provincial and national levels. The RRC, which runs a storehouse in Asosa, has lost all power and authority in the new resettlements and even had to hand over responsibilities for the old settlements to the Resettlement District Party Committee. The RRC now is nothing but a logistic apparatus that distributes aid goods and food rations according to the Resettlement District Party Committee's orders. In addition, the central position of the administrator of the RRC's storehouse was given to a party member. According to the party cadre Simon, in December 1985, 250,642 food rations were handed out to new resettlers in Wollega from this storehouse.

In each settlement of 500 families the party is represented by a group of 10 cadres.[5] In 1985, the party began to recruit the group leaders, who are appointed and not selected, as "peasant cadres." Since it is dangerous to turn down the call to such positions unless one wants to be suspected of being a counterrevolutionary, and since many people hoped to gain material benefits by serving the party, the institutionalization of such positions took place quite swiftly.

In each settlement the resettlers had to build a house for the cadres with a strong fence around it. In front of this house was the central square of the new settlement. In the center of this square a statue made of bamboo sticks and clay was erected, representing a huge five-pointed star with hammer and sickle, the symbol of the Workers' Party of Ethiopia.[6] The huts of the 10 militiamen who were stationed in each new settlement were situated near the cadres' houses. Cadres and militia cooperated on friendly terms, but the technical staff kept a distance from the political center. The cadres received regular payments, but the lower technical staff had to survive with only their minimal expenses covered. The militia were fed on a food-for-work basis by the RRC from the food aid supplies donated to Ethiopia. Militia received wheat flour, sugar and tea. About 1,000 militiamen were fed by the RRC store in Asosa; they also were supplied with new clothing free of charge. In a nearby camp, about the same number of SPLA guerrillas were supplied with 200 quintals of flour, sugar and tea by the RRC. An order was issued to the RRC not to present the receipts on these items in case of investigations of the books by Western delegates. If presenting these books was unavoidable, the delegates were to be informed that these special RRC projects, categories 6 and 7 respectively, supported resettlers who are receiving military training to enable them to defend themselves against "bandits," that is, against the OLF.

Gambella Settlements: Experiments in Ethnic Engineering

This rather efficient organization of the settlements around Asosa differs from the other resettlement areas about which we have direct information. The "success" of the party functionaries, who previously had no experience in resettlement work, may be due to the fact that a five-year-old RRC settlement existed in Asosa, the structure and organization of which could be copied.

The situation in Illubabor province is quite different from that in Asosa. With about 936,000 inhabitants, the Illubabor province is only thinly populated and is divided into two distinct parts: a highland area around the town of Gore inhabited by Oromo, and the lowlands toward southeastern Sudan around Gambella, which are inhabited by different Nilotic peoples.

In the highlands maize and sorghum are grown and large coffee plantations are cultivated. In the lowlands the Anuak grow grains and vegetables on the banks of the Gilo, Akobo and Baro rivers, and fish and hunt in the bamboo forests. In the dry season, the Nuer graze their cattle in this area.

Since the late 1970s, the Ethiopian government has had several plans to speed up the "development" of Illubabor. For example, a coffee plantation covering an area of 10,000 hectares was to be established in the highlands, and large-scale farms were to be set up in the Gilo-Akobo-Baro basin covering 15,000 hectares (Abegaz 1982:210). International organizations and the European Economic Community were approached to finance these projects—without success. Instead, an Ethiopian-Soviet agreement was signed in 1984 to produce sugarcane and cotton on the Aloro River banks. As part of this project, the Soviets started building a dam to stem up the Aloro River for an irrigation system.[7] The project also includes a sugar factory. Anuak refugees in Khartoum reported in April 1986 that two districts of the town of Gambella were destroyed by bulldozers to make room for the Soviet technicians' living quarters.

These plans for irrigated farming caused anxiety and fear among the local Anuak population. The Nilotic population of Gambella traditionally never perceived themselves as part of the Ethiopian state. The international border of southern Sudan meant nothing to them; Anuak, Nuer and other Nilotic groups lived on both sides of the border. Until the decolonization of Sudan, Great Britain had a consulate and an extraterritorial tradepost in the towns of Gore and Gambella. In 1980 the Anuak sent a delegation under Chief David Olimi to Khartoum to ask their former colonial power for its protection against the Ethiopian government's plans, but to no avail.[8]

The development plans for the Gambella region devised in Addis Ababa also provided a way for the government to gain control over this remote border area inhabited by "disloyal" peoples. When the civil war broke out again in Sudan, security problems in Gambella increased. About 110,000 refugees from southern Sudan, mainly Nuer and Dinka, fled into the Gambella region.[9] The Ethiopian government also permitted the SPLA to establish training camps in Gambella and to use the area as a retreat zone. At any given time several thousand SPLA guerrillas are in Gambella. Their strength in this region is greater than that of the Ethiopian army.

The Ethiopian government cannot, however, be absolutely certain of the loyalty of the SPLA forces. On the one hand the Ethiopian government takes advantage of the SPLA's presence and delegates to the SPLA certain regional control functions, such as the capture of escapees from resettlement areas. It also has "supplied" the SPLA with 200 Anuak militiamen, according to reports from Anuak. On the other hand, the Ethiopian security may be aware of the fact that the SPLA is agitating among the local (Ethiopian) Anuak population for its own purposes. According to Anuak refugees, the SPLA proclaims that the struggle of the SPLA also serves to liberate the Anuak in Ethiopia, and that the Gambella region belonged to Sudan anyway. But until now, the SPLA's attempts to recruit fighters among the Ethiopian Anuak have not been successful.

According to the government's plans, 350,000 resettlers will be brought to Illubabor. These people would compose more than one-third (36.3 percent) of the province's total population. Fifty thousand families, or about 250,000 people, are to be settled in the four areas of Abol, Perebong, Akugna and Agenga Gesi – all places near the planned irrigation farms. How far the new settlements will be integrated in these farms remains to be seen. Considering the size of the projects, Gambella's local population had hardly been able to provide the labor on these farms. The resettlement should now have solved the problem. A further 20,000 families or 100,000 people will be "integrated" into the existing Oromo peasant associations in the highlands of Illubabor. The new resettlers would become the largest population group in Gambella, far larger than the Nilotic population. In May 1985, the functionaries responsible in Illubabor told Jacques de Barrin, correspondent for the French newspaper Le Monde, that 125,000 people had already been "settled" (Le Monde 30 May 1985). One year later, journalists were told that 140,000 people had been resettled, 90,000 of them in the highlands and 50,000 in Gambella. One has to be skeptical about the claim that only 15,000 people are supposed to have been resettled between May 1985 and May 1986. The officials did not tell the journalists how many resettlers had died (Tages Anzeiger 11 June 1986).

When the resettlement operations began in 1984, nothing had been prepared in the province for their reception. On 6 December 1984, a delegation of the Australian Development Assistance Bureau visited Gambella, where functionaries told them that 50,000 families would be resettled as of 10 February 1985. Nothing, however, had yet been prepared – no land had been cleared, no machines had been delivered to clear the bush and no tools and implements for the resettlers were available. Work was supposed to start on December 15 (ADAB 1984:13), but the lack of preparations made this impossible.

In mid-January 1985, party cadre Simon, who was working at that time in the party committee of Illubabor, together with some other party members was ordered to prepare the peasant associations in the highlands for the reception of the resettlers within three weeks. At that time the Workers' Party of Ethiopia had just held a three-day seminar for party cadres where head of state Mengistu told hundreds of cadres what they were expected to do during this first "work campaign" in the resettlement operation. When Simon protested that the time allowed for preparation was far too short and that the plans did not take into account the RRC's previous experiences in resettlement, he was suspected of wanting to "sabotage" the "revolutionary campaign." So he ordered the functionaries of the local peasant associations in the highlands where he was in charge to have huts built, to select plots of land and to collect oxen and tools for the new settlers.

We can now better understand the reports we received during our first investigation in the spring of 1985 from refugees from such settlements as

Metu or Alga, who talked of disorientation and lack of organization in the resettlement areas (Clay and Holcomb 1985:116f., 185ff.). Tigrayan refugees coming to the Sudan in 1986 from the resettlement area of Gambella reported similar experiences. Most of the refugees interviewed came from the resettlement camp of Oala; a few came from Finyada. Many people we talked to were flown to Gambella in the early summer and fall of 1985, and thus were able to move into huts that had been built by the Anuak and by students from the towns. "The huts were fragile and could hardly be used," one woman explained. "The rain poured in through the roof and the walls collapsed if one leaned against them. We had to rebuild the huts." Resettlers who were brought before the summer campaign experienced even worse receptions. In some places a few poles had been run into the ground, and the resettlers were told: "These are your huts, build them yourselves." There were strict rules according to which the huts were to be built, and if one did not follow these rules, the party cadres would pull the huts down again.

In 1985 most resettlers were occupied with clearing the bush. They were permitted to cultivate little gardens around their huts. Only a few reported that they had worked on "collective fields." In most places the bush had to be cleared with primitive tools; one person reported that bulldozers had finally pulled out the roots. Bamboo and trees were all cleared away. But it was not always clear in which direction the land was to be cleared. "We were not shown how and what to cut. The cadres never left their tents to

Those resettled in the southwest wreak untold havoc on the environment by cutting thatch for roofs, poles for house construction and clearing forest for fields.

show us, so we cut the nearest ones," one man said. One farmer reported that the settlers had to work from 7:00 A.M. until 2:00 P.M., when the temperature went well above 40 degrees centigrade in the shade. After that they were permitted to eat and to look after their gardens.

The size of these gardens was not standardized; descriptions vary from 0.015 hectares to 0.1 hectares per family. More than half of the people interviewed said that cadres gave them seeds for sorghum, sweet potatoes, oilseed and different kinds of vegetables. The functionaries responsible told the Australian delegation that they would teach the resettlers how to grow vegetables since they had no experience in this. But in 1985 there were no "instructions." "We were given vegetable seeds without knowing what they were. How could we know how to plant them?" reported one refugee. The resettlers had to break the ground with hoes—a technique they found unfamiliar since they used the oxen plow in their homeland. In addition the settlers had to share the few tools they had, since there were not enough hoes for each family to have one.

In 1986, Mohamed Ahmed, secretary of the Gambella Awraja Party Committee, told journalists that "half of the area cleared and plowed by machines" would be given to the resettlers for their own use. "Gambella has the resources to become the breadbasket of Ethiopia one day," Ahmed said. On the way to the "show settlement," which also had a clinic, the journalists passed a long line of East German *Fortschritt* ("progress") tractors. Since collectivization is a point of controversy between the Ethiopian government and potential Western investors, Mohamed Ahmed has rounded up the size of the settlers' private plots to one hectare, as the journalists have duly reported. Also the Asosa officials gave the Tinker-Wise team fantastic figures. In Asosa, the settlers should have received two and sometimes even five hectares of land for their own use (Tinker and Wise, 1986:18). All this is nonsense. In his speech on the WPE central committee's third regular session in September 1985, Mengistu fixed half a hectare as the maximum size of the settlers' private gardens, while in practice settlers in older settlements had gardens of only 0.1 hectare (Wood 1983:527), the exact size also reported by refugees. It is difficult to imagine how settlers could till half a hectare satisfactorily—obviously what Mengistu had in mind—when they are ordered to work a full day on the collective fields, let alone how they could till the five hectares reported by the Tinker-Wise team. The Irish agency Concern, which works in some resettlement sites, says that while the government has officially agreed to a maximum of half a hectare of individually owned plots; as of September 1986 farmers had only 0.1 to 0.3 hectares of land. In many regions of Ethiopia, between one-third and one-half of the peasants till just half a hectare and make a living from it, albeit a precarious one. The "incentive" to work on a collective farm if every settler had such a big garden would be practically nil, which is why the authorities have to keep the gardens as small as possible.[10]

At first the new settlers received their food rations daily. The wheat flour, measured with tin cans and other primitive implements, was infested with mealworms. The wife of a priest told us that, after separating the worms from the flour, only half of the amount remained. Later, groups of seven people received one sack of 50 kg every two weeks. This amounted to less than 500 g per person per day – the limit that was set in Addis Ababa. Pans or other cooking utensils were not provided and the resettlers had to use flattened tin cans, the contents of which the cadres or militia had enjoyed.

Most of the refugees complained that they suffered from a greater hunger than they had ever suffered in Tigray. Health care institutions in Gambella were worse than those in Asosa. New arrivals were given pills to prevent malaria. Material to treat properly the many injuries the people acquired when clearing the bush was not available. Many workers were bitten by snakes, and some refugees reported being attacked by elephants and hippopotamuses. (For highland Ethiopians, Gambella is considered "deep Africa," crowded with "wild beasts and tribes of barbarians." This compounded their feelings of helplessness in their "new country.") In the beginning the unsanitary conditions contributed to the spread of disease. Latrines were built only at a later stage. Those interviewed reported that they did not dare to go into the bamboo jungle to defecate for fear of snakes and wild beasts. In the summer of 1985, one person reported that five to eight people died each day out of about 10,000 resettlers.

In 1985, the settlements in Gambella were less well guarded than those in Asosa. Most of the refugees encountered the cadres only as guards and supervisors at work. Armed with Kalashnikov weapons, the cadres nominated group leaders who had to direct the cleaning of the bush. "We only worked hard when the cadres were around," one person said, but laziness, dissatisfaction and protests were punished with beatings and the other treatments already documented (Niggli 1986:26). Other irregularities were punished with additional reduction of food rations or by withholding food for some time. Only rarely did the resettlers see evidence of the presence of the armed forces in this area. Where settlers were guarded by soldiers, much more brutal treatment was reported. Attempts to recruit militias from the population of new settlers were not successful. Some refugees reported that young, strong, healthy men were taken away and never seen again. They probably were brought to a training camp of the Territorial People's Militia.

During weekly assemblies the cadres set the working goals for the next week and told the resettlers that Ethiopia was everywhere, to the north, south, east and west, and so whether they lived in the north or the south made no difference. Since the cadres spoke only in Amharic, their speeches did not impress the listeners; most of them spoke only Tigrinya. Important messages had to be translated by those who understood Amharic.

Some information obtained during interviews indicates that the cadres started sociocultural experiments directed toward the creation of the "new Ethiopia." One woman reported that in her group the cadres ordered the women to have their hair cut short so they could work better and look like men. They were told that it was not the time to raise children because they had to work and lay the foundation for a better future. Eight pregnant women reportedly were forced to abort their children with an injection. Six of the women never came back to their settlement; the other two had their heads shaven when they returned.

The cadres also told the resettlers to learn the language of the Anuak, their new neighbors, so that they could later marry Anuak. Anuak refugees also report incidents that may be interpreted as attempts at "ethnic engineering." At the moment the Anuak are being pressed to leave their traditional villages along the rivers and to move into the new settlements together with the resettlers. Others have heard that Anuak villages were forcefully depopulated and that the inhabitants were moved to the new settlements. (See Steingraber, "Integrated Settlement," this volume.) It would be logical if the Ethiopian government actually tried to "solve the problem" of the many small ethnic groups with a systematic policy of ethnic mixing. Since the Anuak population totals only 40,000 to 50,000 persons, such a policy would destroy them completely.

The Official Goals of the Resettlement and Villagization Campaigns

The resettlement operation was slowed down in late 1985 and was temporarily stopped in January 1986 due to a combination of internal and external events, the most important of which was the fact that widespread criticism of the resettlement campaign had impeded the massive flow of Western aid on which the government had counted. This in turn caused or strengthened resistance against the resettlement campaign, or rather against its methods and policies, within the circles of power in Addis Ababa. The escape of RRC head Dawit Wolde Giorgis in December 1985, and the later flight to the US of his deputy and temporary successor as chairman of the RRC, Berhane Deressa,[11] in May 1986, are perhaps the most visible but not the most important effects of the power struggle in Addis Ababa.

On the foreign policy front, Ethiopia's rulers used the first half of 1986 to start an "offensive of goodwill" to convince Western governments and aid organizations of the reasonable goals of the resettlement campaign. For the first time, a few selected settlements and new villages were made accessible to foreign visitors and a group of hand-picked journalists.

In domestic policy, however, priorities shifted in 1986. In the previous year, the propaganda was still dominated by agitation for the construction of a "new Ethiopia" by rapidly realizing the resettlement and villagization programs. The two regular sessions of the central committee of the WPE in April and September 1985 were dominated by discussions concerning those two programs. In 1986, the main topic of propaganda shifted to the new constitution. The whole party was called upon to start a large campaign of "discussion" of the draft of the constitution and to propagate it in the various mass organizations.

Based on all published information available, we tentatively interpret the developments in Ethiopia in the following way: in 1985, one part of the party leadership perceived a rapid, and therefore necessarily brutal, collectivization of the rural sector as the only means to avoid the actual collapse of the Ethiopian economy—a collapse caused by a continuous decline of production due, in part, to the drought and famine of 1983-1985. In 1985 this group of "collectivizers" probably was put under pressure because its policy only produced further drastic losses in production, reinforced regional resistance and shocked the Western countries from which the economic planners in Addis Ababa had hoped to secure the main investments needed for a long-range development strategy for the country.

The "collectivizers" in 1986 apparently selected the issue of the constitution as the arena in which to carry out internal power struggles and to use the proclamation of the republic to defeat the exponents of the internal opposition. We perhaps can determine from the changes in personnel and even from purges in the new organs of the republic to what extent the present power struggle was solved. In the logic of these considerations, a new massive start of the resettlement and villagization campaigns cannot be expected before the institutionalization of the People's Republic.[12] The collectivizers rather hastily assumed that this institutionalization would be completed by the time of the twelfth anniversary of the revolution on 12 September 1986. This was not the case. For the central committee's fifth regular session on 7-8 September 1986, only the final text of the constitution was produced, on which a plebiscite will be held. Mengistu said that the plebiscite and the subsequent elections of the organs of the People's Republic will be carried out on Revolution Day, in the new Ethiopian year which began in September 1986 (Radio Addis Ababa 12 September 1986).

The following analysis is based mainly on speeches by Mengistu and other party leaders and ex-Dergue members, held on such ritual occasions as the regular sessions of the WPE's central committee, other party assemblies, trade union meetings and May 1 or September 12 celebrations, of which abbreviated, revised and censored versions are usually broadcast by Radio Addis Ababa. These speeches, which are based on data delivered by the different ministries and written by the ideological department of the party, usually reflect the political will and intentions of the Ethiopian leadership much more accurately than all the "scientific" and "expert studies" of the country's economic situation compiled by the various ministries. One reason for foreign observers' diverse interpretations of the Ethiopian government's politics is that the primary source of information for these visitors, journalists and international experts are the ministries and subordinate technical service staff. These officials, however, lack the political voluntarism in economy and the obstinacy of keeping power that characterizes the Ethiopian leadership.

The "Construction Plan"

In October 1984, simultaneous with the appeal for famine aid to the international community, the WPE institutionalized a "National Committee for the Implementation of the Relief and Rehabilitation Decree" to take charge of all aid operations. The RRC and the responsible ministries were subordinated to this party committee. The chairman of the national committee, head of state Mengistu, is also in charge of the agriculture subcommittee. The ten additional subcommittees are chaired by, among others: Labor and Social Affairs Minister Berhanu Bayeh, in charge of the program's material resources, mainly the foreign aid; Fikre Selassie Wogderess, in charge of the state farms; Fissaha Desta, responsible for logistics; and Legesse Asfaw, responsible for the resettlement campaign.[13]

Legesse Asfaw also presides over the joint committee of party and ministerial departments already mentioned, which directly governs the resettlement areas. Mengistu announced similar double structure for the villagized regions at the WPE's fourth regular central committee session (Mengistu 1986a) and again put it under the chairmanship of Legesse Asfaw (Schille 1986:138). In 1985, Berhanu Bayeh's subcommittee also acquired responsibility for the exaction of the extra "drought tax" introduced in February 1985.

The Relief and Rehabilitation Decree, later usually called simply the "construction plan," has three major elements: (1) the direct feeding of famine victims, (2) resettlement and (3) villagization (Mengistu 1985b). The first two goals were already defined in October 1984. Those people "who fled their home areas because of natural or man-made problems" were to be resettled. This not only included famine victims, but also the so-called "internal displaced persons" who have appeared in growing numbers in the Ethiopian government's statistics since 1978. Pastoral peoples are also to be settled, and finally all unemployed people in the urban centers are to participate in agricultural production, an idea that dates back to the foundation of the first "settlement authority" in the 1970s (Radio Addis Ababa 8 November 1984). This last category was no longer mentioned in 1985, but the settling, or rather resettling, of pastoral peoples is still of great importance.

The decision concerning villagization was made officially at the WPE central committee's second regular session in April 1985.[14] But at that time, as our interviews revealed, the first villagization projects had begun already. The central committee's decision justified the event only after the fact. The institution that actually made the decision in this case, as before, was probably the national committee.

The three major parts of the construction plan were supported by other measures. Serious shortages in the food supply for the urban centers and the government's administrative and ruling apparatus had to be expected because of the drastic drop in agricultural production. A campaign therefore was initiated to collect grain, the results of which were judged satisfactory in September 1985 (Mengistu 1985b), in spite of the fact that large quantities of additional grain had to be imported by the state-owned marketing corporation. The state farms were also expected to make larger contributions in supplying the urban centers. To solve this problem, the state farms made their workers toil harder — usually on a food-for-work basis — and cultivate a few thousand hectares more of new land. The results were worse than expected; the "rise in productivity," in particular, lagged behind (Mengistu 1986a).

In the towns a campaign was started to make the people grow vegetables and tubers in gardens and to raise fowl and small animals in order to reduce dependence on food supplies from the rural areas. In 1985-1986, each town was to "organize cooperatives through its associations and map out and implement plans for self-help," Mengistu declared at the central committee's third regular session. We can assume that the urban unemployed, who originally were to be resettled, will now be invited to work in this "gardening campaign."

The construction plan's motto is to achieve self-sufficiency in food production as soon as possible — an old aim of the Ethiopian government and the main issue of all African leaders since the 1970s, when agriculture was discovered as the motor for development. This goal was specified quantitatively in the 10-year development plan in September 1984. The three primary strategies laid down by the Ethiopian leadership to achieve this goal and the analysis of the present state to be overcome became quite obvious with the acceleration of the socioeconomic transformation in 1985. Their three primary strategies included:

1. Extending government control over all the remaining resources of the country in order to avoid the strangulation of the "modern sector" of the economy by the collapse of traditional agriculture

2. Raising agricultural productivity by introducing "modern" methods of production, by means of the massive extension of mechanized agriculture under the control of the state, primarily in the resettlement areas

3. "Planning" the petty peasant's production through villagization and collectivization.

Overcoming Economic Strangulation by the State

The latest famine in Ethiopia and in other African countries raised many questions concerning the analysis of the problems and the strategies developed to overcome them, which we summarize briefly before explaining the analysis of the Ethiopian leaders.

1. Is drought a climatic and natural event that human beings cannot influence? Or is it the consequence of exploitation of natural resources (deforestation, desertification)?

2. Is the ecological impoverishment of soils cultivated by peasants the result of increasing demographic pressure and archaic production methods? Or is it the result of the marginalization of traditional agriculture by the modern sector to precarious, unsuitable soils?

3. Is famine the result of insufficient production or productivity of small-

holder agriculture? Or is it the effect of the pauperization of this sector and its inability to keep individual stores because of growing land taxes or rents, because of an increasing drain of surpluses by the state or private persons, low price policies and government-controlled marketing, and so on?

4. Does famine affect all peasants of the traditional sector equally? Who profits from famine and who is driven off his land by it?

These four questions indicate the primary strands of the problem. They focus on the relation between the traditional agricultural sector and the modern sector of large-scale commercial agriculture and industry. On the one side are the effects of "modernization," or the so-called "development policy," and on the other side are the issues of power and influence in the relations between the state and the rural population, and the conflicts between those who govern and those who are governed. In the discussion of development policies today, few would debate that among the primary causes of endemic famine in Africa are the modernization efforts of the state, and the disparate opportunities for the various social classes to gain influence on the power structure of the state and to profit from modernization. This implies that famine will continue, the result of the pauperization and marginalization of mainly but not exclusively rural populations, even if production were statistically sufficient.

Interestingly, this discussion has not reached Ethiopian "experts." For many observers, the social and political problems of Ethiopia's peasants were solved with the declaration of the land reform. Therefore they say that the present famine was caused solely by factors beyond human control, such as drought, loss of soil fertility and demographic pressure — all "natural" phenomena. The only artificial cause accepted is civil war.

Of course, the land reform immediately destroyed the economic and political power base of the land-owning class, especially in Abyssinian-colonized southern Ethiopia. But to assume therefore that the peasants have now gained economic or even political power is farfetched, and does not explain on which resources the revolutionary Ethiopian state could rely to expand its bureaucracy and to finance its wars, its industrial projects and its investments in a modern agricultural sector. And, as is well known, the Ethiopian state has directed investments out of its own means only and exclusively into the industrialized agricultural sector, while the traditional sector was offered to the foreign aid organizations as a playing field for development experiments. Even the highly praised Ethiopian government measures for reforestation and soil conservation were financed exclusively by foreign sources.

In the economic policy priorities of the Ethiopian government, the small holders simply did not exist. Instead the government, in order to secure its own resources, helped itself by taking from the peasants whatever it could get. Since the "golden years" of the 1975-1976 land reform, the financial burden imposed on the petty peasants' households has increased rapidly, culminating in the 1985 crisis. The pressure on the peasants to sell their produce to the Agricultural Marketing Corporation at low prices was intensified. The amount of unpaid labor on collective fields belonging to peasant associations, the yield of which goes directly to the state, has multiplied, especially in the 1980s. And finally, the institutionalization of government control over the peasants through peasant associations did not reduce social inequality among the peasants, but only shifted privileges to the minions of the new regime who occupy the peasant associations' boards. For them, famine generated additional profit.

It comes as no surprise that the Ethiopian government's analysis of the causes of the famine does not take these factors into account. The Ethiopian government combines a "natural disaster of international dimensions" (Mengistu 1985b) with the "backwardness" of the Ethiopian peasants in its analysis of the main cause of the famine, and therefore promotes a strategy of "improved control of nature" and a technological revolution of the dominant agricultural production methods.

At the founding of the WPE in 1984, Mengistu declared: "We should rally together to *free farming from the ugly forces of nature,* increasing our production, expanding irrigation and collecting our annual rain water" (Radio Addis Ababa 6 September 1985; emphasis added). "We are *captives of nature,"* Mengistu lamented on a different occasion (Mengistu 1985b; emphasis added), concluding that the entire people has to *"struggle against nature* and emerge *victorious"* (Radio Addis Ababa 19 January 1985; emphasis added). Ethiopians must blame themselves for now being "captives of nature." "Ethiopia has existed as a *symbol of backwardness and a valley of ignorance* for centuries," Mengistu later declared (Mengistu 1985a; emphasis added), and as long as "we do not free our farming from backwardness, we shall not be free from the pressures of climatic changes" (Mengistu 1986c).

The violent language of this approach to ecological issues leaves little hope for real improvement of the ecological situation. In another speech, Mengistu exclaimed that "our main effort is to *eradicate* natural problems and to develop the country for the comfortable livelihood of our people," just after he had called upon the party members to "totally *eradicate"* the "enemy bandits" in Eritrea (Mengistu 1985b; emphasis added).

Struggle against nature, struggle against backwardness and struggle against bandits are the leitmotifs in Ethiopian leaders' speeches. Such themes may be summarized as a "struggle against rural Ethiopia": are not the peasants the bulwark of backwardness, are not the peasants the bandits, do not the peasants represent "nature" that has to be "eradicated" in a painful process of education? The way cadres, militias and bureacrats — all urban people — move peasants back and forth, resettle them, discipline and educate them, drown them in the dirt of holding camps and press them through a tunnel of organized misery to be "reborn" as a new people of a "modern" Ethiopia is in concert with their official discourse and reveals their psychic disposition. "Deliverance from nature" and "deliverance from backwardness" is the deliverance from the people's own rural origins and the deliverance from their internal nature or the peasant in themselves.[15]

In line with this argument, the Ethiopian leaders turn reality upside down in their analysis of the famine's economic consequences. They see the main problem of the famine in the peasants suffocating the modern sector by their "backward habits"; the leaders perceive themselves as "captives of rural Ethiopia." In his speech on May 1, 1986, Mengistu expressed this idea in the following terms:

> The habit of each individual trying to produce only for his own needs is one type of behavior in a backward production system. So in order to be freed from this situation and strengthen agricultural productivity, we should ... make the peasant not just self-sufficient, but allow him to produce enough for the *national consumption*. [Emphasis added.]

The Ethiopian peasants, however, constitute 85 to 90 percent of all "consumers"; as "self-sufficient" producers they meet the largest part of "national consumption," defined as the total consumption of the Ethiopian population. But Mengistu defines "national consumption" as that part of production which exceeds the rural population's actual consumption. His term "national consumption" is identical to a surplus that the rural sector should but, according to his analysis, does not yet achieve.[16] Later in his speech he specifies who should enjoy this surplus as a "national consumer." It should be assured, Mengistu said, "that the peasant produces enough to meet the needs of the urban people and produces all that is necessary for industrial development" (Mengistu 1986c).

Just as the term "national consumption" is reduced to the rural surplus product and the "national consumers" to the urban population and the industry, so the term "national economy" or "national production" is limited to the modern sector, that is, to industrial production and mechanized agriculture. Mengistu uses this terminology in speeches to the labor unions where he defines the working class as that "which is directly related to national production" (Mengistu 1985a), and stresses that the workers first have to help the rural sector to produce "its due contribution to the national economy" (Mengistu 1986b).

This terminology, which places the rural sector quite clearly "outside" the national economy, corresponds to the analogous conception of a geographical and social dualism within the territory of the Ethiopian state. On his extended tour of inspection through the provinces of Hararghe, Bale and Sidamo in the summer of 1985, which was a kind of inventory of the still unexploited national resources, Mengistu stated several times that "until now it was not the Ethiopians who were beneficiaries of our cattle and forestry resources" (Radio Addis Ababa 1 July 1985). The profiteers had been nomads who consumed their own cattle, sold them on local markets or "smuggled" them across the border (whatever that was supposed to mean to pastoral peoples, who have always lived on both sides of the border). At the central committee's third regular session Mengistu complained that "our livestock wealth is being smuggled out of the country and is benefiting outsiders," which is caused by the fact that "our livestock wealth is concentrated in border areas, our inability to provide, in the required amount, goods which our livestock farming compatriots require and our failure to control the contraband trade properly due to the low organizational level of our livestock farming compatriots."

This argument does not make sense in economic terms, since the nomads profit from contraband trade and are not denied their Ethiopian citizenship – a fact the Western Somali nomads, for instance, have painfully experienced. But when Mengistu says that their livestock wealth is not benefiting the "Ethiopians," but "outsiders," he means, of course, that the livestock wealth is not for the benefit of the "national economy" under state control, but rather of those non-Ethiopians or "outsiders," which the nomads are said to be. Their integration into the "national economy" shall now be accelerated, according to the government's plans. With a deliberate conflation of the terms "peasant" and "nomad," Mengistu explained to the UN Undersecretary for African Emergency Operations, Maurice Strong, that the resettlement operation serves "to rehabilitate our *nomad society* and to enable nomads to become productive citizens" (Radio Addis Ababa 20 March 1986; emphasis added).

In full accordance with this conception, Borana nomads, who belong to the Oromo people, were transported to the resettlement area of Metekel in Gojjam (*Christian Science Monitor* 18 October 1985) and Afar, Somali and Oromo nomads were settled in Hararghe and Bale provinces (RRC 1985: 22, 31f.). In this context, Mengistu proclaimed at the central committee's third regular session that "the pastoralists shall be collectivized in suitable areas and commence a stable life style." The mapping out of settlement areas along the borders in the lowlands of Metema, Metekel, Asosa and Gambella is part of this strategy of enforced colonization of the state's territory to the benefit of the "national economy."

Just as the pastoralists' herds roused, as one may say, the greediness of the Ethiopian government, so did "the forests of coffee which are never picked." Therefore, at the central committee's third regular session, Mengistu announced that resettlement would concentrate on these coffee areas in 1985-1986. Traditionally, the local population uses the wild coffee for its own consumption, but given a fair price, the people would cultivate it systematically. Now, however, resettlers are supposed to harvest this valuable cash commodity for the Ethiopian state on a food-for-work basis (the food, of course, being provided by the EEC and Western agencies).

The distinctive simile, by which the Ethiopian leaders liken their "national economy" to an island in an ocean of unexploited border areas and forests, even forests of wild coffee where "nomadic" individuals are producing only "for their own needs," turns upside down the motif of being a "captive of nature," of rural Ethiopia: in this simile, vast, uninhabited areas still exist to be conquered and settled by pioneers.

In fact, serious economic problems are forcing the government to use this simile. As mentioned already, because of the famine the leadership had to fear a collapse of the food supply in the urban centers, and therefore started a campaign to collect grain in rural Ethiopia. By the same token the leaders had to fear a drop in cash crops and other agricultural export products.

The peasants' financial burden nearly doubled as a result of the extra "drought tax" in 1985. Without precautions this burden would have increased the external and internal contraband trade of grain, coffee, qat and cattle.[17] Therefore, in 1984 the national committee had already ordered the coffee harvest to be strictly controlled and dispatched more military and paramilitary forces to fight contraband trade. Mengistu said these precautions were fully successful at the central committee's third regular plenary session and announced an increase in the exports of coffee, incense and myrrh, and particularly in the number of cattle. "As a result of a special campaign which we started this year [1984-1985], we exported 200,000 head of cattle," Mengistu stated, while in the years before, the export of cattle had never exceeded 50,000 head.

The way in which the Ethiopian leaders see the relationship between the peasants' sector and the modern sector of the Ethiopian economy — between "natural" Ethiopia and "profitable" Ethiopia — makes the small holder peasants responsible for the present misery. Such a view reflects their fear of a "state bankruptcy" caused by the decomposition of the social and economic base through chronic famine, and leads as a primary consequence to an enforced raid by the Ethiopian state on the remaining natural resources, which in reality are nothing but the remains of the peasants' and pastoralists' wealth. Government documents say nothing about the way grain, coffee and cattle are being collected.[18] But one may probably correctly assume that local party functionaries were eager to achieve more than the levels expected of them, regardless of the means. In addition, there is no reason to believe these collection campaigns will be stopped, in view of the continuous low rate of agricultural production.

In a second step, the Ethiopian government plans to get at the roots of "backwardness," which means that they aim to revolutionize technology and to reorganize agricultural production along "modern" lines and under strict government control.

The Campaign to Extend Mechanized Agriculture

The government attributes their claim that the "backward peasant" is not able to produce for the needs of the "national economy" to the prevalence of traditional production techniques and a consequent "low rate of productivity." These factors, Mengistu claims, are the root cause of "food shortages" — the WPE's euphemism for famine — and not the drought, which only exacerbated the underlying problem (Mengistu 1986a).

In his speech on 1 May 1986, Mengistu said that "in order to increase agricultural productivity" to such an extent that it would produce enough to supply the towns and support industrial development "it is imperative that research work be expanded and strengthened and that scientific agricultural methods, as well as tractors and various modern agricultural services, be available to the farmer" (Mengistu 1986c). This vague formulation does not reveal who is to be subject or actor in this technological revolution. Is it the individual peasant to whom the various inputs are made available so that he can apply them to his own benefit? This would create the classic "green revolution," in which a class of rich peasants holds the industrial means of production while the majority of peasants are marginalized further.

But this "green revolution" is not what the Ethiopian government plans. Mengistu explained to the WPE group in the All-Ethiopian Trade Union (AEPTU):

> Revolutionary Ethiopia's working class is a class with the dual responsibility of confirming its role as a vanguard class and . . . ensuring that revolutionary Ethiopia's farmers are free from backwardness and *disorganized production* and familiar with modern farming equipment and production methods (Mengistu 1985a; emphasis added).

What Mengistu here calls "disorganized production," from which the peasants are to be freed by the working class, is nothing more than the independent peasant household, where the peasant controls his goals and means of production himself. He exalts the "organized production" of the working class as a model characterized by a hierarchical structure of command, a division of labor imposed from above and the worker's loss of control over the means and the process of production. "Modern farming equipment and methods of production," Mengistu continues in the same speech, require such an "organized process of production." This, he says, "is closely connected to our final goal of laying down and strengthening a socialist base in rural Ethiopia" (Mengistu 1985a). "Socialist base" in this context is synonymous with the "industrialization" of the economy and the "proletarianization" of society. Mengistu spells this out clearly at the end of this speech:

> There is no question that the consciousness, capability and achievement of the working class are of decisive importance to the peasantry which has been suffering under backward production, outlook and life and its gradual transformation to working class and hence, the beneficiary of modern production and civilization.

The first peasants able to enjoy the "gradual transformation" to the working class and profit from the benefits of "organized production" were named by Mengistu during a speech in Bale: "For our compatriots who have suffered from the drought to establish secure lives, they must be vanguard participants in the implementation of the leading construction plan" (Radio Addis Ababa 28 June 1985). The expression "leading construction plan" refers to resettlement.

In this direction the goals of the resettlement campaign are defined clearly. Mengistu told the central committee at its third regular session:

The main objective of the resettlement program is to give the resettlers a chance to carry out modern farming.... As stated repeatedly, the main aim of the resettlement program is to lay a strong foundation for promoting the country's economic growth, as well as making the settlers self-sufficient in food. For this reason, the implementation of the resettlement plan will enable every settler head of family to clear at least half a hectare with his family in the form of a garden to *supplement* his food needs as well as being in a large cooperative farm. The cooperative farm will be managed scientifically with tractors and the advice of agricultural experts [emphasis added].[19]

Note that this model for resettlement only pertains to the so-called "conventional settlement schemes" of Metema, Metekel, Asosa, Gambella and some others. Those peasants who are forced into existing peasant associations within the "integrated settlement schemes" continue to suffer from "backward methods of production." The institutionalization of cooperatives in conventional settlement schemes must be seen as a continuation of the Ethiopian government's strategy to expand state-controlled agricultural production through state farms and cooperatives and to increase the amount of agricultural produce that has to be handled through government channels. In return the government invests in tractors, fertilizers and improved seeds, that is, industrial inputs that were never available to the petty peasants in the past and will not be available to them in the future.[20]

The following calculation, based on figures published by the RRC (1985), demonstrates the extent to which the government hopes to make a "leap forward" through the resettlement scheme. Whether this leap forward can be realized, however, remains an open question. According to the RRC, 276,760 families were to be settled in conventional resettlement areas, approximately 75 percent of the total of 370,000 families that are to be resettled. In 1986, each of these families was supposed to clear and cultivate one hectare of land; in the long run each family will cultivate five hectares.[21] This would amount to 1,383,750 hectares of new land.

In comparison, in 1982 the government calculated that 5.2 million peasant households would cultivate 6,000,000 hectares of land, state farms about 250,000 hectares, and cooperatives about 151,000 hectares (World Bank 1983:i, ii).[22] If each resettled family cultivated only one hectare of land, the total would exceed the area cultivated by state farms, and if the long-range goal of five hectares per family were achieved, the area cultivated by cooperatives would rise nearly eightfold to 1.25 million hectares. In this calculation we have already generously subtracted one hectare per family for the gardens that will supplement food production. Not including an expansion of state farms and the "irrigation cooperatives" of settled pastoralists,[23] this development would lead to a total area of 1.5 million hectares cultivated under government control, the produce of which the government would market. This would amount to one-quarter of the total area cultivated by small holders in 1982.

In 1982, the World Bank calculated that state farms and cooperatives produced about 9 percent of the total agricultural production on 6.25 percent of the cultivated land. Assuming linear proportions, state farms and cooperatives would be able to produce 29 percent of the agricultural output on 20 percent of the land cultivated by the end of the resettlement campaign.

These figures reveal the Ethiopian government targets in order to reach "food self-sufficiency." With about 30 percent of the agricultural production under government control and with the possibility of acquiring the surplus production of small holders through the Agricultural Marketing Corporation,[24] with the terms of trade fixed officially, the Ethiopian government will be able to secure enough food for the urban population[25] and the administrative systems and even to finance industrial development projects through the export of agricultural produce. In this way the government will become self-sufficient in food and independent from peasant producers, a strategy very similar to other African governments' efforts concerning food self-reliance (see Haubert et al. 1985).

"Planning" Small Holder Production

The Ethiopian government's objectives go even further. The creation through resettlements of a cooperative, partially mechanized agricultural sector,[26] according to Mengistu, "should serve as a model for our plans to organize agriculture along modern lines in other parts of our country" (Mengistu 1985b). These plans were set into effect massively and unexpectedly in 1985 with the implementation of the villagization program. Villagization, Mengistu stated at the central committee's fourth regular session on 10 April 1986, "is a basic revolutionary movement which will enable us to restructure rural life in a short period of time."

The main goal of this villagization program, consistent with all measures of the government since 1984, is to eradicate "backward" subsistence economy because "our country's hopes for growth rest primarily on the agricultural sector" and "one of the preconditions that will enable the farmer to shoulder this historic responsibility is collectivization in villages" (Mengistu 1985b).

The conditions under which the villagization campaign's objectives shall be attained are defined rather vaguely, quite in contrast to the resettlement campaign's objectives (see, for example, Clay, Chapter 5). Although official statements use the terms *collectivization* and sometimes *collectivization in villages* almost exclusively, what *kind* of collectivization and what kind of economic reorganization of the agricultural process of production is intended remains unclear. One aim expressed in the resolution of the WPE's second regular central committee session in April 1985 was "to speed up the collectivization of farmers while still maintaining the option of individual farming."

Such language may mean that villagization is to be a gradual process or that peasants should be moved to new villages but should continue farming as independent farmers. If the latter interpretation is intended, then it is not clear how collectivization in villages is to help "hasten agricultural growth"

(Mengistu 1985b), which is described in all official texts as the objective of villagization.

Such interpretation would also contradict Mengistu's short but precise statement concerning the kind of progress to be achieved through villagization: "Placing farmers into collective villages will enable them to promote social production in a short time."[27] In the same speech at the third regular session, Mengistu added that villagization was not an entirely new program: "Forming collectives in villages has previously been going on in certain areas." The collectives mentioned here are the cooperatives that were officially initiated in 1979. Because the peasants stubbornly resisted the idea, the cooperatives never really succeeded.

To hasten the formation of cooperatives within "a short period of time" is therefore one declared objective of the villagization program. The "option of individual farming" that is to be maintained may indicate that the formation of cooperatives in the new villages is to take place on a voluntary basis.[28] Or, it may indicate that a kind of mixed system is to be created, similar to the system of production in the resettlement areas (which are said to serve as a "model"), in which each household is allowed a private garden while the families also have to work on collective fields. This uncertainty is dissolved by the few declarations on how villagization is to change the peasants' way of production. In his speech on May 1, 1986, Mengistu said of the villagization program: "As long as we say we are going to build socialism in our country, then it is important to properly plan needs, production and distribution and there is no alternative but to make the rural areas the beneficiaries of this." But that the "beneficiaries" of planning are in fact the objects of planning is later revealed in the same speech: "Each area should concentrate on the product which it can best produce. The gathering of peasants into villages is one of the principal conditions necessary in order to study and plan *each area's production focus*" (emphasis added).

The Ethiopian leadership thus claims to enforce production objectives in the villagized areas by means of centralized planning and to order concentration on specified products. For this purpose, the labor of the new villagers has to be concentrated in cooperatives and put to work in an "organized" manner, in order "to make adequate use of the soils," as the central committee stated in the final resolution of the third regular session. The "option of individual farming" is reduced thereby to the chaotic transitional phase between the construction of the new villages and the implementation of area-specific production objectives, on which the party bureaus of the administrative regions, together with the concerned ministries, have been working since the summer of 1985.

In the resettlement areas, the revolutionization of agricultural production is based in part on an organizational element (collective work), but mainly on a technological change of the means of production (mechanization and fertilizers). However, the collectivization in villages rests exclusively on an organizational element[29] — realistically, one may say, since the financial and industrial capacities of the Ethiopian state will be stressed already by the realization of the resettlement scheme. Naturally the Ethiopian leaders also vaguely promise to eliminate the shadows of "backwardness" in the villagized areas by using the lamp of "science and technology" (cf. Mengistu 1986c). But for the time being, "modern society" and "socialism" are to be rooted first in the minds of the new villagers. Villagization, Mengistu declared at the central committee's fourth regular session, will "change the farmer's life, his views and his thinking." Therefore the new villages should benefit not only from economic and social services, but also in the first instance from "political" services, as Mengistu expressed clearly at the third regular session of the central committee.

Apart from losing control over his produce and his means of production, the most drastic change in a peasant's life will be the "new working culture" — one of Mengistu's new terms — that will be introduced in the new villages. Why the "new working culture" is necessary becomes clear in the Ethiopian leader's criticism addressed to the peasants: on January 19, 1985, in the midst of the international campaign to rescue the famine victims, Mengistu told an assembly of party cadres, "If some individuals who have toured these [hunger] regions state that the main cause for our hunger is laziness, we should not be hurt, but are obliged to accept this truth." In a longer declamation to the central committee's third regular session, Mengistu made clear that he was not talking about bureaucracy or the party when he used the term "we" in the previous statement:

> Even though emphasis has been placed on supporting the farmers' increasing productivity, especially since the outbreak of our revolution, it is clear that even during years of favorable climatic conditions the productivity of the farmers did not increase at the expected rate. Even though there are many reasons for this, it is possible to say that the main ones are the farmers' failure to make proper use of all the services provided, and, as noted repeatedly, the farmers' inability to correct some work shortcomings which they could have corrected or prevented through their own efforts.

In this speech, Mengistu also vehemently criticized the peasant's "lack of discipline" and said that since achieving a rapid increase in agricultural productivity through technology and research was impossible, the traditional ways of working had to be improved: "Area party members in particular have a responsibility to follow closely the advice and services given to farmers and to make sure that farmers are producing in a disciplined manner."[30]

To summarize, villagization will produce the following changes in rural Ethiopia's pattern of life: the traditional peasant sector will be collectivized without a change in the technological base of production for the time being. Peasant labor will be organized by the state through the ruling party and disciplined in hierarchically structured processes of work under supervision of adequate personnel. The government's planning bureaucracy finally will order the specialization of production (i.e., Village A produces coffee,

Village B produces teff, and so on), which will cause the subsistence economies to collapse. After that the peasants will depend on the government to supply the foods that they no longer are allowed to produce. Thus, their diet will be subject to state control.

This century provides numerous lessons proving that this type of centralized economy does not work — not least the experiments of Ethiopia itself, where neither the state farms nor the cooperatives significantly exceed the peasants' yields per hectare despite the industrial inputs they exclusively get (World Bank 1983:12; Rahmato 1985:72f.). Villagization, which leads to high input and specialized production, will decrease productivity. In fact, this decrease has already begun.[31] Nonetheless, the Ethiopian government wins either way, at least in the short term and providing Western agencies remain willing to make up the difference.

Of course, the government hopes to improve productivity through this pseudoindustrial organization of the traditional agricultural sector and through the division of labor. Many examples, however, suggest that the contrary will result. But in spite of the actual losses in productivity which already have occurred and which will have to be expected in the future, the Ethiopian government still wins. The rural population loses control over its produce, its standard of living can be pressed to an even lower level of minimal subsistence, and an ever increasing amount of agricultural surplus remains in the hands of the government. More importantly, the relation between food production and the production of cash crops now can be defined by the government. After all, the cash crop production of the new villages will benefit first — as soon as the resources are available — from industrial inputs by the government. The ominous slogan "Everything for our motherland," under which Ethiopia's peasants contributed soldiers and money to the government for 11 years, will now include in the "new system" villagization, which shapes and controls every aspect of peasant life.

The Change of Policy, 1984-1985
Within one year, 3.5 million peasants were uprooted by resettlement or villagization — that is, about one-tenth of the total rural population of Ethiopia.[32] This enormous program indicates a fundamental change of the Ethiopian government's policy. The government previously had declared that its objective was to collectivize the peasants in cooperatives, but pragmatic considerations have restrained its action. The reason for this pragmatism was not to emphasize "voluntarism," in order to convince peasants to form cooperatives, but rather to avoid massive losses of agricultural production because of enforced collectivization.

The reasons for breaking with this pragmatism in the fall of 1984 have never been explained by the Ethiopian government leadership. But the change obviously is due to the unexpected extent of the famine which threatened to ruin the state's finances (agricultural exports) and the urban economy (shortages in supply). A revision of the former policy in any direction seemed unavoidable, particularly for a power elite who cannot rely entirely upon the state's administration and, to some extent, even the army, and which has to fight against an armed, ethnically based opposition in every corner of the empire. Didn't the famine prove that something had gone wrong in the past? Didn't it threaten the Ethiopian state's economic survival? Or more precisely: Wouldn't the state's independence and the revolutionary political orientation be affected by the massive international aid on which the state now depended?[33] Didn't famine immediately threaten the current leadership's maintenance of power?

This feeling of being threatened from all sides was expressed clearly by Mengistu at the central committee's third regular session in September 1985:

> We are in a state of war which was declared by our internal and external enemies who oppose our efforts during our long struggle after our great revolution to get rid of backwardness and exploitation. We face not only man-made problems but natural ones, too. Although we are marching towards our objectives without being overcome by this complex situation, we have not yet had the chance to build our national economy *as we would have wished. We still do not produce any defensive weapons* by ourselves to secure the freedom and well-being of our mother country.... In the face of all these odds, we cannot even produce our daily food, we are captives of nature, we die of hunger, and we have to be helped from outside. Of course, there are known forces of international exploitation and their lackeys, who want us to be their permanent dumping ground for their cheap goods and who criticize, discredit and even ridicule our efforts to restrict our life and tastes in order to become self-reliant. Inasmuch as we are overwhelmed by our temporary needs, the question is: If we remain receivers of aid in terms of basics such as food or cover for our heads when the rest of our bodies are naked, then who are we? For whom and for what objective do we stand? What will our country's fate and our people's lot be?... As there is no solution other than depending on our own efforts, creativity, achievements and productivity, let us strengthen our determination, avoid being attracted by cheap and temporary things and march forward for the lasting and important development of the country, true independence and a secure and invincibly honorable existence under the great revolutionary byword: Each for all and all for each! [emphasis added]

The applause at the end of this speech, which was also broadcast by Radio Addis Ababa, probably slipped spontaneously from the bureaucrats' hearts to their hands. In all the hours it took to read the chairman's prepared text, we had no similar spontaneous, emotional response. This passage contained all the ingredients of experienced humiliation, threat and self-doubt ("who are we?"), as well as a heroic incantation of continuous struggle, final battle and tenacious wrestling for "invincible honor." On a more rational level the speech focuses on the analysis of Ethiopia's situation in the following paraphrased statement: We are in a state of war against the class enemies and nature; naked and helpless as we are, we are an easy prey to our enemies, and we will overcome this dangerous situation only by creating our own industrial basis as the foundation of true independence, applying all means and extreme determination.

When writing this speech, the party's ideological department used passages reminiscent — not coincidentally — of Stalin's speeches of 1929 in which he declared the end of the New Economic Policy and the end of tolerance towards the independent peasants by pointing at the aggression of imperialism and stressing industrialization as the only means to maintain the independence of Soviet socialism. Has not Mengistu, on a different occasion, blamed "the influence of imperialism and historical factors" for the predominance of the agricultural sector in Ethiopia (Mengistu 1985a)? The "historical factors," namely the landowning class, were eliminated by the revolution of 1974. Now only "imperialism" — via the dependence of Ethiopia's revolutionary state on the agricultural sector — represents a real threat to the survival of Ethiopian socialism. Traditional agriculture as an "objective" ally of imperialism thus has to be revolutionized and its importance within the Ethiopian society drastically reduced.

The 1984-1985 crisis, when "we stood naked and helpless as captives of nature," therefore called for a drastic change in policy. Without this change, the Ethiopian administration would only have routinely carried out famine relief operations without getting at the roots of the problems. The RRC would have maintained and even strengthened its position as a state within the state and would have become the most important, most dominant economic institution in Ethiopia. That the party deprived the RRC of its power and its responsibility for the relief operations (though the RRC still served as a collector of Western funds) was justified by Mengistu on Revolution Day 1985, in his claim that "the problem was worse last year [1984] and ran out of control" and "therefore, our party was forced right from its inception, to give priority to and concentrate on the task of overcoming it" (Mengistu 1985c).

In this context, the 10-year development plan that had been passed in September 1984 had to be revised partially or supplemented by special emergency plans.[34] The 10-year plan scheduled a gradual institutionalization of cooperatives among peasants so that more than 50 percent of the agricultural produce would be produced by the cooperatives in 1995. The strategies that were to be applied in order to organize the peasants into cooperatives were not described in detail. The first step in the crisis was to redefine the resettlement scheme.

According to information the Ethiopian government gave to Italian political scientist Giordano Sivini in 1986, "It seemed to be necessary to redefine typologies and methodologies in the frame of the 10-year development plan, according to which the RRC originally had planned to resettle [only] 200,000 families within 10 years" (Le Monde Diplomatique July 1986). Mengistu also stressed at the central committee's third regular session that the resettlement plan was part of the 10-year plan, but had been carried out in 1985 on a larger scale than originally intended. In an interview with CBC radio in June 1986, Dawit Wolde Giorgis, the RRC ex-commissioner, reported the conflicts of objectives that were caused by the redefinition of the plans:

There was no way we could find 1.5 million volunteers in northern Ethiopia; therefore, force had to be applied. There was no way either we could adequately supply 1.5 million people in the resettlement areas besides the famine aid program. The government, however, gave priority to the resettlement campaign; therefore, resources had to be taken from famine aid. . . . This happened right at the climax of a crisis when nine million people suffered from hunger and all resources should have been applied to their rescue.

Revision of the resettlement plans in October 1984 appears to have led to internal criticism. Critical arguments can be noticed indirectly in Mengistu's report to the central committee's third regular session in September 1985, a time at which international criticism had begun to be voiced and at which USAID's Peter McPherson still denied the forceful nature of resettlement. Mengistu said that there had been "little opportunity . . . to study the terrain in the resettlement areas," but he added that this would be changed in time for the coming resettlements. He also expressed plans "to transport [the next] settlers before the farming season to enable them to engage actively in production work right from the start." This statement indirectly admits that the first resettlers were brought to unsuitable areas at times that did not take into account the agricultural cycle.

In the same report, Mengistu also defends the forced villagization or collectivization, even though at that time these plans had not yet been criticized by international agencies. Mengistu obviously answers to internal criticism when he asserts that there is no reason for criticism:

> On the basis of the experience gained in Hararghe, we realize that as long as the collectivization of farmers in villages is carried out in a proper manner, *the task will not be as complicated as expected*. . . . If our implementation and the work complies with popular methods, there is no reason why we should not reach our goals [emphasis added].

"Unsuitable resettlement areas," "disruption of the agricultural cycle," "the expectation of difficulties" in the collectivization into villages, and "little opportunity" to prepare for this massive shift of the population were probably points of criticism that referred to the old practice of cautious collectivization and to the expertise of the ministries and the RRC. This criticism probably was voiced within the limits of the present political line, not questioning the revolutionary "essence" of the measures but asking whether the methods of implementation would not be detrimental to the economic objectives of the programs. In short, the critics probably asked whether these massive resettlements and villagization really helped to increase production or whether they instead caused additional reductions, and whether the time of resettlement really was appropriate—that is, whether Ethiopia could afford risking "temporary" production losses when millions of peasants had to be supported by food aid to survive famine.

The critics' arguments were weakened by the fact that they could not respond—without dangerously exposing themselves—to the feelings of threat and to the political motive of maintenance of power or expansion of power which underlay the resettlement and villagization campaigns. The risks the economic critics of these programs had to face became clear in Mengistu's report to the fourth regular central committee session in April 1986. For the first time since the beginning of the forced collectivization campaigns, their character as an element in a "class struggle" was emphasized:

> The villages [villagization] program certainly cannot be established without problems, but our enemies' stance on its necessity and implementation cannot be viewed outside class interests. . . . In a class struggle it is not possible to expect goodwill from all sides and for this reason there is no alternative to struggling mightily for the success of all our objectives.

When the internal argument about the collectivization programs mentions "class struggle," it is cut short — to criticize now would be equal to being a "class enemy" sabotaging the Ethiopian revolution. Using this procedure enables the Ethiopian leaders to co-opt the critics' economic arguments while blocking them politically. At the beginning of 1986, the leaders therefore were able to issue an order to temporarily stop resettlement and to slow villagization without letting the internal critics gain politically. Mengistu could then claim at the central committee's fourth regular session that villagization in all regions "is conducted such that it will not disrupt the harvest." The real meaning of his claim, however, is that the government plans to wait until the harvest for its next (1986) villagization campaign. To assure the critics that this did not represent a fundamental change in the collectivization policy, the party paper, *Serto Ader*, announced that no "alternative to these programs or a shortcut [would] be taken" (Radio Addis Ababa 22 May 1986).

The critics arguments were strengthened, however, by their resemblance to Western criticism. They could argue that not even the resettlements could have been realized without foreign famine aid and that that is why Western criticism should be taken seriously — for "tactical reasons," they probably said, but meaning "strategic" ones.[35] These internal critics can be found in the higher ranks of the Ministry of Agriculture and other ministries concerned with agriculture, as well as in the RRC. They all were forced to hand over the operational responsibility in the resettlement and villagization campaigns to the party; they even lost responsibility for other measures such as the initiation of small agricultural activities in the towns to supplement supplies. These internal critics still use their international contacts to make their controversial view of government policies known, and their "private, confidential" statements are normally interpreted as indications of a possible change of government policy. This misinterpretation of the power of the internal critics is advantageous to the Ethiopian government: it provides mental food to the struggle over the appropriate time to start massive development projects in Ethiopia that occurs among the various (e.g. humanitarian, developmental) lobbies in the West.

But the critics' strength is not without dangers. The zeal by which

Western aid and hardware investors are hawking private opinions of Ethiopian officials may cause political difficulties for them,[36] which will one day develop from simple notes in the files of the security police to a real purge. Recent reports about a purge in the state's administration and the party in the first half of 1986 fit this picture.[37] After all, the party's propaganda had clearly pointed this out to all persons involved in the game.

In his 1986 speeches to the party and to the labor union congress, and in his May 1 address, Mengistu labeled criticism of the collectivization programs as nothing but the effect of an imperialist, mainly US-manipulated defamation campaign. The fact that he mentions external criticism in speeches intended for the Ethiopian public is an indication of the continued doubts and criticism within Ethiopia. But conditions for the critics have worsened: they now are said to be the lackeys of imperialist attempts to gain influence. After the US attack on Libya in April 1986, Ethiopian propaganda stressed this point even more and described Libya's and Ethiopia's situations as similar ones:

> The imperialists and their collaborators have now gone beyond propaganda campaigns and threats.... They will try to make us a target for attack because of our strategic position, our role in the history of the African people [sic] and our potential to be an example for the establishment of strong socialist government in Africa (Radio Addis Ababa 22 May 1986).

The internal threat felt by the leaders during the famine crisis has swollen to an external one, perhaps in the hope of continuing the debated campaigns in a climate of patriotic mobilization which at the same time will suffocate the internal critics. As a test for revolutionary steadfastness in the face of imperialist confrontation, the same broadcast announced the coming proclamation of the Democratic People's Republic.

The 1984-1985 Crisis as a "Revolutionary" Opportunity for the Party

Hard facts about the background of the present power struggle in Addis Ababa are scarce and all interpretations therefore remain provisional. Even the question of who maintains power cannot be answered easily.

Formally, the governmental structures of the Ethiopian state are still in a stage of transition toward their final institutionalization—the establishment of the People's Republic on the basis of the new constitution. At the central committee's fifth regular session in September 1986, the party promised to organize a plebiscite on the constitution and elections in the new organs of the People's Republic within one year. To date, the highest authority of the military dictatorship, the standing committee of the Provisional Military Administrative Council (PMAC), has yet to be dissolved but rarely manifests itself in public. If it convenes at all and issues decrees in its name, it does so in cases involving constitutional changes or reshufflings of the government for which legitimizing by the military dictatorship, the sole representative of state's power, is needed. Thus the PMAC issued the order to establish the constitutional commission, but at the same time proclaimed that this commission should be accountable to the party and not to the

Table 1
Age, Religion and Family Situation

	Tigray		Wollo		REST
	1985	1986	1985	1986	1986
Age	43.3	45.0	24.7	29.0	
Religion:					
Coptic	100.0%	100.0%	5.0%	0.0%	
Islamic			95.5%	100.0%	
Family:					
Married	89.3%	92.1%	64.0%	37.5%	
Resettled:					
Alone	67.8%		46.0%		64.9%
With Some Family	24.0%		36.0%		27.0%
With Entire Family	8.2%		18.0%		8.1%
Without Spouse		81.6%			100.0%
With Some Children		13.3%			20.0%
Arrived in Sudan:					
Without Spouse		89.5%			100.0%
With Some Children		6.7%			0.0%
With Complete Family		0.0%	0.0%		0.0%

Table 2
Where and When Farmers Were Captured for Resettlement

	Tigray		Wollo		REST
	1985	1986	1985	1986	1986
Village Raid	32.1%	0.0%	0.0%	6.2%	2.7%
In Town:					
Market Search	17.9%	32.4%	4.5%	6.2%	37.8%
When Looking for Work	7.2%		4.5%	6.2%	
On a Visit	10.7%	10.8%	9.0%		10.8%
At the Doctor	3.6%	2.7%	4.5%		
Subtotal Town:	39.4%	45.9%	22.5%	12.4%	48.6%
Food Aid Distribution	18.6%	54.1%	72.7%	81.3%	48.7%

PMAC (Radio Addis Ababa 14 February 1986). At present, Mengistu Haile Mariam is addressed first as general secretary of the central committee of the WPE, then as the chairman of the PMAC and lastly as commander-in-chief of the Revolutionary Armed Forces, whereas other members of the standing committee of the PMAC are quoted, but only with their titles in the party and their eventual positions in the council of ministers. The sequence of Mengistu's and the other rulers' titles emphasizes the priority of the party and recalls the position of the army out of which the PMAC originated. The last institution mentioned is always the council of ministers, which directs the Ethiopian administrative bureaucracy. Interestingly, however, Mengistu's chairmanship of the council of ministers is never mentioned, thus stressing this institution's "second class" status.

In the past, most foreign observers have doubted the hierarchy of power structures suggested by the sequence of titles. Particularly interesting and typically misleading were the analyses of the London-based biweekly *Africa Confidential*. Under the headline "Last Tango in Addis," *Africa Confidential* described the founding of the WPE in 1984 as a new disguise for the military dictatorship, a disguise that did not change anything in the actual power structure [*Africa Confidential* 25(19) 1984]. The main argument was that the former politburo of the Commission for Organizing the Party of the Working People of Ethiopia (COWPE), which itself was dominated by the standing committee of the PMAC, moved entirely into the WPE's politburo. It was likewise stressed that high-ranking officers and members of the PMAC and/or the Dergue played an important role in the party's central committee, even though they only held a minority positions.

In a subsequent article, "Farewell to Marx?" [*Africa Confidential* 25(20) 1984], this analysis was carried even further with the argument that, ironically, the foundation of the party had reduced the influence of the "Marxists" and the Soviets, and that the prospects of reanimating Ethiopian Marxism-Leninism were quite gloomy. Basically, *Africa Confidential* argued, the old alliance of the Dergue and opportunistic, secretly anti-Marxist technocrats from the bureaucracy's higher ranks was revived. The party's ideology was nothing but a rhetorical disguise for a fundamentally nationalistic and pragmatic policy to maintain power. As proof it was claimed that only a few engaged "Marxist-Leninists" held leading party positions and that Moscow's minion in the PMAC, Legesse Asfaw, hierarchically stood in the lowest position of PMAC comrades in the politburo.

In the summer of 1985, *Africa Confidential* [26(14) 1985] reported under the headline "Workers' Autocracy" that the party's politburo suffered from a lack of ideological cohesion and that discontent was growing in the army. Mengistu was drawing back more and more and governing as an autocrat, relying on the daily security reports and denunciations from Tesfaye Wolde Selassie, who controls the civil and military secret police as the minister for national and public security. Tesfaye was never a member of the Dergue, but he was "elected" candidate of the party's politburo in September 1984.

Africa Confidential's analysis [26(17) 1985] consequently culminated in the article "End of the Party," which was obviously based on rumors circulating in Addis and which maintained that only "a handful of Marxists" still took the party seriously while the army and the bureacracy had been overcome by feelings of resignation. The party's activities were limited to trivial matters, *Africa Confidential* claimed, such as an enormous output of paper for "ideological discussion" or the introduction of uniforms for every official, styled after the North Korean model.

We think *Africa Confidential*'s analysis pointed in the wrong direction because it did not account for the role the party played in the resettlement and villagization campaigns. For the party, even if dead on paper, did not limit its activities to ideological small talk, but in fact has usurped the major powers of the civil administration within the last two years. The already mentioned National Committee for the Implementation of the Relief and Rehabilitation Decree not only assumed the final control of all relief activities and foreign aid — which at the moment are the state's most important sources of income — but it also channeled all foreign investments, be they in goods or in money, into the revolutionary campaign. Resettlement and villagization are campaigns organized and directed by the party and effectively have deprived the concerned ministries of their responsibilities as well as bypassing regional administrations.

Instead of having the famine crisis administered by the responsible ministries in a routine and pragmatic manner, the PMAC handed it over to the party for its "first work campaign" (Radio Addis Ababa 19 January 1985) and thus made thousands of young party cadres potentates over resettlers and new villagers in distant areas of the country.[38] The crisis gave rise to a second, "socialist" phase of the revolution that was intended to destroy "capitalism" once and for all, even in its incipient peasant form, by proletarianizing the peasantry and thus creating socialism. One must not forget that all liberation movements of the various Ethiopian nationalities are, according to the PMAC and the party, nothing but instruments of imperialist powers.

The state bureaucracy, which was inherited from the empire and modified only in the sense that it was placed under Dergue members' control, would probably not have tackled the famine crisis in a "class struggle" manner. It would have used Western aid to feed famine victims and to rehabilitate small holder farmers, beaming like a cheshire cat about accommodating the military while conspiring with Western donors. In return, the bureaucracy would have bargained for increasing Western engagement in long-term development aid, promising to loosen marketing regulations for agricultural products and to increase assistance for small holder farmers.[39] Had such an operation been successful and had people like RRC ex-commissioner Dawit Wolde Giorgis been able to establish themselves as solicitous fathers of the people, the PMAC as a group of aging military dictators would have been maneuvered further into political isolation, a condition necessary for a successful military coup. Whether high-ranking Ethiopian officials made such calculations remains an open question, but they have motivated the Western governments, particularly the US,[40] to launch massive state and international famine aid.

The PMAC and its strategic brain, Mengistu, would not have stayed in power so long had they not been able to foresee such dangers. The feelings of threat analyzed previously have their origins here. To understand sufficiently the groups within the Ethiopian political elite and to assess possible alliances, the question of who will gain and who will lose in a possible coup against the present government must be answered. The winners would be those in the state bureaucracy who started careers in the administration based on their technical qualifications: the opportunistic technocrats who would not only serve any government but would themselves like to govern. Their allies would include those military officers who have been promoted not for political reasons but because of their military and technical qualifications, and who perceive Soviet influence in the army as strategically, tactically and technologically pernicious and counterproductive. These groups have nostalgic feelings about their former ally, the US, and they hate the Soviet Union — a hatred that extends automatically to the PMAC as the "Soviet proxy."

The losers would not only be Mengistu and the PMAC, but the whole group of politically promoted cadres in the administration, in the party and in the army. This group of new and often younger bureaucrats is a product of the Ethiopian revolution; they are generally called Marxists, though not necessarily convinced Marxists, since that would in any case be an obstacle to any communist party in power.

The "Marxists'" positions in the newly founded party seemed to be weak, since they did not assume controlling positions in the army, the security services or the council of ministers. Such positions were occupied by Mengistu's loyal followers either from the PMAC or from outside.[41] The "Marxists" were given only potentially important positions whose power depended on the extent to which the party would be allowed to develop an overall leadership role: Legesse Asfaw heads the organization department of the WPE, which not only controls the party's activities but also the admission of new members and the assignments of the cadres.[42] The party departments for ideology, economy and nationalities, as well as the control commission, are likewise headed by "Marxists."[43]

The role of the WPE's ideological department has often been underestimated. The department defines the doctrinal and political limits within which "discussions" may take place and according to which all party and administration decisions must adhere. The nationalities department, together with the Institute for Nationalities, founded in 1983, played a decisive role in elaborating the draft of the constitution. The control commission directs the "workers' control committees" that were institutionalized four years ago to battle corruption. They are an important instrument in the control of the state's administration and the economy, and can arrange necessary purges in a nonpolitical manner. The role of the economy department was not clear at first. A few hints indicate that it played an important role in the resettlement and villagization campaigns.[44] The only important party department the Marxists do not lead is the department of the judiciary, administration and defense, currently chaired by Fisseha Desta, third in the hierarchy of the PMAC.

The departments for ideology, economy and nationalities and the control commission were given to "civil" Marxists who, since 1985, have been called the "gang of four." Their head, Shimelis Mazengia, is sometimes named as the closest advisor of the Mengistu [*Africa Confidential* 26(17) 1985; *New African* November 1985]. They seem not only to control strictly the ministries within their range but also to reserve for themselves final decisions concerning changes in personnel within the ministries.

The "action plan" enforced by the national committee in October 1984 probably has strengthened the Marxists' position in the party mainly because the party was commissioned to administer the resettlement and villagization campaigns. One can assume that the position of the technocrats in the party and the government was weakened. The fact that preparations for the declaration of the People's Republic are controlled by the "gang of four," and that the schedule for discussing the draft constitution and for establishing the People's Republic in the summer of 1986 was arranged by Legesse Asfaw's organization department, indicates a future dismissal of conflicts on the highest level — the purge in the intermediate level of cadres is already well under way (see note 37). Legesse's comeback, after he had been declared politically dead in 1984, could not have been quicker or more spectacular. In 1985, he was made popular leader in the resettlement areas; in 1986-1987 he is being allowed to complete the institutionalization of Ethiopian socialism. It is no coincidence, therefore, that rumors were spread in Addis Ababa that the Mengistu loyalists but non-Marxists Tesfaye Gebre Kidan (PMAC member and minister of defense) and Tesfaye Wolde Selassie (head of the secret service and minister of public order) had fallen into disgrace [*Africa Confidential* 27(13) 1986]. Their eventual replacement, as well as other new names that will become known after the coming elections for the Democratic People's Republic, will reveal to what extent the tug-of-war between "technocrats" and "Marxists" can be resolved.

Notes

[1] All figures are quoted in Tinker and Wise 1986:13a.

[2] For information about the new settlement of Asosa, see also Niggli 1986:23-32.

[3] During a quick visit in Asosa in the spring of 1986, the RRC told the Tinker-Wise team that 39 percent of the settlers were already self-sufficient. The RRC predicted that 60 percent of the settlers would be self-reliant in the year 1986-1987. The formulation is misleading; more correctly, the harvest in 1985-1986 covered only 39 percent of the settlers' food needs. The Tinker-Wise team also reports that the harvest has been distributed equally among the settlers (Tinker and Wise 1986:18). But the party cadre Simon, responsible for handing out food rations to the settlers, had no knowledge of this. We presume the settlers' harvest of 1985 (and probably of 1986) was confiscated by the government and sold on its own account, except perhaps for the cheapest quality of maize, which is hard to sell on the market. The steady flow of foreign aid grain allows the government to feed the settlers "gratis," while their modest harvest produces cash for the government. The Tinker-Wise team's lobbying efforts to permit US development aid to Ethiopia should be evaluated in this context.

[4] A peek at this black market sent the Tinker-Wise team into raptures without knowing precisely what was going on. For US policy consumption they wrote in their report: "The local, free enterprise market is thriving" (Tinker and Wise 1986:18).

[5]The general rule for the party deployment in the settler areas is as follows: in every 500-family site exists a cell of at least three members. These cells in turn are subordinated to a party committee of each *amba*, consisting of five cadres. The superior Resettlement District Party Committee is composed of 22 functionaries. Each member of the subordinated cells is assigned to a job for eight months. In total the party has detached 2,000 cadres, thus rotating, in the settler areas (*Probleme des Friedens und des Sozialismus* May 1986:646).

[6]It is interesting to observe the recent shift of political emblems (symbols). At the end of the 1970s, the Provisional Military Council (PMAC) used as their main symbol a stylized ploughshare, thus feigning to be a peasant-based government legitimized by the land reform. The Workers' Party of Ethiopia (WPE) symbol, however, gives priority to the alliance of the working class with the peasantry according to the classic model and is placed, not without irony, in the middle of settlements of uprooted peasants who are going to experience their "socialist transformation" to simple farm hands.

[7]Radio Addis Ababa 1 December 1986. The Aloro project is part of the bigger Baro-Akobo project about which Korn (1986:92) reports. It has recently been extended to a total area of 40,000 to 50,000 hectares. North Korea supports the project with a pilot rice farm. The three state farms Abegaz mentions could be part of the project today.

[8]For a feature on Chief David Olimi, see Hasselblatt 1980:27H.

[9]This is the figure estimated by the UNHCR (United Nations High Commissioner for Refugees) for mid-1986 [*Refugees* 33 (September 1986):9]. The Ethiopian government claims a figure of 180,000 Sudanese refugees in this area (RRC 1985:14).

[10]The German-Swiss journalist group provided the big liberal dailies *Tages-Anzeiger, Suddeutsche Zeitung* and *Frankfurter Rundschau* with almost identical information (*Tages-Anzeiger* 11 June 1986; *Suddeutsche Zeitung* 13 June 1986; *Frankfurter Rundschau* 12 July 1986).

[11]Berhane Deressa is a brother of Dereja Deressa, who was confirmed as general secretary of the Ethiopian People's Democratic Alliance (EPDA) in November 1985. Financially supported by the US government since 1981, the EPDA was mentioned when US government circles discussed the extension of the Reagan Doctrine [e.g., funding liberation fronts] to Ethiopia in the spring of 1986.

[12]At the end of May 1986, the members of the politburo and head of the party commission for economy Fassika Sidelil announced the suspension of the villagization campaign during the rainy season (*Africa Research Bulletin* 30 June 1986:8235C). The resettlement campaign had already been stopped in January 1986.

[13]All four have been members of the Dergue for many years and were "elected" into the WPE's politburo in 1984. Cf. *Africa Confidential* 26(1):2 (January 1985); RRC 1985:9.

[14]In Niggli 1986:82, I incorrectly reported that the decision to start villagization was made at the third regular session in September 1985.

[15]The feature service of the Ethiopian News Agency revealed disgust at the stinking huts of the peasants for its distinguished readers: "A peasant family used to live under the same roof with his possession of livestock. Human beings cohabiting with domestic animals was a reality. This still continues in many parts of the country." The feature continues with, "Toilet is a word whose real meaning for the overwhelming majority [of the peasants] could not understand [sic]," stressing further for its readers the smell of the huts, saying that "cooking food in the bedroom or in the space allotted for cattle in their absence during grazing is not an uncommon scene." All these are "factors of underdevelopment and backwardness" which also limited the peasants' intellectual grip: "Using their mules, horses or donkeys they gazed into the sky to sight an airplane droning overhead." But in that image come the glad tidings: with the villagization the peasants dare to fly into a clean future, leaving behind animals and mud (*Ethiopian Herald* 25 February 1986).

[16]Rahmato (1985:67) wrote that in the early 1980s 82 percent of the agricultural production was consumed, according to the Central Statistical Office, by the peasants themselves, a little bit less even than the 88 percent the peasants form of the whole population.

[17]The government perceives as internal "contraband trade" instances in which private merchants acquired so much of the agricultural surplus because of rising prices on the free market that the state's marketing corporation fell out of competition and could no longer meet its quotas. In 1985, this led to stricter controls of the produce of every peasant association, especially in Gojjam, Shoa and parts of Gondar, and in June 1986, to new regulations concerning internal trade (Radio Addis Ababa 11 June 1986).

[18]Relating to this, Mengistu mentioned at the central committee's third regular session "extensive efforts to *buy* and *collect* grain in the country" (emphasis added).

[19]The somewhat halting official texts correspond to the difficulties of the Ethiopian *langue de bois* to express itself clearly. The English translation follows as literally and elegantly as possible the Amharic original.

[20]The cooperative farms of the settlers correspond best to the "Weland" stage of cooperatives as defined by the cooperative decree of 1979. This decree planned three stages of cooperatives, each differing from the other by a gradual collectivization of the means of production. In the Weland stage all means of production are collectivized and the income of the single members is determined according to their amount of work. A Weland cooperative shall include, ideally, 500 families (which is the case in the new settlements) and 4,000 hectares of land (which has been reduced in the new settlements to 2,500 hectares). Cf. Cohen 1984:21f.

[21]Mengistu speech to the party cadres sent into the settlement areas, Radio Addis Ababa 19 January 1985.

[22]World Bank 1983:i-ii. "The figure of 5.2 million peasant households does not equal the total rural population according to the 1984 census of 37.28 million people, not even if the pastoral population, estimated by the RRC to be 10 percent, is subtracted. Naturally, the World Bank relied on older statistics. But interestingly enough, the Ethiopian Peasant Association, the umbrella organization of all peasant associations, contains only 7.248 million households. Why the P.A. members decrease while population growth continues, is not explained" (*Ethiopian Herald* 5 March 1986).

[23]The 10-year development plan is scheduled to double the state farms' land to 500,000 hectares. This figure still appears to be valid. In the spring of 1986, the WPE delegate mentioned it again while attending a conference in Dakar that was organized by the journal *Probleme des Friedens und des Sozialismus* ("Problems of Peace and Socialism"), a sort of coordinating body of Moscow-oriented communist parties (*PFS* August 1986:1070).

[24]Estimates of the amount of surplus grain of the smallholder sector, which the AMC could acquire before the recent collectivization drive, vary considerably. Wood (1983:528) quotes 30 to 40 percent; Cohen (1984:44), 50 to 60 percent, but he quotes an FAO study that estimates only about 30 percent; Henze (1986:III,24), 50 percent. The private traders have to sell half of their grain at fixed, low prices to the AMC. These restrictions produced black-marketeering, but the peasants benefited least. Refugees from Gojjam told us in the spring of 1986 that one quintal of the best quality of teff had to be sold to the AMC for 45 birr in 1985; private traders paid only 60 birr. The same quintal could be sold on the Addis Ababa market, if available at all, for at least E$250.

[25]According to the census of 1984, the urban population constitutes 11.3 percent of the total population.

[26]"Partially mechanized" for two reasons: machines are planned to be used only for plowing and only for half of the area cultivated in most settlements in the first stage. The other half is to be plowed with the traditional oxen plow. On the basis of these facts, the Tinker-Wise team, lobbying for further US aid to Ethiopia, concludes rather naively that collectivization is to be strictly limited (Tinker and Wise 1986:17). In other words, land plowed by oxen would not be collectivized. But to date the yield of the communally tilled peasant association plots has gone entirely to the state, despite the fact that the peasants worked with their traditional means without pay. Technique alone does not hinder collectivization. The Tinker commission also was taken in by an argument of the Ethiopian government which claims that lowland soils

have to be plowed mechanically because the tsetse flies would kill the oxen, and that mechanization will lead to collectivization since the individual settlers could not buy the tractors themselves. This argument has two flaws. First, FAO projects in Ethiopia, for instance in Anger Gutin, have shown that oxen can survive in tsetse fly areas if veterinary services are provided. In fact, this is the reason for the government's plan to introduce oxen into the settlement schemes. Second, the state could lease out tractors to the peasants organized in a "machine cooperative" who would still remain free to market their produce on their own or in a joint account. Confusion abounds on the Ethiopian connotations of the term *cooperative:* cooperatives in Ethiopia are administered by officials, guided through the central planning bodies of the state, and their yields are divided at a fixed quota and at fixed prices between the state and the peasant labor. The peasants usually receive (though rarely their own produce) just enough to cover their food needs, but even this, according to a number of refugees with whom we spoke, is not always the case.

[27]The English translation of the Amharic original here uses the words "social production," although the term *socialized production* would correspond better to the real meaning.

[28]"Voluntariness" was always encouraged by massive pressure on the still independent members of the peasant associations.

[29]The RRC therefore did not appeal for international help in the form of development aid for the villagized areas in 1985. For those areas, it only requested so-called agricultural packages that consisted of oxen, seeds and tools—the Ethiopian peasants' traditional equipment, and health and social services (RRC 1985).

[30]In the early 1980s, A. P. Wood characterized the government's attitude as follows: "It appears that the government views independent peasant producers as undesirable. Even when grouped in peasant associations, they have the freedom to choose what they grow, and whether or not to sell their produce. Their small plots are said to be operated 'inefficiently' while their land use is not 'optimal' for the local environmental conditions. Grouping these farmers in producer cooperatives is a panacea to a government anxious to control food production, the rural populace and also land use" (Wood 1983:537).

[31]The famine in Hararghe, officially acknowledged at the end of 1985, was caused mainly by the disruption of agricultural production resulting from the villagization of hundreds of thousands of peasants (see Clay, this volume).

[32]The RRC told the Tinker-Wise team that 589,796 persons had been resettled by the beginning of 1986 (Tinker and Wise 1986:13a). And at the central committee's fourth regular session, Mengistu said that 2,839,293 people had been villagized, probably up to the end of March 1986. Villagization continued at least until July 1986 when it was halted temporarily. It then resumed in September and continued through April 1987.

[33]That this problem also gave a headache to Mengistu's Soviet mentors is evidenced in an article in *Probleme des Friedens und des Sozialismus* about "America's hostile, imperialist campaign against Ethiopia." The authors warn that food aid is the "Trojan horse of neocolonialism," claiming that "imperialist circles" try via famine aid to "force upon the Ethiopian government the de-facto recognition of the rebels [meaning the various guerrilla movements]" (*PFS* June 1985: 839, 841). But the final temptation of "imperialism" has always been steadfastly avoided by the Ethiopian government.

[34]At the central committee's fifth regular session in September 1986, Mengistu revealed that a short-term, two-year plan had been passed in 1984, identical to the Relief and Rehabilitation Decree mentioned above. He said that his two-year plan was part of the 10-year development plan. Mengistu announced a three-year plan for the near future, which is based on the experiences of the past two years and which aims to achieve food self-sufficiency by 1989.

[35]Berhanu Bayeh, minister for labor and social affairs, said, "Using aid donated by the international community, which realized that there is no truth in the propaganda campaign (against the resettlements), and by virtue of local support, the resettlement program has been able to save the lives of thousands of our compatriots" (Radio Addis Ababa 8 February 1986).

[36]In the near future one will be able to observe how the resettlement program—no matter what conditions prevail—will irresistibly attract the interest of Western governments' development policy makers and investors, since for the first time Ethiopia presents an opportunity to invest in "agricultural modernization" on a large scale. The Italian government was the first to react and to start action in the Beles Valley in Gojjam: the Italian construction industry benefits there from the immense construction work on dams, tunnels and irrigation and telecommunications systems. It will have a pioneer effect on the decisions of the EEC regarding the resettlement policies.

[37]Dawit Wolde Giorgis in *The Washington Post* (19 June 1986). The Eritrean Liberation Front-United Organization (ELF-UO) on Radio Kuwait (3 February 1986) reported that a coup had failed in January and had triggered a purge in the party and in the third army division. The Ethiopian People's Revolutionary Party (EPRP) reported in *Abyot* (May-June 1986) the removal of higher officials from their party posts and their assignment to embassy functions abroad.

[38]At the end of May 1985, Mengistu talked of 15,000 party cadres and professionals who were active in the resettlement areas alone (Radio Addis Ababa 31 May 1985). About 3,000 of them may have been party members (cf. note 5). Additionally the villagization has mobilized the party machine in the provinces and awrajas so that a considerable part of the estimated 35,000 party members are involved in one or both campaigns.

[39]After the first big collectivization wave of 1984-1985, most Western delegations in the spring of 1986 heard "private" hints about upcoming changes in agricultural policies (for example, see Tinker and Wise 1986). The government characteristically revealed these hints whenever it was seeking increased Western aid. The same thing happened near the end of 1984 when the famine relief operations started. American delegations were fed with the prospects for improved Ethio-US relations, according to US Congress Select Committee on Hunger chaired by Mickey Leland (*Daily Telegraph* 29 November 1984). And Edward Jaycox, first vice-president of the World Bank, reported that the Ethiopian minister of agriculture, in negotiations for loans from the bank, had promised to raise the prices for agricultural products and to support small holder production (*Neue Zurcher Zeitung* 3 December 1984), but the Ethiopian leadership rejected all these policy changes and, in fact, replaced the minister of agriculture. The same type of negotiations with the EEC four months later in the spring of 1985 also went nowhere (Korn 1986:168).

[40]Liberal opponents to extending the Reagan Doctrine to Ethiopia always point to an "overwhelmingly" pro-American attitude on the part of the people and of the government officials. Therefore, even people involved closely in US security and strategic decisions regard the eventual application of the Reagan doctrine to Ethiopia as inappropriate, because it would ruin the chances of a pro-American coup (see Henze 1986a:63ff.). These people believe a coup to be imminent. Henze wrote in the summer of 1986 (1986b:III-31), "Removal of Mengistu could cause his whole 'Marxist-Imperial' system to unravel.... Everybody assumes the military will again play a major role, and hopes that a new group of military rebels will have learned from the mistakes of the Dergue." Korn (1986) plays down American hopes of using famine aid to regain a foothold in Ethiopian affairs. Korn was US ambassador in Addis Ababa from 1982 to 1985.

[41]Three Dergue members control the Ministry of Defense (Lieutenant General Tesfaye Gebre Kidan, standing committee of the PMAC), the army department of the WPE (Fisseha Desta, standing committee of the PMAC) and the political administration of the Revolutionary Armed Forces, the party machine in the army (Brigadier General Gebreyes Wolde Hanna, central committee of the PMAC, former Seded member). The military intelligence is headed by Tesfaye Wolde Selassie, who is not a Dergue member.

[42]The fact that the party's audit commission is headed by the PMAC member Teka Tulu, an Oromo, limits Legesse's power in the party. But Teka Tulu's position is weakened, not only because he is an Oromo, but also because he is said to be involved in corruption cases (Pliny the Middle Aged 1983-1984:9).

[43]Ideology: Shimelis Mazengia (formerly Waz League, then Seded); economy: Fassika Sidelil (Waz League, Seded); nationalities: Shewandagne Belete (Waz League, Seded); control commission: Alemu Abebe (mayor of Addis Ababa during the time of Red Terror, Meison, Seded).

[44]Thus it was Fassika Sidelil who announced the end of the villagization campaign during the rainy season of 1986 (see note 6).

References

Abegaz, H.Y.
  1982   *The Organization of State Farms in Ethiopia After the Land Reform 1975.*
                Fort Lauderdale, FL: Saarbrucken.
African Concord
  1986   Mengistu Under Attack. 13 March. pp. 8-9.
Ahmed, A.A.R.
  1984   A Study on Silt Deposition in the Irrigation Canals of Northern Gezira.
                MS thesis, University of Khartoum.

Ali, O.E.B.
  1983   Reduced Agricultural Productivity in Irrigated Areas with Particular
                Reference to Silting in Reservoirs, Rivers, and Lakes. In R. Ford, ed. *Pre-*
                Assessment of Natural Issues in Sudan. Khartoum: Institute for En-
                vironmental Studies and Program for International Development, Univer-
                sity of Khartoum.

Anonymous
  1987   The Restructuring of Rural Residence Patterns in Hararghe, Ethiopia.
                April.

Australian Development Assistance Bureau (ADAB)
  1984   Report of the Assessment Mission to Ethiopia. 29 November-9 December.
                Canberra: ADAB.

Bulcha, M.
  1983   Some Notes on the Conditions of Oromo, Berta and Other Refugees in
                the Kurmuk District of Blue Nile Province—Republic of Sudan. Uppsala:
                Department of Sociology, University of Uppsala, Sweden. January.

Clark, L.
  1986   Report on the Refugee Influx into Northwestern Somalia. 26 April. Wash-
                ington, DC: Refugee Policy Group.

Clay, J.W.
  1984   Famine in Ethiopia. *Cultural Survival Quarterly* 8(4):1.

  1985   Human Rights Abuses and Deliberate Policies of Starvation in Ethiopia.
                Testimony delivered to US House of Representatives Subcommittees on
                Africa and Human Rights and International Organizations, Committee on
                Foreign Affairs. 16 October.

  1986a   Ethiopia—Feeding the Hand That Bites. *Cultural Survival Quarterly*
                10(2):1.

  1986b   Resettlement in Ethiopia. Testimony delivered to US Senate Foreign Rela-
                tions Committee. 6 March.

  1986c   Refugees Flee Ethiopian Collectivization. *Cultural Survival Quarterly*
                10(2):80-85.

  1987   The West and the Ethiopian Famine—Implications for Humanitarian
                Assistance. Invited paper presented at the 1987 annual meetings of the
                American Anthropological Association, Chicago.

  1988   Famine's Return: Ethiopia Regime Turns Hunger into a Weapon Against
                Its Foes. *San Diego Union.* 8 May.

Clay, J.W. and B.K. Holcomb
  1986   *Politics and the Ethiopian Famine, 1984-1985.* Cambridge, MA: Cultural
                Survival.

Cohen, J.M.
1984   Agrarian Reform in Ethiopia: The Situation on the Eve of the Revolution's 10th Anniversary. Harvard Institute for International Development, Development Discussion Paper No. 164, April.

Cohen, J.M. and N-I. Isaksson
1987   Villagization in the Arsi Region of Ethiopia. Report Prepared by SIDA Consultants to the Ethio-Swedish Mission on Villagization in Arsi Region, December 1-14, 1986. Uppsala: International Rural Development Center, Swedish University of Agricultural Sciences.

Community Aid Abroad — Australia
1986   New Refugees in Somalia Affected by the Ethiopian Government Policy of Villagization. 27 February.

Courier
1986   The Implementation of Socialism Requires a Very Long Period of Time: Interview with Chairman Mengistu Haile Mariam, Ethiopia Head of State. The Courier: African-Caribbean Pacific European Community 99: 26-31.

Dines, M.
1982   Work Camps in Wollega. London: Rights and Justice Committee. Unpublished manuscript.

Ethiopian Embassy
1986   Ethiopia's Resettlement Program: Some Points of Clarification. Press release. 22 January. Washington, DC.

Fathers, M.
1986   Refugees from Ethiopian Tribe Flee Mengistu's New "Socialism." Washington Times. 4 July.

Frado, D.W.
1984   Government and UN Officials Visit LWF World Service Rehabilitation Project in Genale Province, Ethiopia. Lutheran World Information 25/84:6-10.

Glasner, T.
1986   Ethiopia: Old Lands, New Directions. The Courier: African-Caribbean Pacific European Community 99: 16-24.

Grilz, A.
1987   Ethiopia Fights a War of Confusion. Jane's Defence Weekly 7(16):762-764.

Hancock, G.
1985   Ethiopia: The Challenge of Hunger. London: Victor Gollancz Ltd.

Harden, B.
1985   Ethiopia's Farmers Nudged into Villages. Washington Post. 17 December.

Hasselblatt, G.
1980   Schreie im Oromoland. Stuttgart.

Haubert, M. et al.
1985   Politiques Alimentaires et Structures Sociales en Afrique Noir. Paris.

Henze, P.
1986a   The Dilemmas of the Horn. National Interest 1(2):63ff.

1986b   Behind the Ethiopian Famine, Anatomy of a Revolution, I, II, III. Encounter LXVII (1-3) June, July, August-September.

Hollis, R.
1976   Chemical War Regains Favor — Little White Cloud that Explodes. San Francisco Examiner. 31 August.

Hussein, A.A.
1986   Ethiopia's Muslims: In Need of Unity. *Arabia* 1406(July):35.

Hyden, G.
1980   *Beyond Ujamaa in Tanzania: Underdevelopment and an Uncaptured Peasantry.* London: Heinemann.

Ibrahim, A.M.
1984   The Nile: Description, Hydrology, Control and Utilization. *Hydrobiologia* 110:1-13.

ILO (International Labor Organization)
1982   *Socialism from the Grassroots: Accumulation, Employment and Equity in Ethiopia.* Vol. I. Addis Ababa: ILO, Jobs and Skills Programme for Africa.

Indian Ocean Newsletter
1986   Ethiopia: Villagization Resumes. 18 October.

Jakarta Post
1987   RI [Republic of Indonesia] to Assist Ethiopia in Resettlement Programs. February.

Korn, D.A.
1986   *Ethiopia, the United States and the Soviet Union.* London and Sydney.

Kura, A.
1985   Digging One Hole to Fill Another: The Dilemma of Ethiopia's Resettlement Program. Helsinki: University of Helsinki, Department of Environmental Sciences.

Luling, V.
1986   Oromo Refugees in a Sudanese Town. *Northeast African Studies* 8(2/3):131–142.

Lutheran World Federation/World Service in Ethiopia
1983   Genele Rehabilitation Project. pp. 13-18.

Lyon, A., M. McColgan, C. Rostoker and D. Malapel
1986   *Torture and the Violation of Human Rights in Tigray, Ethiopia.* London and Paris: International Federation of Human Rights.

Madeley, J.
1986   Ethiopia Faces New Famine: Villagers Forced to Abandon Crops. *The Observer.* 26 January.

Magistad, M.K.
1987a   Resettlement Drive Presses on Through Scathing Criticism. *Christian Science Monitor.* 18 May.

1987b   Ethiopia: On the Razor's Edge. *Africa Report* May-June:61-64.

1987c   When the Shouting Stops – Ethiopian Relief Revisited. *Development International* July/August:32-35.

May, C.
1986   Ethiopian Policies Blamed in Famine. *New York Times.* 21 May.

Medecins Sans Frontieres (MSF)
1985   *Mass Deportations in Ethiopia.* Paris: MSF. December.

Melander, G.
1980   Refugees in Somalia. Research Report No. 56. Uppsala: Scandinavian Institute of African Studies.

Mengistu Haile Mariam
  1985a   Speech to the WPE primary organization meeting of the All-Ethiopian
          Trade Union Organization, Radio Addis Ababa, 28 August 1985, in
          Foreign Broadcast Information Service, Daily Report: East Africa
          (Washington DC—hereafter FBIS-EA), 30 August 1985, pp. R2-3.

  1985b   Central report to the third regular CC session, Radio Addis Ababa, 2-3
          September 1985, in FBIS-EA, 5 September 1985, pp. R1-11, and 6
          September 1985, pp. R1-9.

  1985c   Address on the 11th anniversary of the revolution, Radio Addis Ababa,
          12 September 1985, in FBIS-EA, 13 September 1986, pp. R1-4.

  1986a   Central report to the fourth regular CC session, Radio Addis Ababa, 10
          April 1986, in FBIS-EA, 14 April 1986, pp. R1-4.

  1986b   Opening speech to the third All-Ethiopia Trade Union Congress, Radio
          Addis Ababa, 30 April 1986, in FBIS-EA, 5 May 1986, pp. R1-4.

  1986c   May Day speech 1986, Radio Addis Ababa, 1 May 1986, in FBIS-EA, 2
          May 1986, pp. R1-4.

  1987   Report to WPE Central Committee. Radio Addis Ababa. 28 March.

Mimouni, J.
  1987   Ethiopie—Ces trois millions de paysans "villagises." *Jeune Afrique* 1364(24
          February):34-36.

Ministry of Agriculture (Ethiopia)
  1985   Villagization Guidelines. Unofficial translation from Amharic to English.

Moghraby, A.I.
  1984   *Water and Land Use in the Blue Nile Basin*. Blue Nile Project. Khartoum:
          University of Khartoum, Institute for Environmental Studies. December.

Niggli, P.
  1986   *Ethiopia: Deportations and Forced Labour Camps—Doubtful Methods in
          the Struggle Against Famine*. Berlin: Berliner Missionswerk. January.

Oromo Liberation Front (OLF)
  1985a   An Open Letter to the Government of the Republic of Italy. 5 February.

  1985b   *Oromia Speaks* 6:1. December. Distributed by the Union of Oromo
          Students in North America, PO Box 21044, Washington, DC 20009.

  1986   The Method of the Implementation of the Villagization Programme and
          Its Consequences. Paper presented at ORA conference, Khartoum.

ORA (Oromo Relief Association)
  1986   The Manner and Implementation of the Villagization Programme and its
          Consequences. Khartoum. November.

Peberdy, M.
  1985   *Tigray: Ethiopia's Untold Story*. London: REST UK Support Committee.

Pfeiffer, E.W.
  1976a   Chemical Weapons Must Be Totally Banned. *Journal of the World Peace
          Council* 6(1):11-13.

  1976b   The Fuel Air Bomb: A New Generation of Binary Weapons. American
          Chemical Society Symposium. pp. 7-9. 31 August. San Francisco.

Pliny the Middle Aged
  1983-84 The Lives and Times of the Dergue. *Northeast African Studies* 5(3),
          Michigan State University.

Prescott-Allen, R. and C.
  1982   The Case for *In Situ* Conservation of Crop Genetic Resources. *Nature and Resources* 18(1). Paris: UNESCO.

Puddington, A.
  1986   The Communist Uses of Famine. *Commentary* April:30-38.

Rahmato, Dessalegn
  1985   *Agrarian Reform in Ethiopia.* Trenton, NJ (American edition).

REST
  1984   Development Work in Tigray. October.

  1985   Progress Report on Shiwata and Agora: Soil and Water Conservation Project. April.

  1985a   "Resettlement" or Coercion? Press release. December.

  1986   Report on Interviews Conducted in Damazine Camp in the Blue Nile Province of Sudan with Tigrayan Refugees Who Have Escaped from Resettlement Camps in South-West Ethiopia. Khartoum. January.

Roberts, A.
  1986   Report on Villagization in Oxfam America Assisted Project Areas in Hararghe Province, Ethiopia. Oxfam America. June.

Rosenthal, R.J.
  1985   The Agony of Refugees Escaping Ethiopia. *The Philadelphia Inquirer.* 18 April.

RRC (Ethiopia's Relief and Rehabilitation Commission)
  1980   Income Levels of Settlers in Rainfed and Irrigated Settlement Schemes. Addis Ababa. September.

  1984   *Review of the Current Drought Situation in Ethiopia.* December.

  1985   *Review of Drought Relief and Rehabilitation Activities for the Period of December 1984-August 1985, and 1986 Assistance Requirements.* Addis Ababa. October.

Rule, S.
  1986   To Ethiopians Who Flee, Somalis Offer Squalor. *The New York Times.* 12 July.

Schille, P.
  1986   Wer lebt, ist noch nicht verhungert. *Der Spiegel.* 18 August.

Sivini, S.
  1986   Une Pause dans le Transfert des Populations en Ethiopie. *Le Monde Diplomatique.* June.

STORM
  1982   Re-grouping and Rehabilitation. 2(3):9-12. London: Rights and Justice.

Svoboda, W.
  1986   Calamity in Mengistu's Countryside. *The Wall Street Journal.* 20 February.

Tinker J. and J. Wise
  1986   Ethiopia and Sudan One Year Later: Refugee and Famine Recovery Needs. Unpublished manuscript. Washington, DC. April.

TPLF/OLF
  1984   The Ethiopian Ruling Junta is to Blame for the Famine. Joint statement by the Tigrayan People's Liberation Front and the Oromo Liberation Front. November.

Tuso, H.
1986   Ye Galla Maret (Oromoland) Policy and the Current Resettlement in the
            South of the Ethiopian Empire. George Mason University.

Twining, K.
1984   Food for the Future: Soil Conservation in Tigray. Relief Society of
            Tigray. July.

US Department of State
1987   Villagization in Ethiopia. Unclassified telegram No. 2675. 22 June. 9
            pages.

Wadhams, S.
1986   Ethiopia. Transcript. Canadian Broadcasting Corporation. 15 June.

Wood, A.P.
1983   Rural Development and National Integration in Ethiopia. *African Affairs*
            82(329):509-539.

World Bank
1983   *Ethiopia, the Agricultural Sector.* Vol. 1. Washington, DC: The World
            Bank. 18 January.

Worldwatch Institute
1986   *State of the World 1986.* Lester Brown et al., eds. New York: W.W.
            Norton.

Wright, K.
1984   Combatting Famine: A Revolutionary Strategy. *Review of African
            Political Economy* 30:100-105. September.

References: Newspapers and Periodicals

Daily Telegraph, London
Frankfurter Rundschau, Frankfurt
International Herald Tribune, European Edition (*IHT*)
Le Monde, Paris
Neue Zurcher Zeitung (NZZ), Zurich
Probleme des Friedens und des Sozialismus, Prague
Suddeutsche Zeitung, Munich
Tages-Anzeiger, Zurich
Washington Post, Washington
Abyot, Paris, Dallas
Africa Research Bulletin
Africa Confidential
Ethiopian Herald, Addis Ababa
New African, London
Refugees, UNHCR, Geneva
Radio Addis Ababa: Complete sample of broadcasts between December 1984 and May 1986,
edited by Foreign Broadcast Informations Service, Daily Report: East Africa (Washington, DC)
Radio Addis Ababa (Mon.): Selected broadcasts between December 1984 and September 1986,
edited by Monitor-Dienst: Afrika, Deutsche Welle, Koln.